Asian Settler Colonialism

Asian Settler Colonialism

From Local Governance to the Habits of Everyday Life in Hawai'i

Candace Fujikane and
Jonathan Y. Okamura

EDITORS

University of Hawai'i Press | Honolulu

© 2008 University of Hawai'i Press
All rights reserved
Printed in the United States of America
13 12 11 10 09 08   6 5 4 3 2 1

Library of Congress Cataloging-in-Publication Data
Asian settler colonialism : from local governance to the habits
of everyday life in Hawai'i / edited by Candace Fujikane and
Jonathan Y. Okamura.
      p. cm.
   Includes bibliographical references and index.
   ISBN 978-0-8248-3015-1 (hardcover : alk. paper) —
ISBN 978-0-8248-3300-8 (pbk. : alk. paper)
      1. Asians—Hawaii—History. 2. Asian Americans—Hawaii—
History. 3. Hawaii—Colonization. 4. Imperialism—Hawaii—History.
5. Hawaiians—Social conditions. 6. Hawaii—Social conditions.
7. Hawaii—Ethnic relations. 8. Ethnography—Hawaii
I. Fujikane, Candace. II. Okamura, Jonathan Y.
   DU624.7.A85A75 2008
   996.9'00495—dc22

                              2008012321

University of Hawai'i Press books are printed on acid-free
paper and meet the guidelines for permanence and
durability of the Council on Library Resources.

Designed by April Leidig-Higgins

Haunani-Kay Trask speaking at the "Stop Racism against Hawaiians" rally held at the University of Hawaiʻi in 1994 to protest racist cartoons and articles by the Asian-dominated student newspaper *Ka Leo o Hawaiʻi*. Photograph by Ed Greevy.

SETTLERS, NOT IMMIGRANTS

Settlers, not immigrants,
        from America, from Asia.
                Come to settle, to take.
                        To take from the Native
                                that which is Native:
                                        Land, water, women,
                                                sovereignty.

Settlers, not immigrants,
                bringing syphilis and leprosy,
                Jehovah and democracy.
                        Settlers, settling
                                our Native Hawai'i,
                                        inscribing their
                                                lies of discovery,
                                                        of penury, of victory.

                Settlers, not immigrants.
                        Killing us off
                                disease by disease, lie by lie,
                                        one by one.

                                                Haunani-Kay Trask

CONTENTS

ACKNOWLEDGMENTS

This book could not have been possible without Haunani-Kay Trask's revolutionary words on Asian settler colonialism in Hawai'i. In her keynote address at the 1997 International Multi-Ethnic Literature of the United States (MELUS) Conference delivered at the newly completed Kamakakūokalani Center for Hawaiian Studies, she stunned audiences by identifying Asians in Hawai'i not as "locals" but as settlers, and her political analysis has effected nothing less than a counterhegemonic transformation of the way that we as Asian settlers see ourselves and our occupation of Native Hawaiian land in a U.S. colony. Her later essay on "Settlers of Color and 'Immigrant' Hegemony: 'Locals' in Hawai'i" crystallized the focus of *Whose Vision? Asian Settler Colonialism in Hawai'i*, a special issue of UCLA's *Amerasia Journal* out of which this book has grown. Eiko Kosasa's extraordinary dissertation, "Predatory Politics: U.S. Imperialism, Settler Hegemony, and the Japanese in Hawai'i" (2004), has also provided clarity of vision for many of the scholars included here.

We would like to thank the following people for their questions, comments, and suggestions during the editing process: Cristina Bacchilega, Mark Chiang, Jeannie Chiu, Ann Curthoys, Monisha DasGupta, Nancy Fan, Cynthia Franklin, Theodore Gonsalves, Julie Ka'ōmea, J. Kehaulani Kauanui, Anne Keala Kelly, Erika Lee, Sharon Heijin Lee, Laura Lyons, Paul Lyons, Kent Ono, Darlene Rodrigues, Drew Saranillio, Eloise Yamashita Saranillio, Naoko Shibusawa, Jon Shishido, Karen Su, Shelley Takasato, and Glen Tomita. Jon Shishido also provided us with much needed technical advice and image editing for this volume.

Amerasia Journal editors Russell Leong, Glenn Omatsu, and Mary Uyematsu Kao nurtured the seeds for this book in *Whose Vision? Asian Settler Colonialism in Hawai'i*. We deeply appreciate the support of the following people who helped to referee the essays for that special issue: Marilyn Alquizola, Alice Yun Chai, Cynthia Franklin, Ruth Hsu, Jacquelyn Pualani Johnson, Brenda Kwon, Laura Lyons, Paul Lyons, Rodney Morales, Brian Niiya, Gayle Fujita Sato, Linda Revilla, Vicky Holt Takamine, and Allison Yap.

It was a pleasure to work with Ann Ludeman, Susan Biggs Corrado and Wendy Bolton, whose careful editing and insightful suggestions helped to sharpen the manuscript.

A special thank you to Masako Ikeda at the University of Hawai'i Press for her profound commitment to this book project and for deftly guiding it to completion.

Some of these essays have appeared in other publications. A version of Dean Saranillio's "Colonial Amnesia: Rethinking Filipino 'American' Settler Empowerment in the U.S. Colony of Hawai'i" appeared in *Positively No Filipinos Allowed: Building Communities and Discourse,* ed. Tony Tiongson, Ricardo Gutierrez, and Edgardo Gutierrez (Philadelphia: Temple University Press, 2006). An early version of Healani Sonoda's "A Nation Incarcerated" appeared in *Colorlines* (Spring 2001). An earlier version of David Stannard's "The Hawaiians: Health, Justice, and Sovereignty" was originally published in *Cultural Survival* 24 (1) (2000).

Hawaiian is not a foreign language in Hawai'i; therefore, Hawaiian words and phrases are not italicized. Words in other languages presented here are not italicized if they are included in English dictionaries (e.g., "issei" and "nisei").

Introduction

Asian Settler Colonialism in the
U.S. Colony of Hawai'i

As indigenous peoples around the world continue to fight for their rights to their ancestral lands and self-determination, Native Hawaiians are engaged in their own struggles for national liberation from U.S. colonialism.[1] It is no coincidence that in their own homeland, Hawaiians suffer from the highest rates of homelessness, unemployment, poverty, health problems, and incarceration for property crimes and substance abuse.[2] Haunani-Kay Trask, a Native Hawaiian nationalist leader and professor of Hawaiian studies at the University of Hawai'i, described Hawai'i as a settler society in essays published in the early 1980s, later reprinted in her 1993 collection of essays, *From a Native Daughter: Colonialism and Sovereignty in Hawai'i*. Trask provides the following definition of settler colonialism.

> Modern Hawai'i, like its colonial parent the United States, is a settler society; that is, Hawai'i is a society in which the indigenous culture and people have been murdered, suppressed, or marginalized for the benefit of settlers who now dominate our islands. In settler societies, the issue of civil rights is primarily an issue about how to protect settlers against each other and against the state. Injustices done against Native people, such as genocide, land dispossession, language banning, family disintegration, and cultural exploitation, are not part of this intrasettler discussion and are therefore not within the parameters of civil rights.[3]

Other Hawaiian critiques of U.S. colonialism, including those by Lilikalā Kame'eleihiwa, Jonathan Kay Kamakawiwo'ole Osorio, and Noenoe Silva, challenge settler historiography and legal discourse in their reexamination of the theft of Hawaiian sovereignty and land.[4] It is in this settler colonial context that *Asian Settler Colonialism* reexamines the past and present roles that Asians have played in the U.S. colony of Hawai'i.

For the past thirty years, the histories and stories of Asian ethnic groups in

Hawai'i have been told primarily through ethnic studies and civil rights frameworks that emerged from the 1968–1969 Third World Strike at what was then San Francisco State College. The Third World Liberation Front (TWLF) brought together African American, Asian American, Latino/a, and American Indian campus groups demanding an autonomous ethnic studies program and community control over curricula and hiring. The TWLF drew critical connections between domestic civil rights struggles in the United States and international human rights struggles in imperial wars being fought in Africa, Asia, and Latin America. In Hawai'i, the anti-war movement and anti-eviction struggles at Kalama Valley, Waiāhole-Waikāne, and Chinatown led people to demand their own ethnic studies program at the University of Hawai'i.[5] As a historical event linking racism in the United States with U.S. imperialism, the Third World Strike reminds us that ethnic studies was founded on the pursuit of justice.

Read in the context of Hawaiian scholarship on U.S. colonialism, however, ethnic histories written about Asians in Hawai'i demonstrate an investment in the ideal of American democracy that is ideologically at odds with indigenous critiques of U.S. colonialism. Although these historical accounts often recognize that Hawaiians have a unique political status as indigenous peoples, they do not address the roles of Asians in an American colonial system. Instead, they recount Asian histories of oppression and resistance in Hawai'i, erecting a multicultural ethnic studies framework that ends up reproducing the colonial claims made in white settler historiography.[6] In their focus on racism, discrimination, and the exclusion of Asians from full participation in an American democracy, such studies tell the story of Asians' civil rights struggles as one of nation building in order to legitimate Asians' claims to a place for themselves in Hawai'i.

In the struggle to make the Ethnic Studies Program permanent on the University of Hawai'i campus, for example, different ethnic groups employed a *terra nullius* argument of land in Hawai'i being "empty" or "belonging to no one," erasing Native peoples and places in order to celebrate their role in the "building" of the settler colony. A 1976 poster announcing an Ethnic Studies Program rally reads, "We working people of Hawai'i cultivate the land and harvest the sea. We build every home, harbor, airport and industry. Through the centuries we've fought loss of lands, evictions, low pay, unemployment, and unsafe working conditions. Yes, we working people struggled for and built Hawaii!"[7] In this and other accounts, the different ethnic groups lay a claim to Hawai'i by claiming the labor that went into building the plantation system, the industries, the roadways, the shopping centers, the schools, and new subdivisions—in short, the physical manifestations of U.S. settler colonialism in Hawai'i.[8]

In his study of anti-Japanese racism in Hawai'i from 1865 to 1945, Gary

Okihiro also argues that the struggles of Japanese in Hawai'i, like those of other minority groups, have helped to make the United States a more egalitarian nation. He writes, "Their persistent resistance to hegemony was not a matter of mere survival but a struggle that resulted in a more democratic America."[9] In this way, the violence of American colonialism is ideologically transformed into "democracy," masking the realities of a settler colony that continues to deny Native peoples their rights to their lands and resources. Moreover, Okihiro asserts a settler claim when he argues that Japanese laborers resisted their exploitation by permanently settling in Hawai'i: "I contend that Japanese persistence in Hawaii, inasmuch as permanent settlement subverted the system of migrant labor, could be interpreted as resistance to an oppressive form of labor."[10] When we read Okihiro's 1991 interpretation of Japanese settlement in the context of Hawai'i's history as a U.S. settler colony, however, we can see that this narrative of Japanese settlement and its affirmation of U.S. democracy actually serves the ends of the United States as a settler state and its occupation of Native lands.

In other accounts, Asian political and economic "successes" in Hawai'i have been represented as evidence of Hawai'i's exceptionalism as a multicultural state, proof that Asians have been able to overcome the racist treatment and policies of the American sugar planters to form what several scholars have described as a "harmonious multiculturalism."[11] Many historians employ a developmental narrative that begins with the colonization of Hawaiians and ends with multicultural democracy in Hawai'i. The story of multiethnic diversity is thus cast as the triumphant "resolution" to Hawai'i's colonial "past." In one such study, Eileen Tamura constructs a generational model of Asian historiography in Hawai'i: the first generation of ethnic histories dating from the 1920s through the 1960s largely written by white social scientists, the second generation of ethnic histories from the 1970s through the 1990s written by scholars about their own ethnic groups, and a third generation of ethnic histories from the 1990s that focuses on panethnic and mixed-ethnic "local" identity.[12] In this trajectory, Tamura argues that second-generation scholarship on Hawaiian sovereignty has been succeeded by "seeds of a new generation of historical scholarship," one that examines "panethnic 'local' identity that has derived from Hawai'i's century-long ethnically diverse society."[13] Such developmental accounts ignore Hawaiians' ongoing struggles for self-determination as well as the tremendous political power some Asian groups have used against Hawaiians as documented in the essays in this book, and in doing so they demonstrate ideological continuities with white settler colonial historiography.

Asian Settler Colonialism calls for a methodological and epistemological shift away from predominant accounts of Hawai'i as a democratic, "multicultural," or "multiracial" state by showing us instead the historical and political conditions of a white- and Asian-dominated U.S. settler colony. It is important to keep in mind that in 1969, at the same time that people of color were united in the Third World Strike, the struggles of American Indians and Hawaiians as indigenous peoples to reclaim their ancestral lands extended beyond a civil rights framework to challenge the very foundation of the U.S. settler state. American Indians who called themselves "Indians of All Tribes" were engaged in the second occupation of Alcatraz Island in San Francisco Bay. Asserting American Indian title to the federal facility by right of discovery, American Indian activists at Alcatraz initiated the Alcatraz–Red Power Movement (ARPM), which led to seventy property takeovers in the ensuing nine years.[14] Similarly in 1976, Hawaiians in the Protect Kahoʻolawe ʻOhana (PKO) were engaged in their own re-occupation of the island of Kahoʻolawe, which had been used since World War II as a site for target practice by the U.S. military. Although some Asians, particularly Japanese Americans who were critical of the U.S. political system after their internment during World War II, supported American Indians at Alcatraz and Hawaiians at Kahoʻolawe in important ways, they used a framework of race and class struggle that did not account for the uniqueness of indigenous struggles for land or their own positions in a colonial context.[15]

In a landmark keynote address delivered at the 1997 Multi-Ethnic Literature of the United States (MELUS) Conference, Trask specifically identified Asians in Hawaiʻi as settlers who benefit from the colonial subjugation of Hawaiians.[16] We have reprinted in this book Trask's more extensive essay titled "Settlers of Color and 'Immigrant' Hegemony: 'Locals' in Hawaiʻi" (2000) where she describes the post–World War II rise of Asians in Hawaiʻi to political power and elaborates on the ideological narratives of immigration that Asian settlers use to claim Hawaiʻi for themselves.

> Our Native people and territories have been overrun by non-Natives, including Asians. Calling themselves "local," the children of Asian settlers greatly outnumber us. They claim Hawaiʻi as their own, denying indigenous history, their long collaboration in our continued dispossession, and the benefits therefrom. Part of this denial is the substitution of the term "local" for "immigrant," which is, itself, a particularly celebrated American gloss for "settler." As on the continent, so in our island home. Settlers and their children recast the American tale of nationhood: Hawaiʻi, like the continent, is naturalized as but another telling illustration of the uniqueness of America's "nation of immigrants."[17]

As Trask points out in her essay, the United Nations Declaration on the Rights of Indigenous Peoples distinguishes indigenous peoples from all others on a particular land base by their indigenous human right to self-determination and self-government; minority populations do not possess this right. In other words, Hawaiians have the right as indigenous peoples to form their own nation; populations considered "minorities" in the U.S. settler state, like the Japanese or the Vietnamese, do not possess this indigenous right to form their own separate nations in Hawai'i. Trask illustrates that the celebration of the "immigrant" success story—a story often used by Asian settler political representatives in Hawai'i—is an attempt to legitimate Asian settler political power made possible by U.S. settler colonialism.

As Native scholars and activists argue in this book, Hawaiians are genealogically connected to their ancestral lands. Momiala Kamahele explains in her essay, "The land is our mother. Native Hawaiians call her Papahānaumoku—'She who gives birth to lands.' As caretakers, Native Hawaiians understand that . . . She creates and ensures a living continuity between the natural world and the human world." Mixed-race Hawaiians are still genealogical descendants of the land despite their settler ancestries; to argue anything less is an act of colonial theft that takes Hawaiians' genealogical heritage away from them. In the U.S. colony of Hawai'i, Asians are settlers who come from their own ancestral homelands where their own genealogical ties lie.

A brief overview of historical events illustrates the colonial process that made possible large-scale Asian settlement in Hawai'i. The Hawaiian peoples suffered a catastrophic population collapse due to diseases brought by foreigners: from an estimated eight hundred thousand to one million Native Hawaiians in 1778, the Hawaiian population plummeted to forty thousand in 1893, the year of the U.S. military overthrow of the Hawaiian government.[18] Foreigners sought increasing control in the governance of Hawai'i, and they were heavily influential in the establishment of a constitutional monarchy in 1840 and the Māhele in 1848, which paved the way for foreign ownership of Hawaiian land.[19] From the early 1850s white American settlers worked aggressively to secure Asian laborers to build their sugar empire. Hawai'i was annexed by the United States in 1898 as a territorial colony, and a white Republican settler oligarchy ruled Hawai'i politically and economically until the mid-twentieth century. In 1954, with the growth of labor unions and return of nisei (second generation) Japanese settlers who had joined the U.S. military during World War II, Japanese children of plantation laborers led the Democratic Party takeover of both houses of the Territorial Legislature.[20] As George Cooper and Gavan Daws illustrate in their book *Land and Power in Hawai'i: The Democratic Years* (1985), the Democrats gained popular support by promising land reform through land taxes and land-use laws that would benefit the working class, but historical records show that they ultimately promoted land development and real estate deals that benefited the Asian and white settlers who came to comprise the political power structure in Hawaiʻi, thus ushering in a new era of Asian settler political ascendancy.[21]

Informed by the work of Trask and other Native scholars who critique the U.S. settler state, the contributors to *Asian Settler Colonialism* work collectively to examine Asian settler colonialism as a constellation of the colonial ideologies and practices of Asian settlers who currently support the broader structure of the U.S. settler state. The contributors investigate aspects of Asian settler colonialism from different fields and disciplines to illustrate its diverse operations and material impact on Native Hawaiians. The essays range from analyses of Japanese, Korean, and Filipino settlement, to accounts of Asian settler practices in state apparatuses, such as the Hawaiʻi State Legislature, the prison industrial complex, and the U.S. military, to critiques of Asian settler representations of their claims to Hawaiʻi in ideological apparatuses such as literature and the visual arts.

Since the focus of this book is the colonial context for indigenous struggles to regain lands and nation, the critical point of difference we emphasize is one that defines a settler state: the structural distinction between Natives and settlers. All Asians, then, including those who do not have political power, are identified in this book as settlers who participate in U.S. settler colonialism. Although Asians in Hawaiʻi are identified in academic disciplines as either "local Asians" or "Asian Americans," we use the term "Asian settler" to emphasize the colonial context in which the essays in this book reexamine Asian settler occupation of Native lands. While "local" is sometimes used as a geographical marker to distinguish "local Asians" in Hawaiʻi from "Asian Americans" on the U.S. continent (as in the Japanese settler organization supporting Hawaiian struggles for self-determination, Local Japanese Women for Justice), it is more popularly used to establish a problematic claim to Hawaiʻi. Other groups in Hawaiʻi besides Asians can also be identified as settlers, but we leave it to those communities to identify their responsibilities to Hawaiians. The essays in *Asian Settler Colonialism* focus specifically on Asians in Hawaiʻi as settlers and the positions they occupy in relation to Hawaiians.

The critiques of Asian settler colonialism delivered by Asian settler scholars in this book do not dishonor the struggles of their grandparents and great-grandparents, the early Asian settler laborers who demonstrated tremendous courage and resourcefulness. As I will later illustrate, the sugar planters established the plantation as an economic base for an American settler colony by exploiting the unstable political and economic conditions in Asian nations resulting from American, British, Spanish, and Japanese imperialism. Hawaiʻi is described in historical accounts as a place that offered early Asian laborers economic opportunities, a political haven from universal conscription or political persecution, or a site from which they believed they could better sustain nationalist struggles in their homelands. On the plantations, however, Asian laborers suffered under horrific conditions of anti-Asian racism. Referred to as "cattle," viewed as "instruments of production," and ordered as "supplies" along with "fertilizer," many Asian laborers were flogged, beaten, imprisoned, and even killed on the plantations.[22]

Honoring the struggles of those who came before us, however, also means resisting the impulse to claim only their histories of oppression and resistance. The Asian settler scholars in this book are now working to restore other complex dimensions to the histories of the early Asian settlers and their descendants, ones that also acknowledge the ways that they are beneficiaries of U.S. settler colonialism. The early Asian settlers were both active agents in the making of their own histories and unwitting recruits swept into the service of empire.

As we are inspired by our family histories of struggle, we also recognize that the suffering of those who came before us does not change the fact that they entered into a settler colony, however temporary or permanent they imagined that settlement to be, and that the large-scale entry of Asians into Hawai'i was made possible by U.S. settler colonialism. In a particularly telling way, much of Asian settler scholarship continues to privilege the United States as the center that defines Asians by their relationship to the white sugar planters. The status of Asians as settlers, however, is not a question about whether they were the initial colonizers or about their relationship with white settlers. The identification of Asians as settlers focuses on their obligations to the indigenous peoples of Hawai'i and the responsibilities that Asian settlers have in supporting Native peoples in their struggles for self-determination.

In our work of mapping out the operations of Asian settler colonialism, we have also been able to identify a settler impulse to concede that Asians are settlers but to deny that all Asians have the political capacity to colonize Hawaiians. In these arguments, Asian settlers who are critical of the term "settler" attempt to make semantic distinctions between (1) the use of the term "settler" to refer to early groups of Asian laborers imported by the plantation owners or recent Asian immigrants who had and have no political power, and (2) the use of the term "Asian settler colonialism," which implies being in possession of the political power to colonize. As settler studies scholars Anna Johnston and Alan Lawson argue, however, inherent in such distinctions is the "strategic disavowal of the colonizing act."[23] In Hawai'i, the collapse of the Hawaiian population and subsequent displacement of Hawaiians physically, politically, and culturally have meant that the condition of being a settler is extricable from the processes of occupation and colonization, and as Johnston and Lawson argue, "Settlers are colonizers in an ineluctable historical and continuing relationality to indigenes and indigeneity." According to these definitions, Asian settler colonialism can be said to commence with the arrival of the first Asian laborers who entered into Hawai'i under the auspices of the white sugar planters' Royal Hawaiian Agricultural Society and occupied Native lands through colonial processes at a time when it was already a nation under siege by Western colonial powers. More recent immigrants, as I will later discuss, are settlers who enter into and occupy the colony of Hawai'i by submitting to the laws set forth by the U.S. settler state.

Other material forces shaping Asian settler colonialism include what Eiko Kosasa, Dean Saranillio, and Peggy Choy describe in their work in this book as the indoctrination of Asian settlers by the "Americanization" movement during and after World War II mobilized by white settlers anxious over the growing Asian population in Hawai'i. Although Eileen Tamura points out that Asians did not become the passive, subordinated workers that the Americanization movement sought to produce, the overall effect of the Americanization movement was unquestioning Asian settler support of the authority of the U.S. settler state. As Tamura points out, "Rather than seek to change the Anglo-American cultural and economic system, the Nisei sought to fit into it. Those who became successful believed in the American system and gained prominence by playing by its rules, not by challenging them."[24] As the arguments of these scholars show, Asian settler support of U.S. colonialism and what we identify as Asian settler colonialism was in place well before the post–World War II political ascendancy of Asian settlers, particularly Japanese and Chinese settlers, and their 1954 Democratic takeover of political power. The year 1954 instead marks a new dimension of an already established architecture of Asian settler colonialism and the legislative means by which Asian settlers not only assumed positions of colonial administration, but also perpetuated the subjugation of Hawaiians through state apparatuses.

The primary concern of this book, however, is Asian settler colonialism as it refers to the present participation of all Asians in Hawai'i in U.S. settler colonialism through different kinds of settler practices, ranging from colonial administration to the routines of everyday life. As the contributors illustrate, all Asian settlers, including colonial administrators, artists, teachers, students, writers, journalists, scholars, and many others who do not see themselves as having a political role to play, support and engage in the U.S. colonization of Hawaiians. Asian settlers who support Hawaiian nationalists play a critical role in bringing about the structural transformation necessary for Hawaiian national liberation, but even supportive Asian settlers, like the contributors to this collection, will continue to benefit from and be a part of the larger system of U.S. settler colonialism until Hawaiians regain their lands and nation. Only by achieving such justice can Asian settlers liberate themselves from their roles as agents in a colonial system of violence.

There are, of course, different Asian settler groups, and the intrasettler racism and discrimination they are subjected to illuminate the complex relations of power among settler groups. Some Asian groups, like Filipinos, remain politically and economically subordinated in Hawai'i, and anti-Filipino racism in Hawai'i is a legacy of Spanish, American, and Japanese colonial violence and occupation of the Philippines. Situating Filipino experiences of racial profiling and discrimination in a colonial framework, however, Dean Saranillio has argued that although Filipinos seek to empower their communities, they do so as settlers in a colonial system. Saranillio writes, "I argue that our current strategy of empowerment does not disrupt the colonial power structures oppressing Native Hawaiians and instead reinforces colonialism by making use of American patriotic narratives." [25] In his essay in this book he argues, "Because the United States invaded Hawai'i, Filipinos, like other settlers who immigrated to Hawai'i, live in a colonized nation where the indigenous peoples do not possess their indigenous human right to self-determination, and because of this Filipinos are settlers." Similarly, Asians who are received in Hawai'i and the United States under U.N. definitions of political refugees, like the Vietnamese, Cambodians, Laotians, and Hmong, do not have political power yet are still settlers in relation to Hawaiians. For Asians who settle in Hawai'i because of histories of colonization in their own homelands, the violence of their own political displacement, in some cases as a result of American military intervention and occupation, only reinforces more strongly our critique of colonialism and its global effects.

As in every settler state, there are differences and power relations that cut across settler populations, between white settlers and nonwhite settlers, among Asian settler groups, between working-class settlers and the settlers who make up the more privileged classes. Vietnamese settlers, for example, occupy a socioeconomically and politically disadvantaged position compared to Japanese settlers. Nevertheless, an analysis of settler colonialism positions indigenous peoples at the center, foregrounding not settler groups' relationships with each other or with the U.S. settler state, but with the indigenous peoples whose ancestral lands settlers occupy. To focus only on the obvious differences among settlers evades the question of settlers' obligations to indigenous peoples. As Eiko Kosasa has argued, "Native Hawaiians are the indigenous people of the islands. It is their nation that is under U.S. occupation; therefore, only Native Hawaiians are colonized. The rest of the population, including myself, are settlers regardless of our racial heritage." [26]

The essays in this book call our attention to the importance of distinguishing Natives from settlers in Hawaiians' struggle for political justice, and in doing so the contributors join indigenous and settler scholars and activists in Australia and the United States in reexamining the positions of immigrants in settler states. [27] Trask's work and the essays in this book point out new directions for foundational as well as recent studies of settler states by scholars such as Donald Denoon, Ronald Weitzer, Daiva Stasiulis, Nira Yuval-Davis, Patrick Wolfe, David Pearson, Anna Johnston, Alan Lawson, Caroline Elkins, Susan Pedersen, and Annie Coombes.[28] In their work, these scholars differentiate conventional, dependent, or franchise colonies like India from settler colonies (later settler states) such as Australia, New Zealand, Canada, and the United States: in conventional colonies, the metropole directs the "outpost" of the colony, which is maintained by a small apparatus of colonial administrators scattered throughout the territory whose power is enforced by the colonial military presence; by contrast, in settler colonies, settlers occupy Native land and rewrite its history as their own. They institute political infrastructures that are designed to benefit settlers economically and politically and to subjugate and eliminate indigenous peoples. As Patrick Wolfe has argued,

> The primary object of settler-colonization is the land itself rather than the surplus value to be derived from mixing native labour with it. Though, in practice, Indigenous labour was indispensible to Europeans, settler-colonization is at base a winner-take-all project whose dominant feature is not exploitation but replacement. The logic of this project, a sustained institutional tendency to eliminate the Indigenous population, informs a range of historical practices that might otherwise appear distinct—invasion is a structure not an event.[29]

Such historical practices range from the Australian settler-colonial policy regarding blood quantum that excluded a substantial proportion of mixed-race Aboriginal peoples from the category of "Aboriginal" to settler claims to academic authority over indigenous culture used to rationalize state policies, including the abduction of Aboriginal children for the assimilationist purpose of "breeding them white"— all practices that illustrate what Wolfe terms "the logic of elimination." What is crucial here is Wolfe's argument that invasion is not simply an event that can be relegated to the past; invasion continues to be constitutive of the very structure of the settler state and its persistent, institutionalized policies of elimination.

As these scholars illuminate the ways that settler states are products of specific material histories and economic systems, some have been highly ambivalent about articulating the roles of immigrants in settler states like Australia and the United States. Because Asians in these non-Asian settler states have been historically subjected to state racism, scholars like David Pearson use what he calls an "analytic triangle" of "aboriginal/settler/immigrant" to represent "immigrants" as occupying a third space that exempts them from colonial responsibilities. Pearson's logic in constructing such a triangle is premised on his conception of the United States as a "post-settler locale," a conclusion derived from his assumption that the "place of aboriginality" in the United States, "given the scale of competing ethnic categories, has a far more muted presence."[30] Similarly, Ronald Weitzer contends that the United States is no longer a settler state because "in the United States and Australia, the indigenous population was forcibly displaced and largely eliminated."[31] Pearson and Weitzer ideologically construct the presence of indigenous peoples as "muted" or "eliminated" in ways that fail to acknowledge their ongoing forms of resistance, and in this way the "vanishing Indian" thesis manifests itself in new ways by representing Native peoples as "disappearing" into a "multicultural" society. Wolfe has critiqued such settler constructions of multiculturalism, underscoring the "primary Indigenous/settler divide": "cultural pluralism is itself celebrated by an assimilationist discourse that seeks to lose Indigenous specificity in amongst the ethnic heterogeneity of immigrant populations."[32] As Haunani-Kay Trask argues in her essay in this book, the failure to identify immigrants in settler states as settlers makes possible the historical fantasy of settler states evolving into "multicultural nations."

In their essays here, Hawaiians demand a recognition of the distinction between Natives and settlers of color, and they stand united with other indigenous peoples all over the world, including Aboriginal and Torres Strait Islander peoples in Australia who also differentiate themselves from ethnic minorities. Aboriginal and Torres Strait Islander peoples have rights to ancestral lands that have been formally recognized in the High Court of Australia's 1992 *Mabo* decision, which acknowledged for the first time Native title to lands colonized by the British. Des Williams, Aboriginal and Torres Strait Islander Commissioner (ATSIC) in 2002, states, "We want recognition of our attachment and ownership of this country. Not just as another ethnic group but as a peoples synonymous with this country."[33] Peter Yu, an organizer of Yawru and Chinese descent who has worked at state, national, and international levels on behalf of indigenous communities, further explains, "First, indigenous Australians are, at a fundamental level, part of the modern Australian nation. Within that nation we have a particular position, for we are Australia's Indigenous people. We are not just another minority ethnic group: we are the first people of this land, and we continue to have our own internal systems, of law, culture, land tenure, authority and leadership."[34]

These arguments on the part of Aboriginal and Torres Strait Islander peoples have influenced the work of scholars in Australia who have also begun to identify Asians as settlers. Ien Ang, Ann Curthoys, and John Docker have argued that although Asians in Australia do not have political power, they are still settlers in relation to indigenous peoples.[35] In her more recent work, Ang points out that the "opening" of Australia to Indochinese refugees, to "non-European—especially Asian—new settlers," implicates them in the colonial process, and Asian settlers have their own responsibilities toward indigenous peoples.[36] Ang writes, "Indeed, non-white migrants have their own moral obligation to work through their relationship to Indigenous Australia."[37] In her own analysis of the differences between indigenous peoples and immigrants that are leveled either by subsuming indigenous peoples into the "multicultural" or incorporating nonwhite immigrants into the "postcolonial," Curthoys concludes, "The continuing presence of colonialism has implications for all immigrants, whether first-generation or sixth. All nonindigenous people, recent immigrants and descendants of immigrants alike, are beneficiaries of a colonial history. We share the situation of living on someone else's land."[38] Docker states simply, "For Aboriginal peoples, migrants are another set of invaders, not brothers and sisters on the margins, not the fellow oppressed and dispossessed."[39]

The work of these Australian settler scholars is critical in pointing to the ways that the status of Asians as settlers is not defined by their political power but by their relationship to indigenous peoples in a settler state. *Asian Settler Colonialism* takes this argument as its premise, but it also expands upon the work being done in settler studies by analyzing the historical and political specificities of a settler colony where some Asian settler groups have come to share colonial power with white settlers. Asian settlers in Hawai'i dominate state institutions and apparatuses, and their legislation and public policies sustain the U.S. settler state. The Native and settler contributors to this book, like other scholars engaged in critiques of empire, map out the present practices of Asian settler colonial administrators in Hawai'i as symptomatic of more widespread settler colonial dynamics.[40] They identify Asian settlers who have obstructed Hawaiians' efforts to regain self-determination, whether in their capacities as U.S. senator, state legislator, governor, director of public safety, or high-ranking military officer. Other contributors examine the colonial practices of Asian settlers who have taken on positions on state boards and committees administering Hawaiian trust assets and issues of self-determination, including Kamehameha Schools / Bishop Estate, the Office of Hawaiian Affairs, and the Akaka Task Force.

In other, less overtly political ways, Asian settlers in Hawai'i actively participate in the dispossession of Hawaiians through their daily identification with and participation in the U.S. settler state. Karen K. Kosasa points out in her essay that each Asian settler has a responsibility toward Native peoples. Asian settler colonialism is as much about the inertia and cynicism that perpetuate current colonial conditions as it is about the aggressive assault on Hawaiian rights. She writes,

> Although many long-time settlers in Hawai'i are critical of the ways the land has been overbuilt by real estate developers and overrun by commercial enterprises, disentangling ourselves from the resulting "amenities" is no easy task. As settlers, many of us are reluctant, even unwilling, to consider how the pleasures of everyday life—dining out, shopping in malls, watching television, and

living in suburban communities—can be part of a larger colonial problem. How can these seemingly innocent activities be "hegemonic"?[41]

As Kosasa illustrates, Asian settler power and privilege have become so naturalized in our lives that that they have become invisible to many in Hawai'i. Each Asian settler, however, is implicated in practices that support existing conditions of U.S. colonialism.

As the essays in this book map out the interlocking state apparatuses of colonial power Asian settlers support and maintain, they also raise questions for Asian settlers about what they can do to change the colonial practices of their own Asian settler communities. The contributors seek to move settlers beyond the paralysis of guilt to an active participation in the struggle for political justice. They map out the colonial and racist practices in Asian settler communities and the U.S. settler state in order to provide Asian settlers with opportunities for intervention and transformation. It is in identifying the United States not as a multicultural democracy but as a settler state that we can more effectively work toward justice for Native peoples and, by extension, for settlers as well.

Some of the essays in this collection do not specifically address Asian settler colonialism in Hawai'i, but they sketch out the larger architecture of U.S. settler colonialism that Asian settlers sustain: these include Mililani Trask's historical outline of the United States' violation of Hawaiians' right to self-determination, David Stannard's examination of interlocking social service organizations that blame Hawaiians for their health crises, and Kyle Kajihiro's account of the impact of militarism on Hawai'i and resistance to it. These essays resonate with and amplify arguments made elsewhere in the book that specifically outline Asian settler colonial practices. When Mililani Trask argues that Native initiatives for Hawaiian sovereignty like Ka Lāhui arose in response to the failure of the Democratic Party to resolve Hawaiians' land claims and demands for self-determination, her arguments enlarge upon Eiko Kosasa and Ida Yoshinaga's critique of the Japanese American Citizens' League (JACL), its defense of U.S. Senator Daniel Inouye, and its operation in service of the Asian settler-dominated Democratic Party. Similarly, Kajihiro's critique of the militarization of Hawai'i recasts our understanding of the "iconography of the World War II nisei vet" largely celebrated as proof that military service enabled Japanese Americans to overcome racial discrimination. Instead, as Kajihiro argues, the mythologizing of the 100th Infantry Battalion and the 442nd Regimental Combat Team "oversimplifies the complex convergence of events and factors that enabled local Japanese to gain power in post–World War II Hawai'i, and it obscures the tragic consequences of this development for Kānaka Maoli." David Stannard's arguments about the settler colonial public policies of social service organizations also take on new dimensions when we consider Eiko

Kosasa's argument that county, state, and federal officials in Hawai'i are largely Japanese.[42]

This collection by Native and settler scholars is not a study or survey of the Hawaiian movement for self-determination, and we urge readers to seek out an extensive body of such works by Hawaiian scholars and activists. The focus of this book is an investigation of Asian settler political practices and ideologies, and the essays here by Haunani-Kay Trask and Mililani Trask that describe Ka Lāhui as a Native initiative for a self-determined sovereignty do so in order to critique present conditions where Asian settlers authorize themselves to sit on state committees and task forces that determine the future for Hawaiians. Their accounts of a Native initiative show us what Hawaiian self-determination would look like without the interference of Asian settlers or the limitations of settler interests.

The essays in *Asian Settler Colonialism* recast and reframe critically our knowledges and the scholarship and practices we engage in. They afford us a new vision of the world, and they demand of Asian settler scholars and readers an interrogation of their interests as settlers and the material consequences of their practices. This interrogation is critical to understanding the system of settler colonialism within which political injustices are reproduced and to seeking out ways of transforming our roles as settlers within it.

The Political Stakes behind the Native/Settler Distinction

On November 23, 1993, Congress passed U.S. Public Law 103-150, also known as the Apology Resolution, which states unequivocally, "The Congress apologizes to Native Hawaiians on behalf of the people of the United States for the overthrow of the Kingdom of Hawaii on January 17, 1893 with the participation of agents and citizens of the United States, and the deprivation of the rights of Native Hawaiians to self-determination." Despite the passage of this law, white and Asian settlers have launched multiple legal assaults against Native entitlements and compensatory programs. Legal cases such as *Rice v. Cayetano, Arakaki et al. v. the State of Hawai'i*, and *Arakaki et al. v. Lingle* have sought to take from Hawaiians what entitlements remain to them after the American military-backed overthrow of the Hawaiian government in 1893. In these cases, white and Asian settlers use civil rights arguments to assert that there are no distinctions between Natives and settlers and that any "preference" given to Native peoples constitutes racial discrimination against non-Hawaiians. In this section, I analyze the arguments that settlers use to equate themselves with Natives in these lawsuits to illustrate the ways that civil rights arguments are often used *against* Native peoples.[43]

Under these lawsuits' colonial classifications of Hawaiians as a racial group,

Native accounts of a genealogical relationship with land are dismissed as "metaphorical." Contributors Haunani-Kay Trask, Mililani Trask, Momiala Kamahele, Healani Sonoda, kuʻualoha hoʻomanawanui, and Kapulani Landgraf challenge these dismissals and call for a political acknowledgment of Hawaiians' genealogical, familial relationship with land in Hawaiʻi. In their arguments we can see the complex significance of land as an ancestor that unites the Hawaiian people while feeding and sustaining their anticolonial resistance. Kahikina de Silva has described Hawaiian nationalists as "'aipōhaku," or "rock eaters."

> The term 'aipōhaku is not used lightly. . . . The eating of stones is not smooth and easy. Gleaning sustenance from them does not make you fat like the kōlea bird that visits Hawaiʻi each winter. But as such unyielding, solid creatures, pōhaku are also the hardened, congealed essence of Papa herself and of the land that makes us kānaka. . . . Those who do, whose mouths eat rock, consequently speak with the solidity and mana of the pōhaku they have absorbed. And, when appropriate, they may even spit those rocks at deserving audiences. The voices of such 'aipōhaku, Trask included, are unmistakable. In an age of dislocation they remind their peers and pōkiʻi that land is not simply a locale; it is our connection to each other, to ancestors gone and descendants to come. And they work endlessly to convince others to politically acknowledge this connection.[44]

De Silva's description of Hawaiian political protests resonates with the 1893 antiannexation song "Kaulana Nā Pua," originally titled "Mele ʻAi Pōhaku" (Rock-eating song). In de Silva's words and in the song we can see the way in which land is central to Hawaiians' survival as a people.

By contrast, settler lawsuits claim that in an American democracy Hawaiians' indigenous rights to land and resources jeopardize democratic ideals of "justice for all." They illustrate precisely what happens when settlers equate themselves with Natives. In the most egregious of ironies, settlers proclaim that Native Hawaiians are depriving them of their civil rights, but they do so in order to use the argument of equal rights to take from Natives their rights and resources as indigenous peoples. In 1996 attorneys representing Harold "Freddy" Rice argued that it is unconstitutional for the state to restrict voting to Hawaiians only in elections for the Office of Hawaiian Affairs (OHA). OHA is a state office charged with disbursing the monies generated by nearly two million acres of "ceded" lands that are held in "trust" by the State for the Hawaiian people.[45] Rice's attorneys used the Fifteenth Amendment, which prohibits states from abridging the right to vote based on race, to argue that the elections deprived Rice of his civil rights. In 2000 the U.S. Supreme Court ruled in favor of Rice, forcing OHA to open its elections to non-Hawaiians. As a result of the *Rice v. Cayetano* decision, other lawsuits followed. *Arakaki et al. v. the State of Hawai'i* (2000) claimed that the *Rice* decision gave non-Hawaiians the right to run in elections for OHA trustees. The district judge ruled in favor of Arakaki, and Charles Ota, a Japanese settler who was a 442nd Regimental Combat Team veteran, a member of the Land Use Commission, and an investor in real estate partnerships, was elected to office.[46] In a March 2002 lawsuit, *Arakaki et al v. Lingle,* the attorneys who filed the suit argued that OHA, the Hawaiian Homes Commission, and the Department of Hawaiian Home Lands programs are unconstitutional because they are race-based and discriminate against non-Hawaiians.[47]

If the language of equal rights and "our democracy" was used for settler colonial purposes by the U.S. Supreme Court in the *Rice* case to level the differences between Natives and settlers, Asian settlers also revealed their own political interests in erasing those differences. In response to the *Rice* decision, former governor Benjamin Cayetano, a Filipino settler, stated publicly, "I've lived in Hawai'i long enough to feel I'm Hawaiian."[48] In Hawai'i, where the word "Hawaiian" is used in reference to those of Hawaiian ancestry, such a statement in and of itself seems merely comical, but Cayetano's remark was politically motivated: as Ida Yoshinaga and Eiko Kosasa point out in their essay, he was acting on the advice of U.S. Senator Daniel Inouye by appointing a Japanese settler as interim OHA trustee following the *Rice* ruling. Charles Ota, the appointee, was also quoted in the media as saying, "I am of Japanese ancestry, but I feel I have been Hawaiian all my life."[49] Cayetano's and Ota's statements thus illustrate how Asian settlers attempt to "indigenize" themselves to protect their political investments in settler control over Native peoples and resources.

As these cases illustrate, an emphasis on "race" and civil rights has historically obscured the political category of the "indigenous" and a long history of Native peoples' struggles for national liberation. As Asian settlers in Hawai'i continue to struggle against different forms of intrasettler racism and discrimination, they can do so with a broader awareness of the effects that civil rights arguments have had for Native peoples. On one register, the erosion of civil rights by the Bush administration in the wake of the 9/11 attacks on the World Trade Center and the Pentagon takes place in a larger colonial context where legislation such as the USA PATRIOT Act (2001) has been used by the colonial state to target not only peoples of Middle Eastern and South Asian descent, but Native peoples who speak out against U.S. colonialism.[50] On another register, as Kamahele illustrates in her essay, Asian and white settlers have used civil rights arguments in their attempts to revise the Hawai'i State Constitution to take from Hawaiians their statutory and constitutional rights to gather resources of the land for Hawaiian cultural practices. The essay by Kosasa and Yoshinaga further examines the ways that Asian settler community organizations like the JACL have used civil rights arguments against Hawaiian nationalists who are critical of Japanese political power.

The Colonial Apparatus of the Sugar Plantations and Asian Settler Labor

Extensive Asian settlement in Hawai'i was made possible by American colonial efforts to secure a labor base for a settler plantation economy. The Kōloa Plantation was established in 1835, and as the first large-scale sugar plantation in Hawai'i it intensified foreigners' desire for title to Native lands. As Lilikalā Kame'eleihiwa has argued, "Recently, much attention has been focused on the 1893 overthrow of Queen Lili'uokalani and the demise of the Hawaiian monarchy. But the real loss of Hawaiian sovereignty began with the 1848 *Māhele*, when the *Mo'i* and *Ali'i Nui* lost ultimate control of the *'Āina*."[51] The Māhele instituted a devastating transformation from traditional communal land tenure to private ownership of land. As Kame'eleihiwa's research shows, the Ali'i Nui believed the Māhele would end the collapse of the Hawaiian population and protect their sovereignty, but those who benefited most were the white political advisers who later started their own plantations.[52]

Thus by 1852, when the first major contract labor group of Chinese arrived in Hawai'i, the Hawaiian Kingdom was already a nation in distress under Western forces of colonialism. As the Hawaiian population continued to plummet, the sugar planters sought to build their empire by securing Asian laborers from China, Japan, Korea, and the Philippines. The planters found that British, American, Spanish, and Japanese acts of imperial aggression created social and political conditions in Asia that helped to facilitate their own efforts in the building of an American settler colony in Hawai'i.[53]

The Royal Hawaiian Agricultural Society was established by the sugar planters in 1850, and it quickly focused on the recruitment of labor from China. In the late 1830s British "gunboat diplomacy" had forced China to open its ports to trade, and Chinese efforts to end the British trafficking of opium into China as well as conflicts over British demands for extraterritoriality led to China's losses in the Opium War (1839–1842) and the Anglo-Chinese War (1856–1860). These international conflicts, the Taiping Rebellion (1850–1864), and other instances of local warfare proved to be devastating for millions of Chinese peasants. Under these conditions, the Chinese government allowed the recruitment of contract labor, and by 1882 the Chinese constituted almost a quarter of the population of the Hawaiian Kingdom.[54] Because the Chinese left the plantations after they had worked off their contracts, many Americans perceived them to be an economic threat, while others attributed the spread of leprosy and smallpox to them.

Anti-Chinese sentiment grew with the increased influx of Chinese redirected to Hawaiʻi after the United States passed the 1882 Chinese Exclusion Act, and successive regulations restricting Chinese immigration were enacted in Hawaiʻi.[55] The sugar planters then turned to securing laborers from Japan.

American gunboat diplomacy had also forced Japanese ports open in 1853, and the Japanese government saw that like China, it, too, was vulnerable to attack by British and American imperial forces. Japan launched a massive program of modernization, rapid industrialization, militarization, and imperialism financed by a new land taxation system that took a tremendous toll on landowners, tenant farmers, and agricultural laborers. The Japanese national slogan during the Meiji period (1868–1912), *"Fukoku kyōhei"* (Enrich the nation, strengthen the military), also shaped the Japanese government's imperialist policies.[56] Under colonial duress, Kalākaua sought to preserve Hawaiian sovereignty from American imperialist interests in 1881 through proposals to Emperor Meiji for a Japan-led "Asiatic federation" including Hawaiʻi, the betrothal of the Japanese prince to his niece, Princess Kaʻiulani, and the immigration of Japanese laborers to Hawaiʻi.[57] The emperor declined the proposals to avoid jeopardizing Japan's hopes for treaty revisions with Western powers, but as Eiko Kosasa reminds us, the Japanese government later considered its emigrating citizens as part of its "peaceful expansion" policy.[58] The first government-sponsored laborers arrived in Hawaiʻi in 1885.[59] By 1900 Japanese settlers constituted the largest settler group in Hawaiʻi, resulting in growing debates over "the Japanese Question."[60] U.S. territorial leaders, planters, and the white settler population grew increasingly anxious over the growing collective organizing power of Japanese labor, conflicts with Japan over Japanese voting rights in Hawaiʻi, and rumors about Japan's plans to annex Hawaiʻi.[61] White laborers proved to be too expensive, and laborers from Puerto Rico, weakened by famine and poverty, were deemed by the planters as "unsatisfactory." The planters sought to return to recruiting Chinese labor, but U.S. annexation in 1898 had made Hawaiʻi subject to the Chinese Exclusion Act barring the immigration of Chinese.[62] The planters then turned to Korea as a cheap source of labor.

Japanese gunboat diplomacy, in turn, had forced Korea to sign the 1876 Treaty of Kanghwa, which was modeled on the treaties that Japan and China had been forced to sign by the British and Americans.[63] Korean nationalism emerged out of Korean resistance to Japanese and Western aggression, and although this resistance had spread throughout the country since 1876, the 1894 Tonghak Rebellion was critical in establishing a grassroots base of national resistance as poor farmers rose up against the imperialist economic policies of Western and Japanese foreign powers, excessive taxation of peasants, and the instability of the Korean government.[64] In response to the Tonghak Rebellion, the Korean government requested Chinese military aid. The Japanese responded by sending their own troops into Korea, and

Japan wrested control of Korea from China in the Sino-Japanese War (1894–1895). The Japanese had defeated the Tonghak army, but the Japanese assassination of Queen Min in 1895 mobilized the activities of the Uibyong (Righteous Army) and its armed struggle against the Japanese.[65] In 1902 the sugar planters enlisted the aid of Horace N. Allen, the American minister to Korea, who convinced Emperor Kojong that supporting American economic interests by setting up an emigration bureau in Korea would help to maintain Korean independence in the face of Japanese imperialism and provide economic relief for Koreans suffering from the effects of famine, a cholera epidemic, and armed conflict.[66] The first Korean laborers arrived in Hawai'i in 1903. Two years later, however, the Korean government prohibited emigration to Mexico and Hawai'i due to reports of Korean laborers being mistreated in Mexico. Japan pressured Korea to close the emigration bureau so that Japan could protect Japanese workers in Hawai'i whose organized work stoppages were being undermined by the planters who hired Korean laborers to replace them.[67] The Philippines became an increasingly attractive new source of labor for the Hawaiian Sugar Planters' Association (HSPA).

The HSPA's recruitment of Filipino laborers illustrates the interlocking operations of American imperialism in Hawai'i and the Philippines. The Philippines had struggled against Spanish colonial domination for more than three centuries. In the nineteenth century peasants defined their struggles against Spanish/Catholic rule in people's movements, from that of the Cofradia de San Jose in the early 1840s to the Santa Iglesia in the 1890s.[68] These movements, the Propaganda Movement (1880–1890) for reform, and armed revolt by the Katipunan founded in 1892 led to the Philippine Revolution in 1896.[69] On June 12, 1898, the Philippines declared its independence, but the United States had also entered into the Spanish-American War, and by the terms of the U.S. peace treaty with Spain, the latter ceded the Philippines, Guam, and Puerto Rico to the United States for $20 million. President William McKinley felt that Filipinos were "unfit for self-rule" after their war with the Spanish, and Filipino nationalists engaged in guerilla warfare to regain control over their nation. One million Filipinos were killed or died from disease as a result of the Philippine-American War.[70] Under American occupation, independent farmers unable to pay rising taxes lost titles to their land, and caciques demanded increasing shares from tenant farmers. In 1906 Albert F. Judd, a member of the oligarchy that overthrew the Hawaiian government, was sent to negotiate with the Philippine Commission governed by William Howard Taft (U.S. president, 1909–1913) for permission to allow the HSPA to recruit Filipino laborers. That same year Filipino laborers arrived in Hawai'i, moving from their own colonized homeland to another colonized space, from one American colony to another.

As these global events and forces indicate, the exodus of Asian laborers from their ancestral homelands and their occupation of Hawai'i were shaped by both U.S. settler colonialism in Hawai'i and imperial contests for control in Asia. The plantation system itself was both a colonial enterprise and a racist system that exploited Asian laborers. As Gary Okihiro has argued, the system of migrant labor was essentially anti-Asian because "it was designed to control and exploit the productive labor of Asians and then to expel them when their utility had ended."[71] Asian laborers were forced to work under conditions that white settlers publicly acknowledged were intolerable for white laborers. In 1921 Walter Dillingham (1875–1963), later hailed by settlers as "Hawaii's greatest builder" because of his role in the dredging and construction of Ala Moana Shopping Center, Pearl Harbor, and Honolulu International Airport, explained that white laborers would not migrate to Hawai'i from the U.S. continent because they could not be expected to do the work that God had created peoples of "variegated colors" to do.[72]

I provide this overview of early Asian settlement to illustrate that it is not colonial intent that defines the status of Asians as settlers but rather the historical context of U.S. colonialism of which they unknowingly became a part. Other Asian settlers recount their family histories of social and political activism but do so within the framework of U.S. colonialism and the complicity of their families as settlers in the growth of a U.S. settler colony. Peggy Choy's own family is widely respected for their commitment to political justice in Hawai'i, and in her essay in this volume she explains the complexity of recognizing the accomplishments of her Korean settler family.

> My own family's stories took place not on their own soil but on Hawaiian soil. They did admirable things for their own community as well as for the home country. However, they were living at a time when the islands were going through a transition from territory to state, a time during which U.S. colonial control over the islands was made more complete. The wider context of colonial domination cannot be ignored. The legacy of their own lives—as ethically as they lived—was tainted with unavoidable complicity.[73]

The oppression of the early Asian settlers does not change the irreducible, substantive issue of indigenous claims to land and nation. Settler arguments that criticize the "essentialism" of the terms the "Native" and "settler" or, worse yet, accuse Native peoples of their own complicity in their colonization fail to address this critical issue of indigenous claims to land and nation. At the same time, Asian settlers who argue that the identification of Asians as settlers "oversimplifies" historical "nuances" actually register the ways that Asian settler complicity becomes lost in demands for "complexity." Furthermore, it is the identification of Asians as settlers that in fact involves a more complex analysis of colonial power in Hawai'i and Asian settlers' maintenance of the colonial system from their differing locations within it.

As ku'ualoha ho'omanawanui argues in her essay in this book, Asian settlers cannot insert themselves into a genealogy of the land in Hawai'i, no matter how long they have lived on it or how much they or their ancestors have suffered on it. Asian settlers have their own long and rich genealogical ties elsewhere, as Eiko Kosasa explains.

> I am a sansei whose grandfather journeyed to Hawai'i in 1898 from Iwate Prefecture in northern Japan. After Tokugawa Ieyasu seized the Ōsaka Castle in the early 1600s, my ancestors fled Ōsaka and settled in the Iwate area where they lived for 400 years. Prior to that they lived in the Ōsaka area for many generations. My genealogical heritage in Japan is long, while it consists of only three generations in Hawai'i. In comparison, the Hawaiian Islands and the continental land mass now called the United States are the genealogical homeland to Native Hawaiians, Alaska Natives, and American Indians. They have lived in this area for thousands of years as peoples and nations. When my ancestors arrived, they entered into a colonial space. Today is no different—we remain Asian settlers in a colonial space. The United States continues to occupy Hawai'i and the American continent in violation of international laws and against the consent of Native nations.[74]

Asian settlers may not be able to identify with the Asian homelands many of them have never seen, but that does not change their condition in Hawai'i: in this colonized location, they are settlers in another's homeland.

In the present political moment, Asian settlers can no longer claim ignorance of the colonial subjugation of Hawaiians. I turn now to substantive evidence of the political power that Asians exercise in Hawai'i in order to provide the larger context for the contributors' critiques of Asian settler colonial administration.

Asian Settler Political Power and Affiliations

In 2005 the demographics of Hawai'i illustrate the extent to which Hawaiians are outnumbered by settlers in their own homeland. Because of the sizable mixed-race population in Hawai'i, there are different ways in which the ethnic distribution of the population is calculated. I present the various U.S. Census and State of Hawai'i Department of Health figures here, even as I will be using as my own primary source the data collected by the Department of Health (see table 1).

The 2000 census data for the population of the State of Hawai'i based on multiple counting of multiracial/ethnic persons, data for "race alone or in combina-

Table 1. Snapshot of Political Power in Hawai'i, 2005

	Percentage of Population (Census)[1]	Percentage of Population (DOH)[2]	Legislature: Senate[3]	Legislature: House	Dept. of Ed. (Admin.)[4]	Dept. of Ed. (Faculty)
Hawaiian	20	22.1	8	10	14	10
White	39	21.1	24	26	20	27
Japanese	24	21.9	40	40	45	34
Filipino	23	15.9	20	14	4	6
Chinese	14	5.8	8	12	5	5
Okinawan[5]	4	–	4	12	–	–
Korean	3	–	4	2	2	1
African American	3	–	0	2	1	0.5
Other	–	13.3	–	–	2	10

[1] 2000 census data for "race alone or in combination" for a total population of 1,211,537.

[2] Department of Health (DOH) figures from the *Hawai'i Health Survey 2000* for a population of 1,156,014. The DOH counts mixed-race Hawaiians as "Hawaiian," mixed-race Caucasian/Asians as "Asian," and those who list Caucasian as their sole race as "Caucasian." The *Health Survey* does not list data for Koreans or African Americans.

[3] Data for the 2005 Hawai'i State Legislature collected from legislators' offices. The DOH's method is used for counting legislators of mixed race. Multiple counting is used for mixed-race Asian legislators (e.g., multiple counting of legislators who are "Japanese/Filipino" as "Japanese" and "Filipino").

[4] Data compiled by the Certificated Transaction Unit for the Department of Education.

[5] The 2000 census lists Okinawans as "Japanese." Population data from the Hawai'i Okinawa Center.

tion" for a total population of 1,211,537, gives us a broad view of the mixed-race population of the state: whites (39 percent), Japanese (24 percent; 4 percent of Hawai'i's population is Okinawan, but they are listed in the census as "Japanese"),[75] Filipinos (23 percent), Native Hawaiians (20 percent), Chinese (14 percent), Koreans (3 percent), blacks or African Americans (3 percent), Sāmoans (2 percent), Vietnamese (1 percent), and "Other Asian" (1 percent).[76] A second set of figures for "race alone" provides the number of people who chose only one race, and the percentages are as follows: whites (24 percent), Japanese (17 percent), Filipinos (14 percent), Native Hawaiians (7 percent), Chinese (5 percent), Koreans (2 percent), blacks or African Americans (2 percent), Sāmoans (1 percent), Vietnamese (0.6 percent), and "Other Asian" (0.3 percent).

Because this book focuses on distinctions between Hawaiians and settlers, the

Department of Health's methods of calculating ethnic distribution figures presents a clearer picture of Hawaiian, Asian settler, and white settler population counts. The *Native Hawaiian Data Book* also uses ethnic distribution figures from the Department of Health's *Hawai'i Health Survey 2000*. According to that survey the ethnic distribution of a population count of 1,156,014 in Hawai'i is as follows: Hawaiians (22.1 percent), Japanese (21.9 percent), Caucasians (21.1 percent), Filipinos (15.9 percent), Chinese (5.8 percent), and "Other" (13.3 percent).[77] The differences between the Department of Health figures and the U.S. Census figures result from the Department of Health's method of counting mixed-race Hawaiians as "Hawaiian," mixed-race Caucasian/Asians as "Asian," and those who list Caucasian as their sole race as "Caucasian." As we can see from all three sets of figures, however, Asian settlers make up the largest group in Hawai'i.

In addition to these population percentages, the 2000 census data regarding the educational, economic, and occupational status of different groups make visible the ethnic/racial stratification of Hawai'i. In his study of this data, Jonathan Okamura concludes that "occupational, income and educational status data from the 2000 U.S. Census for ethnic groups in Hawai'i indicate that Chinese Americans, Japanese Americans and Whites continue to be the dominant groups in the ethnic stratification order, while Native Hawaiians and Filipino Americans continue to occupy subordinate positions"[78] (see table 2).

The subordination of Hawaiians in their own homeland becomes even more striking when we examine other indices that register political power in Hawai'i. Cooper and Daws show in *Land and Power in Hawai'i* that "from 1960 to 1980, Japanese averaged 50% of the total membership of both houses. From 1955 to 1980, the percentage of Japanese Democrats in the Legislature was twice the percentage of Japanese in Hawaii's population. In 1960, when Japanese were 32% of population, they were 67% of Democratic legislators in both houses," and "in 1980, with 25% of population, they were 60% of Democratic legislators."[79] In 1980 Chinese settlers were 5 percent of the population but 10 percent of Democratic legislators. In 1983 the percentage of Filipino Democrats (12 percent) was roughly equal to the percentage of Filipinos in the population. By contrast, in 1980 Hawaiians constituted 18 percent of the population but only 3 percent of the Democratic legislators. Eiko Kosasa extends Cooper and Daws' analysis to examine Japanese political representation in both Democratic and Republican parties and the larger state apparatus. As she argues, "In both 1960 and 1970, *nisei* politicians comprised half of the elected State legislators [Democrats and Republicans] when only a third of the total island population was Japanese."[80] She adds, "One needs only to read the *Directory of State, County and Federal Officials* to find that Japanese surnames pervade the directory during the boom development years of 1960–1980s."

Today, an updated look at the ethnic breakdown of the 2005 Hawai'i State

Table 2. Occupational Distribution within Ethnic Groups in Hawai'i, 2000

Occupational Category[1]	Native Hawaiian[2]	White	Japanese	Filipino	Chinese	Korean
Management, professional, and related occupations	22.8	37.5	36.9	18.3	30.6	27.3
Service occupations	23.7	18.5	14.2	30.8	20.6	24.3
Sales and office occupations	29.0	26.1	32.9	27.7	31.3	33.7
Farming, fishing, and forestry occupations	1.4	0.9	0.8	2.5	0.7	0.7
Construction, extraction, and maintenance occupations	10.9	9.1	8.5	8.8	7.7	7.1
Production, transportation, and material moving occupations	12.1	7.9	6.7	11.9	9.1	7.0

Note: Data from Census 2000 Summary File 2 (SF 2)–100 Percent Data (figures do not always total 100 percent due to rounding off).

[1] Employed civilian population sixteen years and older.

[2] Census categories for race alone or in any combination.

Legislature provides a consistent picture of political power. If we use the Department of Health's method of counting mixed-race populations, the percentages are as follows: Asian settlers collectively constitute 63 percent of the legislature, whites 25 percent of the legislature, and Hawaiians 9 percent of the legislature.[81] A further breakdown of these figures into the different Asian ethnic groups, however, necessitates multiple counting of mixed-race Asian legislators (e.g., multiple counting of legislators who are Japanese/Filipino as "Japanese" and "Filipino"), the final counts totaling over 100 percent (see table 1): Japanese constitute only 21.9 percent of the population of Hawai'i, but they are 40 percent of the Senate and 40 percent of the House of Representatives. (Okinawans are often included in statistics for "Japanese," but separately they are about 4 percent of the Senate and 12 percent of the House.) Whites constitute 21.1 percent of the population, 24 percent of the Senate, and 26 percent of the House. By contrast, Hawaiians constitute 22.1 percent of the population compared to 8 percent of the Senate and 10 percent of the House. The following figures account for other Asian settler groups in the State Legislature: Filipino settlers are 15.9 percent of the population, 20 percent of the Senate, and

14 percent of the House; Chinese settlers 5.8 percent of the population, 8 percent of the Senate, and 12 percent of the House; and Korean settlers about 2 percent of the population, 4 percent of the Senate, and 2 percent of the House.[82]

Okamura further argues that Japanese political power is upheld by a broad base of support from organized labor unions: "The substantial proportion of local Japanese in large public worker unions, such as the Hawaii Government Employees Association [HGEA] and the Hawaii State Teachers Association [HSTA], that can provide endorsements and financial and human resources for campaigning is yet another reason for Japanese election to office."[83] We can also see the degree to which Japanese dominate the Department of Education in both numbers for teacher positions and administrative positions. Data collected by the Hawaiʻi State Department of Education (DOE) in October 2005 illustrate that among 13,207 public school teachers, the largest group continues to be Japanese (34 percent), followed by whites (27 percent), Hawaiians (10 percent), Filipinos (6 percent), Chinese (5 percent), Koreans (1 percent), African Americans (0.5 percent), Sāmoans (0.4 percent), Puerto Ricans (0.3 percent), "Mixed" (6 percent), and "Other" (10 percent) (see table 1).[84] In that same year, among 855 DOE administrative positions, the largest group also continues to be Japanese (45 percent), followed by whites (20 percent), Hawaiians (14 percent), Chinese (5 percent), Filipinos (4 percent), Koreans (2 percent), African Americans (1 percent), Sāmoans (0.5 percent), Puerto Ricans (0.2 percent), "Mixed" (6 percent), and "Other" (2 percent).

The structures of Asian settler power outlined in these statistics go largely unacknowledged, particularly in studies that emphasize either white settler dominance or the "multicultural diversity" of "local society" in Hawaiʻi. If white settlers continue to dominate in economic and political institutions and in educational apparatuses like the University of Hawaiʻi, the figures here provide an overview of the degree to which Japanese and Chinese settlers have also come to command real power economically and politically (see table 2). These last figures for the DOE provide some of the most visible illustrations of the complex interconnections between the materiality of state politics and the ideological production of knowledge. As Japanese settler politicians are supported by Japanese settler teachers and administrators—educators who shape Asian settlers' understanding of their roles in Hawaiʻi—we can see the importance of the ways in which Asian settler histories are interpreted and taught in Hawaiʻi.

Asian Settler Colonial Historiography and Problematic Uses of "Local"

Although "local" identity has been important to the working classes and people of color in Hawaiʻi who used the term in the 1970s as a rallying point in their resistance against forces of commercial, suburban, and resort development, we can also trace the ways in which Asian settler political power in Hawai'i is concealed by evocations of "local" solidarity. As Haunani-Kay Trask argues in her essay, the term "local" is used as a celebrated "gloss" for the term "settler." Like settler historiography in other places that attempts to redeem the settler state by casting it as a multicultural nation, Asian settler historiography in Hawai'i is also premised on a linear emplotment of history that celebrates the multicultural, mixed-race "local" society as a corrective to both Hawai'i's colonial "past" and the "divisiveness" of Hawaiian nationalism. As Noenoe Silva reminds us, "Historiography is one of the most powerful discourses that justifies the continued occupation of Hawai'i by the United States today." [85]

I return here to an examination of Eileen Tamura's essay, "Using the Past to Inform the Future: An Historiography of Hawai'i's Asian and Pacific Islander Americans" (2000), and her assertion that a study of "local" identity provides a "new" direction for a historiography of "Asians and Pacific Islander Americans" in Hawai'i. She frames her argument with a reference to Jonathan Okamura's critique of conservatives who promote the status quo, those who "feel threatened by the Hawaiian sovereignty movement because it distinguished Native Hawaiians from all other ethnic minorities and calls for special rights and privileges for *Na Kanaka Maoli*, the true people of Hawai'i." [86] Yet even with this acknowledgment, Tamura uses "local" as a category to focus on mixed-race peoples and panethnic identifications in order to question the distinction between Hawaiians and non-Hawaiians. Following a lengthy discussion of Hawaiian sovereignty, she asks,

> How does a person, for example, of German, Portuguese, Native Hawaiian, Chinese, and Filipino ancestry self-identify? What about a person who is not a Native Hawaiian but who grew up among Native Hawaiians and identifies strongly with Native Hawaiian culture? How much of our understanding of ethnic identity assumes biological inheritance and how much cultural practices? And what about those in Hawai'i who identify themselves as "local," in which case cultural identity takes precedence over ethnic identity? [87]

In the face of lawsuits threatening Hawaiian compensatory programs and indigenous rights, Hawaiians have answered these questions in terms of genealogy: mixed-race Hawaiians have a genealogical connection to land in Hawai'i however they choose to identify themselves; non-Hawaiians, no matter how long their shared family histories with Hawaiians, do not have this genealogical connection. Tamura's questions, however, are very popular ones in Hawai'i, and they illustrate a settler erasure of Hawaiian identity, either by asserting that mixed-race Hawaiians are not Hawaiian or by arguing that non-Hawaiians "can be more Hawaiian" than Hawaiians. As settler studies scholars Johnston and Lawson note, "The typical settler narrative, then, has a doubled goal. It is concerned to act out the suppression or effacement of the indigene; it is also concerned to perform the concomitant indigenization of the settler." [88]

We can further historicize the popular usage of the term "local" to illustrate the problems that have attended representations of "local" identity. Eric Yamamoto's widely referenced 1979 essay, "The Significance of Local," describes the way the term "local" gained a particular force after 1965, when it was used as a focal point for community control struggles in Hawai'i.[89] In these struggles, working-class tenants sought to challenge their forced eviction from lands slated for suburban and commercial development. Yamamoto defines "localism" in Hawai'i as "a composite of ethnic cultures, emerging in reaction to domination by Western institutions and culture, composed of people of Hawaii with community value-orientations." [90] Newspaper photographs of local people from different ethnic groups linking arms in front of the Waiāhole Poi Factory in a human blockade across Kamehameha Highway against police-enforced eviction shape a collective historical memory of "local" strength and solidarity.[91]

If "local," however, evokes historical memories of the working class protesting their evictions or forming interethnic labor unions, the term has also been used by privileged classes of Asian settlers to claim a history of oppression for themselves. This is not to say that all local Asians fall into these privileged classes, but the term "local" is often used to mask the political power that Asian settlers have historically exercised, often against Hawaiians. As Roland Kotani notes in his 1985 publication *The Japanese in Hawaii: A Century of Struggle*, "During the 1970s and 1980s, Japanese American decision-makers of the Ariyoshi administration rejected the demands of the rising Hawaiian nationalist movement." [92] Kotani cites as examples the eviction of predominantly Hawaiian Hansen's disease patients from Hale Mōhalu, a residential facility, and the Department of Land and Natural Resources (DLNR) evictions of Hawaiians from Sand Island and Mākua Beach to "clear the land" for the development of public parks. He writes,

> Native Hawaiians, who had dominated the public sector work force in Territorial Hawaii, were another ethnic group which expressed resentment about the strong Japanese presence in the Democratic regime. In 1971, Matsuo Takabuki, a prominent Nisei attorney and politician, became the first AJA trustee of the Bishop Estate, the powerful landholding trust established for the benefit of Native Hawaiian youth. A coalition of Hawaiian organizations immediately organized a mass demonstration at Iolani Palace to protest this appointment.[93]

Kotani further details the Ariyoshi administration's refusal to turn over to OHA revenues generated by the ceded lands. Kotani's account provides an important record of the ways that Japanese settler politics operates at the expense of Hawaiians, but without a colonial framework for his analysis he reduces Hawaiians to "another ethnic group" and urges Japanese communities to "fight for a better life for the vast majority of people."

It is also important that we remember the local Japanese politicians and developers who actually constituted the development interests in the 1970s. Although accounts of "local" identity tend to blame the problems of development on Japanese nationals from Japan and white investors from the U.S. continent, Cooper and Daws' *Land and Power in Hawai'i* is monumental in its detailed documentation of the dense interwoven connections among local Asians, development interests, and political institutions in Hawai'i. As they explain, "In those real estate huis, among those real estate lawyers, among those groups of contractors, speculators, developers and landlords, are to be found the names of virtually the entire political power structure of Hawaii that evolved out of the 'Democratic revolution.'" [94]

In account after account, Cooper and Daws illustrate the ways that the Asiandominated Democratic Party negotiated land use and rezoning issues in ways that benefited themselves or those close to them. For example, the Democratic Party supported lease-to-fee conversion bills designed to force landowners to sell land to their lessees for the ostensible purpose of redistributing land from wealthy landowners to poor tenants, but in actuality a "Maryland-type law" was used in the 1980s to target the landholdings of Bishop Estate, a perpetual charitable trust for Native Hawaiians. Such measures sought to take this patrimony from Hawaiians by forcing them to sell trust lands that they were leasing to middle- and upperclass Asians and whites in east and windward O'ahu. As Cooper and Daws write, "Now by the 1980s, the Hawaii lessees who were seeking to own the land on which their homes stood were mainly middle and upper class haoles and local-Asians," while "the beneficiaries of the Bishop Estate were ethnic Hawaiians," resulting in a situation whereby "some of Hawaii's most privileged people [were] seeking land redistribution from the least." [95] There are, of course, working-class Asian settlers who have struggled against Asian settlers who do have political power, but their study points to the ways that the stories of Asian political power have been consistently erased from more popular critiques of "foreign" and "mainland" investors and developers.

Even as I am critical of accounts that represent Asians as part of a multiethnic "local" society rather than as settlers in a colony, my own early work was also part of a move in the 1990s toward politicizing the term "local." In 1994 I published an essay titled "Between Nationalisms: Hawaii's Local Nation and Its Troubled Racial Paradise." [96] In it I argued that "local" Asians in Hawai'i who do not identify either with Asian nation-states or the United States imagine themselves as an unstable "Local Nation" predicated upon anxieties over the illegitimacy of their claims to

Hawai'i. Although my intent was to support Hawaiians, Haunani-Kay Trask incisively criticizes my use of the term "Local Nation" in her essay reprinted in this collection. She writes,

> Ideologically, the appearance of this "local nation" is a response to a twenty-year old sovereignty movement among Hawaiians. Organized Natives, led by a young, educated class attempting to develop progressive elements among Hawaiians, as well as to create mechanisms for self-government, are quickly perceived as a threat by many Asians uneasy about their obvious benefit from the dispossession and marginalization of Natives. Arguing that Asians, too, have a nation in Hawai'i, the "local" identity tag blurs the history of Hawai'i's only indigenous people while staking a settler claim. Any complicity in the subjugation of Hawaiians is denied by the assertion that Asians, too, comprise a "nation." . . . Thus do these settlers deny their ascendancy was made possible by the continued national oppression of Hawaiians, particularly the theft of our lands and the crushing of our independence.

As Trask rightly argues, I had been trying to stake a settler claim by distancing a "Local Nation" of Asians in Hawai'i from Asian Americans on the U.S. continent as well as from whites in the colony of Hawai'i. Like David Pearson and other settler studies scholars, I was attempting to create a "third space" for Asians as another category of the oppressed in Hawai'i. The attempt to ally "Locals" with "Natives," however, created the illusion of a "shared" struggle without acknowledging that Asians have come to constitute the very political system that has taken away from Natives their rights as indigenous peoples.

In Asian settler histories and historiography, the ease with which Asian settlers turn away from Hawaiians' demands for political justice illustrates at base a settler resistance to Hawaiian nationalism and what it might mean for Asian settlers. Asian settlers' persistent celebration of a multicultural "local" community and their contrasting representations of Hawaiian nationalism as racially divisive reveal more about the political interests underpinning the limits of a settler imagination than about the Hawaiian nationalist movement itself. As Asian settler scholars and activists committed to the need for social and political justice that drove the Third World Strike, we need to hold ourselves accountable for the ways our settler scholarship and practices undermine the struggles of Native peoples for their indigenous human rights.

Transforming Asian Settler Colonialism

The essays in this volume also engage the question of how Asian settlers are to correct the political injustices of a settler colony and what form Asian settler support of Native struggles should take. Native and settler contributors caution us about the dangers of settlers who see themselves as "helping" Hawaiians by attempting to direct the sovereignty process or "advising" Native peoples how they should conduct their struggles. In such cases, Asian settlers are unaware of the ways they are motivated by their own settler interests. As Trask argues in her essay,

> The position of "ally" is certainly engaged in by many non-Natives all over the world.... But the most critical need for non-Native allies is in the area of support for Hawaiian self-determination. Defending Hawaiian sovereignty is only beneficial when non-Natives play the roles assigned to them by Natives. Put another way, nationalists always need support, but they must be the determining voice in the substance of that support and how, and under what circumstances, it applies.

Hawaiians will determine the political structure of the Hawaiian nation; Native nationalists remind us that the Hawaiian nation must be built by Native peoples themselves. If settler scholars and activists seek to support Hawaiians in their political struggles, settlers must stand *behind* Natives. As poet ʻĪmaikalani Kalāhele writes to non-Hawaiians in his poem "Huli,"

> If to help us is your wish then stand behind us.
> Not to the side
> And not in front.[97]

The essays presented here underscore the need for Asian settlers to challenge settler ideologies and practices *in their own Asian settler communities*. They call on Asian settler scholars and activists to begin their work in their own home communities, to identify practices in Asian settler communities that obstruct Hawaiian struggles for a self-determined sovereignty, and to work to change those practices. In this volume Asian settlers speak out in support of Hawaiian self-determination, often against the pressures exerted by their own Asian settler communities to silence them. For example, Local Japanese Women for Justice took a stand against Senator Daniel Inouye and the JACL's attack on a Hawaiian nationalist. Peggy Choy also describes her mother Mary Choy, who supported Hawaiians in the Kanaka Maoli Peoples' International Tribunal in 1993 while challenging Korean communities for their failure to address the issue of Native Hawaiian sovereignty.

Asian Settler Colonialism asks Asian settler scholars and activists to expand upon scholarly investigations of settler states and the ways they are maintained. In what ways do Asian settler colonial administrators mobilize state and federal legislation and public policy to deny Hawaiians their rights to their lands, nation, and resources? What are Asian settler rhetorical strategies of self-representation, how do these rhetorical arguments construct the popular Asian settler imaginary, and how are such ideological accounts effective in winning the consent of their Asian settler constituencies? Since political systems are dependent upon culture as an ideological state apparatus, Asian settler scholarship can also examine other areas, such as education, media and advertising, literature, and the visual arts, in order to expose the material contradictions between Asian settler interests and Native struggles. What "lessons" do textbooks in Hawai'i's elementary and secondary schools teach students about the relationships between settler populations and Hawaiians? How are ideologies of multiculturalism and "local" identity used in the media? It is in tracing these complex networks of ideology and the production of meaning that we can expose Asian settler interests in maintaining the status of Hawai'i as an occupied colony. Contradictions between material conditions and ideological representations also point to places of rupture and possibilities for intervention.

The essays ask all Asian settlers to reexamine the conditions of their own lives and the ordinary daily practices they engage in that support the settler state. On a microcosmic level, even seemingly benign conversations that make up the fabric of our daily lives can end up constituting what scholar Erin Wright calls "microaggressions" against Hawaiians or what playwright Alani Api'o calls "a thousand little cuts to genocide."[98] Asian settlers can educate themselves about issues vital to Hawaiians' struggles for self-determination to better understand the political implications of Asian settler practices. On a more collective level, these essays ask Asian settlers to reexamine the ways that their communities are represented in public events and practices and how political representatives and administrators represent Asian settler interests. They ask Asian settlers to speak out against and to change the many ways that their own Asian settler communities obstruct Hawaiians' struggles for justice.

The essays in this volume are organized into two parts: "Native" and "Settler." As we were making editorial decisions about the ordering of essays in this collection, Eiko Kosasa reminded us of Fanon's statement: "The colonial world is a world cut in two."[99] The structure of the book reflects the structure of colonialism in Hawai'i and the lesson from Kalāhele's poem. "Native" comes first; "Settler" follows it and supports it from behind.

Native

The first part, "Native," opens with the work of two Hawaiian nationalists who lay the foundation for the collection as a whole. "Defining the Settler Colonial Problem" features work by Haunani-Kay Trask and Mililani Trask, who broadly define the historical context in which Hawai'i was made into a U.S. settler colony.

"Settlers of Color and 'Immigrant' Hegemony: 'Locals' in Hawai'i," by Haunani-Kay Trask, lays the conceptual foundation for this volume. Trask criticizes Asian settlers—Japanese settlers in particular—who present themselves as champions of Native interests but who obstruct the process of Native self-determination. She argues that "truly supportive Asians must publicly ally themselves with our position of Native control over the sovereignty process. Simultaneously, these allies must also criticize Asian attempts to undermine sovereignty leaders." Trask concludes with a discussion of Ka Lāhui Hawai'i, a Native initiative for sovereignty that represents Native concerns.

Two by Mililani Trask provide us with the historical contexts of U.S. settler colonialism and Hawaiian nationalist resistance. Mililani Trask is an internationally renowned Native Hawaiian leader who in 1993 addressed the U.N. General Assembly on behalf of the indigenous peoples of the world. In "Hawai'i and the United Nations" she recounts the history of U.S. violations of its international trust obligations to Native peoples mandated in the Charter of the United Nations. Among its other trust responsibilities, the United States was to ensure that Hawaiians would be able to develop self-government. Instead, the United States imposed statehood on Hawai'i without providing political alternatives such as independence, thus violating Native Hawaiians' rights to self-government. "Hawaiian Sovereignty" then outlines what that self-government would look like under Hoʻokupu a Ka Lāhui Hawai'i, the master plan for Ka Lāhui Hawai'i.

The following section, "Settler-Dominated State Apparatuses: The State Legislature and the Prison-Industrial Complex," focuses on state apparatuses and Asian settlers who serve as colonial administrators. Asian and white settlers in the State Legislature seek to pass legislative bills that criminalize Hawaiian cultural practices. Momiala Kamahele's essay, "'Īlioʻulaokalani: Defending Native Hawaiian Culture," defines Hawaiian culture in Fanon's words as a "contested culture under colonial domination." Kamahele describes the formation of 'Īlioʻulaokalani, a coalition of Hawaiian hula practitioners who joined forces in 1997 to oppose efforts by Asian and white settler legislators like Randy Iwase and Ed Case to revoke Hawaiian statutory and constitutional rights to access and gather resources of the land. Although the coalition successfully opposed Senate Bill 8, Kamahele concludes that "no matter how hard we work, if we don't have our own nation, if we don't achieve sovereignty, then we will never, never have clearly defined lands or clearly defined rights to practice our culture."

Healani Sonoda's essay, "A Nation Incarcerated," describes the criminalization of Hawaiians and the warehousing of Native Hawaiians into correctional facilities. Asian settler colonial administrators like former directors of public safety Keith Kaneshiro and Ted Sakai, for example, saw during their terms the transferal of hundreds of Hawai'i prisoners to continental facilities. In effect, Hawaiian prisoners were exiled away from their homeland when Hawaiians as a people are pursuing domestic and international claims for sovereignty and lands. Sonoda argues that radical new answers that strive to eliminate the real reasons for and problems behind incarceration will be possible only when Hawaiian land and sovereignty are returned to Natives.

The following section, "Settler-Dominated Ideological State Apparatuses: Literature and the Visual Arts," recognizes the critical importance of ideology in winning the consent of Asian settlers who support U.S. colonialism. In this section ku'ualoha ho'omanawanui and Kapulani Landgraf reveal and document the settler interests inscribed on Native land through literature and art. They then illustrate Native struggles to reclaim the stories and histories of that land with which they have a familial relationship. In "'This Land Is Your Land, This Land Was My Land': Kanaka Maoli versus Settler Representations of 'Āina in Contemporary Literature of Hawai'i," ho'omanawanui argues that Asian settler representations of land in "local" literature often claim Hawaiian cultural values such as a genealogical connection to the land and the "aloha spirit" even as settler literature commodifies land. Even the most supportive Asian settler writers can interpret stories about Native lands only through a settler consciousness. Ho'omanawanui argues that in a colonial context, non-Natives must recognize that Natives have kuleana (rights, privilege, concern, responsibility, authority) over all things Kanaka Maoli, including literature.

Kapulani Landgraf's "'Ai Pōhaku," a series of photographic essays, documents destroyed heiau (places of worship) on O'ahu. Visually, her photographs foreground the places we see every day—Waikīkī resorts, freeways, public schools, military bases, and residential areas—that cover over sacred sites. Landgraf's inscribed photographs, in turn, literally write over those accounts of development to call our attention to the historical processes by which the land was and continues to be colonized by haole as she reclaims the significance of these heiau and their histories. Landgraf uses the word "haole" in reference to "foreigners," encompassing all foreigners, including Asians.[100]

Settler

The first section of part II begins with the "Consequences of Settler Colonialism." In his essay, "The Hawaiians: Health, Justice, and Sovereignty," David Stannard outlines the historical impact of colonization and the resulting complex of interlocking oppressions. Stannard agues that the oppressive colonial conditions maintained by the criminal justice, employment, and education bureaucracies are concealed by social service organizations that attribute Hawaiians' health crisis to the self-destructive practices of Hawaiians themselves, focusing their efforts on "blaming" Hawaiians for what are actually the ongoing effects of colonization.

These conditions, he argues, will not change until Hawaiians are able to achieve the political and economic self-determination they need to support and care for themselves.

In 2008 the United States is a settler state that moves aggressively in the global arena in what it calls its "war on terrorism." The United States has expanded its military bases in Hawai'i to support its economic interests in the Middle East through military attacks on Afghanistan and Iraq, and it continues to provide financial and military support to other settler states like Israel, which has received the largest percentage of U.S. foreign aid. On July 7, 2004, the U.S. military approved the selection of Hawai'i as a site for a Stryker brigade, which entails the acquisition of an additional 24,000 acres of land needed to support the brigade.[101] Kyle Kajihiro examines the normalization and naturalization of the military in Hawai'i in "The Militarizing of Hawai'i: Occupation, Accommodation, and Resistance." Kajihiro provides an overview of the impact of militarism on Hawai'i, then argues that despite the ways that the militarization of Hawai'i is presented as unassailable, this militarism presents contradictions that are openings for intervention and social and political transformation. He concludes by examining key contemporary examples of people's movements challenging the military in Hawai'i, including Native struggles at Kaho'olawe, west Kaua'i, Waikāne, Pōhakuloa, and Mākua.

"Whose Vision? Rethinking Japanese, Filipino, and Korean Settlement" features essays that reexamine the stories we are told celebrating Asian immigration to Hawai'i. Karen K. Kosasa's essay, "Sites of Erasure: The Representation of Settler Culture in Hawai'i," asks us to consider the ways that settlers are involved in the colonization of Hawai'i and Hawaiians through acts of erasure in our everyday lives and artistic practices. Such acts involve settlers' visual production of blankness—blank spaces "emptied" of Native peoples to be filled with settler visions of the American Dream. In their collaborative mixed-media projects, Kosasa and photographer Stan Tomita engage what they call "strategies of exposure" that are "crucial exercises in remembering." As we question the ways that Asian settlers imagine their place on Native lands, we must critically reevaluate the stories they tell to construct a "multicultural Hawai'i."

Eiko Kosasa's essay, "Ideological Images: U.S. Nationalism in Japanese Settler Photographs," provides an overview of the Americanization movement and its efforts to transform the Japanese into patriotic American citizens. Kosasa examines this maintenance of American hegemony in Hawai'i through a dialectic of force and consent visible in family portraits of Japanese settlers taken by Usaku Teragawachi in the 1920s and 1930s. Analyzing the broader meaning of these photographs as they became a part of Japanese settler discourse represented in the 1985 publication *Kanyaku Imin: A Hundred Years of Japanese Life in Hawai'i*,

Kosasa challenges that master narrative of American immigration by situating the "successes" of the Japanese settler community within a colonial system.

Jonathan Y. Okamura's essay, "Ethnic Boundary Construction in the Japanese American Community in Hawai'i," contrasts exclusionary descent-based eligibility arguments used by the politically dominant Japanese American settler population and arguments used in the *Rice v. Cayetano* lawsuit to defend a state law that reserved for Hawaiians the right to vote in elections for the Office of Hawaiian Affairs. Okamura argues that economically and politically dominant groups such as Japanese Americans exclude other groups from participation in their organizations as a way of retaining control over their settler interests and resources; by contrast, Hawaiians, who remain colonized and disempowered in their own homeland, must fight to preserve rights being eroded by a neoconservative political movement.

In "Colonial Amnesia: Rethinking Filipino 'American' Settler Empowerment in the U.S. Colony of Hawai'i" Dean Saranillio argues that Filipinos in Hawai'i are settlers who have been maneuvered by the U.S. settler state against Hawaiians, despite their shared histories of American colonization. Through analyses of works by public educator Joshua Agsalud, Lilo Bonipasyo, a *sakada* (contract laborer) in Virgilio Felipe's biography *Hawai'i: A Pilipino Dream,* and community activist Zachary Labez, Saranillio illustrates the continuities between U.S. colonization of the Philippines and the "Americanization" of Filipinos in Hawai'i. He concludes by contrasting former Hawai'i governor Benjamin Cayetano's opposition to struggles for Hawaiian self-determination with the work of ten Filipina settler activists in Hawai'i who supported Hawaiians opposed to proposed military training on the Windward side of O'ahu.

Peggy Myo-Young Choy's family history, "Anatomy of a Dancer: Place, Lineage, and Liberation," traces Choy's own dance movements back through a family history of resistance in Hawai'i that leaves us with important lessons for Asian settlers to consider. Her aunt's early advocacy for Korean women in Hawai'i and her parents' activism in anti-war demonstrations, anti-development protests, ethnic studies protests, and Hawaiian struggles challenge the myth that we are insulated as individual Asian settler groups from each other and from complicity in the colonial domination of Hawaiians.

We conclude this volume with "Speaking Out against Asian Settler Power," which focuses on the important work of speaking out against the political practices of powerful Asian settlers like U.S. Senator Daniel Inouye and the Asian settler community organizations that support them. In their essay, "Local Japanese Women for Justice Speak Out against Daniel Inouye and the JACL," Eiko Kosasa and Ida Yoshinaga challenge popular assumptions about the ways that Asian settlers like Inouye have "helped Hawaiians." They show us that Inouye, who has accrued an extraordinary amount of political power for himself as a member of the Senate Appropriations Committee, including the Subcommittee on Defense and Military Construction and the Subcommittee on Veteran Affairs, and of the Committee on Indian Affairs, *is* an institution backed by highly visible community organizations like the Japanese American Citizens' League. Kosasa and Yoshinaga challenge Inouye and the JACL for their participation in a smear campaign against Native Hawaiian nationalist Mililani Trask, who had criticized Inouye's attempts to control the process for a self-determined sovereignty for Hawaiians.

* * *

As the essays here show, we cannot transform the settler colony of Hawai'i or the U.S. settler state without first recognizing and making undeniably visible the status of Asians as settlers in a settler state. The essays in *Asian Settler Colonialism* identify Asians as settlers in order to bring about a shift in political consciousness, to identify the problems posed by Asian settler ideologies and practices that reflect their desires for a place in the settler state. For the larger, long-term vision of Hawaiian self-determination to be made a reality, the Native and settler contributors in this volume call on Asian settlers in Hawai'i to reexamine their interests within the U.S. settler state and to hold themselves and their communities accountable for their settler practices. Only through such accountability and anticolonial interventions can we find a way to greater social and political justice.

Notes

1. I use both "Hawaiian" and "Native Hawaiian" in reference to the indigenous peoples of Hawai'i, regardless of federally imposed definitions based on blood quantum.

2. For statistics in this volume, see "A Nation Incarcerated," by Healani Sonoda, "The Hawaiians: Health, Justice, and Sovereignty," by David Stannard, and "The Militarizing of Hawai'i: Occupation, Accommodation, and Resistance," by Kyle Kajihiro.

3. *From a Native Daughter: Colonialism and Sovereignty in Hawai'i*, rev. ed. (1993). Reprint: Honolulu: University of Hawai'i Press, 1999, 25.

4. Lilikalā Kame'eleihiwa, *Native Lands and Foreign Desires: Pehea Lā E Pono Ai?* (Honolulu: Bishop Museum Press, 1996); Jonathan Kay Kamakawiwo'ole Osorio, *Dismembering Lāhui: A History of the Hawaiian Nation to 1887* (Honolulu: University of Hawai'i Press, 2002); Noenoe Silva, *Aloha Betrayed: Native Hawaiian Resistance to American Colonialism* (Durham, N.C.: Duke University Press, 2004). For a discussion of Hawaiian scholarly work on Hawaiian resistance to American colonization, see Silva's introduction to *Aloha Betrayed.*

5. Ibrahim G. Aoudé, ed., *The Ethnic Studies Story: Politics and Social Movements in Hawai'i*, a special issue of *Social Process in Hawai'i* 39 (1999).

6. For a discussion of the colonial claims made by Asian American studies scholars, see Candace Fujikane, "Foregrounding Native Nationalisms: A Critique of Antinationalist Sentiment in Asian American Studies," *Asian American Studies After Critical Mass*, ed. Kent Ono (Malden, Mass.: Blackwell, 2005).

7. Ibrahim, *The Ethnic Studies Story*, x.

8. This narrative of "building Hawai'i" can be found in Asian settler ethnic histories, including those by the Hawaii Laborers' Association, *Facts About the Strike on Sugar Plantations in Hawaii* (Honolulu: Hawaii Laborers' Association, 1920); Joshua Agsalud and Karen Motosue, "Kapuripuri: 75 Years of Filipino Labor," *The Filipinos in Hawai'i: The First 75 Years (1906–1981)*, ed. Juan C. Dionisio (Honolulu: Hawaii Filipino News Specialty Publications, 1981), 80; Virgilio Menor Felipe, *Hawai'i: A Pilipino Dream* (Honolulu: Mutual Publishing, 2002), 188; Ronald Takaki, *Pau Hana: Plantation Life and Labor in Hawaii* (Honolulu: University of Hawai'i Press, 1983), 179; Arlene Lum, ed., *Sailing for the Sun: The Chinese in Hawaii, 1789–1989* (Honolulu: University of Hawai'i Center for Chinese Studies, 1988), 11; Dorothy Ochiai Hazama and Jane Okamoto Komeiji, *Okage Sama De: The Japanese in Hawai'i, 1885–1985* (Honolulu: Bess Press, 1986), 254.

9. Gary Okihiro, *Cane Fires: The Anti-Japanese Movement in Hawaii, 1865–1945* (Philadelphia: Temple University Press, 1991), xv.

10. Okihiro, *Cane Fires*, xiv.

11. Michael Haas, ed., *Multicultural Hawai'i: The Fabric of a Multiethnic Society* (New York: Garland Publishing, 1998), xi. See also Jonathan Okamura's critique in "The Illusion of Paradise: Privileging Multiculturalism in Hawai'i," in *Making Majorities: Composing the Nation in Japan, China, Korea, Fiji, Malaysia, Turkey and the United States*, ed. D. C. Gladney (Palo Alto, Calif.: Stanford University Press, 1994), 264–284.

12. Eileen Tamura, "Using the Past to Inform the Future: An Historiography of Hawai'i's Asian and Pacific Islander Americans," *Amerasia Journal* 26 (1) (2000): 55–85. See also Dana Takagi, "Faith, Race and Nationalism," *Journal of Asian American Studies* 7 (3) (October 2004): 271–288.

13. Tamura, "Using the Past to Inform the Future," 66.

14. Troy Johnson, Duane Champagne, and Joane Nagel, "American Indian Activism and Transformation: Lessons from Alcatraz," in *American Indian Activism: Alcatraz to the Longest Walk*, ed. Troy Johnson, Joane Nagel, and Duane Champagne (Chicago: University of Illinois Press, 1997).

15. I thank Dean Saranillio for the following references on Asian Americans at Alcatraz: Troy Johnson, *The Occupation of Alcatraz Island: Indian Self-Determination and the Rise of Indian Activism* (Chicago: University of Illinois Press, 1996), 118; "Aid to Alcatraz," *Gidra* 2 (1) (January 1970): 3; Marlene Tanioka and Aileen Yamaguchi, "Asians Make Waves," *Gidra* 2 (3) (March 1970): 6–7; Geraldine Kudaka, "Indian Brothers," *Gidra* 2 (4) (April 1970): 22. For an account of local Japanese who supported Hawaiians at Kaho'olawe, see Roland Kotani, *The Japanese in Hawaii: A Century of Struggle* (Honolulu: Hawaii Hochi, 1985), 168–169.

16. Haunani-Kay Trask, "Writing in Captivity: Poetry in a Time of De-Colonization," *Navigating Islands and Continents: Conversations and Contestations in and around the Pacific*, ed. Cynthia Franklin, Ruth Hsu, and Suzanne Kosanke, a special issue of *Literary*

Studies East and West 17 (Honolulu: University of Hawai'i, College of Languages, Linguistics and Literature, 2000), 53. Franklin's introduction to that volume provides an account of Trask's keynote address and audience responses to it.

17. Haunani-Kay Trask, "Settlers of Color and 'Immigrant' Hegemony: 'Locals' in Hawai'i," *Whose Vision? Asian Settler Colonialism in Hawai'i,* ed. Candace Fujikane and Jonathan Okamura, a special issue of *Amerasia Journal* 26 (2) (2000): 1–24. Reprinted in this volume.

18. David Stannard, *Before the Horror: The Population of Hawai'i on the Eve of Western Contact* (Honolulu: University of Hawai'i, Social Science Research Institute, 1989); Kame'eleihiwa, *Native Lands and Foreign Desires,* 81.

19. Osorio, *Dismembering Lāhui,* 11.

20. George Cooper and Gavan Daws, *Land and Power in Hawai'i: The Democratic Years* (Honolulu: University of Hawai'i Press, 1985), 4.

21. See local Asians listed in Cooper and Daws, *Land and Power in Hawai'i,* under "Public Officeholders and Political Figures as Real Estate Investors, Developers, Consultants, Attorneys, Brokers and Salespersons," 15–34.

22. Takaki, *Pau Hana,* 23–24; Lawrence H. Fuchs, *Hawaii Pono: An Ethnic and Political History* (Honolulu: Bess Press, 1961), 49.

23. Anna Johnston and Alan Lawson, "Settler Colonies," in *A Companion to Postcolonial Studies,* ed. Henry Schwarz and Sangeeta Ray (Malden, Mass.: Blackwell, 2000), 365.

24. Eileen Tamura, *Americanization, Acculturation, and Ethnic Identity: The Nisei Generation in Hawaii* (Chicago: University of Illinois Press, 1994), xiv–xv.

25. Dean Saranillio, "Colonial Amnesia: 'Filipino Americans' and the Native Hawaiian Sovereignty Movement," master's thesis, University of California, Los Angeles, 2003.

26. Eiko Kosasa, review of "Forget Post-Colonialism! Sovereignty and Self-Determination in Hawai'i," by Dana Takagi, posted on the Association for Asian American Studies listserv (June 24, 1999).

27. See, e.g., Ann Curthoys, "An Uneasy Conversation: The Multicultural and the Indigenous," in *Race, Colour and Identity in Australia and New Zealand,* ed. John Docker and Gerhard Fischer (Sydney: UNSW Press, 2000); and Ien Ang, "Intertwining Histories: Heritage and Diversity," *Australian Humanities Review* (December 2001).

28. Donald Denoon, "Understanding Settler Societies," *Historical Studies* 18 (1979): 511–527; and *Settler Capitalism: The Dynamics of Dependent Development in the Southern Hemisphere* (Oxford: Oxford University Press, 1983); Ronald Weitzer, *Transforming Settler States: Communal Conflict and Internal Security in Northern Ireland and Zimbabwe* (Berkeley: University of California Press, 1990); Daiva Stasiulis and Nira Yuval-Davis, eds., *Unsettling Settler Societies: Articulations of Gender, Race, Ethnicity and Class* (Thousand Oaks, Calif.: SAGE, 1995); Patrick Wolfe, *Settler Colonialism and the Transformation of Anthropology: The Politics and Poetics of an Ethnographic Event* (London: Cassell, 1999); David Pearson, *The Politics of Ethnicity in Settler States: States of Unease* (New York: Palgrave, 2001); Johnston and Lawson, "Settler Colonies"; Caroline Elkins and Susan Pedersen, eds., *Settler Colonialism in the Twentieth Century: Projects, Practices, Legacies* (New York: Routledge, 2005); Annie Coombes, ed., *Rethinking Settler Colonialism: History and Memory in Australia, Canada, New Zealand and South Africa* (Manchester, U.K.: Manchester University Press, 2006).

29. Wolfe, *Settler Colonialism and the Transformation of Anthropology,* 163.

30. Pearson, *The Politics of Ethnicity in Settler States,* 130, 153.

31. Weitzer, *Transforming Settler States,* 25.

32. Wolfe, *Settler Colonialism and the Transformation of Anthropology,* 168.

33. I thank Ann Curthoys for this and the following reference: http://journalism.uts .edu.au/subjects/oj2/oj2_s2002/rossfinaltwo/repub2/aboriginal.htm

34. See http://www.faira.org.au/lrq/archives/199811/stories/past-truths-are-essential .html

35. In Australia, whites constitute 92 percent of the population, Aboriginal and Torres Strait Islander peoples about 2.2 percent, and Asians 6 percent. The Australian Bureau of Statistics, 2001 census.

36. Ien Ang, *On Not Speaking Chinese: Living between Asia and the West* (New York: Routledge, 2001), 120.

37. Ang, "Intertwining Histories," 8.

38. Curthoys, "An Uneasy Conversation," 32.

39. John Docker, "Rethinking Postcolonialism and Multiculturalism in the *Fin de Siècle*," *Cultural Studies* 9 (3) (1995): 415.

40. Other studies of settler colonialism provide detailed accounts of the practices of settler colonial administrators, such as Weitzer's *Transforming Settler States* and the essays in Coombes' *Rethinking Settler Colonialism.*

41. See also Karen Kosasa, "Thefts of Space and Culture: Kimo Cashman's *Kapu* Series," in *Photography in Hawai'i,* ed. Lynn Ann Davis, a special issue of *History of Photography* (Autumn 2001): 279–287; and "Critical Sights/Sites: Art Pedagogy and Settler Colonialism in Hawai'i," PhD dissertation, University of Rochester, 2002.

42. Eiko Kosasa, "Predatory Politics: U.S. Imperialism, Settler Hegemony and the Japanese in Hawai'i," PhD dissertation, University of Hawai'i, 2004, 283.

43. The current Akaka Bill (also known as the Native Hawaiian Government Reorganization Act of 2005), which promises U.S. federal recognition of Hawaiians as indigenous peoples, has been strongly opposed by many Hawaiians who argue that in its current state it is "more dangerous than beneficial to our Hawaiian community." Curtis Lum and James Gonser, "Group urges OHA to drop support," *Honolulu Advertiser,* October 7, 2005; Keala Kelly, Lehuanani Kinilau, and Haunani-Kay Trask, *First Friday: The Unauthorized News,* aired on 'Ōlelo Community Television, August 5, 2005.

44. Kahikina de Silva, "Introduction: Haunani-Kay Trask," Fall Festival of Writers, University of Hawai'i, Honolulu, November 13, 2003.

45. Melody Kapilialoha MacKenzie, *Native Hawaiians Rights Handbook* (Honolulu: Native Hawaiian Legal Corporation and the Office of Hawaiian Affairs, 1991), 26–42.

46. Cooper and Daws, *Land and Power in Hawai'i,* 29.

47. Vicki Viotti, "Federal Judge Dismisses Lawsuit against OHA," *Honolulu Advertiser,* January 15, 2004; Ken Kobayashi and Gordon Y. K. Pang, "Court Oks Challenge to Taxpayer Funding of OHA," *Honolulu Advertiser,* September 1, 2005.

48. Aired on KITV and other Hawai'i television stations, September 19, 2000.

49. Yasmin Anwar, "OHA's Interim Board Now Complete," *Honolulu Advertiser,* September 17, 2000.

50. USA PATRIOT Act is an acronym for "Uniting and Strengthening America by Pro-

viding Appropriate Tools Required to Intercept and Obstruct Terrorism." The "enhanced surveillance procedures" cited in the act include extending the power of the FBI to investigate private personal records without warrant, without probable cause, and without notification of the person being investigated.

51. Kameʻeleihiwa, *Native Lands and Foreign Desires*, 15.

52. Kameʻeleihiwa, *Native Lands and Foreign Desires*, 299.

53. For a discussion of these global implications of British, American, and Japanese imperialism, see Sucheng Chan, *Asian Americans: An Interpretive History* (Boston: Twayne Publishers, 1991).

54. Wayne Patterson, *The Korean Frontier in America: Immigration to Hawaiʻi, 1896–1910* (Honolulu: University of Hawaiʻi Press, 1988), 4. The earliest Chinese arrived in Hawaiʻi in 1789, but my focus here is on large-scale plantation recruitment.

55. Clarence E. Glick, *Sojourners and Settlers: Chinese Migrants in Hawaii* (Honolulu: Hawaii Chinese History Center and the University of Hawaiʻi Press, 1980), 19–20; Chan, *Asian Americans: An Interpretive History*, 27; Osorio, *Dismembering Lāhui*, 174–180.

56. Kosasa, "Predatory Politics," 75–82; Franklin Odo and Kazuko Sinoto, *A Pictorial History of the Japanese in Hawaiʻi, 1885–1924* (Honolulu: Bishop Museum Press, 1985), 14.

57. Asian settler historians tend to emphasize that Kalākaua invited Japanese laborers to "repeople the islands," but Hawaiian historians emphasize the extreme measures he took to stop the massive deaths of his people. It was under colonial conditions that Kalākaua sought out the Japanese for aid—colonial conditions that later made possible Japanese entry into Hawaiʻi. See Kotani, *The Japanese in Hawaii*, 12; Hilary Conroy, *The Japanese Frontier in Hawaii, 1868–1898* (Berkeley: University of California Press, 1953), 55, 57; Osorio, *Dismembering Lāhui*, 279; Silva, *Aloha Betrayed*, 90.

58. Kosasa, "Predatory Politics," 75–82; Conroy, *The Japanese Frontier in Hawaii*, 47, 53.

59. Conroy, *The Japanese Frontier in Hawaii*, 59–62; Alan Moriyama, *Imingaisha: Japanese Emigration Companies and Hawaii, 1894–1908* (Honolulu: University of Hawaiʻi Press, 1985), 10; Kotani, *The Japanese in Hawaii*, 15–17. An earlier group of 149 Japanese had left for Hawaiʻi without government permission in 1868.

60. Kosasa cites figures from Robert C. Schmitt's *Historical Statistics of Hawaii* (Honolulu: University of Hawaii Press, 1977), 25, in "Predatory Politics," 82. In 1900 there were 61,111 Japanese; 39,656 Hawaiians; 26,819 whites; and 25,767 Chinese in Hawaiʻi. For a discussion of debates on the "Japanese Question," see Eiko Kosasa, "Ideological Images," in this volume.

61. Patterson, *The Korean Frontier in America*, 6–7.

62. Patterson, *The Korean Frontier in America*, 13–14.

63. Chan, *Asian Americans: An Interpretive History*, 13.

64. Yun Pyong-sok, "Korean Resistance to Imperial Japanese Aggression," *Korea Journal* 24 (3) (March 1984): 25–26; Shin Yong-ha, "Conjunction of Tonghak and the Peasant War of 1894," *Korea Journal* (Winter 1994): 64, 70–72. I thank Henry Em and Sharon Heijin Lee for these references.

65. Yun, "Korean Resistance to Imperial Japanese Aggression," 26.

66. See Wayne Patterson, *The Ilse: First-Generation Korean Immigrants in Hawai'i, 1903–1973* (Honolulu: University of Hawai'i Press, 2000), 2; and *The Korean Frontier in America,* 113.

67. Chan, *Asian Americans: An Interpretive History,* 15.

68. Reynaldo Clemeña Ileto challenges developmental narratives of Philippine revolution that begin with *illustrado*-led movements by looking at people's movements. *Pasyon and Revolution: Popular Movements in the Philippines, 1840–1910* (Quezon City: Ateneo de Manila University Press, 1979), 97. I thank Theo Gonzales for referring me to Ileto's critique.

69. Luis V. Teodoro Jr., ed., *Out of this Struggle: The Filipinos in Hawaii* (Honolulu: University of Hawaii Press, 1981), 3.

70. Luzviminda Francisco, "The Philippine-American War," in *The Philippines Reader: A History of Colonialism, Neocolonialism, Dictatorship, and Resistance,* ed. Daniel B. Shirmer and Stephen Rosskamm Shalom (Cambridge, Mass.: South End Press, 1987), 19.

71. Okihiro, *Cane Fires,* xii.

72. Quoted in Fuchs, *Hawai'i Pono,* 228. U.S. Congress, Senate, Committee on Immigration and Naturalization, *Immigration into Hawaii,* Hearings, 67th Cong., 1st Sess., Washington, D.C., Government Printing Office, 1921.

73. Peggy Myo-Young Choy, "Anatomy of a Dancer: Place, Lineage, and Liberation," in *Whose Vision? Asian Settler Colonialism in Hawai'i,* ed. Candace Fujikane and Jonathan Okamura; a special issue of *Amerasia Journal* 26 (2) (2000): 234–252. Reprinted in this volume.

74. Eiko Kosasa, "Asian Americans: Apologists for the U.S. Colonial State," paper delivered at the Association for Asian American Studies Conference, Los Angeles, 2005.

75. Data on Okinawans from the Hawai'i Okinawa Center. I provide separate figures for Okinawans because of the colonial history of Japanese subjugation of Okinawans and its effects of racism against Okinawans in Hawai'i.

76. U.S. Census Bureau, 2001. Summary File 1 Hawai'i.

77. State of Hawai'i, Office of Hawaiian Affairs (OHA), *Native Hawaiian Data Book* (Honolulu: State of Hawai'i OHA, 2002), 9. Data for Koreans and African Americans not listed.

78. Jonathan Okamura, personal communication, November 20, 2004.

79. Cooper and Daws, *Land and Power in Hawai'i,* 42.

80. Kosasa, "Predatory Politics," 283.

81. Data for the 2005 Hawai'i State Legislature collected from individual offices. Some legislators were specifically identified as "Okinawan" while others who are also Okinawan were identified as "Japanese."

82. Koreans are not listed in the *Native Hawaiian Data Book,* so I list the 2000 census figure here.

83. Jonathan Okamura, "Introduction: The Contemporary Japanese American Community in Hawai'i," *The Japanese American Contemporary Experience in Hawai'i;* a special issue of *Social Process in Hawai'i* 41 (2002): xii.

84. Data compiled by the Certificated Transaction Unit for the Department of Education.

85. Silva, *Aloha Betrayed,* 9.

86. Tamura, "Using the Past to Inform the Future," 68.

87. Tamura, "Using the Past to Inform the Future," 69.

88. Johnston and Lawson, "Settler Colonies," 369.

89. Eric Yamamoto, "The Significance of Local," *Social Process in Hawai'i: A Reader,* ed. Peter Manicas (San Francisco: McGraw Hill, 1993 [1979]).

90. Yamamoto, "The Significance of Local," 45.

91. "Waiahole's Tenants, Supporters Block Kam Highway for an Hour to Thwart Any Effort at Eviction," *Honolulu Star-Bulletin,* January 5, 1977, A1.

92. Kotani, *The Japanese in Hawaii,* 165–166.

93. Kotani, *The Japanese in Hawaii,* 165.

94. Cooper and Daws, *Land and Power in Hawai'i,* 12.

95. Cooper and Daws, *Land and Power in Hawai'i,* 427–28.

96. Candace Fujikane, "Between Nationalisms: Hawaii's Local Nation and Its Troubled Racial Paradise," *Critical Mass: A Journal of Asian American Cultural Criticism* 1 (2) (1994): 23–58.

97. 'Īmaikalani Kalāhele, *Kalāhele: Poetry and Art by 'Īmaikalani Kalāhele* (Honolulu: Kalamakū Press, 2002).

98. Erin Wright, "Microaggressions, the First Amendment, and Native Hawaiians: Kūikikalāhiki vs. *Ka Leo o Hawai'i,*" paper delivered at the Association for Asian American Studies Conference, San Francisco, May 2003; Alani Api'o, "A Thousand Little Cuts to Genocide," *Honolulu Advertiser,* February 25, 2001.

99. Frantz Fanon, *The Wretched of the Earth* (New York: Grove Press, 1963), 38.

100. Kapulani Landgraf, e-mail message to author, March 28, 2003.

101. William Cole, "Hawaii's Stryker Brigade Approved," *The Honolulu Advertiser,* July 7, 2004.

PART I

_____

Native

Settlers of Color and "Immigrant" Hegemony

"Locals" in Hawai'i

For a colonized people the most essential value, because the most concrete, is first and foremost the land: the land which will bring them bread and, above all, dignity.

—Frantz Fanon, *The Wretched of the Earth*

The world's indigenous peoples have fundamental human rights of a collective and individual nature. Indigenous peoples are not, and do not consider themselves, minorities. . . . Self-determination of peoples is a right of peoples. . . . Under contemporary international law, minorities do not have this right.

—Sharon Venne, *Our Elders Understand Our Rights: Evolving International Law Regarding Indigenous Rights*

The indigenous Hawaiian people never directly relinquished their claims to their inherent sovereignty as a people or over their national lands to the United States, either through their monarchy or through a plebiscite or referendum.

—U.S. Public Law 103-150, the "Apology Bill"

As the indigenous people of Hawai'i, Hawaiians are Native to the Hawaiian Islands. We do not descend from the Americas or from Asia but from the great Pacific Ocean where our ancestors navigated to, and from, every archipelago. Genealogically, we say we are descended of Papahānaumoku (Earth Mother) and Wākea (Sky Father), who created our beautiful islands. From this land came the taro, and from the taro, our Hawaiian people. The lesson of our origins is that we are genealogically related to Hawai'i, our islands, as family. We are obligated to care for our mother, from whom all bounty flows.

History and Settler Ideology

After nearly two thousand years of self-governance, we were colonized by Euro-American capitalists and missionaries in the eighteenth and nineteenth centuries. In 1893 the United States invaded our nation, overthrew our government, and secured an all-white planter oligarchy in place of our reigning ali'i, Queen Lili'uokalani.[1] By resolution of the American Congress and against great Native opposition, Hawai'i was annexed in 1898. Dispossession of our government, our territory, and our legal citizenship made of us a colonized Native people.

Today, modern Hawai'i, like its colonial parent the United States, is a settler society. Our Native people and territories have been overrun by non-Natives, including Asians. Calling themselves "local," the children of Asian settlers greatly outnumber us. They claim Hawai'i as their own, denying indigenous history, their long collaboration in our continued dispossession, and the benefits therefrom.[2]

Part of this denial is the substitution of the term "local" for "immigrant," which is, itself, a particularly celebrated American gloss for "settler." As on the conti-

On January 17, 1993, Mililani Trask, governor of Ka Lāhui Hawai'i, and Haunani-Kay Trask, director of the Center for Hawaiian Studies, led a commemorative march to 'Iolani Palace, site of the overthrow of the Hawaiian government by U.S. Marines and white sugar planters in 1893. The biggest sovereignty organization, Ka Lāhui Hawai'i, organized the march, which turned out to be the single largest demonstration in the history of modern Hawai'i. More than fifteen thousand people participated, including international visitors from the American continent and the Pacific Islands. Photograph by Bruce Asato (courtesy of *The Honolulu Advertiser*).

nent, so in our island home. Settlers and their children recast the American tale of nationhood: Hawai'i, like the continent, is naturalized as but another telling illustration of the uniqueness of America's "nation of immigrants." The ideology weaves a story of success: poor Japanese, Chinese, and Filipino settlers supplied the labor for wealthy, white sugar planters during the long period of the Territory (1900–1959). Exploitative plantation conditions thus underpin a master narrative of hard work and the endlessly celebrated triumph over anti-Asian racism. Settler children, ever industrious and deserving, obtain technical and liberal educations, thereby learning the political system through which they agitate for full voting rights as American citizens. Politically, the vehicle for Asian ascendancy is statehood. As a majority of voters at mid-century, the Japanese and other Asians move into the middle class and eventually into seats of power in the legislature and the governor's house.[3]

For our Native people, Asian success proves to be but the latest elaboration of foreign hegemony. The history of our colonization becomes a twice-told tale, first of discovery and settlement by European and American businessmen and missionaries, then of the plantation Japanese, Chinese, and eventually Filipino rise to dominance in the islands. Some Hawaiians, the best educated and articulate, benefit from the triumph of the Democratic Party over the haole (white)[4] Republican Party. But as a people, Hawaiians remain a politically subordinated group suffering all the legacies of conquest: landlessness, disastrous health, diaspora, institutionalization in the military and prisons, poor educational attainment, confinement to the service sector of employment.[5]

While Asians, particularly the Japanese, come to dominate post-statehood, Democratic Party politics, new racial tensions arise. The attainment of full American citizenship actually heightens prejudice against Natives. Because the ideology of the United States as a mosaic of races is reproduced in Hawai'i through the celebration of the fact that no single "immigrant group" constitutes a numerical majority, the post-statehood euphoria stigmatizes Hawaiians as a failed indigenous people whose conditions, including out-migration, actually worsen after statehood. Hawaiians are characterized as strangely unsuited, whether because of culture or genetics, to the game of assimilation.

Of course, the specific unique claims of Native Hawaiians as indigenous peoples are denied through the prevailing ideology of "power sharing." Here, power sharing refers to the spoils of the electoral system that are shared, in succession, among "ethnic groups." Politically, power sharing serves to reinforce the colonial position that Hawaiians are just another competing "ethnic group" waiting their turn for political dominance. Disguising the colonial history and subordinated position of Natives, while equating Natives and non-Natives, the ideology tells a false tale of just desserts. Empirically, of course, subjugated peoples cannot willingly share anything. In the case of Hawaiians, we have nothing left to share. Our lands and resources, taken at the overthrow and transferred at annexation to the American government and later to the State of Hawai'i are, literally, not under our control. But the utility of the propaganda of "power sharing" is that it begs the question of why Natives should share power, while reinforcing the refrain that those in power have justly earned their dominant place. Given that Hawaiians are indigenous, that our government was overthrown, and that we are entitled, as a nation, to sovereignty, the argument that we should share power with non-Natives who benefit from theft of our sovereignty is, simply, grotesque.

When the centenary of the American invasion of Hawai'i, overthrow of the Native government, and forcible annexation of the archipelago are commemorated by thousands of protesting Natives in 1993 and 1998, anti-Hawaiian sentiment among growing numbers of Asians and haole is already a political reality. One recent example of this new form of prejudice is the assertion of a "local nation."[6]

Ideologically, the appearance of this "local nation" is a response to a twenty-year-old sovereignty movement among Hawaiians. Organized Natives led by a young, educated class attempting to develop progressive elements among Hawaiians, as well as to create mechanisms for self-government, are quickly perceived as a threat by many Asians uneasy about their obvious benefit from the dispossession and marginalization of Natives. Arguing that Asians, too, have a nation in Hawai'i, the "local" identity tag blurs the history of Hawai'i's only indigenous people while staking a settler claim. Any complicity in the subjugation of Hawaiians is denied by the assertion that Asians, too, constitute a "nation." They aren't complicit in maintaining institutional racism against Natives, nor do they continue to benefit from wholesale dispossession of Native lands and sovereignty. In truth, "local" ideology tells a familiar, and false, tale of success: Asians came as poor plantation workers and triumphed decades later as the new, democratically elected ruling class. Not coincidentally, the responsibility for continued Hawaiian dispossession falls to imperialist haole and incapacitated Natives—that is, not to Asians. Thus do these settlers deny their ascendancy was made possible by the continued national oppression of Hawaiians, particularly the theft of our lands and the crushing of our independence.

This intrasettler competition between haole and Asians is a hallmark of colonial situations. Such contests serve, especially if severe, to mask even further the dispossession and marginalization of Natives. Asians—particularly the Japanese—like to hearken back to the oppressions of the plantation era, although few Japanese in Hawai'i today actually worked on the plantations during the Territory. But at the outset of a new century, it is the resilience of settler ideology that facilitates and justifies non-Native hegemony: "immigrants" who have struggled so hard and for so long *deserve* political and economic supremacy. By comparison, indigenous Hawaiians aren't in power because they haven't worked (or paid their dues) to achieve supremacy. In more obviously racist terms, Hawaiians deserve their fate. We suffer the same categorical character flaws as other Native peoples. To wit, we are steeped in nostalgia or cultural invention; we yearn for the past instead of getting on with the present. Or we are, as a collective, culturally/psychologically incapable of learning how to bend our energies toward success in the modern world.

Against this kind of disparaging colonial ideology, Hawaiians have been asserting their claims as indigenous people to land, economic power, and political sovereignty for at least the last thirty years. Hawaiian communities are seriously engaged in all manner of historical, cultural, and political education. Hālau hula (dance academies), language classes, and varied resistance organizations link cultural practice to the struggle for self-determination. In this way cultural groups have become conduits for reconnection to the lāhui, or nation. Political education occurs as the groups participate in sovereignty marches, rallies, and political lobbying. The substance of the "nation" is made obvious when thousands of Hawaiians gather to protest the theft of their sovereignty. The power of such public rituals to de-colonize the mind can be seen in the rise of a new national identification among Hawaiians. After the 1993 sovereignty protests at the palace of our chiefs,

A Native woman cries as Honolulu police officers from the Specialized Services Division (SWAT) block access to 'Iolani Palace on June 11, 1992. Thirty Native demonstrators were arrested that day. Photograph by Ken Ige (courtesy of the *Honolulu Star-Bulletin*).

Hawaiians, especially the youth, began to discard national identity as Americans and reclaim indigenous identification as Natives.

Re-forming a lāhui that had allegedly disappeared in 1893 continues to serve the process of decolonization on at least two levels. The first is one of throwing off colonial identification as Americans. The second is understanding our Native nation as eligible in both international law and American law for inclusion in policies of Native sovereignty. Hawaiian resistance today is anchored in the increasing knowledge that Hawaiians once lived under their own national government as citizens of the Hawaiian rather than the American nation. Thus the citizenship of our Native people and the territory of our nation—that is, the land base of our archipelago—are the contested ground. *The struggle is not for a personal or group identity but for land, government, and international status as a recognized nation.*

The distinction here between the personal and the national is critical. Hawaiians are not engaged in identity politics, any more than the Irish of Northern Ireland or the Palestinians of occupied Palestine are engaged in identity politics. Both the Irish and the Palestinians are subjugated national groups committed to a war of national liberation. Hawaiians, although not in the stage of combat, are nevertheless engaged in a kind of national liberation struggle. The terrain of battle now involves control of lands and natural resources, including water and subsurface minerals. Any negotiations over settlements other than land involve millions of dollars. By these actions is the lāhui seen to be, and experienced as, a palpable national entity.

If Hawaiians have a pre-contact, pre-invasion historical continuity on their aboriginal territories—that is, on the land that had been ours for two thousand years—"locals" do not. That is, "locals" have no indigenous land base, traditional language, culture, and history that is Native to Hawai'i. Our indigenous origin enables us to define what and who is indigenous, and what and who is not indigenous. We know who the First Nations people are since we were, historically, the first people in the Hawaiian archipelago. Only Hawaiians are Native to Hawai'i. Everyone else is a settler.

Local Asians also know, as we do, that they are not First Nations people. But ideologically, Asians cannot abide categorization with haole. Their subjugation at the hands of haole racism, their history of deprivation and suffering on the plantations, demand an identity other than settler. Faced with insurgent Hawaiians on the left and indifferent or racist haole on the right, young Asians politicize the term "local." Primarily a defense against categorization with haole, especially haole from the American continent, "local" identification has been strengthened in response to "Native" insurgency. As the sovereignty front gains ground and as more Hawaiians assert an indigenous primacy, defensive Asians begin to concoct a fictitious sociopolitical entity based in Hawai'i. Hence the strangely disconnected idea called "local nation."[7]

The projection of a "local nation" as but the latest ideological evolution of "local" Asian identity is a telling illustration of how deeply the threat of Hawaiian nationalism has penetrated the fearful psychologies of non-Natives. Various ethnic groups in Hawai'i are fronting their "local" claims to residency and political ascendance in our aboriginal homeland precisely at the time when organized political power on the part of Natives is emerging. Challenging the settler ideology that "we are all immigrants," Native nationalism unsettles the accustomed familiarity with which haole and Asians enjoy their dominance in everyday Hawai'i. Behind their irritation, however, Asians sense a real political threat. They know the stakes in the various organized sovereignty initiatives are substantial.

The Japanese American Citizens League–Honolulu (JACL–Honolulu) is a recent example of how settlers front their alleged support of Hawaiian sovereignty (the JACL–Honolulu passed a lukewarm sovereignty resolution) while attacking Hawaiian leaders who represent the sovereignty movement.[8] In the fall of 1999 the local Honolulu dailies had a field day attacking Hawaiian sovereignty leader and Office of Hawaiian Affairs (OHA) trustee Mililani Trask because she referred to Senator Daniel Inouye as the "one-armed bandit" in an OHA meeting. Trask explained the nickname was originally given to Inouye by his own Japanese army comrades in World War II. (It was also the nickname commonly used for him by his good friend and former Hawai'i governor, Jack Burns, among others.) The nickname referred to Inouye's admitted theft of jewelry from dead wartime noncombatants. The arm on which he wore the jewelry was later blown off, a fate his war buddies named *bachi,* roughly translated as "bad karma," what we Hawaiians might call hoka, or getting one's just desserts for a bad deed.[9]

Release of Trask's use of the term was done by OHA trustees on the Inouye dole. These were the same trustees Trask had criticized for supporting Inouye's long-standing refusal to include Hawaiians in the federal policy on recognized Native nations. The local newspapers, particularly the right-wing, missionary-descended *Honolulu Advertiser,* ran a biased news story without comment from Trask and a racist cartoon with her cut-off right leg stuck in her mouth.[10]

Never mind, of course, that the "one-armed bandit" epithet was given to Inouye by his own comrades, or that the substantive issue was Inouye's twenty-five-year lock on all federal funding for Hawai'i, which, following Democratic Party procedure, has gone only to Inouye favorites, none of whom support Hawaiian control of Hawaiian lands and entitlements.

In the end, the issue of Inouye's interference in the sovereignty process, including his massive funding to compliant Hawaiian friends, received little coverage in the press. Trask's detailed reply to the *Advertiser* went unreported until Trask called her own press conference to release all information regarding Inouye's control of the sovereignty process. The *Advertiser* then admitted they had received her reply via e-mail but claimed it "wasn't retrieved" by press time. Trask finally paid to have the details of Inouye's political interference printed in the OHA paper.[11]

The JACL-Honolulu, meanwhile, played their customary reactionary role, targeting Trask and successfully obscuring her analysis. In the public controversy that followed, the anti-Hawaiian politics of the JACL were never addressed. The JACL and its spokesperson, Clayton Ikei, published a letter in the *Hawai'i Herald* (a Japanese settler newspaper) and copied it to other media, asking Trask to avoid "future resort to divisive racial and ethnic characterizations" of Inouye.[12]

Neither Ikei nor the membership of the JACL showed any interest in the substance of Trask's criticism of Inouye, namely that he was interfering in a Native process. Following their usual practice, the JACL, like the Japanese membership of the Democratic Party, obscured the issue of their control over Hawai'i politics and Native resources by vilifying a Native leader who criticized non-Native interference by Inouye and his friends.

Politically, the JACL, the Honolulu dailies, and Dan Inouye had once again teamed up to disparage and berate a Hawaiian leader. The JACL continued the familiar role of the Japanese in Hawai'i by opposing Hawaiian control over Native lands, water, and political representation. Inouye's twenty-year refusal to introduce federal legislation recognizing Hawaiians as Native peoples eligible for inclusion in the federal policy on recognized Native nations was never mentioned, let alone criticized by any of the involved parties in the controversy, including the JACL. Clearly and swiftly, the JACL had acted to support the power of the Japanese-controlled Democratic Party while disparaging a Hawaiian leader who sought to analyze and expose that same control.

This collaborationist role of the JACL is in stark contrast to the critical support given to Trask and the sovereignty movement in general by a new group, Local Japanese Women for Justice (LJWJ), formed as a result of the Inouye-Trask controversy. Composed entirely of local Japanese women led by Eiko Kosasa and Ida Yoshinaga, the group published a lengthy piece in the *Honolulu Advertiser* (and later in the *Hawai'i Herald*) criticizing both the *Advertiser* and the JACL for attacking a sovereignty leader. The anti-sovereignty role of certain Japanese leaders in Hawai'i, like Inouye, was also analyzed, as was the role of the JACL in supporting Japanese internment during World War II.[13]

The response of the JACL, written by Bill Hoshijo and David Forman, to their Japanese sisters was swift and nasty. They defended internment of their own people while simultaneously arguing that the war years were a complex and difficult time for all. Refusing to acknowledge their collaborationist role in continuing Hawaiian subjugation, they also once again defended the record of Dan Inouye. True to form, the JACL failed to counter any of the substantive positions their Japanese sisters had argued.[14]

This critical exposure of the JACL frightened their supporters and other Japanese leaders, including one Eric Yamamoto, a professor at the University of Hawai'i law school. For the past several years Yamamoto has been busy publishing scholarly articles supporting "reconciliation" between Hawaiians and some of the Christian churches who benefited from missionization in Hawai'i, including theft of Native lands and complicity in the overthrow of the Hawaiian government.[15] Yamamoto and JACL leaders like David Forman view the JACL as a friend to Hawaiians despite their attack on Trask and her supportive Japanese sisters in LJWJ.

Of course, as a law professor Yamamoto knows full well that no amount of alleged "reconciliation" can equal the return of lands, money, and self-government to the Hawaiian people. Moreover, substantive "reconciliation" would mean Hawaiian control of the sovereignty process from beginning to end. Such Native control, however, is opposed by the JACL and their fellow non-Native travelers.

The role of groups such as the JACL, as well as other Asian supporters like Yamamoto, has clearly been to organize Asians against a nationalist Hawaiian agenda while arguing that everyone in Hawai'i must participate in the sovereignty process.

Of course, the notion that settlers should participate in any form in the sovereignty process is ludicrous. In principle and in practice, Native sovereignty must be controlled by Natives. Just as federally recognized tribes on the American continent do not allow non-Natives to represent their peoples, so Hawaiians should not allow non-Natives to determine our strategies for achieving sovereignty. Simply put, "Native" sovereignty is impossible when non-Natives determine the process.

The current task forces appointed by Senator Daniel Akaka and charged with considering the relationship between Hawaiians and the state and federal governments have sitting non-Native members, including David Forman and Eric Yamamoto. Because of non-Native participation, the principle and practice of Native self-determination is violated. As with the findings of past task forces and commissions, nothing will be recommended that advances Native control over land and waters now enjoyed by the state and federal governments and non-Native citizens of Hawai'i.

There are other Asians, not on the task force, who have decided that the role of a "go-between" is essential to the relationship of Asians and Hawaiians. Predictably, this role highlights the activities of the self-styled and self-appointed mediator, rather than the sovereignty issue itself, as critical to any resolution of conflict. In practice, the "go-between" is a double agent. While professing private support to Hawaiians, such double agents actually lobby our few Asian allies to stay within the Japanese fold—that is, to refrain from publicly criticizing Asians who attack Hawaiian leaders.

Jill Nunokawa, civil rights counselor at the University of Hawai'i, is one among many young, Asian professionals who, when asked, refused to lend public support to Local Japanese Women for Justice. According to Eiko Kosasa, co-chair of LJWJ, Nunokawa expressed the concern that a public defense of Mililani Trask was bad for the Japanese, since Trask was not only criticizing Inouye, but Japanese power in general, including their control of Hawaiian lands and entitlements. Nunokawa told Kosasa that Hawaiians were "going down the race road," and she did not wish to join them there. Tellingly, the Hawaiian sovereignty movement—that is, justice in the form of self-determination—was represented by Nunokawa as the "race road." Here, Native control of Hawaiian lands, waters, entitlements, and, above all, representation at the national level, is thus characterized as a "race" issue.

But the real "race" issue to those who control our lands is not the assertion of Hawaiian claims but the loss of Japanese control. In other words, the fear Nuno-kawa expressed is a pervasive fear Japanese feel about Hawaiian sovereignty, since current Japanese control of Hawaiian lands and waters through their control of the state apparatus is directly challenged by Native sovereignty. The Japanese know that they have, as a group, benefited from the dispossession of Hawaiians. Justice for us would require, among other things, an end to Japanese Democratic Party control over Hawaiian lands and waters. Given that the Japanese as a political bloc have controlled Hawai'i's politics for years, it is obvious that substantive Hawaiian sovereignty requires that Japanese power brokers, specifically Senator Dan Inouye, the JACL, and the rest of the Japanese-dominated Democratic Party, would no longer control Hawaiian assets, including land and political representation.

When movement Hawaiians remark that "Japanese can't be trusted" in the struggle, they are thinking of false friends like Nunokawa, Yamamoto, and the JACL. No matter their much-touted support in resolutions, articles, and personal statements, these alleged Japanese supporters always come down on the side of the reigning Democratic Party, since they are direct beneficiaries of its continu-ing power. As history proves, power is never freely relinquished by those who wield it.

The women in LJWJ, meanwhile, are themselves under attack by Japanese politicos in Hawai'i. Because these women dared to speak publicly against contin-ued Japanese control over Hawaiian lands, resources, representation, and sover-eignty, they have been isolated and severely criticized by the Japanese community. Even members of their families have carried out harsh retribution against them.

Such retribution points up the need for larger and larger groups of critical-thinking Asians to support a form of Hawaiian sovereignty created by Hawaiians, rather than the state or federal governments or non-Hawaiians. Truly supportive Asians must publicly ally themselves with our position of Native control over the sovereignty process. Simultaneously, these allies must also criticize Asian attempts to undermine sovereignty leaders. Until young Japanese leaders such as Nunokawa are willing to stand publicly with Hawaiian leaders such as Mililani Trask and her Japanese female supporters in LJWJ, the anti-sovereignty, anti-Hawaiian effect of groups like the JACL will continue to grow.

While settler organizations like the JACL continue to stir up hatred against Native leaders, the real issue of justice for Hawaiians is intentionally obscured. As enunciated in the Ka Lāhui Master Plan, this justice would mean a "federally recognized" Native Hawaiian land base and government that would establish a nation-to-nation relationship with the American government, as is the case today with nearly five hundred American Indian nations. Such a relationship would mean plenary powers for the Hawaiian nation over its territories. At present, these territories are controlled by the state and federal governments, which regulate public use.

Once Hawaiians reclaim these lands, public and private relationships between Natives and non-Natives will be altered. For example, settlers will have to pay taxes or user fees to swim at Native-owned beaches, enjoy recreation at Native-owned parks, drive on Native-owned roads, fly out of Native-owned airports, educate their children at public schools on Native-owned lands, and on and on. Above all, non-Natives will have to live alongside a Native political system that has statutory authority to exclude, tax, or otherwise regulate the presence of non-Natives on Native lands. The potential shift here frightens non-Natives because it signals the political and economic ascendance of Natives. At the least, Native power means no more free access by non-Natives to Native resources.

Indigenous Peoples and Minorities in International Law

The growing tensions between Asians and Hawaiians in Hawai'i have a corollary in the development of indigenous peoples' human rights in international law. In Article 1 of the United Nations Charter, peaceful relations between nations are seen to depend upon the principles of equal rights and self-determination of peoples. The question that has occupied the Working Group on Indigenous Populations (first convened in 1982 at the United Nations in Geneva) has been the definition of indigenous peoples and the elaboration of their rights. The primary document here is the Declaration on the Rights of Indigenous Peoples. A product of over twenty years' work by indigenous peoples themselves as well as human rights lawyers and jurists, the Declaration is the most complete international document on the rights of indigenous peoples.

The Declaration was preceded by two major studies conducted by the Sub-Commission on the Prevention of Discrimination and Protection of Minorities by U.N. rapporteurs Hector Gros Espiell (1974) and Jules Deschenes (1985), as part of the broad concern regarding the definition and therefore rights of both minorities and indigenous peoples.[16]

In Espiell's study "peoples" were to be considered as, and treated as, categorically different from "minorities." He based his distinctions on U.N. language regarding rights to self-determination and decolonization. He concluded that, under international law, self-determination is a right of peoples and not minorities. The critical link for Espiell was the presence of colonial and alien domination. In addition to being a principle of international law, then, self-determination is a right of "peoples" under colonial domination.

In 1985 a Canadian, Justice Jules Deschenes, submitted a report on minorities to the sub-commission. His discussion of "minority" clarified the relationship between a minority and a majority as critical. He defined "minority" as

> a group of citizens of a State, constituting a numerical minority and in a non-dominant position in that State, endowed with ethnic, religious or linguistic characteristics which differ from those of the majority of the population, having a sense of solidarity with one another, motivated, if only implicitly, by a collective will to survive and whose aim is to achieve equality with the majority in fact and in law.[17]

At the same time Deschenes was conducting his study, another rapporteur, Martinez Cobo, was undertaking a project on indigenous peoples for the sub-commission. His definition of indigenous peoples aided in the clarification of exact differences between minorities and indigenous peoples.

> Indigenous communities, peoples and nations are those which, having a historical continuity with pre-invasion and pre-colonial societies that developed on their territories, consider themselves distinct from other sectors of the societies now prevailing on those territories, or part of them. They form at present non-dominant sectors of society and are determined to preserve, develop, and transmit to future generations their ancestral territories, and their ethnic identity, as the basis of their continued existence as peoples, in accordance with their own cultural patterns, social institutions, and legal system.[18]

In Cobo's final report the identification of indigenous peoples received a great deal of clarification. For example, Cobo argued that indigenous peoples must be recognized according to their own conceptions of themselves. No attempt should be accepted that defines indigenous peoples through the values of foreign societies or the dominant sections of societies. Artificial, arbitrary, or manipulatory definitions, Cobo argued, must be rejected by indigenous peoples and the international human rights community. Finally, Cobo emphasized that the special position of indigenous peoples within the society of nation-states existing today derives from their rights to be different and to be considered as different.

Part of that difference inheres in the *critical identification of historical continuity*. Cobo listed several kinds of historical continuity into the present, including the following.

(a) Occupation of ancestral lands;

(b) Common ancestry with original occupants of these lands;

(c) Culture, in general, including dress, religion, means of livelihood, forms of association, membership in traditional communities;

(d) Language.[19]

Finally, Professor Erica-Irene Daes, the chairperson-rapporteur of the Working Group on Indigenous Populations, has written that "acknowledging the significance of 'territory' may be necessary to address another major logical and conceptual problem: differentiating 'indigenous peoples' and 'minorities.' A strict distinction must be made between 'indigenous peoples" rights and 'minority' rights. Indigenous peoples are indeed peoples and not minorities."[20]

This is a primary distinction because under international law "minorities" do not have the right to self-determination.

The rights of indigenous peoples have also concerned governments whose countries contain a large percentage of indigenous peoples, such as Greenland. In 1991 the Parliament of Greenland argued for a clear distinction between the rights of minorities and the rights of indigenous peoples: "The world's indigenous peoples have fundamental human rights of a collective and individual nature. Indigenous peoples are not, and do not consider themselves, minorities. The rights of indigenous peoples are derived from their own history, culture, traditions, laws and special relationship to their lands, resources and environment."[21]

Finally, Justice Deschenes referred to his country's distinctions between indigenous peoples and minorities in the Constitution Act of Canada, arguing that the United Nations should take guidance from Canada's example and define indigenous peoples and minorities separately.

Specific aspects of the Declaration bear directly upon the differences between indigenous peoples and minority populations. Indigenous peoples are defined by pre-contact, aboriginal occupation of traditional lands. They are not minorities, no matter their number. In other words, the numbers of indigenous peoples do not constitute a criterion in their definition.

While the Declaration covers many areas of concern, certain rights are critical to the distinction that must be made between Natives and minorities. In Article 3 of the Declaration indigenous peoples have the right of self-determination (which minorities do not), and by virtue of that right indigenous peoples can determine their political status.

Political self-determination is tied to land rights and restitution. The doctrine of discovery by which the Americas, the Pacific, and so many other parts of the world were allegedly "discovered" is repudiated. The companion doctrine of *terra nullius* is identified as legally unacceptable. Thus aboriginal peoples have a position from which to argue that traditional lands should be restored to them. In Article 26 indigenous

> peoples have the right to own, use, develop and control the lands, territories and resources that they possess by reason of traditional ownership or other traditional occupation or use. . . . States shall give legal recognition and protection to these lands, territories and resources. Such recognition shall be conducted with due respect to the customs, traditions and land tenure systems of the indigenous peoples concerned.[22]

In Article 4 the Declaration states, "Indigenous peoples, in exercising their right to self-determination, have the right to autonomy or self-government."[23] Interestingly, these rights are considered in Article 43 to "constitute the minimum standards for the survival, dignity, and well-being of the indigenous peoples of the world."[24]

Whole lifetimes have been expended on the process of attempting to move the existing powers of the world to acknowledge and protect indigenous peoples. This process has changed the consciousness of indigenous peoples all over the globe, including Hawai'i. Indigenous peoples can now cite the U.N. Declaration on Indigenous Human Rights in the struggle for protection of their lands, languages, resources, and, most critically, their continuity as peoples.

On the ideological front, documents like the Declaration are used to transform and clarify public discussion and agitation. Legal terms of reference, indigenous human rights concepts in international usage, and the political linkage of the non-self-governing status of the Hawaiian nation with other non-self-governing indigenous nations move Hawaiians into a world arena where Native peoples are primary, and dominant states are secondary, to the discussion.

Ka Lāhui Hawai'i

On the international stage the vehicle that has represented Hawaiians most effectively is Ka Lāhui Hawai'i. Because it is the frontline organization of Hawaiian sovereignty, Ka Lāhui Hawai'i serves as the indigenous party representing Native, as opposed to settler, interests. Through its Master Plan, Ka Lāhui Hawai'i has given concrete policy shape to Native political aspirations. Mental decolonization has led to a first stage of political decolonization. Countering settler American ideology, the Master Plan depends for much of its argument on Native cultural understanding of Hawaiian history, politics, and economics. Like other embodiments of nationhood, the Ka Lāhui Master Plan is both an enunciation of principles and an agenda for political action.[25]

Relying, in part, on international legal standards, the Master Plan endorses the rights and principles contained in four major international documents. These are the Charter of the United Nations; the International Covenant on Civil and Political Rights; the International Covenant on Social, Economic, and Cultural Rights; and the Declaration on the Rights of Indigenous Peoples at the United Nations. Specifically, the rights to self-determination and to self-development are cited in the Master Plan as critical to Hawaiian sovereignty.

In terms of policies regarding the United States, the Plan rejects the current status of Hawaiians as wards of the State of Hawai'i, pointing out that wardship is usurpation of Hawaiian collective rights to land and political power, as well as a violation of Native human and civil rights. Moreover, wardship classifies Hawaiians with children and the incompetent, revealing the racist intent of the classification.

Critically, the Plan rejects American nationality by asserting that self-determination means jurisdiction over lands and territories and internal and external relationships, including the following: the power to determine membership; police powers; the power to administer justice; the power to exclude persons from National Territory; the power to charter businesses; the power of sovereign immunity; the power to regulate trade and enter into trade agreements; the power to tax; and the power to legislate and regulate all activities on its land base, including natural resources and water management activities and economic enterprises.

The current policy of state wardship for Hawaiians whereby the state controls Hawaiian lands and waters is repudiated. Given that the State of Hawai'i has maintained a policy of non-recognition of the indigenous peoples of Hawai'i and has consistently acted as the Native representative despite an extensive record of state neglect and mismanagement of the Native trusts, the Ka Lāhui Master Plan calls for termination of this policy.

Citing the 1993 Apology Bill passed by the U.S. Congress, the Plan notes the Apology acknowledges that "the indigenous Hawaiian people have never directly relinquished their inherent sovereignty as a people or over their national lands to the United States, either through their monarchy or through a plebiscite or referendum."[26]

Therefore, the goals of Ka Lāhui Hawai'i are simple: final resolution of the historic claims of the Hawaiian people relating to the overthrow, state and federal misuse of Native trust lands (totaling some two million acres) and resources, and violations of human and civil rights. Resolution of claims will be followed by self-determination for Hawaiians; federal recognition of Ka Lāhui Hawaiʻi as the Hawaiian Nation; and restoration of traditional lands, natural resources, and energy resources to the Ka Lāhui National Land Trust.

The burden rests with the United States and the State of Hawaiʻi to inventory and restore the lands of the Native trusts, both federally and state held, and to remedy all federal and state breaches of the trust relating to these assets. The federal and state governments must segregate the trust lands from other public and private lands. The United States must allocate not less than two million acres of land (i.e., all the ceded lands) drawn from state-controlled and federally controlled lands to the National Land Trust.

In the area of the National Land Trust, Ka Lāhui identifies the land and natural resource entitlements of indigenous Hawaiians within the entire archipelago. These entitlements include state-held trust lands—that is, Hawaiian Homes lands and ceded lands, marine resources and fisheries, surface and groundwater rights and submerged lands, lands and natural resources under the federal government, energy resources such as ocean thermal and geothermal sources, minerals, airspace, and the trust assets of the private trusts.

Although the Master Plan has many other specific areas relating to various concerns, such as the private Hawaiian trusts, the Plan also delineates an international relationship. Citing Chapter XI, Article 73, of the U.N. Charter, the Plan notes that the United States, as Hawaiʻi's "administering agent," accepted as a "sacred trust" the obligation "to assist the inhabitants of the territory of Hawaiʻi in the progressive development of their free political institutions."[27]

In 1953 the Fourth Committee of the U.N. General Assembly passed Resolution 742, requiring that the inhabitants of territories be given several choices in achieving self-government. These choices include free association, commonwealth, integration (statehood), and independence or "other separate systems of self-government."

The United States never allowed decolonization in Hawaiʻi under the U.N. process, nor did it allow the inhabitants of the territory their right to choose options identified in Resolution 742. The plebiscite in 1959 allowed only one choice—statehood—other than territorial status. By not including other choices, the United States violated international human rights law as well as the human rights of Hawaiians.

Given that Hawaiʻi was removed at the request of the United States from the United Nations' list of Non-Self-Governing Territories in 1959, the position of Ka Lāhui Hawaiʻi is re-inscription of Hawaiʻi on that list, thereby recognizing Hawaiians as still eligible for self-determination. Meanwhile, Ka Lāhui has chosen to develop a culturally appropriate "separate system of self-government" that incorporates Hawaiian values and traditions. As part of this assertion, Ka Lāhui has called for segregation of Hawaiian trust lands and assets from the State of Hawai'i. Additionally, a record of extensive civil and human rights abuses of Hawaiians by the state and federal governments must be established, and strenuous advocacy of Hawaiian rights and claims must proceed.[28]

Natives and "Locals"

Apart from its embodiment of Native aspirations, the Ka Lāhui Hawai'i Master Plan can be read as a perfect illustration of the distance between Natives and "locals" in Hawai'i. The issues before Hawaiians are those of indigenous land and cultural rights, and survival as a people. In contrast, the issues before "locals" have merely to do with finding a comfortable fit in Hawai'i that guarantees a rising income, upward mobility, and the general accoutrements of a middle-class "American" way of life. Above all, "locals" don't want any reminder of their daily benefit from the subjugation of Hawaiians. For them, history begins with their arrival in Hawai'i and culminates with the endless retelling of their allegedly well-deserved rise to power. Simply said, "locals" want to be "Americans."

But national identification as "American" is national identification as a colonizer, someone who benefits from stolen Native lands and the genocide so well documented against America's Native peoples. Here, "identity" is not, as often asserted in Hawai'i, a problem for Hawaiians. It is, rather, a problem for non-Natives, including Asians. We are engaged in decolonizing our status as wards of the state and federal governments and struggling for a land base.

Asians and haole have been thrown into a cauldron of defensive actions by our nationalist struggle. Either they must justify their continued benefit from Hawaiian subjugation, thus serving as support for that subjugation, or they must repudiate American hegemony and work with the Hawaiian nationalist movement. In plain language, serious and thoughtful individuals, whether haole or Asian, must choose to support a form of Hawaiian self-determination created by Hawaiians.

The position of "ally" is certainly engaged in by many non-Natives all over the world. Support organizations like the Unrepresented Nations and Peoples Organization (UNPO), for example, work on a global level to give voice to Native peoples at international forums, and even in their home countries. A few groups in Hawai'i primarily composed of non-Natives (for example, LJWJ) serve the same function.

But the most critical need for non-Native allies is in the arena of support for Hawaiian self-determination. Defending Hawaiian sovereignty initiatives is beneficial only when non-Natives play the roles assigned to them by Natives. Put another way, nationalists always need support, but they must be the determining voice in the substance of that support and how, and under what circumstances, it applies.

Of course, Hawaiians, like most colonized peoples, have a national bourgeoisie—that is, a class that ascends due to collaboration with the state and federal governments. This class serves to counter indigenous nationalist positions. Often, potentially "supportive" locals complain about the confusion surrounding the many sovereignty positions. But the easiest and most defensible position is the one that follows the Ka Lāhui Master Plan. No matter the future leadership of Ka Lāhui, the Plan will remain as the clearest document of this period in Hawaiian history. Non-Natives who support the Plan are, in effect, supporting all the struggles of indigenous peoples that created the Declaration at the United Nations.

Finally, it must be recalled that history does not begin with the present, nor does its terrible legacy disappear with the arrival of a new consciousness. Non-Natives need to examine and reexamine their many and continuing benefits from Hawaiian dispossession. Those benefits do not end when non-Natives begin supporting Hawaiians, just as our dispossession as Natives does not end when we become active nationalists. Equations of Native exploitation and of settler benefit continue. For non-Natives, the question that needs to be answered every day is simply the one posed in the old union song: "Which side are you on?"

Notes

1. See U.S. President Grover Cleveland's message to the U.S. Congress in "The President's Message Relating to the Hawaiian Islands," December 18, 1893, House Ex. Doc. No. 47, 53rd Cong., 2nd Sess., 1893, 445–458, called the Blount Report.

2. See Daniel K. Inouye, *Journey to Washington* (Englewood, N.J.: Prentice-Hall, Inc., 1967); George R. Ariyoshi, *With Obligation to All* (Honolulu: Ariyoshi Foundation, 1997); and Ronald Takaki, *Pau Hana: Plantation Life and Labor in Hawaii, 1835–1920* (Honolulu: University of Hawai'i Press, 1983), and *Strangers from a Different Shore: A History of Asian Americans* (New York: Penguin Books, 1989). Also see various materials published to commemorate one hundred years of Japanese settlement in Hawai'i: Roland Kotani, *The Japanese in Hawaii: A Century of Struggle* (Honolulu: Hawaii Hochi Ltd., 1985); Franklin Odo and Kazuko Sinoto, *A Pictorial History of the Japanese in Hawaii, 1885–1924* (Honolulu: Bishop Museum Press, 1985); and Dennis Ogawa and Glen Grant, *To a Land Called Tengoku: One Hundred Years of the Japanese in Hawaii* (Honolulu: Mutual Publishing, 1985).

3. For a detailed investigation of Chinese and Japanese political ascendancy as a class in post-statehood Hawai'i, see George Cooper and Gavan Daws, *Land and Power in Hawai'i* (Honolulu: University of Hawai'i Press, 1985).

4. Originally, "haole" meant "all foreigners," but it is now used to refer to whites.

5. For statistics on Hawaiian population, housing, land, education, health, prisons, and employment, see Office of Hawaiian Affairs, *Native Hawaiian Data Book, 2006* (Honolulu: OHA, 2006).

6. Candace Fujikane, "Between Nationalisms: Hawai'i's Local Nation and Its Troubled Racial Paradise," *Critical Mass: A Journal of Asian American Cultural Criticism* 1 (2) (1994): 23–57.

7. For an early discussion of the term "local," see Eric Yamamoto, "The Significance of Local," *Social Process in Hawai'i* 27 (1979): 101–115. For later discussions, see Jonathan Okamura, "*Aloha Kanaka me ke Aloha 'Aina:* Local Culture and Society in Hawai'i," *Amerasia* 7 (2) (1980): 119–137; and Eric Chock, "The Neocolonialization of Bamboo Ridge: Repositioning *Bamboo Ridge* and Local Literature in the 1990s," *Bamboo Ridge* 69 (1996): 11–25. Fujikane now appears to have some doubts about her earlier assertion of a "local nation." See "Reimagining Development and the Local in Lois-Ann Yamanaka's *Saturday Night at the Pahala Theater,*" *Social Process in Hawai'i* 38 (1997): 40–62.

8. Japanese American Citizens League Resolution, "Reaffirming Support for the Restoration of Human, Civil, Property and Sovereign Rights of Hawai'i's Indigenous People," adopted at the 1992 JACL National Convention, Denver, Colorado.

9. For the initial news coverage, see *Honolulu Advertiser,* November 10–13, 1999. In a 1989 interview with Mike Tokunaga, Democratic Party insider from the 1950s, Tokunaga recalled a 1959 story where Jack Burns identified Inouye as the "one-armed bandit." Center for Oral History, "Oral History Interview with Mike Tokunaga by Larry Meacham and Daniel W. Tuttle on September 12, 1989," in *Hawai'i Political History Documentation Project, Vol. III* (Honolulu: Center for Oral History, University of Hawai'i, 1996), 1233. In the *Advertiser* story of November 11, 1999, Inouye's Japanese war comrades said they never used the term "one-armed bandit" to describe Inouye. In fact, as pointed out by Richard Borreca in a *Star-Bulletin* column on November 17, 1999, the nickname was used by Jack Burns when Inouye was first running for the U.S. Senate. Borreca claims that Burns used the term "jokingly" when asking why Inouye was planning to run for the Senate rather than the House of Representatives. The source for Borreca's article was Tokunaga's oral history.

In truth, the oral history reveals that Burns was angry at Inouye because the Democratic Party plan was for Inouye to run for the House. Why Burns could call Inouye "the one-armed bandit" without assault by the press is explained by the simple observation that critics of the Democratic Party—in this case, one Mililani Trask—are dangerous to continued Japanese control of the party and, most critically, dangerous to the monumental power that the Democratic Party and the state apparatus wield over Hawaiian resources.

Trask's use of the "one-armed bandit" phrase was a false issue. The real issue was and remains Inouye's control over the sovereignty process. In this instance the issue was lost amidst the well-orchestrated attack on Trask. In fact, the *Advertiser* story and vicious cartoon were perfectly timed to appear before, during, and immediately after Veterans' Day.

In a paid advertisement (titled, appropriately, "Inouye's Legacy to Hawaiians") printed in the February 2000 issue of the OHA newspaper, *Ka Wai Ola,* Trask detailed the *Advertiser* campaign to disparage her and to prevent the airing of critical issues regarding Inouye's interference in the sovereignty process. Needless to say, her side of the story was never printed in the two Honolulu dailies. Significantly, the issue of Inouye's interference in the sovereignty process, which Trask had severely criticized, never saw the light of day. See Mililani Trask, "Inouye's Legacy to Hawaiians," *Ka Wai Ola O OHA*, 17 (2), February 2000, 20–21.

10. Dick Adair, cartoon, *Honolulu Advertiser*, November 12, 1999, A12.

11. "OHA Trustee Won't Back Down," *Honolulu Advertiser*, November 11, 1999, A1; Trask, "Inouye's Legacy to Hawaiians," 20–21.

12. Clayton C. Ikei, representing the JACL. See November 22, 1999, letter to Mililani Trask and the media, reprinted in the local Japanese American community newspaper. Clayton C. Ikei, "JACL Opposes Trask's Comments to Inouye," *Hawai'i Herald*, December 3, 1999, A7; and Pat Omandam, "AJA Group Asks Trask Not to Be Ethnically Divisive," *Honolulu Star-Bulletin*, November 25, 1999, A3.

13. Ida Yoshinaga and Eiko Kosasa, Local Japanese Women for Justice, "Local Japanese Should Understand Inouye's Real Agenda," *Honolulu Advertiser*, February 6, 2000, Focus Section:1, reprinted as "Understanding Inouye's Real Agenda," *Hawai'i Herald*, March 3, 2000, A-4, and reprinted in this volume.

14. Bill Hoshijo and David Forman, Japanese American Citizens League, "JACL Fights against Racism, No Matter Where It Comes From," *Honolulu Advertiser*, February 27, 2000, Focus Section:1, and reprinted as "JACL Speaks Out to Clear the Record," *Hawai'i Herald*, March 3, 2000, A4.

15. See Eric Yamamoto, "Rethinking Alliances: Agency, Responsibility and Interracial Justice," *UCLA Asian Pacific American Law Journal* 3 (33): 33–74. Yamamoto discusses the participation of Hawai'i-based Asian American churches in the public apology by the United Church of Christ (UCC) made to Hawaiians concerning the participation of the churches in the 1893 overthrow of the Hawaiian monarchy. The apology was made by Paul Sherry, president of the UCC, before some fifteen thousand people on the centenary of the overthrow at the palace of our chiefs on January 17, 1993. In discussions with Hawaiian leaders preceding the apology, Paul Sherry responded to my criticism that such apologies were useless to the Hawaiian people. I suggested the UCC return some of the lands the churches controlled in Hawai'i in lieu of an apology. Sherry responded that I was criticizing the church for attempting to receive what he called "cheap grace," an easy forgiveness achieved for very little. Given that reparation monies (totaling over a million dollars) from the church hierarchy went to Hawai'i churches rather than to Native Hawaiians, my conclusions were that while the UCC attained their "cheap grace," we Hawaiians, as usual, received nothing. Also see Eric Yamamoto, *Interracial Justice: Conflict and Reconciliation in Post-Civil Rights America* (New York: New York University Press, 1999).

16. See the discussion of these two studies in Sharon Helen Venne, *Our Elders Understand Our Rights: Evolving International Law Regarding Indigenous Rights* (Penticton, B.C.: Theytus Books, Ltd., 1998), 77–83.

17. Venne, *Our Elders Understand Our Rights*, 80.

18. Venne, *Our Elders Understand Our Rights*, 80.

19. Venne, *Our Elders Understand Our Rights*, 88.

20. Venne, *Our Elders Understand Our Rights*, 146.

21. Venne, *Our Elders Understand Our Rights*, 82.

22. United Nations Declaration on the Rights of Indigenous Peoples (A/RES/61/295), adopted September 13, 2007.

23. Declaration on the Rights of Indigenous Peoples.

24. Declaration on the Rights of Indigenous Peoples.

25. Ka Lāhui Hawai'i, *Ho'okupu a Ka Lāhui Hawai'i: The Master Plan, 1995* (Honolulu: Ka Lāhui Hawai'i, 1995).

26. S.J. Res. 19 (U.S. Public Law 103-150), 103d Cong., 1st Sess., 107 Stat. 1510 (November 23, 1993).

27. Ka Lāhui Hawai'i, *The Master Plan*, 5.

28. Ka Lāhui Hawai'i, *The Master Plan*, 6–8.

Apologies

Slogans of cheap grace
    rather than land:
        "We apologize." But not

        one acre of taro,
            one river of water,
            one handful

          of labor. "We apologize."
           And all our dead
               and barely living, rejoice.

For now we own
    one dozen dirty pages
      of American paper

        to feed our people
          and govern our nation.

Hawaiʻi and the United Nations

The U.N. Charter, "Territories," and U.S. Obligations

Chapter XI of the Charter of the United Nations deals with Non-Self-Governing Territories and calls for international accountability regarding peoples who have not achieved a full measure of self-government. Article 73 reads in part as follows.

> Members of the United Nations which have or assume responsibilities for the administration of territories whose peoples have not yet attained a full measure of self-government recognize the principle that the interests of the inhabitants of these territories are paramount, and accept as a sacred trust the obligation to promote to the utmost, within the system of international peace and security established by the present Charter, the well-being of the inhabitants of these territories, and, to this end:
>
> a. to ensure, with due respect for the culture of the peoples concerned, their political, economic, social, and educational advancement, their just treatment, and their protection against abuses;
>
> b. to develop self-government, to take due account of the political aspirations of the peoples, and to assist them in the progressive development of their free political institutions, according to the particular circumstances of each territory and its peoples and their varying stages of advancement; . . .
>
> e. to transmit regularly to the Secretary-General for information purposes, subject to such limitation as security and constitutional considerations may require, statistical and other information of a technical nature relating to economic, social and educational conditions in the territories for which they are respectively responsible other than those territories to which Chapters XII and XIII apply.[1]

Since Hawaiʻi was a "territory" of the United States in 1945, it is no surprise that the United Nations in 1946 listed Hawaiʻi as a Non-Self-Governing Territory

Kia'āina Mililani Trask leading the January 17, 1993, sovereignty march to 'Iolani Palace. Photograph by Ed Greevy.

under the administration of the United States (Resolution 55[I] of 14 December 1946). Also listed as Non-Self-Governing Territories under the jurisdiction of the United States were Alaska, American Sāmoa, Guam, Puerto Rico, and the Virgin Islands.

From 1946 to 1959, when statehood was imposed on Hawai'i, the United States had (1) a "sacred trust" obligation to the "inhabitants" of Hawai'i detailed in sections a and b above, and (2) an annual reporting obligation to the General Assembly under e above.

America transmitted annual reports on Hawai'i to the U.N. secretary-general from 1946 until September 1959. By letter dated September 17, 1959, the United States notified the U.N. secretary-general that Hawai'i had become a state of the Union in August 1959 and that the United States would thereafter cease to transmit information to the United Nations.

Upon receipt of this letter, the United Nations removed Hawai'i from its list of Non-Self-Governing Territories.

How the United States Violated Its International Trust Obligations to the Native People of Hawai'i

On November 27, 1953, the Fourth Committee of the U.N. General Assembly passed Resolution 742. This resolution was titled "Factors which should be taken into account in deciding whether a Territory is or is not a Territory whose people have not yet attained a full measure of self-government." Part I of the resolution identified "Factors indicative of the attainment of Independence." Part II listed "Factors indicating the attainment of other separate systems of self-government." Part III addressed "Factors indicative of the Free Association of a Territory on equal basis with the metropolitan or other country as an integral part of that country or in any other form."

Hawai'i was made a state of the Union. Our Native people were not given independence nor free association status, nor were we allowed to create our own separate form of government.

The factors listed in Part II of Resolution 742 include

A.2. *Freedom of choice.* Freedom of choosing on the basis of the right to self-determination of a peoples between several possibilities, including independence.

A.5. *Ethnic and cultural considerations.* The extent to which the populations are of different race, language, or religion, or have a distinct cultural heritage, interests or aspirations, distinguishing them from the peoples of the country with which they freely associate.

C.3. *Economic, social and cultural jurisdiction.* Degree of autonomy in respect of economic, social and cultural affairs, as illustrated by the degree of freedom from economic pressure as exercised, for example by a foreign minority group which, by virtue of the help of a foreign power, has acquired a privileged economic status prejudicial to the general economic interest of the people of the Territory; and by the degree of freedom and lack of discrimination against the indigenous population of the Territory in social legislation and social developments.

History verifies that the United States violated the provisions of Resolution 742. The federal ballot used in 1959 did *not* afford the people of Hawai'i "several *possibilities,* including independence," nor were the Hawaiian people given the option to create their own "separate system of government." Consequently, the Native people of Hawai'i were not allowed to exercise the "right to self-determination."

Conclusion

The United Nations never inquired into the statehood plebiscite, nor did the United Nations monitor the process. The U.N. record reveals that the United States was a permanent member of the U.N. committee that received and acted upon America's report on statehood. Subsequent to receiving the report, the U.N. removed Hawai'i from its list of Non-Self-Governing Territories—despite the fact that the United States had violated its "sacred trust" to the Hawaiian people and all the people of the Territory.

Ka Lāhui's Position

Ka Lāhui Hawai'i, a Native initiative for self-government founded in 1987, believes that Hawai'i should be reinscribed on the U.N. list of Non-Self-Governing Territories in order for the process of decolonization to begin. In light of the 1991 Report of the Hawai'i Advisory Committee to the U.S. Commission on Civil Rights, there can be no doubt that the civil rights of the Hawaiian people are being violated. Until these issues are addressed, the United States should be required to file annual reports at the United Nations on the status of Hawai'i and its Native people.

In 1989 Ka Lāhui Hawai'i was able to submit a resolution at the World Conference of Churches Global Consultation in Geneva calling for Hawai'i to be reinscribed on the U.N. list of Non-Self-Governing Territories. In 1993, while attending the World Conference on Human Rights in Vienna, the global indigenous delegates' address to the U.N. Plenary Session called for Hawai'i's reinscription on the U.N. list of Non-Self-Governing Territories. The global indigenous statement was presented to the plenary by Kia'āina Mililani Trask.

Note

1. *United Nations Action in the Field of Human Rights,* U.N. Publications Sales no. E.83. XIV.2 (New York: United Nations, 1993).

Hawaiian Sovereignty

On August 12, 1998, over five thousand Native Hawaiians and non-Hawaiian supporters gathered at ʻIolani Palace to mark the one-hundredth anniversary of the illegal annexation of Hawaiʻi by the United States. The event was not celebratory but was significantly political. The indigenous Hawaiian people had gathered to voice their strong opposition to the overthrow of their Kingdom in 1893 by armed military forces of the United States and to present to the public the historic petition to the U.S. Congress signed by 21,000 Kānaka who, in 1898, successfully opposed the Treaty of Annexation between the United States and the Provisional Government of the Republic of Hawaiʻi. The Treaty of Annexation was never ratified by the U.S. Senate because the pro-annexationist forces could not muster the two-thirds vote needed for ratification.

It is ironic that as the United Nations celebrated in 1998 the fiftieth anniversary of the U.N. Declaration on Human Rights, the indigenous peoples of Guam, Puerto Rico, American Sāmoa, Alaska, and Hawaiʻi commemorated the anniversary of the theft of their lands by America. The gathering was also politically charged because of news that the long-awaited U.N. *Study on Treaties, Agreements and Other Constructive Arrangements between Indigenous Peoples and Nation States* had been tabled at the United Nations in Geneva on July 30, 1998. The treaty study's final report by the special rapporteur, Miguel Alphonso Martinez of Cuba, recommends that Hawaiʻi be relisted on the U.N. list of Non-Self-Governing Territories and decolonized pursuant to U.N. procedures.

Nonetheless, in the United States Hawaiians are excluded from U.S. domestic policy providing Indians and Alaskan Natives with a limited right to self-determination. The U.S. definition of self-determination allows Indians and Alaskan Natives to "control" their lands and natural resources and to develop social and economic projects. This does not, however, apply to Hawaiians. Ka Lāhui Hawaiʻi, the largest sovereignty initiative in Hawaiʻi, has been in existence for twenty-one years. It boasts over ten thousand Native citizens and a long track record of political advocacy in the local, national, and international arenas.

Ka Lāhui Master Plan—Ho'okupu a Ka Lāhui Hawai'i

As a Native initiative for self-government, Ka Lāhui is the best example of how self-determination can work in practice. Founded in 1987, Ka Lāhui had expanded into a nationwide structure with representative bodies throughout the archipelago by 1993.

In 1994 Ka Lāhui created the most comprehensive plan for the attainment of Hawaiian sovereignty yet devised.[1] The Master Plan begins, in Part I, with an endorsement of fundamental principles, including a commitment to peace, disarmament, and nonviolence. There is, as well, a recognition of the inalienable rights of Native Hawaiians and their descendants as called for in the U.N. Charter, the Declaration on the Rights of Indigenous Peoples, and the International Covenant on Civil and Political Rights as well as the International Covenant on Social, Economic, and Cultural Rights.

Rights to "self-determination" and "self-development" follow, including the right to engage freely in traditional activities. But the crucial declaration in this section is the rejection of the wardship imposed by the United States as a result of the policy of "Manifest Destiny" in general and the Tyler Doctrine in particular, which extended that policy to the Pacific.

Later in the Master Plan, the rejection of wardship leads to the assertion of self-determination and sovereignty as attributes of Hawaiian human rights. Historically, Hawaiians tried to escape wardship by entering the Democratic Party— that is, by embracing the reality of American citizenship as they left the dispossession of the overthrow behind them. The very existence of the Ka Lāhui Master Plan revealed the failure of the Democratic Party to resolve the land claims and self-government issues of Hawaiians.

Part I concludes with multiple assertions of jurisdiction by Ka Lāhui Hawai'i. These include the powers to determine membership, to administer justice, to exclude persons from the National Territory, to regulate trade, to tax, and to claim sovereign immunity. This section reveals how Ka Lāhui views itself as a government, albeit one in exile and without U.S. recognition.

Part II addresses how Ka Lāhui functions and lists, among its many accomplishments, the following: formation of a democratic and elective nation whose indigenous citizens exercise the franchise by electing representatives and thereby practice self-determination; the drafting of a constitution that includes spiritual, cultural, and traditional values; and the establishment of a respected international reputation, including membership in the Unrepresented Nations and Peoples Organization (UNPO) at The Hague.

In Part III the Master Plan details the historical relationship with the United States, which evolved from a policy of peace and friendship between 1826 and

1842 into a policy of colonialism under the Tyler Doctrine, which imposed an American sphere of influence on Hawai'i to ward off the predations of Britain and France. All treaties and conventions negotiated between the United States and Hawai'i subsequent to 1842 favored the United States over Hawai'i.

In 1893, through the forces of the United States and the offices of the U.S. minister at the time, the policy of armed intervention (exercised in 1874 and again in 1889, with the landing of U.S. troops on Hawaiian soil) resulted in the overthrow of the Hawaiian government and annexation of the Hawaiian Islands to the United States in 1898. No Native vote in Hawai'i was ever taken on annexation, nor was any vote ever envisioned. In 1900 Hawai'i became American property.

At the creation of the United Nations in 1946, Hawai'i was listed as a Non-Self-Governing Territory under U.S. administration. Such status was considered a "trust" relationship whereby the United States had an obligation to promote the political aspirations of the Hawaiian people toward attaining self-government.

In 1959 Hawai'i became a state. The vote on statehood included only two options: continuation of territorial status or statehood. Neither commonwealth nor independence appeared as choices on the ballot.

Of course, the imperial policy of the United States has continued to be one of non-recognition, denial, and wardship under the State of Hawai'i. This condition of wardship has meant, for example, that the federal government negotiates only with the State of Hawai'i rather than with the Hawaiian people when Hawaiian issues are at stake. The State, meanwhile, has used the lands of the Hawaiian Homes Trust, some two hundred thousand acres, and the Ceded Lands Trust, nearly two million acres, for its own purposes. Meanwhile, the civil rights of Hawaiians continue to be abused, as documented in reports by the Hawai'i Advisory Committee to the U.S. Commission on Civil Rights (December 1991).

Abandonment has been the policy of the Reagan, Bush, and Clinton administrations. All three presidents have asserted that no trust obligation on the part of the federal government exists. In practical terms this has meant no oversight of state actions by the federal government. In 1993 the U.S. Congress passed the Apology Bill, now U.S. Public Law 103-150, in which it is acknowledged that "the indigenous Hawaiian people never directly relinquished their claims to their inherent sovereignty as a people or over their national lands to the United States, either through their monarchy or through a plebiscite or referendum."

Despite the hopefulness that greeted the passage of the Apology Bill in Hawai'i, nothing substantive has changed regarding federal policy toward Hawaiians. While "reconciliation" between the Hawaiian people and the American government is cited, no process or mechanism for reconciliation is included in the bill.

In its Master Plan, Ka Lāhui accepted the U.S. apology and suggested its own process for reconciliation. The goals of reconciliation are listed as follows.

Final resolution of the historic claims relating to the overthrow; to State and Federal misuse of Native trust lands and resources; to violations of human and civil rights; and to Federally-held lands and resources.

The essential elements of reconciliation are: termination of the U.S. policy of non-recognition of Native Hawaiian self-determination, including repudiation of the policy of wardship.

Federal recognition of Ka Lāhui Hawai'i as the indigenous sovereign Hawaiian Nation, including recognition of the jurisdiction of Ka Lāhui Hawai'i over its national assets, lands, and natural resources.

A commitment to decolonize Hawai'i through the United Nations process for Non-Self-Governing Territories.

Restoration of traditional lands, natural resources, ocean and energy resources is to be made to the Ka Lāhui National Land Trust. These lands include Hawaiian Home Lands, the Ceded Lands, and Federally-held Lands. These lands shall be segregated from other public lands.

The process of termination of wardship is detailed in the Master Plan and involves legislation by the State to segregate all Hawaiian trust lands and assets from the general public lands and assets and transfer them to the National Land Trust of the Hawaiian Nation.

The National Land Trust includes all state-held trust lands, surface and groundwater, marine resources and fisheries to the two-hundred-mile limit, energy resources, airspace, and the trust assets of the many private Hawaiian trusts, such as the Kamehameha Schools/Bishop Estate.

In the area of economic development, the Master Plan calls for the establishment of the National Land Trust; jurisdiction over its assets and revenues; the powers of taxation; community-based economic development; and international trade agreements.

On international issues, the Plan reiterates the call for decolonization, self-government, and reinscription on the U.N. list of Non-Self-Governing Territories.

In recent years the State of Hawai'i has attempted to subvert the Hawaiian sovereignty movement through passage of a state law authorizing the creation of the Hawaiian Sovereignty Elections Council (HSEC). Subsequent legislative measures amended the law to delete all references to the right of the Hawaiian peoples to "form a nation of their own choosing" and to authorize the HSEC (a board appointed by the governor) to initiate a vote and constitutional convention. The HSEC law also provided that nothing arising from the vote or convention would "alter . . . amend or change" anything in the State. These limitations mean that

Hawaiians will have a paper nation, but no land, money, or right of self-governance. The State provided two million dollars for the vote.

In response, sovereignty groups and Ka Lāhui Hawai'i called for a boycott of the process. Sixty percent of eligible Hawaiian voters boycotted the election. An additional 10 percent voted no. Despite the overwhelming rejection of the state initiative, the HSEC incorporated a nonprofit organization known as Hā Hawai'i to proceed with a convention that will allow eighty-five Hawaiians to draft a constitution. This process denies the remaining two hundred thousand Hawaiians their right to create a nation of their own choosing.

Throughout Hawai'i, sovereign 'ohana (family) entities and groups are calling for the recognition of their right to self-determination as defined under the International Covenant on Civil and Political Rights (ICCPR). This means that the peoples themselves define their political status and their economic, social, and cultural development.

As the Hawaiian sovereignty movement grows stronger, state and federal governments have increased their activities to circumvent Hawaiian nationhood. Police intimidation, arrests, and criminal prosecution of Hawaiians are increasing as Hawaiians resort to acts of civil disobedience and resistance. Occupations by Hawaiians of traditional sacred places and burial grounds are expanding. Native Hawaiians have begun to use the Apology Resolution, Public Law 103-150, as evidence that the Congress and President Clinton have admitted the illegality of the overthrow, violations of international law, and deprivation of our right to self-determination.

As one Hawaiian kupuna (elder) put it, "Read the Apology Bill. We are the evidence, not the crime. We'll never give up our lands or our culture, and we'll never give up self-determination. We're fighting for our keiki [children] and mo'opuna [grandchildren] now."

Note

1. Find the "Ho'okupu a Ka Lāhui Hawai'i—Ka Lāhui Master Plan" in the appendixes of Haunani-Kay Trask, *From a Native Daughter: Colonialism and Sovereignty in Hawai'i*, rev. ed. (Honolulu: University of Hawai'i Press, 1999), 221–236.

ʻĪlioʻulaokalani

Defending Native Hawaiian Culture

ʻAuʻa ʻia e Kama e Kona moku
   e Kona moku e Kama e ʻauʻa ʻia
      O ke Kama, Kama, Kama, Kama i ka huli nuʻu
         O ke Kama, Kama, Kama, Kama i ka huli au. . . .

Hold fast to and refuse to part with your traditions, oh child of the land
   Defend and protect your way of life
      Keep them precious, for one day your traditions will be taken. . . .

                    —*ʻAuʻa ʻia,* a mele hula

Aloha no kākou. I greet you in the ancestral way of my people. The above mele hula (song/chant that is danced) entreats both the dancer and her people to resist dispossession. It implores Native Hawaiians to maintain a distinctive identity and by so doing legitimate and assert the present condition of Hawaiian resistance.[1] It calls on Native Hawaiians to sustain cultural and political institutions. Holding fast to traditional ways does not mean stagnation; it means cultural survival in the face of colonial oppression.

I am referring here to the meaning of colonialism to Native Hawaiians and its current impact on my people: the eradication of Native Hawaiian rights to access and gather resources of the land. In order to understand our current struggle, allow me to provide our historical circumstances.

My nation, the Hawaiian Kingdom, was overthrown in 1893 and subsequently annexed in 1898 by the United States of America against overwhelming opposition by Native Hawaiians. Hawaiʻi became a U.S. Territory in 1900 and then a state in 1959. Since that time, the U.S. colonial government has maintained our subjugation through the imposition of foreign government and economic systems. The U.S. colonial system is hegemonic—it seeks to dominate every aspect of our lives. Anything Native that links us to our Native national consciousness and is in opposition to the colonizer is systematically destroyed.

In *The Wretched of the Earth* Frantz Fanon writes, "A national culture under colonial domination is a contested culture whose destruction is sought in systematic fashion."[2] Fanon points out that colonialism distorts, discredits, and destroys the national culture of a colonized people because it can be a rallying point of resistance—something the colonizer tries to prevent, at all costs, from happening.

In this essay I refer to the national culture of the indigenous people of Hawai'i whose most visible, identifiable, and expressive form is known worldwide as hula. In modern Hawai'i hula has not been overtly eliminated. Rather, it has been distorted and commodified for the benefit of the tourist industry. Say the word "hula" and images of lithe, brown-skinned maidens, swaying, supple hips, and large, inviting eyes beckon one to a romantic sexual liaison sure to bring erotic delight. These images promote tourism and fill the commercial coffers of multinational corporations. But for those of us who are practitioners steeped in the ancient form of this Native dance, saying the word "hula" brings forth an enormous cultural matrix from which this sacred dance emerged, connecting us back to our ancestors.[3]

During the past three decades two Native Hawaiian movements simultaneously gained Native interest and support—one cultural, the other political. On the cultural front, the ancient form of hula experienced a strong revival as the Native national dance for our own cultural purposes and enjoyment rather than as a service commodity for the tourist industry. On the political front, our struggle to regain control over our Native lands and resources gradually gained Native support as well. These two movements did not interact with each other. Rather, they coexisted on parallel planes even as individuals themselves may have been directly or peripherally involved in both. Although the hula movement embodied practical aspects of Native resistance to colonial domination, many kumu hula (master teachers and keepers of hula) did not perceive hula itself as political, nor did they see the political resistance of Hawaiians as impacting or influencing hula.

However, in the late 1990s political events occurred that would forever change the seemingly separate movements of culture and politics. Kumu hula entered the political arena to defend Native Hawaiian traditional and customary rights to gather resources that ensure the practice of hula and sustain our culture. As a result of this political effort, Native hula practitioners formed a coalition to guard against future colonial laws that could threaten our national culture and our practice of it.

In February 1997 the Hawai'i State Legislature attempted to pass legislation prohibiting the gathering of wood, ferns, flowers, fibers, and cordage used in hula. Since ancient times hula practitioners were protected by a customary right to gather such resources for the dance. However, by the 1990s this traditional gather-

ʻĪlioʻulaokalani hula practitioners at Ua Ao Hawaiʻi, a protest concert held at the Waikīkī Shell. In performances, dancers are usually adorned with lei, but in this concert the dancers are unadorned as a statement of protest. The purpose of the concert was to educate the public about the conservation aspect of hula practices. Photograph by Joe "Bear" Carini (courtesy of Vicky Holt Takamine and the *Honolulu Weekly*).

ing right interfered with the economic interests and plans of developers, wealthy landowners, and business interests. To these settlers, land is a commodity that cannot be exploited to its fullest extent if "strangers," especially "Native strangers," are allowed access to gather the resources of the land, such as flowers, ferns, and fibers. Developers and businessmen wanted to end this legally protected right, which would, by extension, also end our ability to practice in the hula tradition. From the Native nationalist perspective, ending traditional and customary gathering rights is another attempt by settlers to obliterate us as a distinct people.

One of the most powerful means to eradicate Native people is the use of legislative bills. They are strategies to maintain hegemonic control over the Native in a colony. These bills are intended to destroy indigenous national cultures in a purposeful and methodical way. Although the attack on traditional and customary rights to gather resources of the land is generally made in terms of the sanctity of private property, which will ensure economic progress and a better business climate, there is something much less grand and more vicious taking place: an attempt to rid the land of pesky Natives who threaten the colonizer's way of conducting business in Hawaiʻi.

However, the colonizer's attempt backfired. The effort to stop legislative action aimed at eradicating our rights became a rallying point of Native resistance while also increasing our national consciousness as Hawaiians.

I take much inspiration from Fanon and his words. Like him, I see the fight for our national culture as the fight for the liberation of our nation.[4] Our national culture is political precisely because we live under colonial domination where another nation and people have the power to exterminate our way of life and our lives as we struggle to assert that which is rightfully ours. The recent politicization of hula practitioners has moved our resistance struggle to a new dynamic level.

The Cultural Practice

The land is our mother. Native Hawaiians call her Papahānaumoku—"She who gives birth to lands." As caretakers, Native Hawaiians understand that She is the beneficent source of all living things. She nurtures life. She protects without the will to master. She creates and ensures a living continuity between the natural world and the human world. She is the dynamic energy source that powers all life. To practice any aspect of Hawaiian culture, Native Hawaiians turn to the land for guidance.

It follows, then, from Hawaiian oral traditions, that Papahānaumoku is a divine living entity who gives Native Hawaiians the natural world and the resources therein. All living things are Her children, and human beings are but one aspect of the natural world. As human beings, we understand that our obligation is to serve Her. We do so as guardians and stewards of the land. By our service, we are assured of Her care.

The relationship between Native Hawaiians and the land is a familial reciprocal one. Papahānaumoku is our ancestor, our elder to whom we turn for sustenance, strength, and spiritual grounding. We demonstrate our service in familial ways. We show Her respect and revere all Her varied aspects, from the mountains to the sea and all life in between. That is why our chants and hula celebrate and commemorate the beauty and lushness of our land, its bounty and abundance. That is why in performance of our chants and dance we follow a certain spiritual protocol: first, we honor our gods, then our aliʻi (political leaders who are descendants of the gods), and last, the activities of people. In our cultural protocol, gods precede people.

Thus Papahānaumoku nurtures and feeds not only our physical being, but also our psychological and spiritual health; we are born from Her, and we understand that we will eventually return to Her. Papahānaumoku takes care of us, and we take care of Her.

In ancient times, when we took a living thing from Papahānaumoku, such as a tree to make an image of a god, we understood that the god made the tree. In return for the life of the tree, we offered another life: sometimes it was human, sometimes it was animal. But the strictest rules and protocol existed to ensure that each aspect of the taking and giving of life was observed so that the tree would grow again to become a god, and the god would ensure its life.

Besides Hawaiian oral traditions, evidence of a familial intimacy can be found in the Hawaiian language. For example, when we discuss possession, Hawaiian-language terms make a distinction between inherent and acquired possession. Things and people inherent to us are designated with the "o-possessive." Those acquired are designated with the "a-possessive." Thus in the Hawaiian language inherent items include, among other things, the land and one's parents. "My land" becomes in the Hawaiian language not "ka'u 'āina" but "ko'u 'āina," and "my parents" becomes "ko'u mau mākua," two sources from which we are born.[5] Neither is acquired. Both are inherent to us. The land is our parent; we as her children take care of her, for we know she will take care of us. Thus Hawai'i is our motherland.

This understanding is critical to the way Hawaiians practice any aspect of culture and the reason that resources of the land are sacred. When hula practitioners exercise traditional and customary gathering, we establish our presence through protocol when approaching the realm of the uplands or the seashore.

Protocol precedes our gathering of flowers, ferns, fibers, herbal plants, and wood. Protocol is composed of chanted and spoken words. For example, as I go into the mountains or into the sea and gather ferns or shells, there is a chant I must say. As a chanter, I give the gift of my voice to the spiritual guardian of the forest or the sea. Once my presence is established, I ask permission to take one of the "children" of Papahānaumoku in the name of hula to adorn another one of Her "children" in a performance. I express through the words of the chant my deepest appreciation for this appropriation of the living resource of the land. I know that the gift of my voice possesses a mana, or powerful spiritual life force, that offers a replacement for the mana of this other life. It is almost as if I am giving life for life. The life that comes out of me is the sound of my voice, my breath, my chanting, my thoughts, and the words that will invoke the guardians who protect that area. My request is, "Please grant me permission to take and use this fern or body form of the gods to honor the gods. Rest assured that I shall use you with utmost dignity and respect."

Having established my presence, then making my request, I understand that what I gather is not mere adornment for performance. I wear the manifestation of a god. When I take that body form as I prepare to dance and place that fern upon my head, I wear it as a dancer. I know that I have taken the mana of that god, Papahānaumoku, and now embody that god.[6]

As all of these rituals and protocol are used, Native Hawaiian practitioners demonstrate an abiding appreciation for the original source of that fern. Practitioners know that the source of the fern is the gods. But an appropriation is taking place, and a request for the taking allows us an opportunity to give something back because the resources gathered emanate from a deity that made the wood or the fern.

And there is the ceremony of closure. After we have used the fern or flower for our human purposes, we do not discard it like rubbish. These materials from our "mother" are returned to Her loving care in ritual ceremony. Thus in a cyclical pattern is the usage of these plant materials made.

The reason for so much protocol and ritual is the foundational Native perspective that views all living things as one aspect of the natural world, human beings included. Life for life. And in traditional times, it was *literally* life for life.

On a very practical level, hula practitioners are very conscientious about the conservation aspect of our culture. In some hālau hula (dance academies), it is the kumu hula who decides not only what to gather and how much, but, more important, who will participate in the gathering. Only those designated may carry the responsibility. Thus members so designated are very careful not to trample the area. They step lightly and observe each step. A few people participate in the gathering for the entire hālau hula. Sometimes two people gather plant or marine materials for seventeen performers. When gathering, each person spreads out to avoid denuding an area of a particular plant. Conversation is kept to a minimum, if at all. An understanding prevails not to tear plants from the ground and to avoid plucking the young growing plants from the desired matured ones.

In sum, the Native Hawaiian ethic of responsibility to the natural world is commensurate with a recognition and acknowledgment that for every human action and every human condition, the gods have a care. That ethic runs through the structure of the Hawaiian language, as mentioned above, producing a Native identity that is inseparable from the land.

The Bill

Wealthy landowners, development interests, and title insurance companies in Hawai'i are opposed to Native Hawaiian traditional and customary rights.[7] Some of these interests claim that Native Hawaiian rights unduly encumber landowners' private property interests. They allege that the rights of Native Hawaiians to access undeveloped land for various religious, subsistence, or cultural purposes will lead to difficulties in selling, buying, and financing real property in the State of Hawai'i. These same interests claim Native Hawaiian gathering rights as trespass. These settlers hope to eliminate or criminalize Hawaiian cultural practices. For these business interests, land is reduced to a tool for profit. This idea comes from the Western cultural ethic that perceives nature as an object to be mastered and controlled by suppression.

One powerful tool to contain and control "pesky" Natives' rights is the use of legislative bills that turn into law. On January 15, 1997, Senator Randy Iwase pre-filed Senate Bill 8.[8] This bill introduced a process to register all traditional and customary uses exercised on a parcel of land. According to Senate Bill 8, practitioners could not legally exercise a traditional and customary practice without a certificate of registration of Native Hawaiian right.

On February 4 the Senate Committee on Water, Land, and Hawaiian Affairs held a hearing. The room was filled with proponents and opponents of the bill. The committee was co-chaired by Senators Randy Iwase and Malama Solomon. Senator Iwase is an Asian settler. Senator Solomon represented a large Native Hawaiian constituency on the island of Hawai'i at the time and is herself Native Hawaiian.[9] Senator Solomon descends from a long line of respected hula practitioners and kumu hula. Many of us, aware of the bill, were not too concerned that the bill would pass because we believed Senator Solomon would oppose the bill. Further, our concerns were allayed when over 90 percent of the testimony at the hearing opposed the bill. The people who testified were not only Native practitioners, but also scholars, environmental lawyers, activists, law students, high school students, and non-Hawaiian settlers. Of course, testimony supporting the bill included development interests such as construction companies, title insurance firms, and large landowners, including Kamehameha Schools/Bishop Estate.

However, with minor amendments, the bill passed out of the Senate committee and moved on to the Senate Committee on Ways and Means (WAM), which determines the budgetary needs of a bill. We were astonished. But we were also angered when we discovered that Senate Bill 8 passed out of the Committee on Water, Land, and Hawaiian Affairs by unanimous vote. This meant that Senator Solomon voted in support of the bill.

In our view, Senator Solomon had the opportune historical moment to show the Hawaiian community in general and the hula community in particular her support by denouncing Senate Bill 8. Even as co-chair, she could have opposed the bill. Had she done so, Senate Bill 8 would still have gone on to WAM, but she would have secured the respect and support of her constituents and the larger Native Hawaiian community.[10] Senate Bill 8, however, passed out of her committee unopposed.

While the bill was pending in WAM, the hula community organized to oppose and denounce the bill, anticipating the negative impact it would have on Hawaiian culture. This legislative threat became a rallying point of resistance for Native

Hawaiians. That resistance fused culture and politics and took the entire State of Hawai'i by complete surprise. People were shocked that hula practitioners mobilized a defense so quickly and with such force and cultural authority. That is because the general perception of hula practitioners in Hawai'i is that they are a conservative lot, with each hālau hula internally concerned with its own cultural domain.

On a superficial level we discovered that Senate Bill 8 pretended to "harmonize" Native Hawaiian rights with landowner rights. But on closer examination we found that the bill sought to terminate traditional and customary practices particularly if the State believed there would be hardship to the landowner.[11] Key points in the bill included the following: (1) the need to petition for a certificate of registration of Native Hawaiian rights to gather; (2) the certificate itself would "vest in the holder a personal right to engage in Native Hawaiian traditional and customary practices"; and (3) proof that the petitioner of the certificate was indeed Native Hawaiian.

Senate Bill 8 stated that any individuals interested in continuing their customary practice would be required to petition for official recognition of traditional and customary usages. The bill proposed a process to determine and register all traditional and customary usages exercised on a parcel of land. It further proposed that no traditional and customary practices could be legally exercised unless a practitioner possessed a certificate of registration of Native Hawaiian rights. The bill described a cumbersome process whereby Native practitioners would bear the burden of establishing that they were descendants of individuals inhabiting Hawai'i before 1778 through a genealogical chart confirming indigenous status. They would also have to establish proof that the traditional and customary practices they wished to continue were continuous and on identifiable undeveloped land before November 25, 1892.[12] Thus not only did Native Hawaiians have to register certain usages exercised on the land and then be certified to have the right to that usage, but they also had to prove Hawaiian ancestry and provide evidence that an ancestor had exercised the same practice and the same use for the same plant on the same land. If they did not have this proof, the simple act of picking a flower or gathering seaweed along the shore would become a criminal offense.

In addition, Senate Bill 8 required Native petitioners to provide a list of lineal descendants "who will accrue to the benefits conferred by the issuance of a certificate of registration of Native Hawaiian rights." Put another way, without that certificate of registration, any children and/or grandchildren of the petitioner not yet born would not be able to follow the same practice of their ancestor. Thus under this kind of legislation a hula practitioner living in a particular ahupua'a (large land division)[13] would be forced to perform the following:

- file an application stating the cultural use for each parcel of land in a given ahupuaʻa
- research every parcel of land in the ahupuaʻa in which the practitioner lived
- present a certified genealogy confirming race
- prove that the practitioner's ancestors actually gathered the same items before November 25, 1892
- survey the ahupuaʻa and determine if the land was undeveloped
- inventory all land and marine life to be used

It is doubtful that any practitioner would be able to comply with these requirements.

I have been a hula practitioner for four decades, but I am the first in my family to immerse myself in this cultural practice. *Thus by the terms of Senate Bill 8, not only would I be unable to prove continuous practice and be unable to continue it into the foreseeable future, but my daughter and granddaughter would not be able to engage in this practice as well because I would not be able to prove that I had an ancestor before 1892 who danced the hula.* Even if I had an ancestor who was a practitioner, what kind of evidence would be acceptable proof? As one kumu hula said, "The evidence would probably be the flower lei or the fern wreath. But those things are dead. They're all gone. They're in the ʻāina [land]."

To add insult to injury, the bill authorized a state agency, the Land Use Commission, to have exclusive authority and control over the petitioning and certification process. The Land Use Commission is a bureaucracy that historically has not favored Native Hawaiian rights, and it has favored settler interests over Native ones.

The Land Use Commission would be charged with notifying landowners of the individual petitions. The landowners would then have a "reasonable" period of time to respond, and if they did not like the petition of a particular gathering group, the landowner could request a contested case hearing. If the landowner failed to respond, the petitioner could gather resources on the landowner's land as long as the use was reasonable and did not cause hardship for the landowner.

However, if the landowner could prove hardship, the landowner could petition for a termination of the traditional and customary practice. In addition, the Land Use Commission, in concert with the landowner, could impose conditions on the Native practitioner, such as modifying the petition by request of the landowner. Even if the petitioner went to the Land Use Commission, the commission would still favor the landowner.

Another component of the bill attempted to restrict gathering to one's place of residence. However, massive overdevelopment in many ahupuaʻa has obliterated many of the special, sacred sites, resulting in the complete annihilation of Native products necessary for subsistence, religious, and cultural practices. Consequently, many Native practitioners must seek these items beyond their home areas. Kumu hula Vicky Holt Takamine put it most aptly when she said, "My backyard is the Board of Water Supply and my front yard is Pearl Harbor. Where am I going to gather ferns? Where am I going to gather shells for my students? The U.S. military installations in Pearl Harbor have polluted the water." [14]

The most racist part of the bill was that it proposed to force us to prove our race through the certification process, and we would have to bear proof of our race. Who else in this entire state would be subject to those kinds of racist tactics? *Nobody*. Only Native Hawaiians. That is what angered all of us. That is clearly racist. The burden is placed on Native Hawaiians alone to prove indigenous status in our own homeland.

How did this happen? What was the history behind this volatile issue? Many practitioners had never been involved in any kind of legislative fight nor asserted Native rights to anything dealing with culture or identity. The reason is because these things were not part of a practitioner's contextual base in the daily activity of any of the cultural practices. We were too busy in the routines of the practice of our culture, as well as being working people, to be concerned about a landmark court case—*Public Access Shoreline Hawai'i (PASH) v. Hawai'i County Planning Commission*—that had occurred two years before, in 1995. We believed that the State would protect our constitutional rights. But we were so wrong.

Thus when we were alerted to the destructive ramifications of Senate Bill 8, we were pressed into self-education about that *PASH* decision, legal history, land history, and the complex legislative process. We believed, at the time, that the battle would be tremendous, yet it was a challenge we would need to meet quickly.

The Law

Since time immemorial Native Hawaiians have practiced traditional and customary rights to access and gather resources from the land and sea. The State Constitution and the Hawai'i Supreme Court have reaffirmed and recognized these rights, and they have expressly required the State of Hawai'i to protect our Hawaiian heritage. Thus the State has a trust obligation to preserve the rights of the Native people of Hawai'i for future generations.

As we organized, we discovered there was legal protection for our gathering rights. Laws in Hawai'i provide for both statutory and constitutional protection of Native Hawaiian gathering rights. Laws concerning land in Hawai'i during the nineteenth century protected Native tenancy rights to access resources of the land. Eventually, these laws evolved into statutory protection specifically designed to protect Native Hawaiian traditional and customary gathering rights. The key here is the legal right to gather. Thus if an herbalist needs a certain plant for medicinal care and that plant can be found only outside her/his residential jurisdiction, then the gathering can be done where s/he can find the plant—in another district or even on another island.

Statutory protection is provided under the Hawai'i Revised Statutes (HRS), Section 1-1 and Section 7-1.[15] Historically, these two sections are the oldest of Hawai'i law because they date to the mid-nineteenth century, when Kamehameha III divided the lands in Hawai'i in the 1848 Māhele, or land division.

The nineteenth century was a period of intense meddling by foreigners in the economic and political affairs of the Kingdom of Hawai'i. Rights to land became a principal concern, and there was unremitting pressure to give settlers rights to use and to own land. Further, a near collapse in the Native population via the introduction of Western diseases and infectious agents brought successive waves of immigrants to the islands to work on the sugar plantations. High Native mortality was experienced in infancy and adulthood, even from common illnesses such as diarrhea, the cold, and measles. More serious diseases took even greater tolls. In the smallpox epidemic of 1853, thousands of Native Hawaiians died. By 1878, one hundred years after the arrival of the first foreigner, Captain James Cook, the Native Hawaiian population, said to have been about 800,000 at the time of Cook's arrival, had collapsed to 47,500.[16]

Thus in an effort to find some solution to the devastating collapse of the Native Hawaiian population, Kamehameha III reluctantly allowed the land tenure system to change from communal to private property: land, once our mother, was now a commodity. Clearly, when Kamehameha III agreed to māhele the lands of Hawai'i and institute Western private property land tenure, he envisioned a way to ensure Native people's right to use the land, access its resources, and gather material items from the land and the sea.

HRS Section 1-1 states, "The common law of England is declared to be the common law in the state of Hawai'i in all cases except as otherwise expressly provided by the constitutional laws of the United States, or by the laws of the state, or fixed by Hawaiian judicial precedent, or established by Hawaiian usage."[17] What is significant here is the statement "established by Hawaiian usage." Fundamentally, Hawai'i laws are subsumed under English common law, but there are many exceptions that give Hawaiian usage precedence over English common law.

Constitutional protection of Native Hawaiian gathering rights dates back to the last State Constitutional Convention held in 1978. For the very first time, Native Hawaiian traditional practices, customs, and usages in the State of Hawai'i were codified and elevated in the constitution under Article 12, Section 7.[18] That section clarifies the State's obligation to protect and uphold Native rights: "The State reaffirms and shall protect all rights, customarily and traditionally exercised for subsistence, cultural and religious purposes and possessed by ahupuaʻa tenants who are descendants of native Hawaiians who inhabited the Hawaiian Islands prior to 1778, subject to the right of the State to regulate such rights."

By constitutional authority, traditional and customary practices are made an unbroken and sacred right. Native Hawaiian traditional and customary rights now have protected status that engenders in the State of Hawaiʻi a constitutional obligation to protect Native culture. However, that obligation is subordinate to state needs. I recall reading that last statement for the first time during our struggle— "subject to the right of the State to regulate such rights"—and instantly Fanon's words rang clear, that Native Hawaiian culture is the contested culture under colonial domination. The State of Hawaiʻi maintains the hegemonic right to regulate and thereby control Native rights. In other words, no matter how strong the resistance to the colonizer, Native culture will *always* be subjected to and subordinated by state interests and needs. Native culture is still subject to the settler's rules. Although the colonizer has not regulated our rights out of existence, the United States still maintains hegemonic control over Native Hawaiian lands and affairs.

What prompted the emergence of Senate Bill 8? Why were landowners and development interests seeking legislative action to eradicate our legally protected right to access and gather resources?

In 1990 a Japanese company named Nansay Hawaiʻi, Inc., filed an application for a permit to develop a resort complex in Kona on the island of Hawaiʻi in the land division called Kohanaiki. The proposed resort would be built on approximately 450 acres of shoreline area. Nansay planned to build two hotels with more than 1,000 hotel rooms, 330 multiple family residences, a golf course, health club, restaurants, retail shops, and other facilities. Native Hawaiians in the area and a group called Pacific Access Shoreline Hawaiʻi (PASH) protested this development on traditional and customary grounds, as well as environmental grounds.[19] PASH argued that the Hawaiʻi County Planning Commission (HPC) was required legally to recognize and protect Native rights of access and gathering before granting a permit for development. Native Hawaiians in the area explained that their access to shrimp ponds would be severely curtailed or totally abolished by this development. Many Native Hawaiians harvest shrimp for food and as bait for fishing. The HPC rejected the view that Native rights have priority, and PASH appealed. In August 1995 the Hawaiʻi Supreme Court ruled in favor of PASH, reaffirming Native Hawaiians' rights to traditional and customary practices that included Native rights to gather resources from the land. The court further held that land titles in Hawaiʻi confirm only a limited property interest as compared with Western land patents and concepts of property. The two critical points raised by PASH included both constitutional and statutory protection of Native Hawaiian gathering rights as already discussed above.

Wealthy landowners, development interests, and title insurance companies in Hawai'i moved into action. These business interests mounted a defamation campaign alleging that the Hawai'i Supreme Court, by upholding PASH, created a climate of "uncertainty" that would have a negative impact on Hawai'i's economy. Soon a propaganda of fear ensued. Practitioners were characterized as roving bands of Natives entering private property unannounced, taking plants, flowers, and papayas at will. Further, these business interests went to the state legislature during the 1997 legislative session, and Senate Bill 8 and its counterpart, House Bill 1920, were introduced as a specific reaction to the PASH decision affirming Native Hawaiian gathering rights.

The Scene of Protest

Upon close examination of Senate Bill 8 and endless hours of discussion by Native Hawaiian practitioners and supporters about the history behind the bill and its potential impact on Native rights, the conclusion was that the bill was not going to die. Well-respected kumu hula Vicky Holt Takamine said to me, "I tried to stop it as an individual, and other kumu are sending in testimony as individuals, or as leaders of their hālau hula, but it is just not working. We have to do something."

Together, we contacted kumu hula and sympathizers willing to listen and take action.[20] We organized in three days, determined to kill Senate Bill 8. The contested culture burst onto the political scene, asserting that things Hawaiian held extreme importance in Hawai'i. A protest demonstration at the State Capitol for a twenty-four-hour period became the outward expression of that assertion.

Kumu hula throughout the Hawaiian Islands mobilized hundreds of their hula students in an extraordinary feat of grace and power never seen in modern colonial times. Essentially a conservative element of the Native Hawaiian community, practitioners unwittingly participated in the politicization of hula. Thus from the very act of organizing to defend hula was born the union of culture and politics, a union only gradually realized by its practitioners steeped, to a large extent, in the romanticization of hula.[21] Emblematic of that union was the emergence of the 'Īlio'ulaokalani Coalition, Native Hawaiian practitioners committed to defending any encroachment upon Native Hawaiian culture in general and hula in particular.

The protest had two objectives: put the spotlight on an old and customary practice that had its origins in ancient days, while educating the broader public that this conservative community had been shaken from a long slumber and was now awake to do battle and defend Native Hawaiian rights.

The meaning of the name "'Īlio'ulaokalani" refers to the behavior of the 'īlio, or dog. We all know how an 'īlio behaves when it is protecting its master or something it cherishes. The 'īlio fiercely guards anything that is precious to it. When the 'īlio is angered, it will defend its domain. We liked that idea. The remainder of the term refers to the color red in "'ula" and the place from which the 'īlio watches its precious territory, from the heavens, or "okalani." Thus the 'Īlio'ulaokalani Coalition is the defender and protector of our mother, the land, hovering above and watching over Her and all of Her inhabitants—people and all living things. Native culture needs a fierce defender so that Native Hawaiians can survive as a distinct people in our homeland.

At the first organizational meeting the kumu hula present decided on a strategy for the protest. First, they agreed that this effort must be a protest and not a public performance. Second, the protest would occur every hour on the hour by dancing and chanting in the old way. Third, no adornments of any kind or hula costumes were to be worn. And fourth, use of the most sacred hula instrument, the hula pahu (dance drum), would underscore the depth of their commitment to the national culture while also serving as a rallying voice of resistance. Thus they all agreed to allow the most sacred symbol of hula into a political arena and to use this cultural instrument for a most political purpose. The hula pahu became a potent political symbol in 1997.

In traditional times, the pahu was the voice of the heiau (temple). The pahu called the people, the 'aumākua (guardian spirits), the multiple gods, and alerted all people that an important event was about to happen. Furthermore, in a public performance the pahu is always adorned with ferns or some other living plant of our Earth Mother. It is very bad form to present an unadorned pahu in performance. However, for this occasion and purpose, and in this political arena, the kumu hula decided against adorning their drums. This act was in accordance with the affirmation of Hawaiian gathering rights upheld by the *PASH* decision. Protest was our purpose, not entertainment. Kumu hula made it clear that bringing *the* cultural symbol of hula, the pahu, to a political place underscored their mission: to defend Native Hawaiian culture, to defend Native Hawaiian rights.

Uncertain of the number of people who would support our efforts, we gradually assembled at the State Capitol. As the noon hour approached, more people showed up until there was quite a crowd. Hawaiians and non-Hawaiians from diverse economic backgrounds and professions, as well as Native practitioners and those who did not practice the Hawaiian culture, came to support our protest.

At high noon on February 25, 1997, more than one hundred pahu sounded in simultaneous rhythm to the ancient beats of our ancestors. The power of the sound of these pahu overwhelmed everyone. The scene of protest was the rotunda of the State Capitol, located in downtown Honolulu. Seated around the center of the large rotunda area, kumu hula, their students, and supporters began the most ancient and sacred of hula, ʻAuʻa ʻIa—"Hold fast to tradition." Though many of us had danced this hula in the past, this time it held a depth and power that connected us not only to the current political struggle but to a historic ancestral moment in the distant past. Each time the drums sounded, we heard "refuse to part with your traditions." Each time the voices of the kumu hula chanted, we believed the central message, "defend and protect your way of life." And each time the dancers swirled in rhythmic body movements, we implicitly understood our responsibility to "keep traditions precious, for one day they will be taken."

Every hour kumu hula sounded their pahu inside the large rotunda. Every hour one could hear loud chanting in the Hawaiian language directed at the legislators. Every hour scores of hula practitioners danced hula kahiko (ancient hula), all in an effort to convince the State of Hawaiʻi that Native Hawaiian practitioners would no longer remain apathetically quiet while others attempted to circumvent our legally protected rights.

Later, there were reports of legislators in meetings or at the lower level of the State Capitol chambers who heard the drums. One legislator explained that the sound was so awesome it gave him "chicken skin." People at great distances could hear the drums, and it was unnerving for many of the legislators. Nothing like this had ever occurred in the State of Hawaiʻi in modern times. My mother and father were trying to find a parking space five blocks away, and my mother said, "We could hear the drums beating—it sounded so eerie." She expressed the general expectation of most people when they arrived, that a political place would not be one filled with ancient hula, hula dancers, and sacred hula instruments.

However, as one already engaged in the sovereignty movement, I clearly saw a direct connection between politics and culture: Native Hawaiians' struggle for self-determination as an expression of our national culture. Recalling Fanon while at the State Capitol surrounded by hula practitioners from across the state, I realized the political nature of the expression that characterized our national culture; as cultural practitioners in a largely political environment, we asserted through hula that things Hawaiian possessed great significance, and Native Hawaiians would resist colonial imposition.

Politicization of a cultural art form came alive that day.[22] We understood that unless we took action, responsibility for deciding what constitutes the varied aspects of Native Hawaiian culture would be effectively taken from us and legally placed in the hands of the colonizer.

As a significant part of Native Hawaiian national culture, hula reflects the past and present experiences of the people. When that experience involves political struggle, a vibrant hula emerges in such renderings as ‘Au‘a ‘ia, the chant that began this essay. Here is evidence of political dance expressed in traditional times and political expression in the dance. Hula kū‘ē is the term now widely used in the hula community. It means a dance performed to resist, protest, or oppose the status quo. Hula kū‘ē is resistance that is equated with endurance and survival.

Many kumu hula from the outer islands and different hula schools came together to hula kū‘ē. Other practitioners came as well: herbalists, surfers, people who gather in the forests and the ocean. As the night embraced us, a soft rain blanketed the rotunda area. We saw this as a sign blessing our commitment.

A few hours later the sun began to rise. Many of us had hardly slept, too excited by the purpose of our protest. Those of us who stayed the night moved away from the rotunda to the east side of the capitol. There, we called up the sun as our ancestors did in ancient times through chant. It felt good to hear the power of human voices in unison with one purpose. It empowered us to stop Senate Bill 8.

We knew that the bill was now held in the Senate Committee on Ways and Means, whose co-chairs were Senators Lehua Fernandes Salling and Carol Fukunaga.[23] A few days before the protest vigil, we mobilized the hula community and other practitioners and supporters to call and send faxes to these co-chairs to stop Senate Bill 8. According to staff members in Senator Fernandes Salling's office, they began receiving phone calls and faxes from the senator's constituency and others demanding to know what would be her course of action. The senator and several office staff members closely reviewed the bill and were startled by the bill's contents and its proposals.

Meanwhile, I contacted Mililani Trask, attorney and one of the founding members of ‘Īlio‘ulaokalani, to get some idea of the status of Senate Bill 8.[24] Trask knew the legislative system and was familiar with many of the legislators. We spoke on the phone as one hundred pahu resonated throughout the rotunda, tensions mounting. Trask assured me of Senator Fernandes Salling's opposition to Senate Bill 8 and her support of Native Hawaiian rights, but the senator still had to convince her co-chair. In a move that would later cost her the co-chair spot on the most powerful committee in the Senate, Senator Fernandes Salling refused to schedule a hearing for Senate Bill 8. What did this mean? Was the bill really dead?

Hopeful at the possibility that the bill could die, I announced to a crowd of several hundred people that Senate Bill 8 would not be scheduled for a hearing. I explained that due to the efforts of one brave Native Hawaiian senator, the bill could die. The cheers were deafening. I cautioned the crowd that the legislative session had just barely begun and that anything could happen. But it seemed we had won.

The ten o'clock hour was at hand. It had now been twenty-two hours since we began this protest. Tired yet invigorated, we gathered at the rotunda in the center of the capitol at the sound of the conch shell. All the local media, camera crews, and newspaper reporters were there capturing the moment. Rumors circulated that Senators Solomon and Iwase wanted to address the crowd and explain their position. Unimpressed, we proceeded. The pahu sounded; voices rose in chant. Emboldened and flushed with hope, hundreds of hula practitioners moved in unison to ancient hula.

Suddenly, Senator Solomon appeared. Kumu hula and leader of the ʻIlioʻulaokalani Coalition Vicky Holt Takamine left her pahu and approached Senator Solomon. Both moved to the microphone. Cameras zoomed in. Everyone watched in tense anticipation as the drama unfolded. Other legislators leaned over the balcony to listen and observe. Holt Takamine quieted the throng. Meanwhile, Senator Solomon, seeing Senator Iwase, gestured for him to join her at the microphone. Both senators explained their decision to move the bill out of their committee. Senator Solomon disingenuously exclaimed that she voted in opposition to the bill. Astonished by her blatant attempt at a cover-up, I quickly moved to the microphone. The crowd shouted at her, some calling her a liar. Somehow, she believed we were not informed on the status and movement of the bill. But she was dead wrong. At the microphone I pointed out the fact that I had the voting record of each legislator on the Senate Committee on Water, Land, and Hawaiian Affairs on this bill. Senator Solomon, along with all the other committee members, had cast an affirmative vote supporting Senate Bill 8. The booing and hissing continued.

Then Senator Iwase, coerced by Senator Solomon, stepped up to the microphone. Defending the bill he introduced, he affirmed the landowners' and developers' position. His tone, too, demeaned our efforts. He constantly referred to us as "you people," saying that we must "learn" to discuss the issue and that right now "you people" are "too emotional." What he meant, of course, was that we were "too emotional" to discuss this issue in a rational manner. This angered the already hostile crowd because he spoke to us as if to a group of children disrespectful of a legislator's power and authority.

Kumu hula Pua Kanahele, from the island of Hawaiʻi, moved to the microphone amid more shouts from the crowd. Countering Senator Iwase, Kanahele reminded him that many in the crowd had college degrees and taught at the university level, and that many had professional careers. Thus we had "learned" how to discuss and analyze issues by gathering the facts at hand before making a decision. She stated very plainly that it was legislative efforts such as Senate Bill 8 that ignited concern among practitioners of Native Hawaiian culture. With Senators Iwase and Solomon near the microphone, the crowd chanted, "Kill the bill! Kill the bill!" A sea of handheld signs reflecting that sentiment surrounded the rotunda.

With pressures mounting, Senator Solomon took the bill and, in a gesture of profound theatrics, tore it up before the people and the cameras. The crowd went crazy. It made for good news copy. It was on the six o'clock and ten o'clock evening news, and by the next day it was the lead story in all of the newspapers.

Exhausted but elated, we ended the protest as we began it: dancing to 'Au'a 'ia. The hula pahu sounded once more as scores of hula practitioners moved as one with a power and force not seen in a long time. And there was my daughter, pregnant with my future grandchild, dancing with her ancestors.

We could not believe our success at our first attempt at political activism. Yet a widespread uneasiness prevailed among the practitioners. There was still a good two months remaining before the end of the legislative session, and we knew anything could happen. We realized that, like Dracula, Senate Bill 8 could rise again. Though we laughed and understood the humor, we were tentative. We were political innocents treading on new political ground that felt like quicksand—ever shifting, ever partial; we little understood the legislative process or what the backlash could stir up.

The irony remains that credit for the bill's demise was given not to Senator Fernandes Salling, but to Senator Solomon. It would not be until the summer of 1997 that we discovered how the Senate majority chose to deal with one of their own. Punished for her actions in the spring, Senator Fernandes Salling was removed as

On February 26, 1997, protesters celebrated the successful twenty-four-hour vigil at the state capitol opposing Senate Bill 8. The bill sought to eradicate Native Hawaiian gathering rights. Photograph by Dennis Oda (courtesy of the *Honolulu Star-Bulletin*).

co-chair of the Ways and Means Committee. The most plausible explanation for her removal from the most powerful committee in the Senate is that she posed a threat to the maintenance of colonialism. The powerful agents of the dominant culture made certain that any attempts to support the assertion that things Hawaiian have any great political significance would be eliminated.

As for Senators Solomon and Iwase, whatever their suggestions and their words, these two legislators serving as agents of the hegemonic culture came to us not as public servants yet still expected civil service. They sought but did not get the hospitality or aloha that they had always expected and received. Though we "won" and felt warm with victory, this moment gave us pause. For in the heat of battle, we understood that what was valuable to them in their own terms was status, power, and dominance—the status of a political official institutionalized in the Hawai'i State Legislature with the political clout to dominate and oppress us. This was clearly illustrated twelve months later in the 1998 legislative session, when yet another bill emerged seeking once again to terminate our cultural rights.

The Aftermath

After Senate Bill 8 was killed, two resolutions pertaining to the regulation of traditional and customary rights emerged. Senate Ways and Means co-chairs Carol Fukunaga and Lehua Fernandes Salling introduced Senate Concurrent Resolution 230, with text identical to Senate Resolution 114 (SCR 230/SR 114). The resolution sought to fund a study of traditional and customary gathering rights by the William S. Richardson School of Law at the University of Hawai'i at Mānoa in consultation with the 'Īlio'ulaokalani Coalition and members of the Hawaiian community and other local interests. The resolution was referred to the Senate Committee on Water, Land, and Hawaiian Affairs. This was the very same committee that passed Senate Bill 8. Wounded by the public throttling they both received at the hands of Native practitioners, Senators Iwase and Solomon did not schedule a hearing on the resolution, and it died in committee. Neither senator made any serious effort to resolve this issue.

Meanwhile, in the House of Representatives, House Concurrent Resolution 276 and House Resolution 197 (HCR 276/HR 197), introduced by Representative Ed Case, proposed some discussion with all interested parties to seek common ground on the appropriate regulation of traditional and customary rights.

House Resolution 197 attempted to address the gathering-rights issue by providing community dialogue in the fall of 1997. Landowners, title companies, and business interests, along with Native Hawaiian practitioners, participated in several months of community meetings throughout the state. But this effort did not work.

Business interests do not understand our cultural concerns. The ʻĪlioʻulaokalani Coalition decided to continue a dialogue with one of the larger business entities called Pacific Business Roundtable, which is a consortium of businesspeople who seemed genuinely concerned. But even that effort failed.

By the 1998 legislative session, more bills similar in nature to Senate Bill 8 began to appear. Representative Case introduced legislation designed, in essence, to eliminate our right to gather from the land. At one hearing, Representative Case pressed kumu hula Vicky Holt Takamine to define the size of the parcel of land that would be acceptable to practice traditional and customary gathering rights. Was it one acre, seven hundred square feet, or what? She responded by saying that if a lauaʻe (fern) is growing on the road or freeway and is needed for a cultural practice, then she will stop to gather that fern. That road or freeway could be on federal, state, or city land that is developed. Later in conversation, Mililani Trask commended Holt Takamine. She added that places like Hilo Bay on the island of Hawaiʻi are developed land, but the ʻopihi (limpet sea creature), which is a Hawaiian delicacy that must attach itself to rocks to survive, does not know that it is attaching itself to developed or undeveloped property. If Native Hawaiians see the ʻopihi on the rocks at the pier, they will pick it and eat it. We are saying that it does not matter whether the land is developed or undeveloped. Confining the gathering to strictly undeveloped land severely restricts the ability of Native Hawaiians to practice our culture. Gradually, we realized that the government could deprive us of our constitutionally protected rights by the issuance and passage of a bill—an instrument of tremendous power wielded like a scythe to cut down the roots and branches of our culture.

This is clear: no matter how many times we go to the state legislature to fight for our traditional and customary right to practice our culture, the odds will always be against the Native Hawaiian practitioner. We expect the struggle to continue.

This is the contested culture under colonial domination. I feel ambivalent about the success of our efforts. I was happy that many in the hula community got involved in a very political way. That a Native woman in a position of power, Senator Lehua Fernandes Salling, stood by her principles gave me some hope. But I was dissatisfied; I still harbor a measure of discontent because I know that no matter how hard we work, if we do not have our own nation, if we do not achieve sovereignty, then we will never, never have clearly defined rights to land or to the resources we need to practice our culture in our own way.

The denial of the existence of Native Hawaiians as a distinct people is a way of legitimizing the State's claim to our ancestral lands. Destroying the right to traditional and customary practices eliminates the conditions necessary for the national culture to flourish. Thus from my perspective, Native Hawaiians have become victims of a conscious and persistent effort of destruction directed against them. Presently, cultural resilience among Native Hawaiians remains within the colonial frame, one in which we are subject to a sustained effort to destroy us.

There is no suspension of the national culture during a political struggle for national liberation.

'Au'a 'ia e Kama e Kona moku. . . .

Notes

1. I provide a loose translation of the ancient mele hula. The principal belief is to hold on to that which defines a Native Hawaiian: genealogical bloodlines tied to the land that identify a cultural tradition distinct to a land-based people. In some circles this mele hula is attributed to a Maui Ali'i Nui (High Chief) named Kamalalawalu, who struggled to impart the correct kinds of political decisions to benefit the welfare of his people in changing times. Repetition of parts of an Ali'i Nui's name recalls the mana, or spiritual and political life-force of that individual, hence the repetition of "Kama" here several times. In other circles, 'Au'a 'ia conveys the idea that each individual is responsible for the conservation of one's cultural practices. As kumu hula Kaho'onei Panoke said in a recent conversation when asked what this mele hula means to him, "I think of my responsibility to the land, my people, and my culture."

I capitalize the "N" in the term "Native," borrowing the argument made by Haunani-Kay Trask to underscore the geographical and ideological difference between that which is indigenous versus that which is Western and foreign. By emphasizing the use of the capitalized "N" in "Native," I turn against the self-alienation of the colonized Native Hawaiian and instill an awareness in the colonizer of our own historical and cultural tradition, which embraces a realization of the deformations suffered at the hands of colonialism. Use of the term "Native" invokes the old sense of humiliation while simultaneously rejecting the colonial stereotype and lending expression to a heightened consciousness of decolonization. See Haunani-Kay Trask, *From A Native Daughter: Colonialism and Sovereignty in Hawai'i*, rev. ed. (1993). Reprint: Honolulu: University of Hawai'i Press, 1999.

2. Frantz Fanon, *The Wretched of the Earth* (New York: Grove Press, 1963), 237.

3. See Momiala Kamahele, "Hula as Resistance," *Forward Motion* 2 (3) (1992): 40–46; and Trask, "'Lovely Hula Hands': Corporate Tourism and the Prostitution of Hawaiian Culture," in *From a Native Daughter*, 136–147 .

4. Fanon, *The Wretched of the Earth*, 233.

5. Trask, "From a Native Daughter," in *From a Native Daughter*, 116. I am indebted to Trask for this remarkable insight into our Hawaiian language. This is linguistic proof that land, like parents, was never "owned."

6. Today, those who call dance movements scripted to Christian text and danced within the context of the Christian Church "Christian hula" are not considered to be hula practitioners in the true sense of that term. It is unfortunate that this phrase is used for a religion that historically denigrated Native peoples and their cultural practices. People in a Christian church who dance to a Christian dance are appropriating the sanctity of one form of

religious expression for another. Many of us who are hula practitioners and traditionalists see a real problem with calling this Christian dance "hula."

7. This discussion is confined to one of two legislative bills introduced in the 1997 Hawai'i legislative session that viewed traditional and customary rights as an encumbrance on the land. House Bill 1920 was assigned to the House Committee on Hawaiian Affairs, whose chairman was Representative Ed Case (District 23, Mānoa). This bill did not concern Native practitioners because it was deferred early in the legislative session. House Bill 1920 tried to create the judicial process for traditional and customary gathering rights so that in case of conflict, there would be a process for dealing with the Land Use Commission, the developers, and contested case hearings. For an excellent legal analysis of both Senate Bill 8 and House Bill 1920 within the context of legal and historical precedence, see D. Kapua Sproat, "The Backlash against PASH: Legislative Attempts to Restrict Native Hawaiian Rights," in *University of Hawai'i Law Review* 20 (1998): 321.

Property and development interests in Hawai'i, such as the Land Use Research Foundation (LURF) and the Pacific Legal Foundation (PLF), and their financial supporters are opposed to Native Hawaiian traditional and customary rights. The PLF has characterized Native Hawaiian traditional and customary rights to gather as trespass, thereby attempting to criminalize all Native practitioners. Business interests profit from outright development and clearly target the elimination of Native Hawaiian gathering rights, viewed by them as encumbrances on the land.

8. Senator Randy Iwase represented District 18 on the island of O'ahu. It includes portions of 'Ewa District (portions of Crestview and Seaview, Waipi'o, Mililani, Waipi'o Acres) and a portion of Wahiawā District (Wheeler Army Air Field). Office of Elections, State of Hawai'i, "Factsheet: Geographic Descriptions for Senatorial Districts," http://www.hawaii .gov/elections/facts/Senbdy.htm

9. Senator Malama Solomon represented District 1 on the island of Hawai'i. It includes North Kohala District (Hāwī, Hala'ula), Hāmākua District (Kukuihaele, Honoka'a, Pa'auilo, 'O'ōkala), North Hilo (Laupāhoehoe and Honohina), portions of South Hilo District (Hakalau, Honomū, Pepe'ekeo, Onomea, Pāpa'ikou, Pauka'a, portion of Hilo), portions of North Kona District (Kailua-Kona, Honokāhau, Makalawena, Ka'ūpūlehu, Pu'uanahulu), and South Kohala District ('Anaeho'omalu, Waikoloa, Puakō, Kawaihae, Waimea). Office of Elections, "Factsheet."

10. Senator Solomon was not re-elected in the 1998 election after serving in the state legislature for nearly two decades.

11. Hawai'i State Senate, SB 8 (Honolulu: Nineteenth Legislature, 1997).

12. On November 25, 1892, the Kingdom of Hawai'i reorganized the judiciary, repealing the relevant section in the 1859 Civil Code and adopting language similar to that found today in Haw. Rev. Stat. Sec. 1-1. See Session Laws ch. LVII, Sec. 5 (1892).

13. An ahupua'a is a large, wedge-shaped land system extending from the mountains to the sea. In a subsistence society, all the material, spiritual, and psychological needs of the people could be found in such a self-sufficient ahupua'a. These land systems provided such necessities as fresh water, wood products from the mountains, other foods from the sea, and fishponds.

14. Other elements of Senate Bill 8 restricted gathering to undeveloped land. These lands were defined as being "without structures or improvement," "without grading," and "without building permits." A vacant lot without a permit would be considered undeveloped land, but if it had a permit, then practitioners could not gather on it even though it was vacant. If the land did not fall under this category, the Native Hawaiian practitioner was denied the certificate, effectively terminating her/his right to gather.

15. *Hawai'i Revised Statutes: Comprising the Statutes of the State of Hawai'i, Consolidated, Revised and Annotated* (Honolulu: Published by authority, 1985).

16. David Stannard, *Before the Horror: The Population of Hawai'i on the Eve of Western Contact* (Honolulu: University of Hawai'i, Social Science Research Institute, 1989).

17. *Hawai'i Revised Statutes.*

18. *Proceedings of the Constitutional Convention of Hawaii of 1978* (Honolulu: Chief Clerk of the Convention, State of Hawaii, 1980).

19. See the decision of the Hawai'i Supreme Court in *Public Access Shoreline Hawai'i v. Hawai'i County Planning Commission,* 79 Hawai'i 425, 903 P.2d 1246 (August 31, 1995).

20. Founding members include myself; kumu hula Vicky Holt Takamine; Pua Kanahele, an internationally acclaimed kumu hula who resides on the island of Hawai'i; Frenchy DeSoto and Hannah Springer, trustees of the Office of Hawaiian Affairs; and other kumu hula and practitioners, including Manu Boyd, Keali'i Reichel, Mililani Trask, Kaho'onei Panoke, and Mapuana de Silva.

21. Well-known kumu hula Mapuana de Silva, ambivalent about her involvement in defending Native rights, remarked to me that if this effort became too political, she would not hesitate to leave. In our company was a respected kupuna (Hawaiian elder) who was surprised by de Silva's admonition. Gently, I responded that politicization of hula had already begun the minute we organized to resist colonial power.

22. See articles by Dennis Oda, "All Pau; Aloha!" *Honolulu Star-Bulletin* (February 17, 1997); and Catherine Kekoa Enomoto, "Dance of the Red Dog: Kumu Hula Unite and Realize Their Power in the Push for Sovereignty and Preservation of Culture," *Honolulu Star-Bulletin* (December 31, 1997).

23. At the time, Senator Lehua Fernandes Salling represented District 7, which included the island of Ni'ihau and parts of the island of Kaua'i, including a portion of Kawaihau, Līhu'e, Koloa, and Waimea districts. Senator Carol Fukunaga represented District 12 on the island of O'ahu, which includes portions of Honolulu.

24. At the time of this protest vigil, Mililani Trask was the Kia'āina (leader) of the Native Hawaiian sovereignty initiative Ka Lāhui Hawai'i. She was unable to attend the protest vigil because of a prior commitment.

A Nation Incarcerated

Twenty-three hours in a lifeless cell,
day after day, it's the same old hell.
Who knows why? I'd like to know.
I wish I knew the answer for this,
to release his soul from captivity.
Oh lord, hear his plea.
Show him a picture,
or give him an answer that will help him.
He wants to free his body,
he wants to free his mind.
He's been in prison too long.
Here's his song.

—Warren Kaʻahanui, "Rusty Old Steampipes"

Native Hawaiians are being imprisoned in alarming numbers in our own ancestral homeland, making Hawaiʻi's incarceration rate one of the fastest rising in the country.[1] With increasing deportation of Native inmates to U.S. continental private prisons, criminalization is yet another tool of American colonial power to control Native lands and deny Hawaiians sovereignty.

In 1820 the first Calvinist American missionaries arrived in Hawaiʻi to "civilize" Natives by criminalizing their cultural practices.[2] At first sight, these missionaries proclaimed Hawaiʻi's indigenous peoples to be "savage," speculating that they had indeed found the missing link between brute and man.[3] Imposing their perverse sense of morality upon the Native peoples, they were instrumental in instituting settler laws in Hawaiʻi, criminalizing traditional Hawaiian cultural ways, including hula,[4] surfing,[5] and the Native language.[6] Hawaiians were charged with vagrancy, whereas for millennia we freely traveled to the mountains and ocean to gather food and fish. For these colonial crimes, Hawaiians were imprisoned and fined.[7]

In 1895, two years after the overthrow of the Hawaiian monarchy, Prince Jonah Kūhiō Kalanianaʻole joined other Native Hawaiians in an unsuccessful attempt to restore Queen Liliʻuokalani to her throne. They were discovered, arrested, and tried for treason. Prince Kūhiō spent almost a year in prison, criminalized for his attempt to right the injustices of American imperialism (courtesy of the State of Hawaiʻi Archives).

Though we were an independent nation, Hawai'i was colonized because of American imperial, strategic interests in the Pacific and Asia. The United States supported the illegal overthrow of our government in 1893 and stole two million acres of Native lands. By the time the United States annexed the Hawaiian Kingdom in 1898, white and Asian settlers outnumbered the Native population three to one, with Japanese laborers constituting the largest settler group.[8]

Today, the ratio is approximately 80 percent settlers to 20 percent Natives.[9] Local Japanese settlers have ascended to ruling-class status and, with white settlers, direct the American colonial system. Now a colonized people, Hawaiians inhabit the islands' lowest socioeconomic strata, with nearly half of the Hawaiian population classified as poor or low income.[10] For Hawaiians, land is familial, the source of material, cultural, and spiritual existence and political power. One devastating outcome of land dispossession today is the disproportionate rates of incarceration of Native adults and children.

After more than a century of violent colonial rule, poverty-stricken, landless Hawaiians are now stereotyped as criminals in Hawai'i. Settlers institute laws and policies to maintain their control over Hawai'i's lands and resources, warehousing Native Hawaiians into correctional facilities.

Settler Racism

> We have a race of people that find out that the lifestyle that they were accustomed to is outlawed and with a severe penalty, the prisoner is punished inside the prison and outside the prison by the government and society, the children suffer ostracism in school and society, males in prison can no longer devote time to their families. . . . When people look at prisons they only see the highly negative aspects, like rape and murder and don't see spitting on the sidewalk and trespassing as the crime. Society and government are the real culprits for the victimization and present day situation of the Hawaiian Prisoner stereotype.
>
> —Keoni May, a former Hawai'i correctional
> facility guard, "Hawaiians in Oahu Prison"

The United States is a racist, settler colonial country built upon Native peoples' lands. Colonizers imposed their education, health, housing, and criminal justice systems on Hawai'i (the colony), reflecting racist policies enforced in the continental United States (the metropole). Hawaiian studies professor Haunani-Kay Trask defines racism as a "historically created system of power in which one racial/ethnic group dominates another racial/ethnic group for the benefit of the dominating group."[11] According to Trask, this dominating group controls economic, cultural, and political power by controlling the "monopoly of the means of violence."

Prospering within this colonial system, Japanese settlers today wield the institutional power to be racist against Hawaiians supported by the brute force of the U.S. military and state police apparatus. Since the 1954 Democratic Party takeover, Japanese settlers have many times held the majority and leadership in the state legislature, while Native legislators have consistently remained the legislative minority.[12] Japanese settlers have held the most powerful state executive positions of governor and lieutenant governor for twenty-four years. For six years, 1996–2002, Japanese settlers directed the Hawai'i Department of Public Safety (DPS), the agency that oversees all adult county jails, state prisons, and inmates. Keith Kaneshiro was director from 1996 to 1998, and Ted Sakai ran the department for four years, from 1998 to 2002. During their terms hundreds of Native Hawaiian inmates were sent to continental facilities, where they have suffered from gang violence and rape and have found drugs more accessible than in Hawai'i facilities.[13]

American incarceration has always been conducted along racial and class lines. On the continent, blacks are approximately six times more likely to go to prison than whites.[14] The primary racial tension in Hawai'i is not between whites and people of color, but between white and Asian settlers and Hawaiians. Hawai'i's indigenous peoples are incarcerated at a higher rate than white and Asian settlers. In 2002 Hawaiians were 22 percent of Hawai'i's population, yet constituted 38 percent of the male inmate population and 44 percent of the female inmate population.[15] Japanese settlers were also 22 percent of the population, yet they constituted only 6 percent of Hawai'i's male inmate population and 4 percent of the female inmate population. Furthermore, whites made up 21 percent of Hawai'i's general population (comparable to the general Hawaiian population), yet ranked number one in arrest rates, making up approximately 35 percent of all arrests. The systematic advantage of white privilege in Hawai'i's colonial judicial system, however, ensures that whites make up a considerably smaller percentage of the inmate population than Natives.[16] While Hawaiians constitute approximately 26 percent of all arrests in Hawai'i, they are more likely to be incarcerated after going through the colonial legal process than any ethnic group. Recent statistics establish Hawai'i's indigenous male and female inmate population at 39 percent, but many state correctional facility workers estimate a Native inmate population closer to 60 percent.[17] The disproportionate incarceration of Hawaiians contradicts Hawai'i's lovely "melting pot" image presented by white and Asian settlers and testifies to the violence of institutionalized racism against Native Hawaiians.

Disturbingly, Hawai'i's indigenous peoples live in a state with one of the fastest rising incarceration rates in the United States, ranking number one in 1997.

Hawai'i's increasing incarceration is part of a U.S. national trend with a record two million inmates in America in 2000.[18] In the colony of Hawai'i, white and Asian settlers carry on the American legacy of incarceration along racial and class lines within the framework of local systems of power that subjugate Hawai'i's indigenous peoples.

Landlessness and Poverty

> We were, in effect, using the prisons to contain a growing social crisis concentrated in the bottom quarter of our population. . . . A growing prison system was what we [Americans] had instead of an antipoverty policy.
>
> —Elliott Currie, *Crime and Punishment in America*

Japanese settler control over the islands does not reflect the "industriousness" of settlers, but rather reveals the systematic advantage any colonial structure gives settlers over indigenous peoples and Native lands. While Asian settlers celebrate their "success" on Native ancestral lands, Hawaiians live in poverty.[19] With settlers running banks, corporations, and policy boards, Hawaiians become excluded as a group from economic advancement. Hawaiian unemployment rates are triple that of Japanese settlers and double that of whites.[20] Whites hold economic power in America, with average household earnings almost double those of black households. Japanese settlers in Hawai'i hold a similar income advantage over Hawaiians.[21] Not surprisingly, the most common serious offenses committed by Hawaiians are categorized as property crimes.[22] National research repeatedly links low income and unemployment to incarceration rates. Although entitled to approximately two million acres of prime, valuable land in Hawai'i that was stolen by the United States and is now held in trust by the State of Hawai'i for the *benefit* of Native Hawaiians, 45 percent of all Hawaiians are living in poverty.[23]

Contrary to settlers' stereotype of Native criminal "violence," the top offenses in adult Hawaiian arrests are nonviolent theft, a poverty-related crime, and "all other offenses," which are minor and consensual crimes (e.g., trespassing and drug paraphernalia) where many times there is no "victim."[24] As the poorest group in Hawai'i with the highest unemployment rate of the six major ethnic groups,[25] Native Hawaiians are overrepresented in Hawai'i's jails and prisons.[26] Numerous statistical studies show that unemployed individuals are more likely to be arrested and incarcerated. This economic status often compounds the problems of Native Hawaiians who are arrested. When considering a pretrial supervised release for a defendant, the judge makes his or her determination based on middle-class standards, for example, whether the defendant has a job, a stable home (the same address for a year), or substance abuse problems. Most poor people, however, are unemployed, under-educated, and have no stable residences (some are homeless). Many Hawaiians are doomed to incarceration because of their poor economic and housing circumstances, the root of which lies in American colonialism and settler racism. Furthermore, Native Hawaiians remain in jail before trial because their families cannot afford fifty or one hundred dollars for bail. Thus they have a greater chance of incarceration even before conviction. As Hawai'i's economy continues to worsen, so will the incarceration rate in Hawai'i.

Criminalizing Drug Use

> The war on drugs is a political war, waged not by scientists and doctors but by police officers and politicians. Under more fortunate circumstances, the prevalence of drugs in American society—not only cocaine and heroin and marijuana but also alcohol and tobacco and sleeping pills—would be properly addressed as a public-health question. The American Medical Association classifies drug addiction as a disease, not as a crime or a moral defect. Nor is addiction contagious, like measles and the flu.
>
> —Lewis H. Lapham, "A Political Opiate,"
> in *The Crisis in Drug Prohibition*

Criminalizing drug abuse among Native Hawaiians, rather than treating it as an illness caused by the hopelessness of colonialism, contributes to the high incarceration and recidivism rates for Hawaiians. If drug addiction were treated as a medical problem and not a crime, as in many European countries like Portugal and Great Britain, the prison "problem" would significantly decrease.[27] Sakai estimated that roughly 85 percent of Hawai'i's inmates have substance-abuse problems; however, as director of the DPS, he provided treatment for fewer than 20 percent of them.[28] Hawaiians are one of the two ethnic groups in Hawai'i with the greatest "prevalence of substance abuse and treatment need."[29] For Hawai'i's indigenous peoples, drugs are the manifestation of daily life struggles.

National statistical data link drug use to crime, especially property crimes that include theft and larceny, the most serious crimes for which Native Hawaiians are arrested. Drug users often live in poverty and rob to support their habit. Substance abuse is a major contributing factor for Native Hawaiian incarceration, and drug-related arrests are on the rise in Hawai'i. In 2001 Honolulu ranked first (by a wide margin) in the United States for crystal methamphetamine use by arrestees.[30] Crystal methamphetamine is a volatile and very addictive drug that dominates the lives of many in poor, rural, Native Hawaiian communities. Rather than providing treatment for drug addiction in poor communities, white and Asian settlers who benefit from the dispossession of Hawaiians continue to criminalize drug use, putting more Hawaiians in jails and prisons.

In the U.S. colony of Hawai'i many Hawaiian families have only these legacies to pass down to indigenous youth, who will continue to suffer under the white and Asian settler racist regime. Recent statistics reflect that from grades eight through twelve, Native Hawaiian students' use of alcohol, tobacco, and other drugs is usually higher than that of students from other groups.[31] With an average of five thousand Hawaiian children being arrested each year, it comes as no surprise that in 2001 Native children made up nearly half of the Hawai'i Youth Correctional Facility's population.[32] The cycle of drug abuse and incarceration is perpetuated in the next Hawaiian generation.

Over the years gaps in social services that help reduce substance abuse and recidivism among Hawai'i's inmates have been brought to the attention of state leaders, but with very few results. The few transitional and drug treatment inmate programs that have been initiated under white and Japanese settler rule usually ensure no meaningful change for Native inmates. By underfunding proven programs or expecting community humanitarians to volunteer their services, the settler-controlled State of Hawai'i sets up needed inmate programs to fail. Furthermore, existing social service inmate programs like substance abuse treatment and transitional housing are limited in their scope of services or are not holistic enough in their approach. For Native Hawaiian inmates these programs are only "Band-Aids" for the socioeconomic symptoms of the underlying problem—colonization. Through this Band-Aid approach the State creates a façade that they are addressing the problems of Hawaiian over-incarceration in progressive ways. This is done out of their own self-interested desire to avoid international attention over the blatant racism that exists against Hawaiians, whose culture is the number one commodity for Hawai'i's tourist industry. For white and Japanese settlers, the purpose of Native Hawaiian inmate social service programs is not to empower inmates but to pacify the misgivings of Hawaiian families, U.S. constitutional watchdogs like the American Civil Liberties Union (ACLU), international human rights abuse observers,[33] and, most important, the potential tourist.

During his term Sakai publicly stated that he supported the idea of rehabilitative programs for Hawaiian inmates, but he attempted to rationalize the DPS' "inability" to implement restorative justice and wellness-center programs recommended by the state legislature. It is important to quote his "Response to Senate Concurrent Resolution No. 62, Twenty-first Legislature, December 2001" in its entirety to illustrate settler logic.

Dear Mr. Speaker and Members of the House,

Senate Concurrent Resolution No. 62, S.D.1, H.D.1 requests that the Department of Public Safety, in consultation with the Department of the Attorney General, the Prosecuting Attorney of each County, the Police Department of each County, and private groups such as the 'Ohana Ho'opakele, implement programs of restorative justice and establish wellness centers to reduce the rate of incarceration and increase opportunities for inmate rehabilitation, particularly among native Hawaiians.

The Department of Public Safety supports the intent of this resolution which ably presents the rationale behind promoting programs that contribute to resolving crime on a broader basis than just punishment of offenders. However, our limited resources prohibit us from carrying out the actions requested.

This Resolution requests that we review and implement alternatives to transferring inmates to mainland correctional facilities. We do not have much choice in this matter. The inmates who are on the mainland have been sentenced to prison terms for felonies. There are four facilities in Hawaii that focus on these offenders. Each of them is filled to capacity. The Halawa Correctional Facility, the only facility in Hawaii capable of housing medium and close custody male inmates, is about 200 inmates over its maximum capacity. We would welcome alternatives, so long as they are appropriate for the population. That is why we support proposals for medium and minimum-security treatment facilities.

The Department has always advocated for expanded treatment options and alternatives to incarceration for those offenders that are eligible and that can benefit from these kinds of programs. To this end, we proposed funding for treatment programs for qualified offenders on pre-trial release, probation and parole. Such programs reduce the rate of incarceration and increase opportunities for rehabilitation for all offenders.

The department has also supported establishing restorative justice programs and wellness centers to reduce the rate of incarceration and increase opportunities for inmate rehabilitation. We presently participate in the group convened by the Department of the Attorney General to expand restorative justice programs in the State. Hawaii County has already made much progress in this area and is an example of what can be accomplished when the criminal justice system works hand-in-hand with the community. We are also interested in promoting wellness centers as community and culturally based alternatives to incarceration.

The Department supports the intent of SCR 672, H.D.1, S.D.1 and respectfully recommends that the Legislature review the contents of this resolution and considers assigning this task to the Legislative Reference Bureau for further study.

Very truly yours,
Ted Sakai
Director[34]

In this letter Sakai argues against instituting wellness centers because of "limited resources." Instead of being an advocate for the prisoners and requesting that the legislature provide such resources, Sakai suggests instead that Hawai'i County stands as an example that the system is working well with the community. Other evidence, however, proves otherwise.

One example of the settler society's pacifying tactics is Act 161, passed in 2002 by the Hawai'i State Legislature after years and hundreds of testimonies submitted on the need for more inmate substance abuse treatment programs by inmate advocates like Kat Brady of the local Community Alliance on Prisons. In Act 161 the State recognizes that drug abuse continues to be a scourge for inmates, and recidivism is the norm rather than the exception. Recognizing the failure of the existing corrections system and following the lead of other states like Arizona, California, and New Mexico, Act 161 mandates drug treatment for first-time minor drug offenders who are nonviolent, requiring them to enroll in substance abuse rehabilitation programs. So far, out of the forty-five inmates deemed eligible for this program, only twelve have been released, three are awaiting openings in substance abuse programs in order to be released, and one has been denied release altogether.[35] Although it seems like a step in the right direction, the language of the act ensures that less than 1 percent of the total inmate population is eligible for this program, and those eligible may still end up serving hard time because of the lack of substance abuse programs in Hawai'i.

Private Prisons: Deporting the Native

> While government-run prisons are often in gross violation of international human rights standards, private prisons are even less accountable.
>
> —Angela Davis, "Masked Racism: Reflections on the Prison Industrial Complex"

The over-incarceration of Hawaiians creates overcrowded prisons. Since 1992 the State's "solution" has been to deport inmates, 40 percent of whom are Hawaiian, to distant facilities on the continental United States. This deportation policy recalls the U.S. Indian Removal Act of 1830, the "Trail of Tears," which removed the Creeks, Seminoles, Cherokees, Chickasaws, and Choctaws from their ancestral lands so whites could settle there. The removal of Native Hawaiian inmates from the island colony is an attack on the larger Hawaiian community as we press forward with domestic and international claims for sovereignty and lands. The removal policy further disintegrates Hawaiian families and leaves Native inmates vulnerable to the despotism of private prisons far from home.

Native inmates are sent to private prisons owned by multinational corporations like the Corrections Corporation of America (CCA), the largest private corrections business in the United States, with prison facilities in other countries, including Australia.[36] Currently, 32 percent, or 1,169, of all Hawai'i male inmates are housed in three CCA correctional facilities on the U.S. continent: the Florence Correctional Center, the Central Arizona Detention Center, and the Diamondback Correctional Facility, located in two states.[37] Hawai'i's women inmates are being held in the Central Oklahoma Correctional Facility in McCloud, operated by Dominion Group, a private corporation. It costs the State double per inmate daily to house prisoners in Hawai'i rather than in U.S. continental private facilities. The DPS cites costs of $105 a day to house a prisoner in Hawai'i compared to $58 a day on the continent.[38] In order to gain the monopoly on Hawai'i inmates, CCA offered the State financial incentives to house all Hawai'i inmates in their facilities at a discount: the State initially received a dollar discount per inmate daily (this agreement expired in 2001).[39] With annual profits exceeding $20 million for inmate deportation, state and corporate interests overshadow the well-being of prisoners and their families.

Prison corporations like CCA profit by contracting cheap prison labor to private businesses. In Hawai'i's facilities, manufacturers and the State pay inmates to produce goods at rates outrageously below minimum wage: 38 cents to 99 cents an hour.[40] When Hawai'i inmates are deported to continental facilities, their pay plummets to 14 cents to 38 cents an hour. This type of "slave labor" is allowable under the Thirteenth Amendment of the U.S. Constitution, which abolishes slavery except for those that "have been duly convicted."[41] With the slave system of the old South preserved in the U.S. correctional system and the number of prisons throughout the United States continually rising, American corporations soon will no longer have to utilize third-world cheap labor. U.S. prisons, which hold a disproportionate number of blacks, Hispanics, Native Americans, and Native Hawaiians, will be able to provide practically free labor in America.

Prison corporations handle lucrative contracts between prisons and phone service providers. MCI, AT&T, and Sprint charge exorbitant rates for calls; prison corporations reap between 50 and 60 percent of generated revenues.[42] In one year the California and Florida prison systems profited by a total of $37.9 million from

"Boogie" Kealoha Kekahuna is a Hawaiian inmate who was deported without notice to his family to correctional facilities on the U.S. continent. In protest against his forced exile from his homeland and to symbolize his Native cultural identity, Kekahuna tattooed his face in the Hawaiian warrior tradition. This photo was taken in 2000 at Diamondback Correctional Facility in Oklahoma (courtesy of "Boogie" Kealoha Kekahuna).

phone revenues alone. Hawai'i residents pay up to thirty dollars for a half-hour call to family members incarcerated on the continent. For some inmates the excessive cost of these calls severs family ties. Currently there is a class-action lawsuit being filed on behalf of "all persons who receive and/or pay for telephone calls from inmates in CCA facilities."[43] Through deportation, the State of Hawai'i, CCA, and other corporations profit off a colonized, poverty-stricken indigenous community. The commodification of Hawaiians by the government and corporations, however, is not new. Like the prisoner-for-profit assault on Native Hawaiians, Hawai'i's tourist industry is supported by the State, which receives $70 million in tax dollars annually to exploit Hawai'i's indigenous peoples and cultures.[44]

With the help of Native collaborators, white and local Japanese settlers maintain their oppressive control over their financially lucrative commodity: the Hawaiian people. In 2000 Protect Our Native 'Ohana (PONO), a Native Hawaiian inmate advocate group, protested the deportation of Native Hawaiian inmates to private U.S. continental facilities.[45] The protest was staged with signs in front of the Asian settler governor's office that read "Hawai'i's #1 Export = Native Hawaiians."

No Solutions in a Settler Society

> So successful has the prison been that, after a century and half of "failures," the prison still exists, producing the same results, and there is the greatest reluctance to dispense with it.
>
> —Michel Foucault, *Discipline and Punish: The Birth of the Modern Prison*

Although the State of Hawai'i is cognizant of the correctional system's failures, it is business as usual for its Corrections Department. Michel Foucault, the famous French philosopher on social torture, points out that under the guise of rehabilitating "criminals," the modern prison system's true purpose has always been that of maintaining silent, invisible (but nonetheless violent) social control, allowing one class to dominate another.[46] Today, white and Japanese settlers utilize the prison system as a means of controlling the indigenous population. In this respect Hawai'i's corrections system has been an overwhelming success for settlers.

While most white and Japanese settlers have never seen the inside of a colonial prison, most Hawaiians have family members or friends who are or were incarcerated. Human rights abuses in continental prison facilities run rampant, almost unchecked. A horrifying example is that of Hawaiian women held at the Central Oklahoma Correctional facility who reported having been stripped, drugged, and repeatedly raped by staff, resulting in at least one forced into abortion. They are in the process of filing suit.[47] Despite these conditions, Hawai'i's female inmates were still sent to the Oklahoma facility. With these types of sexual abuses against Native inmates almost commonplace within Hawai'i State facilities as well, the DPS, controlled by Japanese settlers, takes the precaution of injecting incoming female inmates with doses of Depo-Provera, a powerful birth control drug that prevents inmate pregnancy for three months.[48] The dehumanizing conditions that Hawaiian inmates must endure are life shattering, traumatic, and genocidal.

Unfortunately, the cycle of incarceration for Hawaiian families will continue.

While Hawaiian children make up 27 percent of all juvenile arrests in Hawai'i, they constitute 46 percent of the Hawai'i Youth Correctional Facility population, many of whom later "graduate" into adult facilities.[49] The State of Hawai'i rarely invests in developing and expanding alternative programs that intervene early on with "career criminals," and when they do intervene the results are minimal. Instead, the settler-controlled State reinforces the colonial cycle of incarceration for Hawaiian families. With few or no alternatives available, Hawaiian children, who have the worst education statistics in the State, have little chance at remaining part of "free" society in Hawai'i. For those Hawaiian youth living in poverty who fall prey to drugs, their risk of incarceration is greater than any of their peers, especially in a racist settler society that stereotypes Natives as the quintessential criminal. The missionary objective of 1820 to criminalize the Native has been institutionalized within the political, social, and economic power structure of present-day Hawai'i.[50]

The major socioeconomic factors discussed earlier that plague Native Hawaiians and contribute to their high incarceration rate—racism in Hawai'i's judicial system, poverty, and drug abuse—are interrelated, materializing from U.S. colonization of indigenous minds, bodies, and lands. As tools for maintaining settler colonial rule in Hawai'i, prisons were built in our homeland specifically to warehouse the indigenous population.

In an earlier version of this essay I argued that culturally based, treatment, and holistic programs are necessary alternatives to deportation and incarceration.[51] However, after serving for a year as the cultural specialist for the Office of Hawaiian Affairs (OHA), a state agency mandated to help Hawaiians, I've experienced firsthand how Hawaiian programs are almost always set up to fail in a settler-controlled state bureaucratic system that creates arbitrary barriers to funding and success with the help of opportunistic Native collaborators. While Hawaiian-focused rehabilitative programs may restore the spiritual, cultural, and physical well-being of Native inmates and help reintegrate them into their families and communities, the effects may be diminutive or only temporary. The "rehabilitative" answers for indigenous inmates need to focus on the return of land and sovereignty to the Hawaiian people. Without land and sovereignty, Hawaiians will remain the hapless victims of a flourishing settler society that benefits from criminalizing, incarcerating, dehumanizing, deporting, and exploiting the Native.

As the most heinous manifestation of colonial rule in Hawai'i that perpetuates the human exploitation and depravity of the old U.S. slave system, prisons in Hawai'i need to be abolished. Radical new answers that holistically strive to eliminate the real reasons for and problems behind incarceration will be possible only when Hawaiian land and sovereignty are returned to Natives. Under foreign systems of power, Hawaiians have endured mass death, oppression, torture, and disenfranchisement, and today we have been degraded to criminal status in our own homeland.

We have become a nation incarcerated.

Notes

Epigraph: "Rusty Old Steampipes" is a popular Hawaiian blues song written by Warren Kaʻahanui, a Native Hawaiian inmate serving a life sentence, and was performed by the Mākaha Sons of Niʻihau (*Mākaha Bash 3 Live at the Shell*).

1. The terms "Native Hawaiian," "Native," "Hawaiian," and "indigenous" refer to the descendants of the original inhabitants of the Hawaiian archipelago who occupied these islands prior to 1778. For incarceration rates, see United States Department of Justice, *Bureau of Justice Statistics Bulletin*, NCJ 170014 (Washington, D.C.: GPO, 1998), 4.

2. First "contact" with Europeans in 1778 and subsequent colonial rule was and has been violent. The Native population suffered an 85 percent collapse over the fifty years following contact. David Stannard, *Before the Horror: The Population of Hawaiʻi on the Eve of Western Contact* (Honolulu: University of Hawaiʻi Press, 1989), 43–45. See also "The Hawaiians: Health, Justice, and Sovereignty" in this volume.

3. Lilikalā Kameʻeleihiwa, *Native Land and Foreign Desires* (Honolulu: Bishop Museum, 1992), 139.

4. Dorothy B. Barrere, Mary Kawena Pukui, and Marion Kelly, *Hula: Historical Perspectives* (Honolulu: Bishop Museum, 1980).

5. The gambling, sexual, and religious practices and the "immoral" costumes associated with surfing were outlawed by 1830. American missionaries believed that Native Hawaiians should be spending their time working for settler plantations, not surfing. Native Hawaiians caught surfing could be charged with vagrancy along with other crimes against the Christian sense of morality. Frequently attacked in the newspapers by missionaries, surfing had all but disappeared by the mid-1800s. Ben Finney and James D. Houston, *Surfing: A History of the Ancient Hawaiian Sport* (San Francisco: Pomegranate Books, 1996), 54–57; Arthur H. Klein, *Surfing* (Philadelphia: J. B. Lippincott Company, 1965), 27.

6. Samuel M. Kamakau, *Ruling Chiefs of Hawaiʻi*, 2nd ed. (Honolulu: Kamehameha Schools, 1992), 298–299; Eric Kapono, "Hawaiian Language Revitalization and Immersion Education," *International Journal of the Sociology of Language* 112 (1994): 125.

7. Sally Engle Merry, *Colonizing Hawaiʻi: The Cultural Power of Law* (Princeton, N.J.: Princeton University Press, 2000), 73.

8. Ralph S. Kuykendall, *Hawaiʻi: A History* (New York: Prentice-Hall, 1950), 210.

9. State of Hawaiʻi, Office of Hawaiian Affairs (OHA), *Native Hawaiian Databook* (Honolulu: State of Hawaiʻi, OHA, 2002), 9.

10. *Native Hawaiian Databook*, 31. According to the National Center for Children in Poverty, "poor" in Hawaiʻi refers to those with an income below 100 percent of the Federal

Poverty Level (FPL), and Hawai'i's "low income" refers to those with an income below 200 percent of the FPL.

11. Haunani-Kay Trask, *From a Native Daughter: Colonialism and Sovereignty in Hawai'i*, rev. ed. (1993). Reprint: Honolulu: University of Hawai'i Press, 1999, 252.

12. Linda K. Menton and Eileen H. Tamura, *A History of Hawai'i*, 2nd ed. (Honolulu: University of Hawai'i Press, 1999), 285.

13. "Riots rock CCA Prison in Oklahoma," *Prison Legal News*, December 1999, 16; Kevin Dayton, "Oklahoma Prison Called Drug Haven by Inmates," *Honolulu Advertiser*, August 15, 2001, A1; Linda Burton, "Hawaiian Women Prisoners File Suit Over Sex Abuse, Torture in Oklahoma Private Prison," *Prison Legal News*, May 2002, 6; "Sent Away: Hawai'i Prisoners on the Mainland," *The Honolulu Advertiser*, October 2–4, 2005.

14. United States Department of Justice, "Bureau of Justice Statistics: Criminal Offenders Statistics." http://www.ojp.usdoj.gov/bjs/crimoff.htm.

15. *Native Hawaiian Databook*, 9, 29.

16. State of Hawai'i, Office of the Attorney General, *Crime in Hawai'i 2001: A Review of Uniform Crime Reports* (Honolulu: Research and Statistic Branch, Crime Prevention and Justice Assistance Division, 2002), 13, 107.

17. *Native Hawaiian Databook*, 29. As a volunteer at the Hālawa Medium Security Correctional Facility, I was able to interview numerous staff members, including guards, educators, and clerks. They all estimated a much higher number of Native Hawaiians being incarcerated in Hawai'i. From their experience working at Hālawa they believe the percentage of Native Hawaiian inmates is somewhere between 60 and 80 percent.

18. The U.S. Department of Justice predicted, "If recent incarceration rates remain unchanged, an estimated 1 of every 20 [American] persons (5.1%) will serve time in a prison during their lifetime."

19. See, e.g., Asian settler autobiographies like Senator Daniel Inouye's *Journey to Washington* (Englewood Cliffs, N.J.: Prentice-Hall, 1967) or former governor George Ariyoshi's *With Obligation to All* (Honolulu: University of Hawai'i Press, 1997).

20. State of Hawai'i Department of Business, Economic Development and Tourism (DBEDT), *The State of Hawai'i Data Book 2000: A Statistical Abstract* (Honolulu: State of Hawai'i DBEDT, 2001), 379.

21. United States Census Bureau, "Summary File 3," *Census 2000*. www.census.gov

22. *Native Hawaiian Databook*, 25

23. *Native Hawaiian Databook*, 31.

24. *Native Hawaiian Databook*, 25; *Crime in Hawai'i 2001*, 13.

25. According to the *Native Hawaiian Databook* the six major ethnic groups in Hawai'i are Hawaiians, whites, Japanese, Filipinos, Chinese, and Koreans.

26. *The State of Hawai'i Data Book 2000*, 379.

27. United States Drug Enforcement Administration, "The Changing Face of European Drug Policy." DEA 02023. http://www.usdoj.gov/dea/pubs/intel/02023/02023.html.

28. Lynda Arakawa, "Anti-Drug Programs Get Push At Capitol; Critics Say Addicts Need More Treatment, Not More Prisons," *Honolulu Advertiser*, March 5, 2000, A1.

29. United States Department of Health and Human Services Center for Substance

Abuse Treatment, "Executive Summary," *Substance Abuse and Treatment Needs: Survey Estimates for Hawai'i* (Rockville, Md.: GPO, 1998).

30. Karen Blakeman, "Meth Violence Tear at Hawai'i, Use of Drug Epidemic Here," *Honolulu Advertiser,* December 22, 2002, A1, A6.

31. *Native Hawaiian Databook,* 19.

32. State of Hawai'i Department of Human Services, Office of Youth Services.

33. The rates of incarceration and inmate deaths for the Aboriginal peoples of Australia are so ridiculously high that Australia has been the focus of massive international attention and criticism for its racially discriminatory acts of human rights abuses, including criticism from the U.N. Office of the High Commissioner for Human Rights and Amnesty International. See Gary Trujillo, "Australia: Justice System Working against Aboriginals, Says Report," *Institute for Global Communications,* http://igc.apc.org.

34. http://www.hawaii.gov/psd/documents/reports/r5scr62.pdf

35. Debra Barayuga, "Oahu's Overcrowded Prisons: Freeing Up Space," *Honolulu Star-Bulletin,* November 10, 2002, A1, A8.

36. Angela Davis, "Masked Racism: Reflections on the Prison Industrial Complex," *Colorlines* (Fall 1998); Anne Dutney, "Private Prison Companies—A CCA Perspective," Australian Institute of Criminology Conference, Melbourne, June 16–17, 1997, 2; Kevin Dayton, "Prisons for Profit: Inside the Big Business of CCA," *The Honolulu Advertiser,* October 3, 2005, A6.

37. This information was received through various phone interviews conducted by me with Howard Komori of the State of Hawaii Department of Public Safety in June 2002.

38. State of Hawai'i Department of Public Safety, "Response to Act 259, Section 66 Session Laws of Hawai'i," Report to Legislature, December 2001, 2; Kevin Dayton, "Keep Transferring or Build Here? Costs, Economics Not That Simple," *The Honolulu Advertiser,* October 3, 2005, A1.

39. Kevin Dayton, "Prison Debates Weighs on State," *Honolulu Advertiser,* December 5, 1999, A1, A4.

40. This information was obtained through numerous interviews with inmates both at Hālawa and Florence Correctional Center in 2001 while I was still working as a volunteer at Hālawa Medium Security Correctional Center.

41. United States, *The Constitution of the United States with Index and the Declaration of Independence,* 19th reprint (Washington, D.C.: GPO, 1997), 25.

42. "Prisons Cashing in on Inmate Phone Calls," *Naples Daily News,* September 1, 1999, http://www.naplesnews.com/today/business/d182056a.htm

43. Gary A Draizen, letter to author, March 18, 2001.

44. State of Hawai'i, Hawai'i Visitor's Authority, *2002 Hawaii Tourism Authority: 2002 Annual Report to the Hawaii State Legislature* (October 31, 2002), 25.

45. "Inmate Advocates Voice Opposition to Transfer," *Honolulu Star-Bulletin,* June 8, 2000, A5. I am the co-founder of PONO.

46. Michel Foucault, *Discipline and Punish: The Birth of the Prison* (New York: Vintage Books, 1979 [orig. 1975]), 277.

47. Burton, "Hawaiian Women Prisoners File Suit Over Sex Abuse," 6–7; Dayton, "Keep Transferring or Build Here?" A5.

48. Christine Donnelly, "Inmates Sues over the Death of Her Fetus in Prison." *Honolulu Star-Bulletin,* December 3, 1999, A10.

49. *The State of Hawaiʻi Data Book 2000; Crime in Hawaiʻi 2001,* 13; State of Hawaiʻi Department of Human Services, Office of Youth Services (2001).

50. *Crime in Hawaiʻi 2001,* 168.

51. Healani Sonoda, *Colorlines* (Spring 2001) 9–11.

"This Land Is Your Land, This Land Was My Land"

Kanaka Maoli versus Settler Representations of ʻĀina in Contemporary Literature of Hawaiʻi

Kaʻina (Introduction)

> This land is your land, this land is my land
> from California to the New York island
> from the redwood forest to the gulf stream waters
> this land was made for you and me.
>
> —traditional American folk song

> I ka ʻōlelo no ke ola, i ka ʻōlelo no ka make
> In the language is life, in the language is death.
>
> —traditional Hawaiian proverb

In *Representation: Cultural Representations and Signifying Practices* (1997), cultural studies critic Stuart Hall argues that the act of representation, which he defines as "the production of meaning of the concepts in our minds through language," is closely tied to identity and knowledge.[1] In examining the positioning of people of color as "Other" by hegemonic white powers, Hall focuses on the discursive practices of representation identified by Michel Foucault, who was concerned with the effects and consequences—the *politics*—of representation, or who has the *power* to represent whom.[2] Are there differences in representation by different groups of people based on their positions of power? Foucault and Hall conclude that the answer to this question is a resounding "yes."

In this essay I focus on the differences between the representations of ʻāina (land) in contemporary literature of Hawaiʻi, popularly referred to as "local literature."[3] I argue there is a distinction between representations of ʻāina in Kanaka Maoli (Native Hawaiian) literature and Asian and other settler or "local" literature.[4] The main differences in representation between these two literatures center on how ʻāina and Kānaka Maoli are described and portrayed, as well as the inclusion, use of, and attitudes toward language—ʻōlelo Hawaiʻi (Hawaiian language), English, and Hawaiʻi Creole English (HCE, commonly referred to as "pidgin") in particular. These differences in representation exist because Kānaka Maoli and settlers are operating from different cultural paradigms and different language bases. Such differences are important to note as Hall states that "the emphasis in the discursive approach is always on the historical specificity of a particular norm or regime of representation: not on language as a general concern, but on specific languages (meanings) and how they are deployed at particular times, in particular places."[5] While Hall isn't referring specifically to ethnic languages, I believe that it is relevant in this context, since the Kanaka Maoli worldview, as espoused in our ʻōlelo makuahine (mother tongue) and our cultural traditions, is based on a very different relationship to Hawaiʻi than that of settlers who speak English or HCE. Because of this, our understanding and representation of ʻāina, reflected in our ongoing political activities as well as our literature, are unlike that of Asian settlers. This is particularly obvious in their continued nostalgia for plantation "roots" that go back less than two hundred years, while ignoring Kanaka Maoli roots that go back centuries. These differences are also apparent in settlers' continued references

Courtesy of *Kauaʻi Times*, December 14, 1990

to Hawai'i as a "landscape," "geography," and "environment," English words that connote a Western-based understanding of what land is, terms that overshadow and negate Native understandings of land as 'āina, which for Kānaka Maoli is familial.

Like other indigenous peoples, Kānaka Maoli have continually fought to represent ourselves in various social, political, and economic venues because we are often marginalized and oppressed by dominant hegemonic forces, which in Hawai'i today include Asian and haole (white) settlers.[6] This is as apparent in the contemporary literary scene as it is in Hawai'i politics. Kanaka Maoli writers are fighting to retain and regrow our literary sovereignty through an assertion of our indigenous voices against a backdrop of haole and Asian settlers who continually try to usurp, undermine, and misappropriate our traditions using a variety of political hegemonic tropes, from American ideals of "freedom" and "democracy" to the mislabeled and misleading Hawai'i Visitors and Convention Bureau (HVCB) concept of "aloha spirit." Thus while the cartoon above refers specifically to Japanese nationals in a broader context, "local" Asian settlers have come to make up the political structure in Hawai'i, and they participate in the land (and literary) dispossession of Kānaka Maoli. In this context "freedom" represents the ability to dispossess indigenous peoples for the purpose of possessing their familial lands.

While there are many Kanaka Maoli organizations that differ on the specifics of what Kanaka Maoli political and economic sovereignty could look like, the common goals shared among them include self-government and the reestablishment of a land base from which Kānaka Maoli can live, work, and dream, free to practice our culture and develop our own way of life without being interfered with, controlled, or oppressed by non-Natives with a different social, political, economic, or moral agenda.[7] The growing assertion of literary sovereignty on the part of Kanaka Maoli writers today is but a small part of the larger movement for self-determination.

Kanaka Maoli versus "Local" Literature

The establishment of acceptable categories of what is contemporary literature of Hawai'i has been in flux for the past several decades. This literature is sometimes called "local" literature, which embraces a mixture of regionally based writing and ethnic or culturally based writing. This literature is regional in that it is set in Hawai'i, populated by characters living here who uphold American values but see themselves as different from those living on the U.S. continent or European/Asian homelands. It is also viewed as ethnic or culturally based because it incorporates HCE, or an HCE-derived vernacular.

Kanaka Maoli literature is often incorporated into the broader category of "local" literature. This seemingly positive and inclusive move has been problematic. What the proponents of "local" literature fail to acknowledge is that folding Kanaka Maoli literature into this category is oppressive, first because there is an erasure of our centuries-long Native literary tradition,[8] an erasure that Kanaka Maoli literature scholar Kaʻimipono Kaʻiwi Kahumoku describes as a move that "denies our status as Native people."[9]

Second, the inclusion of Kanaka Maoli literature under the generic term "local" is problematic because there are political tensions between Kānaka Maoli and non-Natives, the consequence of the inability of haole and Asian settlers to understand that Kānaka Maoli have a different relationship to Hawaiʻi, which means we have a different literary movement as well.[10] Kanaka Maoli writer and publisher Māhealani Dudoit describes it thus:

> While "Local" literature is a movement not unlike other regional movements, the Kanaka Maoli literary movement was and is part of a nationalist movement; i.e. the dynamics of nation-building in literary form. So, as the local community here wishes to distinguish itself as culturally different from the non-local and from the continent, it is not involved in nation-building with all the political and identity issues which are brought into play. Thus the objectives and the stakes are worlds apart.[11]

Kanaka Maoli literature is literature produced by Hawaiians, and it distinguishes itself from "local" and other modern literatures in several ways.[12] First, we recognize our oral traditions as being part of our literature. Second, "authorship," typically defined in Western terms as an individual and credited process, is less important. It is not uncommon for Kānaka Maoli to compose moʻolelo (compositions) in hui (collectives) and for texts to be either uncredited to any individual author or to be credited to a pseudonym. This practice reflects two important Kanaka Maoli cultural values: the collective approach to a task and the concept of haʻahaʻa (humility), where one downplays oneself. These values reflect Kanaka Maoli cultural values as accurately as haole ideas of credited and individual authorship reflect the Western cultural values of individual achievement and celebrity. For Kānaka Maoli, a composer did not necessarily "own" a text (as dictated by American copyright laws today); in fact, it was common practice for a composer to give a composition to the person or persons being written about, whereupon it became theirs, the composer relinquishing all "copy" or performance rights.

In addition, colonial academic authorities assume that moʻolelo belong to an unowned oral tradition. University of Hawaiʻi professor of political science Noenoe K. Silva specializes in Hawaiian and political movements with an emphasis on Hawaiian language, and she points out that haole scholars "don't notice or credit the vast majority of moʻolelo and mele published from 1834–1948 which are *signed* with author and composer names. It serves the colonial project to pretend there are no authors. It facilitates both colonial theft of kūpuna (ancestor) knowledge, and it aids in perpetuating the myth of backwardness and savagery."[13]

All of these factors speak to a different paradigm, a cultural perspective that enlarges the Kanaka Maoli concept of literature and is much more inclusive of a variety of Kanaka Maoli voices. One of the myths perpetuated by settlers is that Kānaka Maoli are not a "literary" people with a "literary" tradition, and that excuse has been used to exclude or marginalize Kanaka Maoli writers from Hawaiʻi-based literary anthologies.[14] Yet over seventy nineteenth-century Hawaiian-language newspapers flourished from the 1830s to the 1940s, with a large number of Kanaka Maoli writers published during that period.[15] While many of these writers are not recognized outside the Kanaka Maoli communities, that should not preclude their voices from being heard, nor should it preclude Kānaka Maoli from being considered literary. It is important to understand the breadth of Kanaka Maoli literary expression as we speak against the constraints of the "local" label.

Moʻokūʻauhau, Aloha Spirit, and Other Cultural Misappropriations

> Sharing a common enemy, local culture has often been characterized as a culture of resistance against the dominant white culture and rooted in the struggles of the working class of Hawaii's sugar plantations.
>
> — Eric Chock, Darrell Lum, Jim Harstad, and Bill Teter, eds.,
> *Growing Up Local: An Anthology of Poetry and
> Prose from Hawaiʻi*

The lumping together of Kanaka Maoli and "local" writers assumes a common alliance and background, assumes shared values, themes, and literary metaphors, and assumes a position of "solidarity" of "writers of color" against a common enemy—all things haole. Yet on closer inspection it is not difficult to see that there are some obvious differences, the most important being that Kānaka Maoli are indigenous to Hawaiʻi. Everyone else is a settler.

The claim for a genealogical connection to Hawaiʻi has been made by "local" writers such as Darrell H. Y. Lum. In his 1986 introduction to an anthology of "local" literature titled *The Best of Bamboo Ridge*, Lum, a Hawaiʻi resident who traces his Chinese heritage back through Hawaiʻi's sugar plantation era, writes, "For many islanders, it doesn't take a lot of digging to find one's roots in the soil of Hawaii's sugar plantations: grandparents or great-grandparents who immigrated to the islands as contract laborers. No wonder, then, the local literature which *Bamboo Ridge: The Hawaii Writers' Quarterly* has published over the years has echoed this island life."[16] Lum is a founding editor of Bamboo Ridge Press, which was established "to publish literature by and about Hawaii's people," giving "special attention . . . to literature that reflects an island sensibility"[17] to provide "an alternative to the mainstream, white literary canon."[18] While Bamboo Ridge claims to be a literary journal for *Hawai'i* writers, what it has actually become is a literary journal run by Asian American settlers publishing (mostly) other Asian American settlers who trace their "island roots" back to Hawai'i's sugar plantations and no farther, meaning there is little if any reflection and/or recognition of the indigenous population of Hawai'i.[19] Lum's claim to a Hawai'i-based genealogy for non-Native settlers is echoed by Asian American critic Stephen Sumida, an American ethnic studies professor from Hawai'i currently based in Seattle, Washington. In his book, *And the View from the Shore: Literary Traditions of Hawai'i* (1991), Sumida writes,

> The local poet Phyllis Thompson, a migrant teacher from the mainland in the 1960s, once told me that in the native Hawaiian way, personal introductions include these questions: What are you called (i.e., your given name)? Who is your family (i.e., your surname and genealogy)? Where are you from (i.e., your neighborhood or district)? And who is your teacher (i.e., your school or the way of thought to which you are loyal)? It occurs to me that, without their knowing its Hawaiian origins, locals expect this genealogical exchange, this fine ritual of personal introductions, not for judging the superiority of one person over another, but for learning facts that relate somehow to inner values of the individual, on the one hand, and to already existing social and cultural connections on the other. This local ritual is expressively a way for two people to begin discovering their relationships with each other, however distant, in order to talk stories that sprout on common ground. It is a way to begin weaving their histories together—and this defines friendship, or an aspect of it, local style.[20]

Lum, a creative writer, and Sumida, a literary critic, share similar political views on the concept of "local." Twelve years after his introduction to *The Best of Bamboo Ridge,* Lum picks up Sumida's argument and stretches it even further by evoking a claim to the land through genealogy for settlers and their descendants built on culturally rooted Kanaka Maoli traditions. In the introduction to Bamboo Ridge's latest literary anthology, *Growing Up Local,* Lum writes,

> The "What school you went?" question has its roots in the Native Hawaiian way of identifying oneself by *geography* and *genealogy*. . . . This impulse to establish how we are related is critical to understanding local culture and local literature. The question . . . rather than being a question that divides us, is

fundamentally an effort to discover how we are connected. This sense of family and community characterizes local literature. Like all families, the stories and poems in this collection may be marked by conflict, disagreement, and discord, yet retain a fundamental bond to the islands and local culture. As diverse as these pieces are, each one has an honesty of voice, a strong and sure sense of place, and a sense of *genealogy* that invites us to share the experiences of being local.[21]

Here Lum attempts to link the relatively short "local" experience to that of long-standing Kanaka Maoli history through two tropes, moʻokūʻauhau (genealogy) and ʻohana (family). This attempt, however, fails to be convincing since Kānaka Maoli don't separate ʻāina (or what Lum calls "geography") from moʻokūʻauhau, as our genealogy is derived from the land, which makes us ʻohana to it. What Lum and Sumida refuse to acknowledge is that there are historical and cultural differences that separate Kanaka Maoli genealogical claims to the land and local/settler claims, and their conflation of these claims is a colonial appropriation echoed by so many "local" writers.

Furthermore, this conflation of Native and settler claims makes no distinction between the tremendous gap in time between Native and non-Native arrivals to the islands: the first Western explorer didn't "discover" Hawaiʻi until about two thousand years after the first Kānaka Maoli made landfall; "immigrants" to Hawaiʻi (starting with the Calvinist missionaries in 1820) didn't arrive for another half century after that. Therefore, any claim to "Hawaiian" roots by settlers through the plantations goes back a mere 150 or so years; the Kanaka Maoli claim goes back at least two millennia. Why, then, is Lum trying to specifically link Asian settlers to a Kanaka Maoli tradition? Again, it is colonial for settlers to claim Kanaka Maoli traditions and land.

By extension, our literary themes, forms of expression (genres), and metaphoric expression, especially about ʻāina, differ greatly from the much-celebrated settler perspective. One example is that while Kānaka Maoli have continued to protest the overthrow of our government in 1893, the subsequent annexation to the United States in 1898, and all threats to Kanaka Maoli land tenure, gathering rights, and related issues since then and have written extensively in the Hawaiian language, in English, and in HCE about these issues from that time to this, there is no significant literature written by Asian or haole settlers that supports Kanaka Maoli claims, which run deeper than saccharine sentiment and fond recollection for the "good old (plantation) days."

While the "local" label has been constructed by some Asian settlers in Hawaiʻi to differentiate themselves from their continental Asian American counterparts, there is little difference in attitude and philosophy on the part of either group toward the indigenous Kanaka Maoli population and our ancestral home: both groups view Hawai'i as a commodified resource, not as an ancestor; a picturesque setting for people-centered stories, not as a character in mo'olelo. They also share the dominant American ideology that America (including Hawai'i, their fiftieth state) is a land of equality, opportunity, liberty, freedom, and justice for all. Perhaps the most damaging of all is that they perpetuate the myth that we are a nation made up of *only* immigrants. In other words, there is a complete erasure of the Native and a denial of our distinct culture and literary style. On this point Native Hawaiian nationalist, scholar, and poet Haunani-Kay Trask comments,

> The issues before Hawaiians are those of indigenous land, cultural rights, and survival as a people. In contrast, the issues before "locals" have merely to do with finding a comfortable fit in Hawai'i that guarantees a rising income, upward mobility, and the general accoutrements of a middle-class "American" way of life. Above all, "locals" don't want any reminder of their daily benefit from the subjugation of Hawaiians. For them, history begins with their arrival in Hawai'i and culminates with the endless re-telling of their allegedly well-deserved rise to power. Simply said, "locals" want to be "Americans." [22]

Furthermore, the sociopolitical history of Hawai'i prior to annexation and through statehood has influenced the differing political perspectives inherent in the two literatures: Kānaka Maoli have always maintained a position ma hope o ka 'āina, standing firm behind the land and our right to manage it, while to the settler Hawai'i is merely real estate, a land base from which to flex one's hegemonic power, participate in capitalism and the "American dream," rape the resources, and reap the benefits of the land. It is Hawai'i's colonial status that makes it an attractive destination for Asian immigrants: mass Asian immigration to Hawai'i sugar plantations in the nineteenth century was a result of U.S. imperialism. Settlers of Asian and haole descent have swollen in numbers and greatly outnumber Native Hawaiians, outranking us in every positive social, political, and economic realm. [23]

He Ali'i ka 'Āina, He Kauwā ke Kanaka? The Land Is a Chief, Man Is Its Servant?

> The literature of local writers has a distinct sensitivity to ethnicity, the environment (in particular that valuable commodity, the land), a sense of personal lineage and family history, and the use of the sound, the languages, and the vocabulary of island people.
>
> —"local" writer Darrell Lum, *The Best of Bamboo Ridge*

> Ideally, local literature is not exactly ethnic writing and it's not exactly
> regional writing either. It reflects both ethnic culture as well as
> physical environment. But relationship to landscape, how geography
> affects you, is very hard to define. A lot of the time it's not very
> important. It's hard to be genuinely mystical about rocks. That's one
> thing transient mainland poets have been criticized for—relating to
> landscape in that way.
>
> —"local" writer Eric Chock, "An Interview with Eric Chock"

In order to understand the cultural relationship Kānaka Maoli have with the ʻāina, one must first look to the ʻōlelo kumu (source language). There are many words in Hawaiian to describe land—ʻāina, honua, papa, one, puluwai, ʻāina hānau, kulāiwi, one hānau, ʻāpaʻa, mahakea, lepo, ʻalaea, iwi—the most important of which is ʻāina. Handy, Handy, and Pukui write,

> *ʻĀina* also conveys the sense of arable land. It is essentially a term coined by
> an agricultural people, deriving as it does from the noun or verb *ʻai,* meaning
> food or to eat, with the substantive *na* added, so that it may be rendered either
> "that which feeds" or "the feeder." *ʻĀina* thus has connotations in relation to
> people as conveying the sense of "feeder," birthplace, and homeland. In this
> sense it entered also into the compound *ma-ka-ʻaina-na,* meaning the com-
> mon people or country folk in general as distinguished from the aliʻi and their
> entourage. The broad social concept contained in [makaʻainana] was for the
> Hawaiian derived from *ʻāina,* meaning land, which in its turn is a derivative
> of the word meaning food, primarily cultivated food, and specifically in many
> uses, taro.[24]

Thus ʻāina is the land that can nurture and sustain life by providing food, including the majority of environments from the ocean to the highest mountaintops; it
is the land that provides food for all living things, not just humans. The difference
between Kanaka Maoli sentiments about ʻāina and haole thinking about land is
easily demonstrated in the following equational form.

Hawaiian: ʻāina → food → nurturing/sustaining → *value of family*
haole: land → real estate/commodity → buying/selling → *monetary value*

For Kānaka Maoli, the value of the ʻāina is not monetary; it is familial. Furthermore, the specific allusion to taro (or kalo) made by Handy, Handy, and Pukui
evokes the familiar relationship in another way, as Hāloa-naka, the first kalo plant,
is the elder sibling of the Hawaiian people, reaffirming the familiar relationship to
ʻāina through the word itself. The land sustains us, nurtures us like a family member. Thus in our culture the values of aloha ʻāina (love for the land) and mālama
ʻāina (caring for the land) are fundamental. But for non-Natives land is a com-

modity that can be bought and sold; it is the monetary value land possesses in haole culture that accelerated Kanaka Maoli dispossession of 'āina.[25] And since settlers have benefited and prospered from this dispossession, and continue to do so, we are not and cannot be true political allies as long as they continue to deny Kanaka Maoli land claims, and we will not have parity in discussions in "local" literature on land. Kānaka Maoli have practiced mālama 'āina for over two thousand years and countless generations. In comparison, any claim by more recently arrived haole and Asian settlers to understanding this ancient and primary cultural concept of land as mother is disingenuous.

Hawaiian words for people are related to words for land, demonstrating the close relationship between the two in our culture: "maka'āinana" (steward of the land), "kama'āina" (child born on the land), and "kupa" (sprouting from the land). "Kupa" and "'āina" are also linked through the term "kupa 'ai au" (Native born who is long attached to the place), "*lit.* Native eat[ing] long time [from the land]."[26] The word "iwi" (bones), a metaphorical reference to people, is synonymous with both being Native to a place ('ōiwi, kulaiwi) and being one's homeland (kulaiwi, kuapuiwi, ko kō iwi 'āina hānau).[27]

The word "papa" also demonstrates the familial link between Kānaka Maoli and 'āina. "Papa" means one who is Native born, "especially for several generations."[28] It also refers to the Earth Mother, Papahānaumoku. Papa is generically any flat surface, plain, stratum, or foundation; thus her name translates to "foundation who gives birth to islands."

In one creation story of Papahānaumoku and Wākea (Sky Father), a keiki alualu (miscarried fetus) is born to them. After the child is buried outside the home, a kalo plant, which they name Hāloa-naka, "quivering stalk with long breath," grows from the spot. The next child born to them is also named Hāloa and is said to be the progenitor of Kanaka Maoli people.[29] Thus Kānaka Maoli aren't masters over the land, as in the Judeo-Christian tradition set forth in the book of Genesis in the Bible, but are the subservient younger siblings of the 'āina and the mea 'ai, "fruits" of the land, most directly, the kalo plant Hāloa-naka, our elder sibling.

Further demonstrating the connection between Kānaka Maoli and 'āina is the relationship among the words "hā" (breath), "Hāloa" (the kalo plant and ancestor with the long breath, which itself suggests immortality through the production of offspring), and "aloha" (love, affection, compassion, mercy, sympathy, kindness, grace, and charity).

Thus in the Kanaka Maoli worldview the connection between Kānaka and 'āina is not just theoretical; it is direct. And it is a connection that does not exist between non–Kānaka Maoli and Hawai'i. Settlers to Hawai'i have not claimed this story of Papahānaumoku or dispossession from her as their history, even those who have taken to calling themselves "kama'āina," "children of the land," as a way to distinguish themselves from new and transient residents, such as tourists, the military, and recent immigrants.

Some settlers, representatives of mainstream hegemonic power, have attacked Kānaka Maoli, claiming we have invented these traditions of mālama ʻāina without context. Former University of Hawaiʻi anthropology professor Jocelyn Linnekin, a haole, has argued that our important cultural value of aloha ʻāina was "made up" by contemporary Kānaka Maoli during our struggle to stop the bombing of Kahoʻolawe island beginning in the 1970s.[30] Revered Kanaka Maoli scholar Mary Kawena Pukui, however, states that aloha ʻāina "is a very old concept, to judge from the many sayings (perhaps thousands) illustrating deep love of the land."[31] That Linnekin, a haole professor, has often been called on by settler colonial administrators in the State of Hawaiʻi as an expert on Kanaka Maoli culture speaks to the larger issue of settler power. By repeatedly trying to redefine Kanaka Maoli culture in a non-Native paradigm, these settlers in power seek to eradicate Kanaka Maoli culture, or at least control it to fit their own agenda, typically detrimental to Kanaka Maoli people.

Darrell Lum tries to tap into the Kanaka Maoli worldview linking Kānaka to ʻāina through genealogy when he describes settler writers as having a "distinct sensitivity to ethnicity, the environment (in particular that valuable commodity, the land), a sense of personal lineage and family history."[32] But the problem with Lum's attempt at expressing aloha ʻāina and equating settler sentiment for ʻāina with that of Kānaka Maoli is that he describes the "beloved" land we share in colonial sentiments: it is a "commodity," not an ancestor; it is an "environment," a setting, a landscape, not family. And its value is not in its ability to provide food, or to nurture life, but in its monetary worth.

Lum's interpretation of aloha ʻāina is driving home "to a nice little house in the suburbs: a modest twenty-year old single wall, three bedroom, two bath place with a carpet going for $150,000 or so . . . on leased land."[33] Dennis Kawaharada, then an English professor at Kapiʻolani Community College, a writer, and publisher, responded by stating that "Lum wants us to feel sympathy for this 'typical' islander because his $150,000 house is on leased land; another response might be 'At least he has a three-bedroom, two-bath house; the majority of islanders can't afford that.'"[34] Lum's obvious bourgeois attitude does not reflect Kanaka Maoli sentiment; it reflects—not surprisingly—middle-class American values. University of Hawaiʻi English professor Rodney Morales, who is also a Hawaiʻi-based writer, comments that "while the colonized [i.e., "locals"] have made great strides (from books published to awards to a growing audience), some, in succumbing to the benefits of compromise and dilution as they play out a distinctly American Dream, show that they have bought into the colonial construct."[35] Thus there is no difference between haole colonial views on land and Asian settler views like Lum's, despite his professed "love" for Hawaiian land, one of several cultural values he thinks Kanaka Maoli culture shares with Asian cultures.

> The immigrant laborers shared more than a common enemy.... They entered a Native Hawaiian culture that valued interpersonal relationships and love for the land. Their own values of family loyalty, obligation, and reciprocity coincided with those of the Native Hawaiians: an orientation that valued harmony between people, minimized personal gain or achievement, and shared natural resources. This cultural accommodation on the part of Native Hawaiians and immigrant labor was born out of a tradition of hardship, struggle, and conflict that counters the romantic notions of blended cultures, the melting pot, or a multiethnic Hawai'i based on a democratic sharing of cultures.[36]

It is quite presumptuous on Lum's part to equate the theft of Kanaka Maoli political power through the overthrow of our government in 1893 with "cultural accommodation." It is preposterous to argue that discrimination against Asian settlers, while real, can in any way be equated with the loss of the Hawaiian nation and our right to self-determination. The overwhelming social, psychological, political, and economic effects of such a devastating historic event on Kānaka Maoli have been well documented in a variety of ways by a number of sources. Moreover, this colonial assault has been multi-pronged, continuous, and unrelenting since the arrival of Captain Cook in 1778. It has long been the goal of the first haole colonizers to wipe out Kanaka Maoli self-determination (if not Kānaka Maoli outright), control our land base, and dictate the confines of our being. The goals of Kānaka Maoli, like those of other Native peoples worldwide, have been the reclamation of our land base, the right to self-determination and self-government, and the right to practice our culture in the manner that we choose. The goals of Asian settlers, like those of the haole Americans they pretend to despise yet secretly idolize, are to thrive in a capitalist environment and reap the benefits of hegemonic dominance. So while Lum and other Asian settlers pretend to side with Kānaka Maoli against our alleged "common enemy"—haole—they do not understand that they are linked with the haole because of their shared American values.

Because neither Lum nor Chock are Kānaka Maoli, and because neither speaks nor understands the language and all its nuances, they are unable to see 'āina from a Kanaka Maoli perspective and thus repeatedly describe it in foreign terms: "landscape," "geography," "environment," "nature"; these concepts translate into foreign ideologies such as environmentalism. Environmentalists have no relationship to the land they are protecting. In fact, many times "protect the environment" means "no humans allowed"—Native or otherwise. More often than not fences are erected around forests, no-fishing zones established in the sea, and Natives are forced away from the land; Natives are depicted as harmful to the "natural" environment rather than as members of its family.

Natives see these issues differently than settlers do: ʻāina does not translate to "landscape" because landscape implies a pristine, panoramic view of the land devoid of human beings; by being "land that feeds," ʻāina automatically includes humans—at least Natives—because, first, we are the ones being fed, and, second, we are descended from the land and are *related to* and not *separate from* elements of "nature": taro, seaweed, fish, rocks. By extension, mālama ʻāina does not equate to "environmentalism" because the mandate to the ʻāina is the same as mālama/aloha ʻohana (care for, cherish the family): we care for/love the land in the same way we care for our elders, our siblings, our spouses, and our children, and by doing so, we *maintain our relationship* with those we are caring for, whether it be our human family, earthly family (Papahānaumoku, Hāloa the taro), or spiritual family (through the presence of our ʻaumākua, or spirit guardians who physically manifest themselves in nature).

In the Hawaiian world, pōhaku (rocks) are created, in part, from the volcano goddess Pele, whose very name means "lava." This is another way Kānaka Maoli connect genealogically to the ʻāina and demonstrate a relationship with it. Noted kumu hula (hula master) Pualani Kanakaʻole Kanahele addresses this point by stating,

> The notion that a rock exists as an inanimate object, especially in its creative stages, is totally foreign to the Hawaiian. Rock, especially fresh lava flow, has a spirit, and with the assumption of a spirit, procreation is possible. Thus, this belief that Pele (the volcano deity) is magma. Pele is lava, and that she is the one who controls the outpouring of this energy is within this dualistic concept. Pele is the creative force whose name signifies the physical and the spiritual essence of newly formed land.[37]

In quoting Kanahele in her own work, Manulani Aluli Meyer, a professor of education, reflects that "it is a valuable and logical exercise to argue the spiritual nature of rocks . . . rocks have spirit, magma is Pele."[38]

In their ignorance of Kanaka Maoli culture, Lum and Chock presume to speak for Natives. So when Chock states that "it's hard to be genuinely mystical about rocks. That's one thing transient mainland poets have been criticized for—relating to the landscape that way,"[39] he is demonstrating two things. First, he is describing his own colonial perspective through his use of the words "mainland" and "landscape." Second, he is taking a typical non-Native approach to rocks, assuming a human superiority and separateness. I would like to address both of these individually.

Contrary to Chock's opinion, Kānaka Maoli were and still are "genuinely mystical" in composing, chanting, and singing about rocks; as part of the 'āina, rocks are a primary metaphor in our poetry *and* we are related to nā pōhaku (rocks) through ancestors such as Papahānaumoku and Pele. An extension of 'āina, pōhaku are alive to us, and they contain great mana (supernatural or divine power). A good example is the anti-annexation mele commonly known as "Kaulana Nā Pua" (Famous are the children), originally titled "Mele 'Ai Pōhaku" (Rock-eating song).[40] The song is credited to Kanaka Maoli Ellen Kekoaohiwaikalani Wright Prendergast. According to haole missionary descendant Ethel M. Damon, the song was written in January 1893, just after the overthrow of the monarchy.[41] Damon writes that Prendergast was at home in Kapālama when some guests were announced, members of the Royal Hawaiian Band on strike: "'We will not follow this new government,' they asserted. 'We will be loyal to Liliu [*sic*]. We will not sign the haole's paper, but will be satisfied with all that is left to us, the stones, the mystic food of our Native land.' So they begged her to compose this song of rebellion. . . . Soon the mele was well known among Hawaiians."[42]

The first stanza clearly states Kanaka Maoli loyalty to the Hawaiian government and their rejection of haole colonization. The poetic images are also land based—Kānaka Maoli are not just keiki (offspring), they are pua (flowers), beautiful products of the 'āina; while they are in support of the sovereign representative, they are ma hope, behind the 'āina, who plays a double role of representing and being represented by the ali'i (sovereign leader).

Kaulana nā pua a'o Hawai'i	Famous are the children of Hawai'i
Kūpa'a ma hope o ka 'āina	Ever loyal to the land
Hiki mai ka 'elele o ka loko 'ino	When the evil-hearted messenger comes
Palapala 'ānunu me ka pākaha.	With his greedy document of exhortation.[43]

The second stanza metaphorically describes the response from the people—the entire archipelago responds to the summons to stand firm behind the land. Again, the intertwining of place names and chiefly names is deliberate, each recalling the other as islands were traditionally given epithets honoring beloved ancestral rulers of those places.

Pane mai Hawai'i moku o Keawe	Hawai'i, island of [chief] Keawe answers
Kōkua nā Hono a'o Pi'ilani	[Maui and] the "Bays of Pi'ilani" assist
Kāko'o mai Kaua'i o Mano[kalanipō]	Kaua'i of [chief] Mano[kalanipō] lends support

Paʻapū me ke one [o] Kakuhihewa.   And so do the "sands of [chief]
                                       Kakuhihewa" [Oʻahu].

The phrases "Hawaiʻi, moku o Keawe," "Nā hono aʻo Piʻilani," "Kauaʻi a Manoka-
lanipō," and "Ke one [o] Kakuhihewa" are common epithets poetically describing
the islands of Hawaiʻi, Maui, Kauaʻi, and Oʻahu, linking the land to the Aliʻiʻaimoku
(sovereign) of that land: Keawe, ruler of Hawaiʻi; Piʻilani, chief of Maui; Mano-
kalanipō, Kauaʻi's head; and Kakuhihewa, Oʻahu's leader. The term "ʻai" in "Aliʻi-
ʻaimoku" evokes both meanings of "food" and "chief," which is not coincidental,
as the principal job of the Aliʻiʻaimoku was to be a competent manager of both the
land and the people, able to provide adequate food for his people.[44] This is much
more traditional and meaningful than the silly, Americanized epithets attached to
the islands today, describing Hawaiʻi as the "Orchid Isle," Maui as the "Valley Isle,"
Kauaʻi as the "Garden Isle," and Oʻahu as the "Gathering Place," epithets commonly
promoted in all aspects of local culture, from tourism (pre-recorded information
played in flight on Aloha Airlines when passing over or approaching one of these
islands) to commerce (Kauaʻi's newspaper titled *The Garden Island,* or Hawaiʻi's
"Orchid Isle Motors" auto dealership).

The phrase "paper of the enemy" refers to the annexation document. In actuality, two anti-annexation petitions were circulated among Kānaka Maoli to be
forwarded to the U.S. Congress. One was only recently rediscovered by Noenoe
Silva.[45] Virtually every Native man, woman, and child able to sign his or her
name to the anti-annexation petitions did so, a resounding, unified voice against
annexation.

ʻAʻole aʻe kau i ka pūlima	No one will fix a signature
Ma luna o ka pepa o ka ʻenemi	To the paper of the enemy
Hoʻohui ʻāina kūʻai hewa	With its sin of annexation
I ka pono sivila aʻo ke Kanaka.	And sale of Native civil rights.

The fourth stanza makes a direct reference to rocks and defiantly proclaims that
Kānaka Maoli would rather eat rocks than become annexed to the United States.

ʻAʻole mākou aʻe minamina	We do not value
I ka puʻukālā a ke aupuni	The [U.S.] government's promises of money
Ua lawa mākou i ka pōhaku	We are satisfied with the stones
I ka ʻai kamahaʻo o ka ʻāina.	The wondrous food of the land.

Here, rocks are described as "ka ʻai kamahaʻo o ka ʻāina," "the wondrous (or mystical) food" of the ʻāina, the "land that feeds."

The last stanza is linked to the first stanza, where loyalty for Liliʻuokalani is
directly stated. Here the intertwining of Liliʻuokalani and the land equates the ʻāina

with the sovereign through the line "Ma hope mākou o Lili'ulani" (We support the sovereign Lili'uokalani).[46]

Ma hope mākou o Lili'ulani	We back Lili'u the royal one
A loa'a 'ē ka pono a ka 'āina	Who has won the rights of the land
(A kau hou 'ia e ke kalaunu)	(She will be crowned again)
Ha'ina 'ia mai ana ka puana	Tell the story
O ka po'e i aloha i ka 'āina.	Of the people who love the land.

Moreover, there is a deeper meaning to this mele Hawaiians call kaona (underlying, poetical meaning), which is a hallmark of Kanaka Maoli writing. A former student of mine, Kawika Winter, shared the kaona of this mele with me as he learned it from kūpuna Eddie Ka'ana'ana and Lydia Hale.

The song is not talking about literally eating stones. This saying, "Ua lawa mākou i ka pōhaku / I ka 'ai kamaha'o o ka 'āina" (We are satisfied with the stones / The wondrous food of the land) refers to the food which stones provide. It is with stones that we build our terraces to grow kalo—the staple food of the Hawaiian people. It is with stones that we cook the kalo in the imu. It is with stones that we pound our kalo into poi. It is with stones that we carve the poi board. It is with stones that we carve our canoes to go fishing. And it is with stones that the foundations of our houses were made. This song is talking about stones being the wondrous food of the land. What it is really saying is that it is our traditions as a Hawaiian people that will carry us on as a people. Money cannot and will not ever be able to do that. Realizing that this is a protest song, you can see why the words were phrased in such a way that the overthrowers of the Hawaiians would not be able to understand. It was only meant for Hawaiians to understand.[47]

Thus the kaona of the mele is much deeper than it originally appears, as it is speaking not only of stones, but the function and importance of stones within Hawaiian culture. Chock's presumption reveals his settler mentality.[48]

An example of this concept would be the extensive mo'olelo surrounding the Hawaiian volcano goddess, Pele. The word "pele" means lava, and what is lava but rock? She is an enigmatic figure in Hawaiian mo'olelo, the only akua (god) to have an entire genre of hula dedicated to her; she is worshipped as a human ancestor as well as a deity; she takes the shape of old woman, beautiful temptress, liquid lava, and solidified rock; she commands the elements of storms through her brothers Kauilanuimaka'ehaikalani and Kamohoali'i. But most important, despite the continuous and strident efforts to stamp out Hawaiian gods, she has maintained her visibility and power through her continuous presence in the form of volcanic eruptions, carving and shaping the land at her will.

In an attempt to silence criticism by visiting continental writers who claim Hawai'i writing focuses on "nature themes," Lum, like Chock, has made statements downplaying what he calls "standing-in-awe-of or ain't-it-beautiful nature writing."[49] Clearly this ignores or sweeps away Kanaka Maoli tradition: the vast majority of writing about "nature" (our family) *is* standing-in-awe *and* ain't-it-beautiful writing; it is celebratory and respectful.

A prose example of Kanaka Maoli "in-awe-of-nature" writing comes from the mo'olelo of Kaluaiko'olau. In 1887 Kaua'i native Kaluaiko'olau was diagnosed with leprosy and ordered to the leper colony situated on the isolated northern Kalaupapa peninsula of the island of Moloka'i. Ko'olau refused to part from his 'āina and his family, both of which he loved dearly. Described as a hero by the Kanaka Maoli community and an outlaw by haole authorities, Ko'olau fled to the safety of the rugged and isolated Kalalau Valley in the Nā Pali region of Kaua'i with his wife and young son, where they successfully evaded the Provisional Government's soldiers. After the death of her husband and son from the disease, Ko'olau's wife Pi'ilani left the refuge of the valley to return to Kekaha, where the rest of their family still lived.[50] Upon hiking out of the valley, Pi'ilani stopped to chant a mele mahalo (song of appreciation) to the valley. In this short segment, taken from the English translation by kupuna Frances Frazier, Pi'ilani addresses four specific places in Kalalau and describes her affection for each.

> I gaze upon you, o 'Ohe'oheiki [Little Bamboo], and your abundance; it was you who gave refuge from the dizziness of the summer days and the winter nights. It was your sweet flowing breast and kindliness, your welcoming hands to the wanderers; you were the heaven above and the earth below—you are the parent, the refuge. For you is this breath which sighs a greeting to you. Love to you, Kaluamoi [the moi fish hole], the hospitable bosom in which time was passed. It was your heights that veiled and obscured us from the pursuers, peered at by the stars blown away from the mountain peak, revealing brightly the heights where the waterfalls speak. O Limamuku [Chopped Limb], O Limamuku indeed! For you is this throbbing deep within, for you these tears which fall so freely, for you is this pain which tears at the breast—the lehua blossoms are scattered by the pelting of the pouring rain. Who would not feel the pain—here are the gusts of grief that will not be assuaged—farewell, farewell to you, the place of refuge where there is no ridgepole, farewell to the nest which gave ease to me and my husband and my child, farewell to your steeps, so difficult of access, farewell to the sweet singing voices of your babbling streams. The eyes will turn away from seeing you, yet always they will gaze inwardly, where love dwells. You are consecrated, you are marked—farewell to you. I still hear your murmuring voice, O Stream of Waimakemake [Desired

Water], whose cool waters eased our burning thirst. My love to you, you are always before my eyes, in my remembrance, farewell to you.[51]

The deep love and appreciation Pi'ilani feels for the 'āina is quite apparent in this moving passage. It is not, however, a particularly exceptional piece in the sense that it was and still is quite common for Kānaka Maoli to hold such deep sentiments for our beloved 'āina, so much so that there is a very large genre of our literature dedicated to wahi pana, or places celebrated in story.

Kūpa'a i ka 'Āina: Wahi Pana from a Kanaka Maoli Perspective

In Hawaiian culture the telling of mo'olelo is important because of the different emphasis on place than that found in Western tales. For example, Hawaiian wahi pana stresses the storyteller's knowledge of a place, which is revealed in the detailed setting of the mo'olelo. The 'āina was not merely a setting or backdrop, but an integral part of the plot. This is done through the use of place names in both poetic and nonpoetic ways. Kānaka Maoli are connected to the land through mo'okū'auhau (genealogy), which are remembered and recalled through story. Mo'okū'auhau are more than just lists of names of illustrious ancestors; as each name is recounted, a story is triggered in memory, which imparts knowledge of that place. This would have been more apparent in more traditional times, when Kānaka Maoli had a more intimate connection with land through their direct stewardship of it, but while we are more colonized and more urban today, these mo'olelo are still a part of us.

The poetry of place names is important in recalling the particular history or significance of a place and could be entertaining as well as educational, since, as University of Hawai'i linguistics professor Samuel Elbert states, "In their imaginations people ally the place with amusement and affection to the wondrous events of the past."[52] One example from the Pele epic is the little islet of Mokoli'i, located off the coast of Hakipu'u at the dividing point between the moku (districts) of Ko'olauloa and Ko'olaupoko on the windward side of the island of O'ahu. "Moko" is an older form of the word "mo'o" (lizard, "dragon"-like creature),[53] and "li'i" is "small" or "tiny." Thus the name is rendered as "Little Lizard." It refers to a mo'o of the area slain by Pele's younger and most favored sister, Hi'iakaikapoliopele (Hi'iaka-in-the-bosom-of-Pele), who was on her way from the volcano to the island of Kaua'i to fetch Pele's lover, Lohi'au. When Hi'iaka killed the giant mo'o, part of its body fell into the bay; the island represents the tip of the mo'o's tail that is sticking up out of the water.[54]

Today this island is incorrectly labeled "Chinaman's Hat" or "Keoni's Poi Pounder" because of its shape, which approximates these two items. It is interesting to note that "local" writer Dean Howell has probably done the most damage in appropriating the land for Asian settlers by writing and publishing an illustrated children's story titled *The Story of Chinaman's Hat*.[55] The cover illustration depicts a sleeping Chinese man, sitting in an upright position under water, the island positioned on his head like a hat. The story begins in China, and the main protagonist is a Chinese boy with a fictional and derogatory name, Lick Bean. One day, Lick Bean wanders into the Fong Family Herb Shop, where he buys and consumes some herbs guaranteed to make him bigger. He swims to Hawai'i, where he is a giant to the dwarf-sized Hawaiian royalty. He places his now diminutive hat on the Ali'i Nui (High Chief). Of course, this action ignores cultural protocol where one would never stand above the ali'i or touch his sacred head, actions forbidden and punishable by death.

The Hawaiians in turn are so "pleased" with the gift that they weave a very large lauhala hat for him, which then turns into land. Later Lick Bean returns to normal size and goes back to China. The story ends with the Hawaiian ali'i gazing out to the island Mokoli'i, where Lick Bean's "spirit still rests beneath the island." The description of the text on the back cover reads, "Chinaman's Hat is a small island off the east coast of the island of Oahu, Hawaii and is a popular scenic spot. It is frequently photographed because of its remarkable resemblance to a Chinese straw hat. *The Story of Chinaman's Hat* is an original legend describing how this uniquely shaped island was created." There is, of course, a photograph of Mokoli'i, inviting the reader to view Mokoli'i anew, now that the "remarkable resemblance" of that island to a straw hat has been explained. This "remarkable resemblance" is of course subject to cultural interpretation. Howell's book celebrates the "originality" and individuality of authorship, a positive thing in Western literature. It completely erases the Native perspective of the 'aina as mo'o, a living entity that Hi'iaka—a female, no less—overpowers. On the one hand, it presents a racist depiction of Chinese culture; on the other hand, it has led to the insertion of a hegemonic narrative that inscribes an Asian settler history onto the land.[56]

For Kānaka Maoli, Mokoli'i doesn't exist in isolation as "Chinaman's Hat" does. The small ahupua'a (land district) of Hakipu'u, which is the closest land area on the main island, supports the Hi'iaka mo'olelo, as it is rendered as haki (to break, broken) and pu'u (hill, back), or "Broken Back," referring to the spine of the lizard. Metaphorically, the word "pu'u" refers to a problem or obstacle.[57] Because the mo'o is an obstacle in Hi'iaka's journey, she overcomes the obstacle by the act of haki, breaking and thus destroying it.

Wahi pana are also a recounting of place names, and this is sometimes prominently placed in the plot of the mo'olelo. Here, Elbert explains that "the teller becomes a reporter of detail rather than a re-teller of adventure. To the outsider, such detailed lists of places are boring, but not so to the narrator or [the] Hawaiian audience. Listed in travel-guide order, the places bear witness both to the story's veracity and the teller's memory." [58] The presentation of wahi pana in the Hawaiian language lends a poetic sense not meaningful in English. On this point Kanaka Maoli kumu ʻōlelo Hawaiʻi (Hawaiian-language teacher) Larry Kimura has observed that "the Hawaiian attention to detail . . . sound[s] silly in English . . . [as] it cannot be done properly in that medium." [59] Thus once again we see the importance of the Native language, since the mere mention of a specific place name recalls to the educated mind the countless number of moʻolelo associated with that place, preserving both the name and the story of the area.

The colonial views of ʻāina expressed by Lum and Chock are reflected in local literature, where Hawaiʻi is merely a setting, a backdrop to the plot, and is thus treated and described differently from Native-produced literature. One example is the island of Molokaʻi and how it is depicted in Lois-Ann Yamanaka's novel, *Blu's Hanging* (1997). It is important to critique Yamanaka's work from this perspective since she has received national recognition and critical acclaim for her work. The novel focuses on the Ogata children and their struggles to cope with the death of their mother and the threats posed by adults in the small community of Kaunakakai, particularly a twenty-year-old local Filipino man who molests his eight- and thirteen-year-old nieces. While Yamanaka does not claim Kanaka Maoli heritage, outside of Hawaiʻi where distinctions between Natives and settlers are ignored, she is hailed by many as a "Native Hawaiian" writer. One example is Jamie James' review of Yamanaka's novel *Heads by Harry* in the *Atlantic Monthly* (February 1999). His article, "This Hawaii Is Not for Tourists," sums up two thousand years of island history in the space of three short paragraphs; it begins with the stereotypical American images of "grass skirts, ukuleles, pupu platters, [and] Don Ho," culminating with the ignorant statement that "the islands never had a Native bard to explain them to the rest of the world. . . . Now Hawaii has found a bard of sorts, the novelist Lois-Ann Yamanaka." [60] He goes on to describe Yamanaka as the "first talented Hawaiian writer of fiction" who is "poised to be the first major voice of the new Hawaiian literature." He then lists Milton Murayama, Darrell Lum, Sylvia Watanabe, and Nora Okja Keller—all Asian settlers—as having "produced significant fiction about Hawaiian themes, written in authentic Hawaiian vernacular." [61] James is not the only writer to make such an egregious error; in a letter defending their decision to award the 1997 Association for Asian American Studies (AAAS) Fiction prize to Yamanaka for *Blu's Hanging* despite criticisms of the book's controversial depictions of its Filipino American characters, then Fiction Award chair Caroline Chung Simpson also describes Yamanaka as a "Native Hawaiian writer" who "offers a local insider's critical perspective of the effects of U.S. imperialism on contemporary Hawaiian culture and various Asian-Pacific American groups." [62] For better or worse, Yamanaka has become a recognized voice of "authenticity" for the islands. Like Lum and Chock, she narrates the "feel good" immigrant success story, and she erases the character of the 'āina; it simply becomes a backdrop for human-centered drama.

Throughout *Blu's Hanging* the descriptions of the main town of Kaunakakai, where the Ogata family lives, is described only in negative terms of being hot and dusty; Miss Owens, a haole teacher from the American Midwest, "hates" Moloka'i, yet her negative description is never disputed by Ivah, or any other "local" character in the novel. In Yamanaka's description, Kaunakakai is a wretched place: rusting signs, abandoned homes, skinny dogs roaming lethargically through the streets, and "swirling red pineapple field dust" everywhere.[63] Aunt Betty describes it as a "godforsaken, hot-as-hell town," and Ivah's views echo Aunt Betty's.

> It's so hot in this town that babies wear diapers only, men go without shirts, windows and doors stay wide open, and people seek out the shade of a mango tree, or a lanai where there's a breeze. Inside, ceiling fans whir and standing fans with blue-cool plastic blades collect oily dust in a blue-gray blur. That's why Mama said steam, don't fry—it's so hot here that when you're standing over a pan of bubbling oil, your sweat rolls off your eyebrow, lands in the hot oil, and wham, it shoots you right in the face.[64]

Ivah has a very Western conception of the need to escape a wretched small town. Her desperate existence in Kaunakakai and her negative attitude toward that place is typical of non–Kanaka Maoli colonial views of immigrants trying to find their place in America rather than connecting to the 'āina as a place of nourishment and sustenance. Thus descriptions of other parts of Moloka'i are absent.

The tentative connections Yamanaka makes to 'āina are ignored by fellow Asian settler writer Marie Hara, who describes Yamanaka's writing in a book review as exhibiting alternately "the family's sadness in a bleak and depraved landscape" and "deeply felt love for this particular earth" throughout a novel that "celebrates the little known beauty spots" of Moloka'i.[65] Curiously, despite the glaring omission of Kānaka Maoli from the novel and the centrality of its Asian settler characters, Hara closes her article by saying that Yamanaka celebrates the "children of the land," and she asserts that "there is a lot of truth right there in place and in language" because Yamanaka is "willing to go places no writer of Hawai'i imagined before." Like Chock, Lum, and Yamanaka, Hara exhibits the same distance to 'āina when she proclaims that the Ogata children are able to somehow "survive" their childhood, "enduring a surreal hometown Kaunakakai, full of cynical teachers and bigots."[66] Kaunakakai seems to be full of negative images and not much else.

Very few places are mentioned by name, and the two that are, Phallic Rock and Hālawa Valley—both important images with detailed mo'olelo in Kanaka Maoli culture—are rendered insignificant in this novel. The full name of the phallic stone Nānāhoa is Ka 'Ule o Nānāhoa, or "Nānāhoa's penis," probably named for the shape of the pōhaku, which stands about six feet high. It was believed that women who performed the right prayers and ho'okupu (offering) and who slept on the stone overnight would become pregnant.[67]

Hālawa Valley is also rich with cultural significance.[68] Thought by archaeologists to be one of the original and thus oldest settlements in Kanaka Maoli history, this single valley on the east side of the island boasts many specifically named features, including a name for each type of wind that comes through the valley; Kanaka Maoli traditions recognize eighteen names in all.[69]

None of Yamanaka's descriptions of Moloka'i come close in comparison with Kanaka Maoli poetry describing the island. In the numerous mele composed by Kānaka Maoli about Moloka'i, not one describes the island or Kaunakakai in the same dismal and oppressive tone that Yamanaka employs.[70] In contrast, Moloka'i native Ida Hanakai Ah Yat's mele "Moloka'i Nui a Hina" (Great Moloka'i, child of Hina)[71] describes the island as nani (lovely) and a place that is waiwai nui (of great importance). Matthew Kāne's "Moloka'i 'Āina Kaulana" (Moloka'i, a celebrated land) describes Moloka'i as ku'u one hānau (my beloved homeland), ka heke nō ia i ka'u 'ike (the best I know), a beautiful place that commands admiration (he nani kū kilakila). Hālawa Valley is kaulana (celebrated), ho'ohihi (entrancing), kāhiko (adorned), and aloha nō 'ia (greatly loved). Kanaka Maoli musician Malani Bilyeu's contemporary mele "Moloka'i Sweet Home," written in English, differs from Yamanaka's portrayal in that he represents Moloka'i with loving sentiment reflective of Kanaka Maoli values of 'āina as cherished, echoing the older tradition exemplified by Ah Yat and Kāne.

> I feel your evening breeze tonight
> Moloka'i, I am longing for your laughter
> I'll gaze upon your silent shore
> And reminisce that sweet embrace of ginger.
>
> As New York City walls close in
> I long for the touch of an island
> Moloka'i, Moloka'i—sweet home.[72]

One could argue that since the main narrator in *Blu's Hanging* is an unreliable child narrator, her perception of the land she lives on is skewed by her poverty and her dysfunctional family life. Yet Kānaka Maoli live in similar conditions and do not typically write about 'āina with such negativity. While Ivah supposedly is "growing up local" in Kaunakakai, Yamanaka's bias toward O'ahu (often seen as the "center" of the State of Hawai'i because it is the center of economics and politics) is clear in the conclusion, with Ivah escaping her oppressed life, leaving for

Mid-Pacific Institute, a private college preparatory school located in Honolulu. In other words, the answer to Ivah's dilemma that Yamanaka provides is for Ivah to flee to Hawai'i's center of capitalism, to pursue the American dream, pushing for her "equal opportunity" to compete in a free society.

Yamanaka is by no means alone in her scant descriptions and character relationships to the land. Well-known stories by Lum himself, such as "Beer Can Hat" and "Paint," are devoid of any references to places identified by Kanaka Maoli histories or stories. Instead, settings identified as "local" consist of manmade structures—McKinley High School, "Kaneohe Hospital," freeways, recycling plants—and not the land itself. One could argue that the vague setting makes the stories more universal: it could be Makiki or Mission Viejo, Pearl City or Portland. Yet the lack of Kanaka Maoli histories anchoring these stories to Hawai'i (other than characters speaking HCE) speaks against Lum's waxing poetic about the "shared" value of "love for the land" and a genealogy to it "shared" by Kānaka Maoli and Asian settlers.

Perhaps most disturbing about the work of Lum, Chock, and Yamanaka is the absence of Kanaka Maoli characters in their stories. There are only a few shadowy background Kanaka Maoli characters in *Blu's Hanging,* despite the fact that the book is set on Moloka'i, a small island with a large number of Kanaka Maoli residents. The political reality is not that Kānaka Maoli have physically disappeared. We have disappeared only in the sense that we have no political power and are thus an afterthought, if thought of at all, in the discourse of the hegemonic "powers that be" in Hawai'i—haole and Asian settlers.

What appears to be happening in the world of "local" literature is that "local" is being defined through a linguistic rather than physical "landscape." In other words, what locates the literature as "local" is the use of HCE. Lum has stated that "while ethnicity and class play important roles in defining local culture's resistance to the dominant Western society, the bonds that tie it together are the common values, common history, and common language... Hawai'i Creole English."[73] This perspective echoes Chock's comments from a 1983 interview: "Writers, whatever their race, wherever they come from, have to recognize that they are writing in a tradition—or several traditions. You can't say you were created in a vacuum. You learn your words from somewhere. The way you speak is particular to your culture and to your subculture, to your ethnicity."[74] This reference to HCE again denies the presence of the Native language, a Native existence, and an extensive Native history, all of which are reduced in his view to the last one hundred and fifty years: genealogy and shared claim to the land through HCE.

Trask, however, counters this argument by saying that "a celebration of pidgin English becomes a gloss for the absence of authentic sounds and authentic voices."[75] She is referring to the "identity crisis" that Asian settlers feel in the literary world: they are no longer based in a homeland. While they are in reality Asian American, they feel "different" from their continental Asian counterparts, who identify themselves as "American," and thus have cloaked themselves with a "local" veil, claiming a "local" voice through Hawai'i Creole English. Yet the authentic sound and voice of Hawai'i is 'ōlelo Hawai'i, the Hawaiian language, not HCE.

The Quest for Kuleana

> Some non-Hawaiians assert they are Hawaiian writers, and their work part of the canon of Hawaiian literature. . . . Here, an immigrant/settler consciousness is attempting to dispossess our Native people through the backdoor of identity theft. Contemporary writers who claim, through generational residence in Hawai'i, that they are Hawaiian . . . confuse the development and identification of our indigenous literature. Asian writers who grew up in Hawai'i and claim their work as representative of Hawaiian literature or of our islands are the most obvious example. By asserting a special island identity, these local Asian authors . . . hope to separate themselves from Asian writers elsewhere in the American imperium. Their claim to difference is precisely that they are local, that is, they are "from" Hawai'i. This kind of settler assertion is really a falsification of place and culture. Hawai'i has only one indigenous people: Hawaiians. Hawaiian culture is our culture; it does not belong to everyone but only to us.
>
> —Haunani-Kay Trask, "De-Colonizing Hawaiian Literature"

One of the fundamental aspects of Polynesian culture is the idea of communal responsibility, which Hawaiians call kuleana. Kuleana (rights, privilege, responsibility, and authority) includes the many ways these principles are present in our lives: individually, socially, professionally, and culturally. In traditional society, kuleana was divided in three primary ways: by rank or class (chiefs, commoners), by age (children, young adults, elders), and by gender (male, female). This division of responsibility, privilege, and authority is also applicable to the discussion of what falls in the realm of Native and non-Native authority. In a Western context, mere study, scholarship, and devotion of one's life to a particular topic is enough to give one "authority" on the topic; thus many non-Natives can and do claim authority in various realms to which they have no genealogical or cultural connection: Native languages, Native cultures, and Native people, through disciplines such as linguistics, anthropology, and religion, as well as through such colonial institutions as "democratic" governments, education systems, and even marriage.

Yet from a Native perspective, clearly they don't have—and can never have—kuleana in Native realms of scholarship, knowledge, and experience.

While not all non-Native scholars, writers, and critics are hostile to nā mea maoli (all things indigenous), even those who are supportive of Kānaka Maoli sometimes assert themselves into Kanaka Maoli kuleana with a settler consciousness. One example is Hawai'i-based writer and publisher Dennis Kawaharada. In Rodney Morales' essay on the politics of "local" literature, he describes Kawaharada as being critical of the "ignore-the-Native" practices of peers like Chock and Lum.

> In [his] essay, he [Kawaharada] talked about how the "local literature" that had been developed by the "grandchildren of Asian immigrants" was constructed upon a "nostalgia for family and homeland," and then stated, "and if you write it in pidgin English and refer to local landmarks like King Street and Diamond Head or Tantalus, you've got a regional flavor that has some appeal for a local, if not a national, audience. . . . But this literature is not local in the same sense that Hawaiian stories are local." Kawaharada went on to claim that this literature was "neo-colonial" partly because it "embodie[d] values of the American way of life."[76]

Morales goes on to link Kawaharada's criticism of Bamboo Ridge with that of Hawai'i-based writer Richard Hamasaki, who "felt that there was a need for non-Native Hawaiians to learn more about and respect the cultures and values of Hawai'i's indigenous people."[77] Both Hamasaki and Kawaharada have been critical of the exclusionary practices of Bamboo Ridge Press, namely the fostering of a small number of some Asian and a few haole settler writers; as contemporaries of Chock and Lum, so they should.

Yet despite their good intentions, the question becomes one of kuleana—where do they, and other non–Kanaka Maoli, fit into the realm of Kanaka Maoli literature? In the 1970s and 1980s, Hamasaki created a successful Hawai'i-based literary journal, *Seaweeds and Constructions,* which published Kanaka Maoli poets such as Wayne Westlake, Joseph Balaz, and Dana Naone. Kawaharada, who worked for a time with Chock and Lum at Bamboo Ridge Press, went on to form Kalamakū Press, where he has been ambitiously printing collections of previously published Hawaiian mo'olelo; over the past decade, Kawaharada's press has put out six publications based on Hawaiian mo'olelo. Four are anthologies of previously printed Kanaka Maoli material: *Hawaiian Fishing Legends: With Notes on Ancient Fishing Implements and Practices* (1992), reprinted that same year as *Hawaiian Fishing Traditions [by] Moke Manu and Others, Nanaue the Shark Man and Other Hawaiian Shark Stories [by] Emma M. Nakuina and Others,* (1994), *Voyaging Chiefs of*

Havai'i [by] Teuira Henry and Others (1995), and *Ancient O'ahu: Stories from Fornander and Thrum* (1996). One, *The Wind Gourd of La'amaomao* (1990), is an original English translation by Sarah Nakoa and Esther Mookini of a previously published Hawaiian-language novel, *He Mo'olelo Hawai'i o Pāka'a a me Kūapāka'a, nā kahu 'iwikuamo'o o Keawenuia'umi, ke ali'i o Hawai'i, a o nā mo'opuna ho'i a La'amaomao [A Hawaiian Story of Pāka'a and Kūapāka'a, the attendants of Keawenuia'umi, the sovereign of Hawai'i, the grandchild of La'amaomao]* (or *Ka Ipumakani o La'amaomao*), by Moses Nakuina. A Hawaiian-language reprint of Nakuina's *Ka Ipumakani o La'amaomao* (1902), which itself is based on an older, orally passed down traditional mo'olelo, was published by Kalamakū Press in 1991. Besides these collections of Hawaiian mo'olelo, Kawaharada has also published two collections of his own essays: *Storied Landscapes* (1999) and *Local Geography: Essays on Multicultural Hawai'i* (2004).

Morales describes Kawaharada as a "staunch defender of Native Hawaiian rights and values" and positively relates Kawaharada's efforts in founding his press "in part to recover and publish Native Hawaiian folktales."[78] Kawaharada's efforts have helped to make Kanaka Maoli mo'olelo more readily available to the general public. But it is time to consider that this may be the kuleana for Kanaka Maoli publishers such as 'Ai Pōhaku and the more recently established Kuleana 'Ōiwi Press. With the exception of *The Wind Gourd of La'amaomao*, all of the mo'olelo that Kawaharada has been reprinting were originally published in English by haole "authorities" such as Abraham Fornander and Thomas Thrum, who rarely credited Native sources, often referring to them as anonymous "informants." In addition to republishing these works, Kawaharada himself has written the introductions and notes for *The Wind Gourd of La'amaomao* and all of the anthologies, with the exception of the collection of shark mo'olelo *Nanaue the Shark Man and Other Hawaiian Shark Stories*. For this collection, he included a reprint of haole folklorist Martha Warren Beckwith's "Hawaiian Shark Aumakua."[79]

So how has Kawaharada's publishing of Kanaka Maoli mo'olelo empowered Kānaka Maoli? So far, all it has done is shift the course of the conversation and "territorial rights" over Native literary resources from being between white settlers to being between white and Asian settlers, or what Trask calls "the struggle between Haole and Asians for local authenticity," which she argues is "rather like the fight between earlier and later immigrants: the indigenous is wholly denied."[80]

I applaud Kawaharada's efforts to take Bamboo Ridge to task in his critical essays. And I appreciate his professed support of Kanaka Maoli literature and Kanaka Maoli writers. But when he inserts himself into a position of authority in place of a Kanaka Maoli voice by publishing anthologies of Kanaka Maoli literature, writing the introductions to these anthologies that could have been penned by a Kanaka Maoli scholar and claiming a central position of knowledge and authority on Kanaka Maoli moʻolelo in his collection of personal essays, I must evoke the question of kuleana. Under American laws and practices, Kawaharada has the right as a businessman to pursue publishing rights and profit from his entrepreneurship. But from an indigenous cultural perspective, Kawaharada does not have kuleana over the telling or retelling of Kanaka Maoli moʻolelo. And it is not as simple a matter of just not being Kanaka Maoli: even within Kanaka Maoli culture, there are traditionally different kuleana over various aspects of culture, moʻolelo included: some moʻolelo were kapu by rank, gender, profession, and even island, district, or family association. As Kānaka Maoli have become more aware of our cultural practices and have become bolder in asserting our cultural rights and voicing concern over matters of kuleana, it is no longer enough for non–Kānaka Maoli to say they support us; they must actively demonstrate it as well.

Kawaharada's *Storied Landscapes* is disturbing because it perpetuates settlers' practice of claiming Hawaiʻi for their own. By asserting himself as the narrator throughout the essays, Kawaharada reframes the view of the ʻāina for the reader through a non-Native lens; while Kānaka Maoli are present (such as Nainoa Thompson, the master navigator of the voyaging canoe *Hōkūleʻa*), they are not permitted to speak or share their manaʻo (thought, idea, belief) of the ʻāina to which they are genealogically connected. Even the title of the book reveals a settler bias, as the term "landscape" implies a pastoral scene devoid of Kānaka Maoli, a *terra nullius* waiting to be conquered, colonized, settled. Ironically, one of Kawaharada's main points in this collection is to point out and criticize "the strategy of colonization through the usurping of the native voice in storytelling."[81] Kawaharada criticizes Jack London for inserting "his own racist notions" into his story "Koʻolau the Leper," yet fails to see how he is inserting *himself,* a settler, into the land and culture he is trying to represent in this book, a land and culture not his own.

Kawaharada's insertion of self as narrator of an indigenous Hawaiian moʻolelo is most evident in the opening essay, "A Search for Kūʻula-kai." After a brief opening paragraph that introduces Hāna, Maui, as the setting for the Kūʻulakai moʻolelo, Kawaharada goes on for several paragraphs detailing his experiences growing up on Maui and visiting Hāna, which he identifies, along with his interest in fishing, as establishing his "kuleana" to write on this topic.

> During my childhood in the 50's and early 60's, my family visited Hāna once a summer.... What brought me back to Hāna in 1991, two decades after my last visit, was the story of the Hawaiian fishing god Kūʻula-kai.... I was interested in such fishing traditions because my father, who died in 1971 when I was 20, had been both a fisherman and a boat-builder.... The story of Kūʻula-kai

evoked memories of my boyhood fishing trips with my father and our summer car rides to Hāna.[82]

Nearly sixty paragraphs in length, Kawaharada's narrative focuses on himself and
his family experience for about one-third of the essay. It is admirable that part
of what Kawaharada is trying to do is interrogate his "colonial education," which
had taught him "nothing about Hawaiian traditions." He says, "Was it possible to
claim to know, to be a part of, to dwell comfortably in a place without honoring
ancestral spirits and traditions which humanize every landscape?"[83] Yet that is
exactly what Kawaharada does throughout the collection of essays, inappropri-
ately laying claim to a place and to knowledge of that place. Kawaharada seeks
out the story of Kūʻulakai "as a way to remember my father." He continues that it
is also "to honor some ancient gods of Hawaiʻi."[84] But how is that demonstrated in
the essay, or throughout the collection? Instead, what Kawaharada is doing is typical of what settler writers like Lum and Chock before him tend to do—condense
Kanaka Maoli and settler history, culture, and attitudes into something "local" in
which parity of values is claimed. He writes,

> For kamaʻāina (children of the land) place names are important as an expres-
> sion of affection for the land which provides sustenance, and as essential
> reminders of the characters and resources of each place. (Haole writers, like
> London, who re-tell Hawaiian stories often leave out place names; but read-
> ers familiar with traditional stories find such tellings uninformed because we
> expect specific details about the setting.)[85]

Unlike ancient times, the terms kamaʻāina and Kanaka Maoli are no longer
exclusively synonymous with each other. As Houston Wood has pointed out in
Displacing Natives (1999), kamaʻāina is a term that has been appropriated by settler
haole. It is also a term appropriated by Asian and other settlers and is often used
synonymously with the term "local." Wood writes,

> The practice of pretending innocence while securing hegemony, for example,
> informs common usage in the islands of the word "kamaʻāina." According
> to Pukui and Elbert's *Hawaiian Dictionary*, before Euroamericans arrived
> kamaʻāina referred to Kanaka Maoli who were born to a particular locale.
> Early explorers, missionaries, and settlers left this meaning unchanged, but
> later immigrants and Euroamericans born in the islands increasingly desired
> to possess land not only by deed and lease but also through the claim that
> Hawaiʻi was their "home." "Kamaʻāina" was thus transformed from a concept
> denoting Native-born into a term meaning "island-born," or even merely
> "well-acquainted with the islands." By adopting a Native word to describe

themselves, Euroamericans obscured both their origins and the devastating effects their presence was having on the Native-born. . . . Many of these newly self-named kamaʻāina were now even asserting they knew more about "authentic" Hawaiian culture than did Kanaka Maoli themselves.[86]

As Wood argues, "it is as often kamaʻāina Asians as kamaʻāina Caucasians who claim to 'become Polynesian' while dancing the hula or while fishing at ancient Native Hawaiian fishing spots."[87] Wood then offers a series of examples where he is equally critical of the "kamaʻāina Asian" Bamboo Ridge Press. In critiquing Stephen Sumida's *And the View from the Shore,* he concludes, "Such rhetoric linking the Hawaiian people's experience of having their land colonized and their nation overthrown with stories of immigrant plantation struggles undermines claims for indigenous rights and reparations."[88] This comment is much more widely applicable than to just Sumida's text.

In *Storied Landscapes,* Kawaharada's concern is that fiction "often melts into fact in the reader's mind; and what appears to be fact is often fiction."[89] He says that if we read London's stories with these assumptions, we risk believing they are true. The same can be said for Kawaharada's essays: if we assume that anyone has kuleana over Hawaiian culture, history, and the (re)telling of it through our moʻolelo, then it isn't difficult to understand why most haole and Asian settlers in Hawaiʻi argue there is no difference between themselves and indigenous Kānaka Maoli, despite the vast differences in kuleana that do exist.

It is encouraging that Kawaharada's press has recently published a collection of art and poetry by Kanaka Maoli poet ʻĪmaikalani Kalāhele. By doing so, Kawaharada, like Hamasaki before him, is providing a venue for Kānaka Maoli to speak rather than be spoken for. It suggests some hope that if the issue of kuleana is properly addressed, then Kānaka Maoli and Asian settlers can coexist in a way that is mutually beneficial.

Yet even the most supportive non–Kānaka Maoli can still get caught in non-Native rhetoric. At the end of his essay, Morales proposes four new directions for local literature, the first of which, he suggests, is "to get more into the indigenous culture, the host culture of Hawaiʻi."[90] Again, this idea of "host" culture alludes to Kānaka Maoli happily accommodating all comers. In her poem "Host Culture (Guava Juice on a Tray)," Kanaka Maoli poet Mahealani Kamauʻu stridently opposes the haole-imposed and repressive concept of what "host culture" is supposed to mean, referring to it as "euphemistic bull shit," stating, "They act like / they was invited / like all these years, / we been partying / Or something; . . . / Whoever thought up / That crap / Deserves to get whacked."[91]

While it is nice that "a growing number" of non–Kānaka Maoli are "interested" in the "host culture," I am a skeptical Kanaka Maoli writer, poet, and scholar of Kanaka Maoli literature who has witnessed far too many examples of what this means: the taking over of our kuleana by non-Natives.[92] In the literary realm of the past century, this list is headed by haole such as Abraham Fornander, Thomas G. Thrum, William Westervelt, William Hyde Rice, Martha Warren Beckwith, Katherine Luomala, and Nathaniel B. Emerson. In more contemporary times, this list has expanded to include Frederick B. Wichman, grandson of William Hyde Rice. Through the Asian-controlled Bamboo Ridge Press, Wichman has published *Kaua'i Tales* (1986), *Polihale and Other Legends* (1991), *More Kaua'i Tales* (1997), and *Pele Mā, Legends of Pele on Kaua'i* (2001), stories that were provided by mostly *unnamed* and *uncredited* Kanaka Maoli sources.[93] Through the University of Hawai'i Press, Wichman has published *Kaua'i: Ancient Place-Names and Their Stories* (1998) and *Pua Ali'i o Kaua'i: Ruling Chiefs of Kaua'i* (2003). Other Kanaka Maoli writers and/or scholars were known and publishing at the time—Wayne Westlake, Joseph Balaz, John Dominis Holt, Haunani-Kay Trask, Dana Naone Hall (who edited Bamboo Ridge's *Mālama: Hawaiian Land and Water* in 1985), Rubellite Kawena Johnson—so why not empower them to publish mo'olelo of our 'āina and kūpuna, instead of another non-Hawaiian?

The list also includes haole American studies professor Glen Grant, most known for his storytelling and collections of ghost stories related to Hawai'i. He capitalized on this fame and had been tapped by publishers like Mutual Publishing and the University of Hawai'i Press to write introductions to several different republications of older Kanaka Maoli texts, such as Lili'uokalani's autobiography, *Hawaii's Story by Hawaii's Queen*. Why are non–Kanaka Maoli editors and publishers profiting from Kanaka Maoli mo'olelo and Kanaka Maoli scholarship, especially when Kanaka Maoli writers, publishers, scholars, and the general Kanaka Maoli community work with and translate these texts in ways that are culturally knowledgeable and appropriate?

In her essay "Against Extinction: A Legacy of Native Hawaiian Resistance Literature," Māhealani Dudoit addresses this concept of kuleana as one vital for survival.

> I think it is not surprising that an independent people should strive for their independence as a people. Nor is it surprising that Hawaiians should have called forth their tremendous powers of spiritual and intellectual expression through words in their struggles to protect their kuleana. For precisely in our struggle to preserve our political sovereignty and our relationship to the land do we struggle against our extinction.[94]

Kuleana over nā mea Hawai'i (all things Hawaiian) is certainly something Kānaka Maoli have struggled with for a long time, and our quest to gain control over our land, gathering rights, language, culture, customs, and now literature continues as we struggle for nationhood. White and Asian settlers in Hawai'i should know that Kānaka Maoli aren't going to go away anytime soon, and we will not allow our Native voices to be silenced.

Ha'ina 'ia mai 'ana ka puana (Conclusion)

Ha'ina 'ia mai 'ana ka puana, "thus the story is told." While there is no standard opening to a Kanaka Maoli mo'olelo (such as "Once upon a time"), our mo'olelo as told through mele frequently conclude with this line. The stories of my Kanaka Maoli ancestors were passed down through oral tradition for countless centuries; for over a hundred years many have been preserved on paper in the Hawaiian-language newspapers, a legacy to Kānaka Maoli of that generation of our illustrious storytelling past. These stories survive through the hā, the breath of life, the essence of aloha that nurtures and sustains us.

The vast majority of Kanaka Maoli mo'olelo and mele are called pana; storied or legendary places are called wahi pana, the songs composed for them mele pana. By far this is one of the largest categories of mo'olelo and mele: thousands upon thousands of these mo'olelo and mele have been catalogued and published over the years, although they haven't always been well understood, especially by non–Kānaka Maoli. Many exist in untranslated forms in Hawaiian, others exist only on deteriorating microfilm copies of old Hawaiian-language newspapers, not having been reprinted or republished since they originally appeared during the nineteenth and early part of the twentieth centuries.

Settler writers and scholars must acknowledge Native kuleana over all things Kanaka Maoli, including literature. This is particularly important in regards to sociopolitical and economic status because these influence areas of culture, such as language and literature. Darrell Lum concedes at one point that "an immigrant people may never know the deep connection to the land that perhaps only Native Hawaiians can fully appreciate."[95] Yet there is no attempt at bridging or understanding this divide, which could come through wider publication of Kanaka Maoli writers by Bamboo Ridge Press, or more vocal support for Kanaka Maoli endeavors. Morales cautions the "Bamboo Ridge gang" to be careful, as they are creating a community that is positioning "Native Hawaiians as a *they*." He says that "telling a story or writing a poem is one thing. Defining a community that you're less and less a part of, that's something else."[96] Settler writers need to acknowledge their place as settlers and ours as Natives.

I will end with a poem by Kanaka Maoli poet, artist, and musician 'Īmaikalani Kalāhele. It is written about sovereignty, yet it speaks to the realm of Native kuleana, literary and otherwise.[97]

The source
of
my origins
lie
beneath my feet,

the breath
in my chest
originated
in Pō

the destiny
of my race
is
plunged into
my gut
and
infesting
my veins

with a new
nationalism,
old spiritualism,
and a need
to make wrong
right
now.

Notes

The title of this essay is taken from a political cartoon that appeared in the *Kaua'i Times* (December 14, 1990) at the height of Japanese investment in Hawai'i. The cartoon is a parody of Woodie Guthrie's patriotic song "This Land Is Your Land, This Land Is My Land," a song every American child learns at some point during elementary school. The intent of this song is clear from the lyrics given above: the erasure of the Native population and the indoctrination of every citizen into the American ideological myth that this is a land of equality, opportunity, and freedom. I have twisted the perspective a bit more from the *Kaua'i Times* version to imply a Native perspective. An alternate end line for this stanza is, "God bless America for you and me."

1. Stuart Hall, *Representation: Cultural Representations and Signifying Practices* (London: SAGE Publications Ltd., 1997), 17.

2. Hall, *Representation*, 5.

3. There are several excellent articles available that discuss the politics of how "local" identity is constructed. See Haunani-Kay Trask, "Settlers of Color and 'Immigrant' Hegemony: 'Locals' in Hawai'i," *Whose Vision? Asian Settler Colonialism in Hawai'i*, a special issue of *Amerasia Journal*, ed. Candace Fujikane and Jonathan Okamura (Los Angeles: UCLA Center for Asian American Studies, 2000) (see also "Settlers of Color and 'Immigrant' Hegemony: 'Locals' in Hawai'i" in this volume); Candace Fujikane, "Reimagining Development and the Local in Lois-Ann Yamanaka's *Saturday Night at the Pahala Theatre*," *Women in Hawai'i: Sites, Identities, Voices*, ed. Joyce N. Chinen, Kathleen O. Kane, and Ida M. Yoshinaga, a special issue of *Social Process in Hawai'i* 38 (1997); Jonathan Y. Okamura, "The Illusion of Paradise: Privileging Multiculturalism in Hawai'i," *Making Majorities: Constituting the Nation in Japan, Korea, China, Malaysia, Fiji, Turkey, and the United States*, ed. D. C. Gladney (Stanford: Stanford University Press, 1998); and Eric Yamamoto, "The Significance of Local," *Social Process in Hawaii* 27 (1979).

4. "Kanaka Maoli" will be used as an adjective to denote ideas, concepts, and things "Hawaiian." "Kānaka Maoli" with the kahakō, or macron, will be used to refer to the plural noun "Hawaiian people."

5. Hall, *Representation*, 6.

6. "Haole" originally meant "foreigner" but now refers to Caucasians, particularly Americans and Europeans. Samuel Elbert and Mary Kawena Pukui, *Hawaiian Dictionary*, rev. ed. (Honolulu: University of Hawai'i Press, 1986), 58.

7. For more information, see H. Trask, *From a Native Daughter: Colonialism and Sovereignty in Hawai'i*, rev. ed. (1993). Reprint: Honolulu: University of Hawai'i Press, 1999; and www.kalahui.org, or http://www.hawaiiannation.org, which has links to other sovereignty sites.

8. Generically termed mo'olelo, Kanaka Maoli literature has existed in oral forms for thousands of years mainly through the genres of oli (chant), mele (song), mo'okū'auhau (genealogies), and ka'ao (stories), although it also includes myth (more correctly defined as stories of gods), legends, and history. These genres are further broken down into specific categories based on style or theme (e.g., kanikau are dirges, mele pana are songs that celebrate places). Since a system of writing was established in the 1820s, Kanaka Maoli litera-

ture has expanded to include written forms of these traditional genres of moʻolelo and has also incorporated and adapted new forms based on foreign structures (the romance epic, for example). While Kanaka Maoli–produced literature was originally written in Hawaiian after Hawaiian-language medium schools were banned in the latter part of the nineteenth century, Kanaka Maoli literature has come to embrace literature written not only in Hawaiian, but also in English, HCE, or any combination of the three.

9. Personal communication, 2002.

10. Kānaka Maoli are local, but not all locals are Kanaka Maoli.

11. Personal communication, 2002.

12. According to J. Van Dyke, "The term 'Native Hawaiian' is defined in section 201(a)(7) of the Hawaiian Home Commission Act, 1920, ch. 42, 42 Stat. 108 (1921), reprinted in 15 HAW.REV.STATE.Ann.331 (Mitchie 1997) . . . as referring primarily to persons with 50% or more Hawaiian blood." "The Political Status of the Native Hawaiian People," http://www .nativehawaiians.com/documents/pol_hawn.pdf, fn. 3. "Part-Hawaiian" refers to those with less than the 50 percent blood quantum. However, federal laws can be confusing, as in other federal statutes, "the term 'Native Hawaiian' is used to cover all persons who are descended from the people who were in the Hawaiian islands as of 1778, when Captain James Cook" arrived. It is important to note that blood quantum distinctions have not come out of Kanaka Maoli culture (i.e., prior to colonization, Kānaka Maoli never discriminated against each other along the lines of blood quantum, which is separate from cultural protocols regarding moʻokūʻauhau, or genealogical lines). As they are terms that have been used as weapons against Kānaka Maoli to divide our communities, many Kānaka Maoli reject the colonial terms altogether in favor of the indigenous term "Kānaka Maoli," the real (maoli) people (kānaka).

13. Personal communication, 2002.

14. For an excellent discussion of this issue, see the "Editor's Note" of ʻŌiwi: A Native Hawaiian Journal, vol. 1, ed. Māhealani Dudoit (Honolulu: Kuleana ʻŌiwi Press, 1998), 1–8.

15. See Helen G. Chapin, Shaping History: The Role of Newspapers in Hawaiʻi (Honolulu: University of Hawaiʻi Press, 1996); and Esther T. Mookini, Hawaiian Newspapers (Honolulu: Topgallant Publishing Co., 1974).

16. Eric Chock and Darrell H. Y. Lum, eds., The Best of Bamboo Ridge: The Hawaii Writers' Quarterly (Honolulu: Bamboo Ridge Press, 1986), 4.

17. Excerpted from "About Us," Bamboo Ridge Press, http://www.bambooridge.com.

18. Eric Chock, "The Neocolonialization of Bamboo Ridge: Repositioning Bamboo Ridge and Local Literature in the 1990s," Bamboo Ridge: A Hawaii Writers' Quarterly (Spring 1996): 12.

19. An excellent analysis of this situation is found in Dennis Kawaharada, "Local Mythologies, 1979–2000," Hawaiʻi Review 56 (Spring 2001): 185–225.

20. Stephen Sumida, And the View from the Shore: Literary Traditions of Hawaiʻi (Seattle: University of Washington Press, 1991), xvii.

21. Eric Chock et al., eds, Growing Up Local: An Anthology of Poetry and Prose from Hawaii (Honolulu: Bamboo Ridge Press, 1998), 12. Emphasis added.

22. H. Trask, "Settlers of Color and 'Immigrant' Hegemony," 20.

23. Data compiled from several sources, such as the Native Hawaiian Data Book (Hono-

lulu: Office of Hawaiian Affairs, 1998). See also the *State of Hawai'i Data Book 2006*, online at http://www.oha.org. Despite Hawai'i being promoted as "The Health State," due mainly to skewed statistics based on a large Asian and haole population, Native Hawaiians consistently outrank all other ethnic groups in every negative health category, having the highest rates of illness such as heart disease, cancer, diabetes, and asthma; highest rates of infant mortality; and highest rates of alcoholism, drug abuse, and tobacco use. We also have the poorest social and economic statistics, with the highest rates of prison incarceration at both the juvenile and adult level, and highest rates of welfare, illiteracy, poverty, and homelessness. Papa Ola Lōkahi, *Native Hawaiian Health Data Book* (Honolulu: Papa Ola Lōkahi, 1992). Health statistics links for these and other categories available through the Hawai'i Medical Library online site at http://hml.org/WWW/nativehawaiian.html.

24. E. S. Craighill Handy, Elizabeth Green Handy, and Mary Kawena Pukui, *Native Planters of Old Hawaii: Their Life, Lore, and Environment* (Honolulu: Bishop Museum Press, 1972), 45. Because of the depth and complexity of the Hawaiian language, this is really an oversimplification, as the meanings of the root word 'ai (food, esp. fruits and vegetables; to rule, as over land or people; to eat) and its relationship to related words such as ai (sexual reproduction); aina (sexual intercourse), 'aina (meal), and 'āina (land) connotes a more intertwined relationship than otherwise indicated. Elbert and Pukui, *Hawaiian Dictionary*, 9, 11.

25. I am referring here to the Māhele, or privatization of lands, that occurred in 1843–1848, during the reign of Kauikeaouli, Kamehameha III. For an excellent analysis of the Māhele and its results, see L. Kame'eleihiwa, *Native Lands and Foreign Desires, Pehea Lā e Pono Ai?* (Honolulu: Bishop Museum Press, 1992).

26. Elbert and Pukui, *Hawaiian Dictionary*, 184.

27. Elbert and Pukui, *Hawaiian Dictionary*, 184.

28. Elbert and Pukui, *Hawaiian Dictionary*, 316.

29. Kame'eleihiwa, *Native Lands and Foreign Desires*, 24.

30. J. Linnekin as cited in J. Tobin, "Cultural Construction and Native Nationalism: Report from the Hawaiian Front," *Asia/Pacific as Space of Cultural Production*, ed. Rob Wilson and Arif Dirlik (Durham, N.C.: Duke University Press, 1995), 152–153. Tobin's essay provides an insightful discussion of the extended debate argued primarily between Linnekin and Hawaiian studies professor Haunani-Kay Trask.

31. Elbert and Pukui, *Hawaiian Dictionary*, 21. One example that Pukui cites is the mele "Kaulana Nā Pua," discussed in depth later in this essay.

32. Chock and Lum, *The Best of Bamboo Ridge*, 4.

33. Chock and Lum, *The Best of Bamboo Ridge*, 3.

34. Kawaharada, "Local Mythologies, 1979–2000," 191–192.

35. Rodney Morales, "Literature," *Multiculturalism in Hawai'i*, ed. Michael Haas (New York: Garland Press, 1998), 108.

36. Chock et al., *Growing Up Local*, 12.

37. Pualani Kanaka'ole Kanahele, "Kīlauea: Creation and Procreation," *Pleiades: The Journal of the University of Hawai'i Community Colleges* (1990): 62, cited in Manulani Aluli Meyer, *Ho'oulu: Our Time of Becoming: Hawaiian Epistemology and Early Writings* (Honolulu: 'Aipōhaku Press, 2003), 103.

38. Meyer, *Hoʻoulu*, 103.

39. Eric Chock, interview by J. Watson and L. Ball, *Hawaiʻi Review* (special supplement, fall 1983): 2.

40. It was also known as "Mele Aloha ʻĀina" (Patriot's song). S. Elbert and N. Mahoe, *Nā Mele o Hawaiʻi Nei, 101 Hawaiian Songs* (Honolulu: University of Hawaiʻi Press, 1970), 64.

41. Elbert and Mahoe state that the mele was written in 1893. The mele was published in the first volume of the *Buke Mele Lāhui* in 1895, although the *Buke Mele* suggests the song was previously published in *Ka Makaʻāinana* or another Hawaiian newspaper from where it was gathered.

42. Damon, quoted in Elbert and Mahoe, *Nā Mele Hawaiʻi*, 64. One source asserts that this mele protested annexation, as "the [provisional] government, which had just overthrown Queen Liliʻuokalani, was offering money to anyone who would sign the petition in support of Hawaiʻi's annexation to the United States. It is said this song was sung to Liliʻuokalani under her window while she was imprisoned in ʻIolani Palace" (http://www.namamonoeau.com/kaulana.html).

43. Elbert and Mahoe, *Nā Mele Hawaiʻi*, 64.

44. See Kameʻeleihiwa, *Native Lands and Foreign Desires*.

45. The other has not yet been found. For more information, see N. Silva and N. Minton, comps., *Kūʻē: The Hui Aloha ʻĀina Anti-Annexation Petitions, 1897–1898* (Honolulu: Noenoe K. Silva and Nālani Minton, 1998); N. Silva, "Ke Kūʻē Kūpaʻa Loa Nei Mākou: Kanaka Maoli Resistance to Colonization," Ph.D. dissertation, University of Hawaiʻi, 1999; and N. Silva, *Aloha Betrayed: Native Hawaiian Resistance to American Colonialism* (Durham, N.C.: Duke University Press, 2004).

46. Liliʻulani is not a misspelling of Liliʻuokalani. Elbert and Pukui, *Hawaiian Dictionary*, 206.

47. Personal communication, November 2001.

48. It may be interesting to note that the mele has a rather happy tune, which has been described as masking the true meaning of the lyrics from non-Hawaiian speakers. This is evident in Peter Moon's remake (*Tropical Storm*, Panini Records, 1979), a very jazzy, rock-and-rollish rendition that doesn't treat the mele in a dignified manner. Peter Moon is an Asian settler musical contemporary of Lum and Chock.

49. Chock and Lum, *The Best of Bamboo Ridge*, 3–4.

50. For a more in-depth study, see my article, "Hero or Outlaw? Two Views of Kaluaikoʻolau," *Navigating Islands and Continents: Conversations and Contestations in and around the Pacific, Selected Essays*, ed. Cynthia Franklin, Ruth Hsu, and Suzanne Kosanke, a special issue of *Literary Studies East and West* 17 (Honolulu: University of Hawaiʻi at Mānoa College of Languages, Literature, and Linguistics, 2000), 232–263.

51. F. Frasier, *The True Story of Kaluaikoʻolau, as Told by His Wife Piʻilani* (Līhuʻe, Kauaʻi: Kauaʻi Historical Society, 2001), 42–43; my own translation of place names.

52. S. Elbert, "Connotative Values of Hawaiian Place Names," *Directions in Pacific Traditional Literature*, ed. Adrienne L. Kaeppler and H. Arlo Nimmo (Honolulu: Bishop Museum Press, 1976), 124.

53. The term "moʻo" is difficult to render in English, as it typically refers not to the little, benign geckos common in Hawaiʻi households today, but large, dragon-like creatures that

could be fierce and deadly. However, the word "dragon" is fraught with European, American, and Asian cultural connotations. The incommensurability of the symbols moʻo and dragon once again demonstrates how Kanaka Maoli cultural paradigms differ from those of haole and Asian settler cultures.

54. One of the most accessible sources of this story, albeit not the best, is Nathaniel B. Emerson's *Pele and Hiiaka, A Myth from Hawaii* (1915). Emerson based his story on several previously published versions by Kanaka Maoli writers from 1860 to 1906. With only one exception, these moʻolelo were all printed in the Hawaiian language and are therefore inaccessible today to non-Hawaiian-language speakers. The sole English-language version, titled "Hiʻiaka: A Hawaiian Legend by a Hawaiian Native," was published in the newspaper *Pacific Commercial Advertiser* in 1883 by Emma Nakuina, who published under her Hawaiian name, Kaili. The son of American missionaries, Emerson was raised in the islands and was a fluent speaker of the Hawaiian language. Today most Hawaiian scholars agree that while Emerson has, in previous generations, been upheld as a preserver of Hawaiian traditions, he was little more than a plagiarist who capitalized on his knowledge of the language and his connections in the Hawaiian community by publishing English renditions of sacred stories and selling them for money. Unfortunately, because many people today do not speak, read, or understand Hawaiian, Emerson's English-language text is relied upon as an "authoritative" text, which it is not. See also E. Sterling and C. Summers, *Sites of Oahu* (Honolulu: Bishop Museum Press, 1993), 181–182; and Anne Kapulani Landgraf, *Nā Wahi Pana o Koʻolaupoko* (Honolulu: University of Hawaiʻi Press, 1994), 10.

55. Dean Howell, *The Story of Chinaman's Hat* (Honolulu: Island Heritage, 1990).

56. See references to "Chinaman's Hat" in Maxine Hong Kingston, *China Men* (1980); reprint: New York: Vintage, 1989.

57. Elbert and Pukui, *Hawaiian Dictionary*, 358.

58. An excellent example is found in S. Elbert, "Connotative Values of Hawaiian Place Names," where he recounts the moʻolelo of the fish goddess Laenihi en route to find her brother a wife. In one short paragraph, eighteen wahi pana are listed in her travels from Molokaʻi to Maui. *Directions in Pacific Literature,* ed. Adrienne Kaeppler and H. Arlo Nimmo (Honolulu: Bishop Museum Press, 1976), 125.

59. Larry Kimura, "Native Hawaiian Culture," *Native Hawaiian Study Commission Report* (Washington, D.C.: U.S. Government Printing Office, 1985), 177.

60. Jamie James, "This Hawaii Is Not for Tourists," *Atlantic Monthly* (February 1999), 90.

61. James, "This Hawaii Is Not for Tourists," 91.

62. C. Chung Simpson, "Statement on the Selection of *Blu's Hanging* for the 1997 AAAS Fiction Award," letter dated March 9, 1998.

63. Lois-Ann Yamanaka, *Blu's Hanging* (New York: Harper Perennial, 1998), 32.

64. Yamanaka, *Blu's Hanging,* 65.

65. Marie Hara, "Blu's Rising," *Honolulu Weekly,* June 4–10, 1997, 10.

66. Hara, "Blu's Rising," 10.

67. C. Summers, *Molokai: A Site Survey* (Honolulu: Bishop Museum Press, 1971), 30. Moʻolelo surrounding the Nānāhoa can be found in 27–31.

68. See Summers, *Molokai,* 160–175.

69. Eleven winds are identified in Summers, *Molokai,* 160. Nakuina lists eighteen in

all. They are: Hoʻolua, Hoʻolua Noe, Hoʻolua Kele, Hoʻolua Pehu, Hoʻolua Kaʻipou, Hoʻolua Wahakole, Hikipua, Hakaano, Laukamani, Puʻuohōkū, ʻOkia, Ualehu, Laʻikū, Nāulu, Kēhau, Kaipali [Koipali], Līanu, and ʻEhukai. M. Nakuina, *He Moʻolelo Hawaiʻi o Pākaʻa a me Kūa-pākaʻa, nā kahu ʻiwikuamoʻo o Keawenuiaʻumi, ke aliʻi o Hawaiʻi, a o nā moʻopuna hoʻi a Laʻa-maomao* [A Hawaiian Story of Pākaʻa and Kūapākaʻa, the attendants of Keawenuiaʻumi, the sovereign of Hawaiʻi, the grandchild of Laʻamaomao] (Honolulu, 1902), 69–70. The only wind name found in Summers and not in Nakuina is Kaʻao (160). Kaipali (Nakuina) and Koipali (Summers) are probably variants of the same name.

70. Other examples include "Hīhīwai" and "Ka ʻŌpae" by Dennis Kamakahi; "He Kama a Hina," "Kaulana Wale nō ʻo Molokaʻi," and "Kāʻana" by John Kaʻimikaua; "Molokaʻi Cowboys" by Ernie Cruz Sr.; "Koʻolau" by Waymouth Kamakana; "Kalamaʻula" by Hanna Dudoit; "Me Molokaʻi" by Ivy Hanakahi Wu; and the traditional mele "Ua Nani Molokaʻi" and "Ka Paniolo Nui o Molokaʻi."

71. Hawaiian goddess associated with healing and the moon. See M. Beckwith, *Hawaiian Mythology* (Honolulu: University of Hawaiʻi Press, 1972); and L. Kameʻeleihiwa, *Nā Wāhine Kapu, Divine Hawaiian Women* (Honolulu: ʻAi Pōhaku Press, 1999).

72. M. Bilyeu in R. Morales, *Hoʻihoʻi Hou, A Tribute to George Helm and Kimo Mitchell* (Honolulu: Bamboo Ridge Press, 1984), 43.

73. Chock et al., *Growing Up Local*, 13.

74. Chock interview by J. Watson and L. Ball, 1.

75. H. Trask, "De-Colonizing Hawaiian Literature," *Inside/Out: Literature, Cultural Politics, and Identity in the New Pacific*, ed. Vilsoni Hereniko and Rob Wilson (Durham, N.C.: Duke University Press, 1995), 170.

76. Morales, "Literature," 120.

77. Morales, "Literature," 120.

78. Morales, "Literature," 116.

79. This article was originally published by Beckwith in *American Anthropologist* 19 (4) (Oct.–Dec. 1917): 503–517.

80. Trask, "De-Colonizing Hawaiian Literature," 170.

81. Dennis Kawaharada, "A Twisted Tale: Jack London's 'Koʻolau the Leper,'" *Storied Landscapes: Hawaiian Literature and Place* (Honolulu: Kalamakū Press, 1999), 96.

82. Kawaharada, "A Search for Kūʻula-kai," *Storied Landscapes: Hawaiian Literature and Place* (Honolulu: Kalamakū Press, 1999), 1–4.

83. Kawaharada, "A Search for Kūʻula-kai," 5.

84. Kawaharada, "A Search for Kūʻula-kai," 7.

85. Kawaharada, "A Twisted Tale," 92.

86. Houston Wood, *Displacing Natives: The Rhetorical Production of Hawaiʻi* (Lanham, Md.: Rowman & Littlefield Publishers, Inc., 1999), 41.

87. Wood, *Displacing Natives*, 50.

88. Wood, *Displacing Natives*, 51.

89. Kawaharada, "A Twisted Tale," 97.

90. Morales, "Literature," 127.

91. Mahealani Kamauʻu, "Host Culture, Guava Juice on a Tray," *ʻŌiwi: A Native Hawaiian Journal*, vol. 1, 135.

92. See H. Trask, "Coalitions between Natives and Non-Natives," *From a Native Daugh-*

ter: *Colonialism and Sovereignty in Hawai'i* (Monroe, Maine: Common Courage Press, 1993), 247–262.

93. The topic of my master's thesis in religion was a Pele moʻolelo published in the Hawaiian language by a Kanaka Maoli, Moke Manu. Wichman published a portion of Manu's moʻolelo in *More Kauaʻi Tales* (Honolulu: Bamboo Ridge Press, 1997) without crediting him. This is probably due, in part, to his use of the English translation by Mary Kawena Pukui, which is in the Bishop Museum archives. In Wichman's collection, Pukui is barely mentioned, and Manu is not mentioned at all. Wichman also admits to making changes to the moʻolelo as he sees fit to make them more "entertaining," disregarding the original intention of the moʻolelo (see *Polihale and Other Kauaʻi Legends* [Honolulu: Bamboo Ridge Press, 1991], 182). Not only are Wichman and Bamboo Ridge Press profiting from Kanaka Maoli texts and Kanaka Maoli scholarship, but they are also distorting the moʻolelo by making indiscriminate changes to the original text.

94. M. Dudoit, "Against Extinction: A Legacy of Native Hawaiian Resistance Literature," *The Ethnic Studies Story: Politics and Social Movements in Hawaiʻi*, ed. Ibrahim G. Aoudé, a special issue of *Social Process in Hawaiʻi* 39 (Honolulu: Department of Sociology, University of Hawaiʻi at Mānoa, 1999), 246.

95. Chock et al., *Growing Up Local*, 13.

96. Morales, "Literature," 115.

97. ʻĪmaikalani Kalāhele, "Manifesto," *He Alo ā He Alo (Face to Face): Hawaiian Voices on Sovereignty* (Honolulu: American Friends Service Committee, 1993), 151. Kalāhele is noted for combining visual images with texts, as he has done here. The moʻo image is a particularly powerful cultural image, as it is both the land, as indicated in the earlier discussion of Hiʻiaka and her slaying of Mokoliʻi, as well as an important ʻaumākua figure.

'Ai Pōhaku

The Hawaiian landscape is a document of cultural history. The arrival of the haole to Hawai'i brought a distinct entrepreneurial view of the land. The Hawaiian significance of places was hidden behind haole technology and architecture. Resort, military, industrial, residential, and highway development ravages our 'āina. Man has replaced the gods. Man has forgotten their names. These images are from a series called "'Ai Pōhaku," an attempt to rediscover the significance of destroyed heiau on the island of O'ahu.

"Kahehuna Heiau"

"Āpuakēhau Heiau"

"Kukuiokāne Heiau"

"Ka'akahaimauli Heiau"

"Pākākā Heiau"

PART II

Settler

DAVID STANNARD

The Hawaiians

Health, Justice, and Sovereignty

It has been over thirty years since the psychologist William Ryan introduced the phrase "blaming the victim" into the language of social analysis.[1] Victim blaming, Ryan explained, was an insidious technique newly employed by apparently sympathetic and liberal social scientists and politicians for dealing with the terrible suffering of America's poor and abused. In contrast to older ideologies that dismissed those living at the margins of society as inherently inferior beings deserving of their fate, the new ideology of the victim blamers happily acknowledged historical injustice as the principal cause of such things as poverty and ill health, and then went about the business of trying to change the consequences of that past injustice—that is, change the victims themselves—without addressing the ongoing oppression that was in fact the true cause of the problem.

Today, almost four decades later, the blaming-the-victim syndrome is alive and well in the United States, and nowhere is this more evident than in Hawai'i's treatment of its indigenous people.

* * *

The Hawaiians were one of the last large-scale indigenous societies to be encountered by Western adventurers. At daybreak on January 18, 1778, in the midst of a voyage from Tahiti to the western coast of North America, sailors aboard two British ships under the command of Captain James Cook unexpectedly sighted the smallest of the high islands in the Hawaiian chain. In retrospect, it is not difficult to understand why Cook and his crews were astonished at what they had stumbled upon, since Hawai'i—a string of eight major islands, the largest of which is more than six times the size of Tahiti—is the most isolated archipelago on earth, more than two thousand miles in every direction from the nearest inhabited lands.

First settled by Polynesians well over a millennium earlier, the Hawaiian Islands had by far the largest population and the most complex and hierarchical political system in all of the island Pacific. Estimates of the all-island population size have varied over time, increasing dramatically in recent years. The first attempt at a systematic population estimate for the islands in 1778 was carried out by an officer on board one of Cook's ships. His total came to approximately 400,000. The most recent revised estimate puts the figure at closer to 800,000.[2]

But whatever the population at the moment of Western contact, it did not remain that large for long. In their lengthy isolation the Hawaiians had been spared the ravages of every major epidemic disease (smallpox, typhoid, yellow fever, measles, and others) that had long infected much of the rest of the world, and they had no previous exposure to treponemic infections (such as syphilis) or to tuberculosis. The observations of those sailing with Cook unanimously support the findings of modern studies of skeletal remains that at the moment of Western contact the Hawaiians were extraordinarily strong, healthy, and free of serious infectious disease.[3] Unfortunately, the men on Cook's ships were so universally infected with syphilis and gonorrhea that they had been too weak to sail when originally scheduled to leave Tahiti, and tuberculosis—which at the time affected nearly half the people in England—was active and widespread among Cook's officers and crews.

Venereal disease and tuberculosis were already spreading among the Hawaiians by the time Cook's ships departed the islands for good in 1779. Seven years later the surgeon on board a French frigate that visited a remote part of Maui wrote that the *majority* of Natives there had become infected with venereal disease.[4] And six years later still, Captain George Vancouver, who had been with Cook in Hawai'i in 1778–1779, revisited the islands and reported finding massive depopulation virtually everywhere.[5]

From this point on account after account by European and American explorers reported on the visible ravages of newly introduced disease among the Hawaiians and on the precipitous decline of this formerly robust population. Major epidemics were not uncommon—typhoid in 1804; influenza in the mid-1820s; mumps and whooping cough in the 1830s; measles, mumps, and whooping cough in the late 1840s; smallpox in the 1850s; Hansen's disease (then known as leprosy) throughout the latter part of the century—and in *each case* as much as 10 percent of the population was wiped out.

Ghastly as these scourges were, the most devastating long-term damage done to the islands' population occurred in the *wake* of these epidemics and, additionally, as a consequence of widespread tuberculosis and venereal disease among the people. Year after year, with virtually no periods of relief, disease-caused infertility and subfecundity produced recorded birth rates so low that, even in the absence of epidemics, missionaries and others routinely predicted the imminent extinction of the Hawaiians.[6]

In 1831 the first official all-island census counted only 130,000 people. At best—if the 1778 population had been only about 400,000—that meant a decline of nearly 70 percent in just over fifty years, roughly twice the proportional devastation of the Black Death in medieval Europe; if, as is far more likely, the population in 1778 was closer to 800,000, the 1831 population represented a half-century decline of almost 85 percent. And it remained in free fall. By 1850 the population was less than 85,000. By 1890 it was down to 40,000. And, finally, in 1900—in the immediate aftermath of the U.S. seizure and annexation of the sovereign Hawaiian nation—it reached a nadir of just over 37,000, an overall collapse of at least 90 percent, and probably more than 95 percent, since 1778.[7]

New immigrants continued to come to Hawai'i, and with each new wave the Natives were pushed ever further from the corridors of influence and power. As the twentieth century progressed, however, the number of Hawaiians began to grow again, thanks to intermarriage, with consequently rising numbers of so-called "part" Hawaiians, though the size of the "full" (unmixed) Hawaiian population continued to decline. Today the number of full-Hawaiians is well under 10,000; the number of part-Hawaiians is in excess of 220,000. But both separately and together they remain the unhealthiest and most oppressed people in the islands.

* * *

The State of Hawai'i is proud to call itself "The Health State." And not without reason. Overall life expectancy in Hawai'i is almost seventy-six years for males and more than eighty-two years for females—in each case roughly four years greater than the national average.[8] Since Hawai'i is unique as the only state in which no single race or ethnic group constitutes a majority of the population, this across-the-board index of well-being is extraordinary.

But for Hawaiians the story is very different, with life expectancy, according to U.S. Census reports, of less than sixty-five years for males and less than seventy-two years for females. These are by far the lowest life expectancies of any major population group in Hawai'i. The combined male-female rate is approximately the same as the overall state and national figures of half a century ago—and is roughly equivalent to that of such countries as El Salvador, Paraguay, Nicaragua, and the Dominican Republic today.[9]

The pattern of mortality is especially telling. Below one year of age the Hawaiian death rate is more than double the overall state average. Between one and four years of age it is triple the state figure—and so on, through early adulthood. In every age category up to age thirty the Hawaiian death rate is never less than double, and often is triple, the equivalent general mortality rate in the islands. Indeed, with just under 20 percent of the state's population, Hawaiians account for nearly 75 percent of the state's deaths for persons less than eighteen years of age. Only after age seventy does the Hawaiian mortality rate fall below the state average—and that is because at that point there are relatively few Hawaiians left to die: after seventy years of age fully 64 percent of the state's non-Hawaiian population is still alive, compared to barely 40 percent of the Hawaiian population. Particularly alarming is the fact that while, as expected, the mortality rate for non-Hawaiians *decreased* significantly between 1980 and 1990, for both full- and part-Hawaiians it actually *increased* in that period.[10]

The causes of this exceptionally high mortality rate are numerous, and not only numerous, but, like the mortality rate itself, they are worsening. For example, between 1980 and 1990 rates of death from heart disease, cancer, stroke, and diabetes either declined significantly or held steady for non-Hawaiians, while for Hawaiians they all increased, and in some cases increased dramatically. Moreover, for *full*-Hawaiians the rate of death from cancer and stroke was three and a half times that of non-Hawaiians; for heart disease it was four times that of non-Hawaiians; and for diabetes it was nine times that of non-Hawaiians.[11]

These and similar reports have set off alarms in the Hawai'i health and social service communities. Professional agencies, both public and private, have aggressively sought out the principal reasons for this health crisis, and they have found them in the easily labeled "abnormal" behavior of Hawaiians themselves. That is, the state's social pathologists have focused their efforts almost entirely on blaming the victim.

Hawaiians, it turns out, have the highest rates of any group in the islands of obesity, smoking, and both acute and chronic drinking. Teenage motherhood among Hawaiians is almost double the state average, while the maternal substance abuse rate is much higher among Hawaiians than non-Hawaiians: two and a half times higher for fetal alcohol syndrome; three times higher for cocaine use; and almost five times higher for methamphetamines. More than one-third of the state's confirmed child abuse and neglect cases are found in Hawaiian families.[12]

Following a ritualized, vague, and gratuitous acknowledgment of tragedies in the past—the conveniently distant nineteenth-century past—the diagnoses of the helping professions in Hawai'i relentlessly focus on the Hawaiians' own allegedly self-destructive practices in the present. Programs have been set up to teach Hawaiians healthier eating habits; drug and alcohol rehabilitation units have been established; birth control and perinatal care services are in place—and more. Many of these are laudable activities, no doubt. But in locating the problem *within* the victims themselves, the institutions and agencies that would help the Hawaiians out of their present condition consistently ignore the routine oppression and discrimination Hawaiians face in everyday life—oppression and discrimination that is the root cause of the seemingly deviant behavior that is so upsetting to the social and behavioral scientists.

Consider, for example, just four very visible potential areas of concern—areas in which the major social service agencies have little or no action-oriented interest: housing, income, education, and criminal justice.

Hawaiians represent roughly 20 percent of the state's population, but they occupy less than 10 percent of the housing units in the islands—and the percentage of units rented by Hawaiians that contain six or more persons is more than double the state average. Yet despite these crowded conditions (and the potential for multiple incomes per household), more than one out of four Hawaiian rental households have total incomes below the official poverty threshold—a rate almost double that for the state at large.[13]

Some Hawaiians, of course, do own their own homes. But those homes are far and away the lowest in value among all ethnic groups in Hawai'i, and the percentage of Hawaiian families in owner-occupied homes who receive public assistance and/or have incomes below the poverty level is almost twice the state average.[14] In brief, whether they rent or own their housing units, Hawaiians tend to be far more impoverished and to live in the worst and most crowded conditions of any people in the islands.

And whether they rent, own, or are homeless (the sight of Hawaiian families permanently camped in public parks and on beaches is commonplace), Hawaiians have the highest unemployment rate of all ethnic groups in the state. They represent more than 28 percent of the individuals receiving Aid for Dependent Children, almost triple the percentage of any other identified group. They constitute the largest percentage of families in the islands that are living below the poverty line, more than double the statewide average. And the proportion of Hawaiians in the categories of persons who earn less than $10,000 a year and less than $5,000 a year is more than twice those rates for all other groups combined.[15]

As for education, the higher the level, the lower the participation of Hawaiians. Statewide in the elementary and secondary public school systems more than 25 percent of students are Hawaiian and just under 75 percent are non-Hawaiian. At the community college level 16 percent of the students are Hawaiian, while 84 percent are non-Hawaiian. At the main campus of the University of Hawai'i less than 9 percent of the students are Hawaiian; more than 91 percent are non-Hawaiian. And of recent MA, PhD, JD, and MD degrees awarded by the university, barely one-half of 1 percent went to Hawaiians, while more than 99 percent went to non-Hawaiians.[16]

This drastic situation, with its debilitating, long-term social consequences, has indirect causes ranging from institutional racism in the professional workforce (that systematically locks Hawaiians out and thereby discourages belief in the value or efficacy of higher education) to the need for young and impoverished

Hawaiians to care for families at a much earlier age than non-Hawaiians (thereby forcing them prematurely into low-level jobs that preclude time for educational pursuits). But more direct causes of the undermining of Hawaiian educational opportunity are conscious public decisions by government and education leaders—such as dramatic recent increases in higher education tuition levels, while the university and the state legislature refuse to fund requests for tuition waivers or other educational aid specifically targeted for Hawaiians. Remedial academic programs for all groups that may incidentally benefit Hawaiians address none of the real reasons for their gross under-participation in education at the higher levels. In fact, like nutrition training for the desperately poor and hungry, such programs only reinforce the perception that Hawaiians are to blame for their own educational shortcomings.

It is perhaps within the criminal justice system, however, that evidence is most vivid regarding the true reason that Hawaiians persistently rank at the bottom of virtually every index of social well-being.[17] Throughout the past decade and more Hawaiians have constituted the overwhelming plurality of adults in Hawai'i sentenced for felony convictions. Almost 40 percent of state prison inmates are Hawaiian, double their proportion of the general population and twice the rate of any other group.[18] It is commonly assumed, therefore, that criminal behavior among Hawaiians also is disproportionately large. But actually—despite the fact that, like African Americans in the rest of the United States, Hawaiians are particular targets of police investigation and harassment—Hawaiian arrest rates are no higher than the proportion of Hawaiians in the population at large.

Put differently, although Hawaiians constitute two out of every five inmates in the prisons, they represent only *one* out of every five arrestees for all crimes, both Part I Index offenses (crimes of violence and serious property theft) and Part II Index offenses (lesser crimes such as vandalism, prostitution, and drug possession). Indeed, even among Part I offenses, Hawaiian arrest rates are highest for nonviolent crimes such as auto theft and burglary and lowest for violent crimes like murder, rape, aggravated assault, and arson—for which, combined, their arrest rate actually is lower than their proportion of the state population.[19]

The only possible explanation for this enormous disparity between arrests and incarceration is that Hawaiians are singled out by the court system for especially harsh treatment. Apart from the sheer injustice of this deliberate practice, its effect on other indices of social well-being is nothing short of debilitating. The cruelly disproportionate criminalization of huge numbers of Hawaiians not only cripples those individuals' life chances, but also undermines every aspect of their families' existence—from income loss to emotional stability. Thus it is not at all surprising to discover that Hawaiians have more than double the statewide rate of families containing children under the age of eighteen that are headed by females (with no adult male present) or that Hawaiian families receive all forms of public assistance at two to three times the rate of other groups.[20]

What is particularly devastating, however, is that this entire complex of interlocking oppressions has become the fundamental source of a widely held self-fulfilling prophecy that labels Hawaiians as incorrigibly deviant—and treats them as such. Within the juvenile justice system, for example, the same pattern observable regarding Hawaiian adult arrests and convictions not only exists, but is also growing worse. During the middle years of the 1990s well over *half* of all minors incarcerated in state correctional facilities were Hawaiian—a figure more than 50 percent higher than the Hawaiian juvenile arrest rate for all offenses.[21] And, as with Hawaiian adults, that arrest rate was roughly equivalent to the proportion of Hawaiians in the state's overall juvenile population.

Despite the fact, then, that Hawaiians demonstrably do not commit significantly more crimes than would be predicted by their mere proportional presence within the state's population, the justice system in Hawai'i is embarked on a patently transparent campaign to incarcerate and thus create a multigenerational class of Hawaiian criminals. In so doing it is meshing its efforts with those of other social service and social control units that consistently declare the Hawaiians at fault for their own misery. Within each institutional category, then—health, housing, employment, education, criminal justice, and more—the racist mistreatment of Hawaiians is, simultaneously, both cause and consequence of the discrimination and suffering that is meted out by each of the other overlapping agencies. And palliative efforts confined to addressing mere symptoms of oppression (nutritional counseling, remedial school programs, menial job training, and the like) only serve to distract attention from those symptoms' fundamentally racist and institutionally systemic roots.

In his original analysis of the "blaming the victim" phenomenon, Ryan described "ideological warfare against the poor in the interest of maintaining the *status quo*" as "one of the most detestable forms of Blaming the Victim."[22] The Hawaiian people today are victims of a concerted ideological war that is being waged against them, as indigenous people, by both public and private sector agencies. Direct assaults by the criminal justice, employment, and educational bureaucracies are effectively concealed by the social service organizations that relentlessly find that the fault of the Hawaiians' poverty and ill health lies within the Hawaiians themselves.

So the suffering continues. And so it *will* continue until the Hawaiians' ongoing struggle for political and economic self-determination achieves a measure of success sufficient for the Hawaiians to support and to care for themselves—as they did for many long centuries before that winter of 1778, when the first European ships came into view on the distant horizon.

Notes

An earlier version of this essay was originally published in *Cultural Survival* 24 (1) (2000).

1. William Ryan, *Blaming the Victim* (New York: Pantheon Books, 1971).

2. James Cook, *The Three Voyages of Captain James Cook Round the World*, volume VII by James King (London, 1821), 118–119; David E. Stannard, *Before the Horror: The Population of Hawai'i on the Eve of Western Contact* (Honolulu: University of Hawai'i Press, 1989).

3. The accounts of Cook and his officers are conveniently collected in J. C. Beaglehole, ed., *The Journals of Captain James Cook*, volume III in two parts (Cambridge: Hakluyt Society and the University Press, 1967). Among the more extensive osteological surveys, see Charles E. Snow, *Early Hawaiians: An Initial Study of Skeletal Remains from Mokapu, Oahu* (Lexington: The University Press of Kentucky, 1974); and Sara L. Collins, "Osteological Studies of Human Skeletal Remains from the Keōpū Burial Site," in *Moe Kau a Hoʻoilo: Hawaiian Mortuary Practices at Keōpū, Kona, Hawaiʻi*, Toni L. Han et al. (Honolulu: Bishop Museum Department of Anthropology Report 86-1, 1986).

4. M. Rollin, M.D., "Dissertation on the Inhabitants of Easter Island and the Island of Mowee," in J. F. G. de la Pérouse, *A Voyage Round the World Performed in the Years 1785, 1786, 1787, and 1788*, 2 vols. (London, 1799), II:337–338; see also I:341.

5. George Vancouver, *A Voyage of Discovery to the North Pacific Ocean and Round the World, 1790–1795* (London, 1798), I:158–160, 187–188.

6. See David E. Stannard, "Disease and Infertility: A New Look at the Demographic Collapse of Native Populations in the Wake of Western Contact," *Journal of American Studies* 24 (1990): 325–350; reprinted in Kenneth F. Kiple and Stephen V. Beck, eds., *Biological Consequence of the European Expansion, 1450–1800* (London: Ashgate, Ltd., 1997).

7. Reports on the missionary and subsequent government censuses of the nineteenth century can be found in Robert C. Schmitt, *Demographic Statistics of Hawaiʻi, 1778–1965* (Honolulu: University of Hawaiʻi Press, 1968), 42–43; and Eleanor C. Nordyke, *The Peopling of Hawaiʻi*, 2nd ed. (Honolulu: University of Hawaiʻi Press, 1989), 178. Both of these sources, however, severely underestimate the population of the islands prior to the existence of censal records; see discussion in Stannard, *Before the Horror*, 4–14, 50, 59–60, 103–146.

8. *State of Hawaiʻi Data Book* (Honolulu: State Department of Business, Economic Development, and Tourism, 1995), 64, table 2.10.

9. Mark Eshima, compiler, *Native Hawaiian Data Book* (Honolulu: Office of Hawaiian Affairs, 1998), 404, table 6.1; Robert C. Schmitt, *Historical Statistics of Hawaiʻi* (Honolulu: University Press of Hawaiʻi, 1977), 52, table 2.6; *The Statistical History of the United States from Colonial Times to the Present* (Stamford, Conn.: Fairfield Publishers, 1965), 25, Series B 92-100.

10. Eshima, *Native Hawaiian Data Book*, 414, table 6.67; Mele A. Look and Kathryn L. Braun, *A Mortality Study of the Hawaiian People, 1910–1990* (Honolulu: The Queen's Health Systems, 1995), 8, figure 1.

11. Eshima, *Native Hawaiian Data Book*, 428, table 6.74.

12. Eshima, *Native Hawaiian Data Book*, 430, table 6.75; 394, table 6.55; 372–373, tables 6.41–6.41a; 284, table 5.11.

13. Eshima, *Native Hawaiian Data Book,* 92, table 2.7; 111, table 2.17; 112, table 2.18; 114, table 2.19; 124, table 2.25.

14. Eshima, *Native Hawaiian Data Book,* 120, table 2.2; 142–143, table 2.35 and figure 2.35.

15. Eshima, *Native Hawaiian Data Book,* 584, table 8.42; 268, table 5.4; 50, table 1.24; 542, table 8.18; 516–517, table 8.5 and figure 8.5.

16. Eshima, *Native Hawaiian Data Book,* 206, table 4.2; 222, table 4.10; 220, table 4.9; 232, table 4.14.

17. See also Healani Sonoda, "A Nation Incarcerated," in this volume.

18. Eshima, *Native Hawaiian Data Book,* 486, table 7.13.

19. Eshima, *Native Hawaiian Data Book,* 470, table 7.5; 474, table 7.7.

20. Based on calculations drawn from Eshima, *Native Hawaiian Data Book,* 104, table 2.13; 270, table 5.4; 276, table 5.7; 278, table 5.8.

21. Eshima, *Native Hawaiian Data Book,* 494, table 7.17; 472, table 7.6; 476, table 7.8.

22. Ryan, *Blaming the Victim,* 210.

KYLE KAJIHIRO

The Militarizing of Hawai'i

Occupation, Accommodation, and Resistance

> Militarization is a step-by-step process by which a person or a thing gradually comes to be controlled by the military or comes to depend for its well-being on militaristic ideas. The more militarization transforms an individual or a society, the more that individual or society comes to imagine military needs and militaristic presumptions to be not only valuable but also normal. Militarization, that is, involves cultural as well as institutional, ideological, and economic transformations.
>
> —Cynthia Enloe, *Maneuvers: The International Politics of Militarizing Women's Lives*

The forces of militarism and imperialism have indelibly shaped modern Hawai'i. At the crossroads of Asia-Pacific commerce, Hawai'i has long been a centerpiece of U.S. military strategy. Over a hundred years have elapsed since the United States of America militarily intervened in the sovereign Kingdom of Hawai'i and forever changed the course of Hawaiian history, and still militarism continues to exert a powerful influence over the social, economic, and cultural affairs of Hawai'i.

Militarism in Hawai'i cannot be reduced to a simple product of military policy. Instead, it must be understood as the result of a complex interaction of forces, including the political and economic fears and ambitions of global powers; the way key actors in the local society either resisted, accommodated, or collaborated in the process of militarization; the deployment of strategies to normalize and maintain militarism; and the interplay of ideologies of race, class, and gender that not only justified but often encouraged the expansion of empire.

While most histories of Hawai'i have overlooked the central role of the U.S. military, a few social critics have attempted to describe the militarization of Hawai'i. Some have emphasized the role of global forces and events in the militarization of

Hawaiʻi.[1] Others have analyzed how certain civilian sectors, in the pursuit of their own interests, collaborated in the militarization of Hawaiʻi.[2] More recent studies have illuminated how militarism relies upon various discursive strategies to cloak itself in an aura of inevitability and naturalness and "produce processes of militarization that are hidden in plain sight."[3] While U.S. military hegemony today seems nearly unassailable, militarism in Hawaiʻi has its contradictions and weaknesses, what Ian Lind calls "structural sources of tension."[4] These contradictions present openings for intervention and social change.

Militarism in Hawaiʻi has developed through the push and pull of local, national, and global interests over time. Often these interests converged; sometimes they competed against each other. As Lind suggests, "despite surface appearances, militarism is inherently unstable."[5] Throughout the different phases of militarism in Hawaiʻi, the interests that most often prevailed were that of colonizers and settlers. In this contest Kānaka Maoli, the indigenous people of Hawaiʻi, lost the most.[6] But they also resisted and sometimes changed the course of militarism in Hawaiʻi. Their movements represent hope that people can transform Hawaiʻi socially, culturally, politically, and environmentally from an occupied nation, disfigured by war and addicted to militarism, into a free state, a model of nonviolence and of just social, cultural, economic, and environmental conduct.

This essay (1) briefly surveys the history and current status of militarism in Hawaiʻi; (2) considers some of the impacts of militarism in Hawaiʻi; and (3) examines some key contemporary examples of resistance to militarism.

The Militarization of Hawaiʻi

The development of U.S. military institutions in Hawaiʻi was driven by a desire to expand the United States' trade with Asia and its influence in the Pacific. As a vital refueling and provisioning stop on transpacific trade routes, Hawaiʻi was considered key to economic and military hegemony in the Pacific. Not to be outdone by European colonial powers that were snatching up colonies in the Pacific, U.S. President John Tyler in 1842 claimed Hawaiʻi as part of the U.S. sphere of influence. This so-called Tyler Doctrine extended the racist ideology of "Manifest Destiny" into the Pacific.

In 1873 General John M. Schofield and Lieutenant Colonel Burton S. Alexander, disguised as tourists, secretly surveyed Hawaiʻi for suitable naval ports. Upon spying Ke Awalau o Puʻuloa (the Kanaka Maoli name for Pearl Harbor, meaning "the many harbors of Puʻuloa"), Schofield concluded, "It is the key to the Central Pacific Ocean, it is the gem of these islands."[7]

Hawaiʻi's haole (white) elite, the sugar planters and merchants, leveraged U.S. desire for a naval base in Hawaiʻi to their own advantage. They forced King David

Kalākaua to enact the "Bayonet Constitution"[8] and sign a Treaty of Reciprocity with the United States that gave the U.S. exclusive access to Pearl Harbor in exchange for lowering the tariff for Hawai'i-grown sugar.

On January 16, 1893, when King Kalākaua's successor, Queen Lili'uokalani, attempted to enact a new constitution to restore Native Hawaiian power in the government, U.S. foreign minister John Stevens, conspiring with haole leaders, landed American troops from the USS *Boston*. On January 17, with American guns aimed at 'Iolani Palace, the haole leaders deposed the Queen and declared a new provisional government. U.S. President Grover Cleveland condemned the U.S. military intervention as an illegal act of war against a friendly nation and called for the restoration of the Kingdom of Hawai'i. Anti-annexation forces successfully held off two attempts to ratify treaties of annexation. However, the political winds shifted against Hawai'i in 1898. With the outbreak of war with Spain, the U.S. military stepped up efforts to seize Hawai'i. On July 6, 1898, Congress passed a simple joint resolution purporting to annex Hawai'i. Nearly overnight, Hawai'i was transformed into the hub of the United States' vast military enterprise in the Pacific and a launch pad for its imperial thrust into Asia.

U.S. occupation ushered in a period of unprecedented military expansion in Hawai'i. Construction of a naval base at Pearl Harbor began in 1900, and it was soon followed by Fort Shafter, Fort Ruger, Fort Armstrong, Fort DeRussy, Fort Kamehameha, Fort Weaver, and Schofield Barracks. Brigadier General Montgomery M. Macomb, commander of the U.S. Army, Pacific (Hawaiian Department) from 1911 to 1914, stated, "Oahu is to be encircled with a ring of steel."[9]

In the territorial period leading up to World War II, Hawai'i's haole oligarchy formed an alliance with the military establishment. The military and the haole elite shared two key interests: the industrialization of the islands and the maintenance of white settler rule in Hawai'i.

The bombing of Pearl Harbor on December 7, 1941, provided the justification and opportunity for the military to bring Hawai'i under military discipline.[10] Plans for concentration camps and martial law, which had been in the works for years, were quickly implemented. As martial law took effect, Japanese community leaders were arrested and put in concentration camps. In his study, *Cane Fires: The Anti-Japanese Movement in Hawaii, 1865–1945*, Gary Okihiro describes how the Japanese in Hawai'i were driven to "superpatriotism" by anti-Japanese racism.

The nisei [second-generation Japanese] plight was an essential part of the military's strategy for maintaining economic and political stability. Nisei were driven to patriotism, with virtually no other choice. Furthermore, the definition of patriotism, as determined by Hawaii's political and military leaders, meant subordination to their will whether that meant quiet acceptance of inequality or complicity in the destruction of things Japanese.[11]

In response to this anti-Japanese reaction, many young Japanese men enlisted in the U.S. military to prove their loyalty to the United States. After the war Japanese American veterans returned home with heightened expectations of social and economic advancement. Many of them were educated on the G.I. Bill and entered business and government.

Ironically, even as the war unleashed intense racism against Hawai'i's Japanese community, it hastened the demise of the old plantation power structure and brought what Lind called a "military-industrial-revolution" that opened up new economic and social possibilities for Asians in Hawai'i.[12] World War II and the U.S. military facilitated the transformation of Hawai'i's Japanese into "Japanese Americans." The heroism and sacrifice of nisei veterans became legend, but the powerful iconography of the World War II nisei vet was used to expedite the forced assimilation, the Americanization, of Hawai'i's Japanese. War was the theater in which the nisei redeemed themselves in a grand morality play, where individuals from an oppressed group could overcome racial discrimination by demonstrating unquestioning loyalty to the United States and making enormous personal and collective sacrifices in war. Men like U.S. Senator Daniel Inouye, former U.S. Representative Spark Matsunaga, former governor George Ariyoshi, and former Bishop Estate trustee Matsuo Takabuki became celebrated icons in that mythology. But this story oversimplifies the complex convergence of events and factors that enabled Japanese settlers to gain power in post–World War II Hawai'i, and it obscures the tragic consequences of this development for Kānaka Maoli.

The nisei veterans' rise to political power in the so-called "Democratic Revolution" of 1954 was made possible in part by the organization of the militant International Longshoremen's and Warehousemen's Union (ILWU), which had won a string of significant organizing victories in the plantations and docks after World War II. However, the nisei veterans joined the anti-communist witch hunts of the late 1940s and early 1950s to drive radical voices out of the movement.[13] Matsuo Takabuki, a nisei veteran who became one of the most influential men of the postwar era, recalls in his memoirs, "The Burns group and I worked with my 442nd and 100th Battalion friends to take over these precincts from the ILWU faction."[14]

The sweeping reforms promised by the Democrats reaffirmed colonial American values—assimilation, individualism, and middle-class aspirations of material wealth, status, and power. George Cooper and Gavan Daws observe that "the vast majority of Hawaii's elected Democrats turned out not to be revolutionaries, but just practical politicians with an eye to bringing some new social groups into positions of relative affluence and influence."[15] Takabuki himself admits, "Our social and economic goals were not revolutionary. We wanted to accelerate the changes that had begun during the war, not destroy the system."[16] The new Democrats saw statehood as the ticket to "first-class citizenship."

The Cold War brought massive military expenditures to Hawaiʻi, and this, coupled with the expansion of corporate tourism, ushered in a period of unparalleled economic growth. As Cooper and Daws observe, the Democrats rose to power in "the biggest boom in Hawaii's history."[17] In their rise to power, the Democratic leadership in Hawaiʻi forged a new partnership with the military. Looking to modernize Hawaiʻi's economy but lacking the capital to do so, the young Democrats "embraced defense spending as a welcome alternative" to the plantation economy.[18] By the 1940s military spending had overtaken sugar and pineapple to become the largest source of revenue for the islands. Democrats sought to leverage their influence to maximize the benefit from these expenditures and maneuvered themselves into key congressional posts where they would have influence in military appropriations.[19]

As Haunani-Kay Trask, a professor of Hawaiian studies and an activist, writes,

> For our Native people, Asian success proves to be but the latest elaboration of foreign hegemony. The history of our colonization becomes a twice-told tale, first of discovery and settlement by European and American businessmen and missionaries, then of the plantation Japanese, Chinese, and eventually Filipino rise to dominance in the islands. . . . As a people, Hawaiians remain a politically subordinated group suffering all the legacies of conquest: landlessness, disastrous health, diaspora, institutionalization in the military and prisons, poor educational attainment, and confinement to the service sector of employment.[20]

The State of Militarized Hawaiʻi

Today, despite some military "downsizing," Hawaiʻi remains one of the most highly militarized places on the planet, a "linchpin" of U.S. empire in the Asia-Pacific region. The military controls 205,925 acres, or roughly 5 percent, of the total land in Hawaiʻi,[21] down from a peak of 600,000 acres in 1944.[22] On Oʻahu, the most densely populated island, the military controls 85,718 acres out of 382,148 acres, or 22.4 percent of the island. The military also controls vast Defensive Sea Areas—submerged lands in Kāneʻohe Bay, from Pearl Harbor to Koko Head and off the west shore of Kauaʻi.[23] Throughout the archipelago, the combined armed services have twenty-one installations, twenty-six housing complexes, eight training areas, and nineteen miscellaneous bases and operating stations.[24]

The U.S. Pacific Command (USPACOM) has 300,000 military personnel in the theater (one-fifth of the total U.S. active-duty military force), including 100,000 forward-deployed troops in the western Pacific.[25] In 2000 there were 33,930 armed forces and 50,804 military dependents stationed in Hawai'i. Combined with the 112,000 veterans living in Hawai'i, the military population totaled 196,734, or 16 percent of Hawai'i's total population of 1,211,537.[26] Today the military is the second largest "industry" in Hawai'i behind tourism, with expenditures totaling approximately $4.39 billion, or 9.8 percent of the gross state product.

The Department of Defense is currently undergoing a series of dramatic changes that will have an impact on the future of the military in Hawai'i. Technological advances have brought about what some military commentators have termed a "Revolution in Military Affairs (RMA)." The Bush administration military strategy embraces these changes, focusing on high-tech weapons systems, such as missile defense, leaner and more mobile force structures, and a nuclear posture that relies on the threat of nuclear first-strike. At the same time, the administration is willing to close bases and reduce troops in order to afford these expensive new weapons.

Hawai'i's congressional delegation has consistently supported the expansion of military troops and infrastructure. Recently the army embarked on a multiphase "transformation" to reconfigure its war-fighting capabilities for future conflicts. As part of this transformation, the army proposed the largest expansion in Hawai'i since World War II.[27] However, the military expansion in Hawai'i runs counter to the national military trend.[28] Selection of Hawai'i as one of six sites to receive an Interim Brigade Combat Team is a reflection of the political clout of Hawai'i's congressional delegation and their relationship to Kaua'i-born Army Chief of Staff General Eric Shinseki, who was a key proponent of the Stryker Brigade concept.

"Just the Way Things Are"

The military maintains its hegemony in Hawai'i through a complex and diffuse network of power and persuasion that has yet to be thoroughly analyzed. It has been able to mask its imperial function by infiltrating civilian institutions (schools, universities, corporations, local government, media, tourism, charities, religious institutions) and managing public discourse. Furthermore, economic dependency keeps the military tightly enmeshed in the social fabric of Hawai'i.

Enloe observes that "militarization is such a pervasive process, and thus so hard to uproot, precisely because in its everyday forms it scarcely looks life threatening."[29] Moreover, Ferguson and Turnbull write, "The narratives of naturalization imbricate military institutions and discourses into daily life so that they become 'just the way things are.' The narratives of reassurance kick in with a more prescriptive tone, marking the military presence in Hawai'i as necessary, productive, heroic, desirable, good." [30]

Flashpoints between the community and the military provide glimpses of what militarism looks like, how it functions, and how it can be challenged in Hawai'i. The following sections review some of the significant impacts and sources of conflict between the military and Kānaka Maoli: land, environment, and cultural survival.

Impacts: Militarizing the ʻĀina

Land is a central and continuing source of conflict between the military and Kānaka Maoli. The militarization of land has resulted in the alienation of Kānaka Maoli from their ancestral lands; the loss of subsistence and cultural resources; and the contamination of the air, land, and water with toxic waste, unexploded ordnance, and radiation. At its root, the conflict between Kānaka Maoli and the military over land involves a fundamental clash between the Kanaka Maoli relationship to a living ʻāina (literally "that which feeds") and the Euro-American concept of "land" as flat and lifeless real estate.

In the Kanaka Maoli cosmology, the ʻāina is the physical manifestation of the union between Papahānaumoku (Papa who gives birth to islands), the Earth Mother, and Wākea, the Sky Father. As an ancestor of humans, the ʻāina could not be owned or sold. Lilikalā Kameʻeleihiwa writes that "the 'modern' concepts of aloha ʻĀina, or love of the Land, and Mālama ʻĀina, or serving and caring for the Land, stem from the traditional model established at the time of Wākea." [31]

Militarization greatly accelerated the dispossession of Hawaiian lands. In 1898 the U.S. seized nearly 1.8 million acres of former national and crown lands of the Kingdom of Hawai'i. Existing in a kind of legal limbo, these so-called "ceded lands" are held in a quasi-trust status by the federal government and the State. In 1959, when Hawai'i was admitted as a state, the military retained control of approximately 180,000 acres of "ceded lands," while the rest reverted to the State as trustee.[32] Approximately 30,000 acres that were returned to the State were immediately leased back to the military for sixty-five years.[33] In most cases the rent paid by the military was one dollar for the term of the lease. Today 54 percent of military-held land, approximately 112,173 acres, is so-called "ceded land," commonly understood by Kānaka Maoli to be stolen land.

The military also illegally seized Hawaiian Home Lands.[34] In 1983 a federal-state task force concluded that 13,580 acres of Hawaiian Home Lands were improperly withdrawn through presidential executive orders. Of these improperly transferred lands, 1,356 acres in Lualualei, which could have supported four thousand housing units, were removed from the Hawaiian Home Lands inventory by the navy for its ammunitions storage and radio communications complex. Homestead lands were also improperly withdrawn for military training in Humuʻula, Hawaiʻi, and for munitions storage in Waimea, Kauaʻi.[35] In a 1999 land-swap agreement between the state and federal governments to settle the improper transfer, the Department of Hawaiian Home Lands received 580 acres at Barbers Point in exchange for the land at Lualualei.[36]

Other lands in Hawaiʻi were seized by the military through condemnation, a practice that peaked during World War II. Citizens filed lawsuits to prevent the taking of land or to obtain adequate compensation for lands near Pearl Harbor and in Lualualei, Kāneʻohe, Kahoʻolawe, Waikāne, and elsewhere, usually unsuccessfully.

Impacts: Cultural Genocide

Land alienation, a form of colonial violence, has contributed to the cultural decline of Kānaka Maoli by not only severing the genealogical ties between Kānaka Maoli and the ʻāina, but also by disrupting their ability to practice and transmit their culture to future generations. The violence continued as the military transformed the land, destroying or altering natural and cultural resources and blocking access to military-controlled areas. In the process they destroyed or disrupted Kanaka Maoli means of food production (fishing areas, fishponds, and agricultural systems for kalo, or taro, and ʻuala, or sweet potato), natural resource acquisition (forests, minerals, medicinal and spiritual plants), and use of cultural sites (religious sites, burials, sacred features of the landscape).

Statistics illustrate the legacy of colonization: Kānaka Maoli have the highest rates of homelessness, poverty, disease, and crime.[37] They have the lowest educational achievement and life expectancy.[38] Kānaka Maoli make up 36.5 percent of persons incarcerated for felony charges.[39]

By facilitating population transfer of Americans to Hawaiʻi, the military has also had a profound impact on Hawaiʻi's culture and political demographics. In 2000 the military population, including dependents and veterans, reached 16 percent of Hawaiʻi's population, nearly eclipsing the Kanaka Maoli population of 239,655, or 19 percent of the total population.[40]

The flood of settlers stripped Kānaka Maoli of their political sovereignty, land, and cultural rights, in many ways resembling the population crises of other occupied nations, such as Tibet, East Timor, and Palestine, where the colonizer uses systematic population transfer as a policy of conquest and occupation. Economic pressures and cultural and political displacement result in nearly one-third of Kānaka Maoli living in diaspora.

Impacts: Environmental Assault

In Hawai'i the military has left a trail of environmental disasters, the full extent of which is yet to be fully comprehended. *The Military Contamination and Cleanup Atlas for the United States—1995* identified 405 military-contaminated sites designated for cleanup in Hawai'i, 6 of which are listed as "superfund" sites (highly contaminated sites that receive priority funding for cleanup). The report does not include Johnston Island, Waikāne Valley, Kaho'olawe, or Mākua nor the dozens of forgotten military training areas and camps that have not yet been designated for cleanup. The cost for cleanup of all the polluted sites in Hawai'i would run into the billions of dollars.[41]

Some examples of the military's environmental impacts include jet fuel, oil, and organic solvents in the soil and groundwater at Pearl Harbor, Hickam Air Force Base, and other military sites; PCBs at numerous military bases; radioactive waste;[42] the destruction of native ecosystems by live-fire training; unexploded ordnance; high-powered radio facilities emitting electromagnetic radiation; sonar tests that harm marine mammals;[43] and nerve-gas testing and disposal.[44]

Kānaka Maoli, recently immigrated Asians and Pacific Islanders, and low-income communities face the greatest threat from the military's environmental assault. Many Asians and Pacific Islanders subsist on fish and shellfish from Pearl Harbor's contaminated waters. The Wai'anae District, with the largest concentration of Kānaka Maoli and some of the worst health, economic, and social statistics in Hawai'i, bears the burden of the Lualualei Naval Magazine and Radio Facility and Mākua Military Reservation, which occupy a full third of the land in Wai'anae.

Kīpuka of Resistance

Despite the intense level of militarization in Hawai'i, Kānaka Maoli and local people continued to resist military intrusions and disruptions. The complete history of this resistance is yet to be written. I briefly survey a few examples of resistance from the 1970s to the present.

In the 1970s, as urbanization began to encroach on rural communities, a wave of land struggles erupted. Rural communities in Hawai'i had long held out as pockets of resistance to the forces of capitalism and imperialism, what University of Hawai'i ethnic studies professor Davianna Pōmaika'i McGregor has called "cultural kīpuka."[45]

The struggles that emerged to protect these traditional communities from urbanization were also kīpuka for the formation of social movements. Communities began to resist, aided by young local activists who took inspiration from the civil rights, antiwar, and national liberation movements of the 1950s through the 1970s. Kanaka Maoli activism was also influenced by Native American occupations of Alcatraz Island and Wounded Knee. The land struggles that erupted in the 1970s—such as those at Kalama Valley and Waiāhole—sowed seeds of leadership, inspiration, strategy, and momentum for other struggles to take root and grow. Various strands of the movement came together in the effort to free Kaho'olawe from military occupation and destruction, which in turn kindled other struggles and helped give birth to the modern Hawaiian sovereignty movement.

Kaho'olawe: Aloha 'Āina

Kaho'olawe, also known as Ko Hema Lamalama o Kanaloa,[46] is the smallest of the major islands in the Hawaiian archipelago, measuring approximately 28,000 acres. The island is sacred to Kānaka Maoli and considered to be kinolau (multiple physical forms; an embodiment) of Kanaloa, god of the sea. Inhabited for more than a thousand years, Kaho'olawe contains some of the richest and most intact cultural sites in Hawai'i.

The navy began bombing Kaho'olawe in 1940. With the declaration of martial law in 1941, the entire island was taken over by the navy. From 1941 to 1967 the island and its surrounding waters were off limits to the public. In 1952 an executive order by President Dwight Eisenhower gave the navy formal jurisdiction over Kaho'olawe but stipulated that the navy was to rehabilitate the island and return it to the public in a "reasonably safe" condition when no longer needed by the military.

In 1969 protests ensued when a five-hundred-pound bomb was found over seven miles across the channel on Maui land leased to then Maui mayor Elmer Carvalho. In 1971 Carvalho and the environmental group Life of the Land sued to stop the bombing and sought an environmental impact statement (EIS) for the navy's use of the island. The navy released a hastily prepared EIS in 1972, and the lawsuit was dismissed.

The Hawai'i State Senate passed a resolution requesting that the navy immediately look for alternatives to the bombing in 1974. The legislature issued a report in 1978 dismissing the military's claim that Kaho'olawe was irreplaceable.

Hawaiian activists, many of whom had gained experience in other land struggles, felt that it was time to take back Kaho'olawe. On January 4, 1976, the Protect Kaho'olawe Association (later renamed the Protect Kaho'olawe 'Ohana or PKO) staged the first in a series of bold land occupations of Kaho'olawe during scheduled naval exercises to protest the bombing and to assert Kanaka Maoli cultural rights. The protest was organized by the Aloha Association. While the navy apprehended most of the thirty-five protesters who attempted to make the crossing from Maui, nine managed to get on the island. They included George Helm, Walter Ritte Jr., and Dr. Emmett Aluli of the Moloka'i group Hui Alaloa; Kawaipuna Prejean and Stephen Morse of the Hawaiian Coalition for Native Claims; Ian Lind of the American Friends Service Committee; Ellen Miles; Kimo Aluli; and Karla Villalba. The Coast Guard captured seven of the nine within a few hours, but Ritte and Aluli eluded the military for two days before turning themselves in.[47]

The PKO planned to complete five landings symbolizing the five fingers of limahana (the working hand). The completion of the five landings symbolized the completion of the tasks and laulima (many hands working together).[48] In the ensuing acts of civil resistance, many activists were arrested. These actions led to a cultural and spiritual awakening and a deepening of political conviction for all who were involved.

Kaho'olawe became a lens for the movement that brought into focus the issues and dynamics of U.S. occupation. In January 1977 George Helm wrote about the reasons for the fourth occupation of Kaho'olawe: "Call me a radical for I refuse to remain idle. I will not have the foreigner prostitute the soul of my being, and I will not make a whore out of my soul (my culture)."[49] During the occupation Helm wrote in his diary, "The occupation of the military reservation is not so much a defiance as it is a responsibility to express our legitimate concern for the land of the Hawaiian. . . . We are against warfare but more so against imperialism."[50]

That same year that protests began the PKO filed a lawsuit against the navy alleging violations of environmental and cultural preservation laws as well as Kanaka Maoli religious freedom. In February 1977 Judge Samuel King denied two requests, one by the PKO and one by the Maui County Council, to issue temporary restraining orders against navy bombing. Later that year the PKO won a court victory when federal judge Richard Wong ruled that the navy violated both the National Environmental Policy Act (NEPA) and an executive order that required the preservation of historic sites. The navy was ordered to redo its 1972 EIS but was allowed to continue training.

As the movement spread, local and international solidarity became an important element of the campaign to stop the bombing. Hawaiian organizations, unions, religious organizations, and even the state government adopted resolutions calling for an end to the bombing. The Nuclear Free and Independent Pacific movement pressured foreign governments to withdraw from joint military exercises on Kaho'olawe. In 1984 Japan withdrew from RIMPAC exercises.[51] Delegations from the PKO also visited Culebra and Vieques in Puerto Rico to learn from and lend support to struggles there to end military destruction of their islands.

In 1977 two young activists "disappeared" crossing the channel between

Kaho'olawe and Maui: George Helm, the charismatic president of the PKO and a musician, and Kimo Mitchell, a commercial fisherman and National Park Service ranger. Their deaths fueled a sense of urgency and deepened convictions in the movement as it generated wider public support.

The PKO lawsuit led to a 1980 consent decree that limited navy training on the island, mandated unexploded ordnance cleanup from one-third of the island, and allowed PKO to have regular access to the island. Following the consent decree, the entire island was placed on the National Register of Historic Places in January 1981. Archaeologists had discovered a wealth of prehistoric sites, which confirmed the cultural and spiritual significance of the island.

The consent decree was controversial within the PKO movement. Supporters of the consent decree argued that the agreement was necessary for Kānaka Maoli to exercise their culture. Critics countered that the agreement compromised fundamental principles and weakened the movement politically.

The PKO continued to press for an end to the bombing. Under the consent decree the PKO organized cultural accesses to the island at least six times a year. Although the navy argued that the island was essential to national security, they eventually lost interest in Kaho'olawe. In what was largely seen as a political move to boost the sagging election campaign of Hawai'i Republican congressional candidate Pat Saiki, in 1990 President George H.W. Bush issued an executive order discontinuing the bombing of Kaho'olawe. Saiki lost the election, but the bombs were finally silenced.

In November 1990 Congress enacted Senate Bill 3088, which established the Kaho'olawe Island Conveyance Commission to recommend the terms for returning the island to the State. In 1993 a state law created the Kaho'olawe Island Reserve Commission (KIRC) to oversee cleanup, restoration, and resource management of a Kaho'olawe cultural reserve. This statute also specified that the island would eventually be transferred to a Native Hawaiian nation upon gaining recognition from the U.S. government. Title X of the fiscal year 1994 Department of Defense Appropriations Act transferred Kaho'olawe to the State and appropriated $400 million to clean up and restore the island. Unlike base cleanup projects that were conducted under the Base Realignment and Closure Act or other federal environmental laws, the Kaho'olawe cleanup authorized and funded as a special project the largest unexploded ordnance (UXO) removal effort ever attempted.

In 1998 the Navy began to clean up unexploded ordnance. In *Memorandum of Understanding between the Navy and State of Hawai'i*, the Navy agreed to the "removal or clearance of all unexploded ordnance from the surface of the island."[52] The navy was to clear another 25 percent of the island to a depth that would allow "reasonably safe use." However, in 2000 the navy reported that it would not be able to meet these goals. When the cleanup operation wrapped up in 2003, only one-ninth of the island was safe enough for unrestricted human activity. The KIRC and PKO did not pursue legal and political options for holding the federal government accountable for its cleanup obligations.

Kahoʻolawe activists encountered challenges and contradictions to their own success. Victory required them to play politics in order to secure funding for cleanup and restoration, and activists' energies were consumed by administrative and bureaucratic functions of overseeing the restoration and transfer of the island. Nevertheless, the Kahoʻolawe struggle blazed a trail that others would continue.

Sowing Seeds of Resistance

Kahoʻolawe was the first contemporary struggle to directly confront the U.S. military as an imperial force in Hawaiʻi, and it helped to illuminate the contradictions of U.S. occupation and militarism. A few of the struggles against militarism that followed are briefly described below.

Hālawa Valley/H-3 Freeway In 1963 the Oahu Transportation Study called for a trans-Koʻolau freeway. The freeway was justified as a defense highway to connect Kaneohe Marine Corps Air Station (now Marine Corps Base Hawaii) and Pearl Harbor. In the early 1980s the legal challenge by the Stop H-3 Association successfully blocked the route through Moanalua Valley on the basis of cultural and historic preservation laws. The State realigned the project to Hālawa Valley. While the federal court blocked the second route on environmental grounds, in 1984 Senator Inouye succeeded in passing legislation that exempted the H-3 from applicable environmental laws. After a legal challenge by the Office of Hawaiian Affairs, the freeway's path was realigned around an ancient loʻi kalo (taro terrace) on the Kāneʻohe side of the Koʻolau mountains. Kānaka Maoli maintained that the site was connected to Kukui-o-Kāne Heiau, a sacred temple to the god Kāne, but the Bishop Museum disputed their claims. Parts of the heiau were destroyed.

On the leeward side, in Hālawa Valley, the freeway bisected an entire religious site complex, dividing the men's heiau from the women's heiau—Hale-o-Papa. In April 1992 a group of women started an encampment to protect Hale-o-Papa until their eviction in August of that year. Later that same year, in a demonstration organized by the Hālawa Coalition, thirteen people were arrested for blocking cement trucks entering Hālawa Valley, at a cost of more than $200,000 to the State.[53] After a thirty-seven-year struggle, H-3 was completed at a cost of $1.3 billion, or $80 million a mile, which, according to some, made it mile for mile the most expensive roadway ever built. At the inaugural Trans-Koʻolau Run, protesters urged runners to abandon the route. A group of Kānaka Maoli and supporters have continued to mālama (care for) the sites at Hale-o-Papa.[54]

Nohili/Pacific Missile Range Facility In the early 1990s the army sought to utilize the navy's Pacific Missile Range Facility (PMRF) on west Kaua'i for Strategic Target System (STARS) missile launches. The Nohili Coalition, Hawai'i Ecumenical Coalition, Sierra Club, and others vigorously opposed the launches, citing the threat to endangered species, the possibility of explosions, the release of toxic waste products, and the desecration of Kanaka Maoli cultural sites. The sandy dunes of west Kaua'i are known to be an ancient burial place for Kānaka Maoli. Despite successful efforts by the community to force the army to do an EIS, launches commenced in 1993. During the first launch, twenty-one persons were arrested for civil resistance. Fourteen more were arrested for climbing the fence of the base during the second launch. Although the STARS program was de-funded by President Bill Clinton in 1996, a new threat emerged in 1997—the Theater Missile Defense program. The navy sought to expand its launch and tracking facilities into Ni'ihau and other Northwest Hawaiian Islands. Although expansion into Ni'ihau has been halted due to disagreements between the State and the owners of Ni'ihau over environmental laws, missile defense testing has accelerated under the Bush administration. Since the terrorist attacks on the World Trade Center and the Pentagon on September 11, 2001, the military has permanently restricted public access to the prime fishing, surfing, and recreation beaches near the PMRF.

Waikāne/Marine Corps Waikāne in the Ko'olaupoko District of O'ahu is rich in lore,[55] sacred sites, and traditional lo'i kalo (taro fields). In 1899 Lincoln McCandless acquired land in Waikāne and built a tunnel through the Ko'olau mountains in order to sell water to central O'ahu sugar growers. During World War II the army took control of 1,061 acres in Waikāne and adjoining Waiāhole to be used for training and bombing. The McCandless heirs granted the government a lease that was extended after the war and assumed by the Marine Corps in 1953. The McCandless heirs also gave a 187-acre parcel to the Kamaka family to settle a disputed land title.

In 1975 the Kamaka family and the McCandless heirs gave the marines notice to vacate, which they did on July 1, 1976. The Kamaka family farmed the land between 1976 to 1983, not knowing that it was contaminated with unexploded ordnance; the marines had told them it was clean. In the original lease, the military had agreed to clean the land before vacating. However, in 1989 the Marine Corps instead condemned the land and fenced it off. The Kamaka family lost their land, and Waikāne remains "off limits."

Pōhakuloa Pōhakuloa on the island of Hawai'i is located high on the "saddle" between Mauna Kea, Mauna Loa, and Hualalai. The military established the Pōhakuloa Training Area (PTA) in 1956. Encompassing 116,341 acres, 84,815 acres of which are "ceded lands," the PTA is the largest U.S. military training area in Hawai'i and the largest outside the continental United States. The army has identified 150 sites and 1,000 archaeological features within the PTA. It is the home to twenty-one endangered species of plants and animals, one of the highest concentrations of endangered species of any army installation in the world.

The military conducts major training activities, including bombing and artillery training, on twenty-three ranges. In 1981 Aloha 'Āina Life Education Center, Greenpeace–Hawai'i Island, and the Fund for Animals–Hawai'i Island sued the army to halt training for failing to comply with environmental laws.[56] The suit, however, was dismissed.[57] In 1993 activists protested Japan's Ground Self-Defense Force training at Pōhakuloa. Houseless Kānaka Maoli joined the protest, pointing out the fact that Kānaka Maoli die waiting for homes while the military bombed Hawaiian Home Lands. The army proposes to acquire another 23,000 acres under its transformation program.

Imua, Ke Ola Pono o Mākua (Go Forward in Justice, Mākua) In the 1970s Kanaka Maoli activists carried the inspiration of the Kaho'olawe movement to Mākua Valley. Today, Wai'anae groups continue the struggle to free Mākua.

Mākua, which means "parents" in Hawaiian, is believed to be one place where Wākea (Sky Father) and Papahānaumoku (Earth Mother) came together to create life on earth. Kānaka Maoli consider Mākua to be part of a large wahi pana (sacred area) extending from Kea'au around Ka'ena to Kawaihāpai. At Ka'ena, the westernmost tip of the island, is a leina-a-ka-'uhane (soul's leap), a large rock where souls of the dead are believed to leap into the spirit realm. Mākua is rich in mo'olelo ka'ao (historical accounts). The great cave Kāneana was once a home for the demigod Māui and his mother Hina.[58] One tale tells of a shark-man, Nanaue, who lived in Kāneana cave. He would enter the sea through an undersea passage and meet with the female mo'o (lizard/dragon spirit) of Ko'iahi Stream who would come down to the sea during heavy rains. The two would turn into beautiful human forms and make love on Pōhaku-kū-la'i-la'i in the crashing surf.[59]

Another mo'olelo ka'ao about Hi'iaka-i-ka-poli-o-Pele and her sister Pele, the volcano goddess, recounts the adventures and miraculous deeds of Hi'iaka in the Mākua vicinity. In what could be read as an allegory for the present struggle in Mākua, Hi'iaka restored the life of a Mākua girl who was killed by an evil, invading kūpua (supernatural spirit). Hi'iaka fought and defeated the intruder, who had killed the girl because she refused his advances. Hi'iaka then taught the girl's parents to use medicinal forest plants of Mākua to heal their daughter.[60]

The valley contains at least three documented heiau sites and numerous other ancient sites, while the beach contains many burials. Waters offshore have always been important fishing grounds. Mākua also contains critical habitat for numerous native species, including over forty endangered species, some of which are found nowhere else in the world.

The military first began using a small area in Mākua Valley for a gun emplacement in 1929. Troop maneuvers were conducted at Mākua through the 1930s.

In December 1941, with the outbreak of World War II and the imposition of martial law, the military took control of the entire western tip of Oʻahu, including Mākua. By June 1942 the remaining private citizens were ordered to leave, and their lands condemned. In May 1943, at the request of the secretary of war, the Territorial government issued the army a revocable permit for the "duration of the present war and six months thereafter."[61] The permit stipulated that the army must restore the valley to "satisfactory" condition at the expiration of the permit.

The evictions and destruction of the community traumatized Mākua residents. Mākua native Walter Kamana recalls, "I was small, used to run when the plane come in. The plane had no respect for people living in the valley. Only had one small church. You ever seen your church get bombed one Sunday? I seen that, small boy. I seen my church get taken away by a bomb."[62]

After World War II, a decades-long struggle ensued between the army and the Territorial government over control of Mākua. In 1964, over the objections of Hawaiʻi's Governor John A. Burns, President Lyndon Johnson signed Executive Order 11166 designating 3,236 acres of the valley as a training facility.[63] The State leased an additional 1,515 acres to the army for sixty-five years for a mere dollar.

The military used Mākua for a wide variety of military training. The valley was bombed and strafed from the air, bombarded by battleships, invaded by amphibious assault teams, pounded by mortars, howitzers, and rockets, and burned with napalm. In the 1960s a man scavenging for scrap metal was killed.[64] The explosions, uncontrolled dumping of waste, and leakage from unexploded ordnance have released tons of toxic chemicals that contaminate the soil and groundwater.

Fires, of which there have been more than 270 over the last ten years, have caused serious harm to endangered species and human settlements. In 1970 the army allowed a fire to burn overnight before the State Forestry Division was notified. The blaze went out of control and moved toward Kaʻena and Kuaokalā. It burned 1,525 acres before rains extinguished the fire two days later. State forester Herbert Kikukawa wrote to the army that the 1970 fire "converted the entire valley floor from dryland forest to a dense stand of highly flammable grass."[65] In 1995 another fire scorched over half of the valley's 4,700 acres and burned the shelters of families living across the highway, and in 2003 shifting winds ignited a wildfire that scorched over 2,000 acres and killed several populations of endangered plant species.

Kānaka Maoli continued to use and live on Mākua Beach during the years of military occupation despite periodic harassment by the police and state authorities. In 1965, when the Mirisch Corporation filmed the motion picture *Hawaii* in Mākua Valley, the State issued an order to evict Mākua beach residents.[66] Before long, Kānaka Maoli had resettled the beach.[67]

In the 1970s Hawaiian activists made conscious efforts to link the movements for Kahoʻolawe and Mākua. Members of the Protect Kahoʻolawe ʻOhana discussed strategy at Mākua beach. Walter Ritte is quoted as having said, "Once we unite behind Kahoolawe, we can move to the next problem."[68] In 1976 the Mākua Valley Reclamation and Restoration Association, the Hawaiian Coalition of Native Claims, and the Nānākuli-Waiʻanae Community Association organized a large rally at Mākua in solidarity with activists who were then occupying Kahoʻolawe.[69] Protesters defied the military fence and marched into the valley. For many, it was the first time seeing the devastation of the ʻāina.

When Hurricane Iwa struck in November 1982, forty families were displaced from Mākua beach. As the families attempted to rebuild their village, the State blocked resettlement. Mākua residents and supporters formed the Kōkua Mākua ʻOhana to rebuild and resettle Mākua beach. Hundreds rallied at Mākua to support the right for beach residents to live a traditional lifestyle.[70] On January 22, 1983, as residents began to rebuild their homes, the state arrested six persons for "obstructing governmental operations." Refusing to stand for the judge or recognize the jurisdiction of the State court, the defendants said that because of the illegality of the military overthrow of 1893, the U.S. did not have title to the lands of Hawaiʻi.[71]

In 1992 the army applied for a permit to operate an Open Burn/Open Detonation (OB/OD) site in Mākua, which would have increased the amount of hazardous waste disposed there. Unbeknownst to the community until then, the army had conducted OB/OD activities in Mākua for many years without a permit. An Environmental Protection Agency (EPA) study documented that up to 2,500 tons of ammunition have been destroyed in a single year, with an average of 560 tons destroyed per year.[72] The community strongly opposed the OB/OD activities and forced the army to drop its plans and close the OB/OD site. The newly formed grassroots environmental justice group Mālama Mākua demanded that the army do an EIS for all of its activities in Mākua.

Meanwhile, the beach community at Mākua had grown to nearly two hundred people. Mākua had become their puʻuhonua (refuge) for families who had been ravaged by the Western system and whose broken lives and families were healed by the ʻāina. However, in 1996 beach residents were forced to organize the Mākua Council to fight yet another eviction. Despite numerous rallies and growing community support, on June 16 of that year hundreds of police invaded Mākua, cutting off media access to the scene and evicting the last residents from the beach. Some residents torched their homes in defiance. Sixteen persons were arrested and eleven later convicted for "trespassing." The standoff with the beach community was a glaring example of the contradiction between the landlessness and poverty of Kānaka Maoli and the military occupation of Hawaiian lands.[73]

Although the occupation of Mākua beach ended, confrontations over training continued. On Easter morning in 1997, the Hawai'i Ecumenical Coalition and Mālama Mākua led a sunrise service on the shore, blocking a Marine Corps amphibious landing scheduled for that day. That victory has been commemorated every Easter in a sunrise service at Mākua. In September 1997 the marines again planned to hold an amphibious landing at Mākua. This time they announced their plans only days after thousands of mourners had gathered at Mākua beach to memorialize beloved Hawaiian musician Israel Kamakawiwo'ole, who once lived at Mākua beach and whose ashes were scattered in its waters.

Outraged at the military's arrogance, the community prepared for a confrontation. Religious structures were defiantly built in the path of the invading troops. A paepae (foundation platform) was dedicated to Papahonua and symbolized the new foundation for a community in Mākua. Another kuahu (shrine) was dedicated to Kanaloa, god of the sea, and linked Mākua spiritually to Kaho'olawe.

As tensions mounted and calls for civil disobedience went out in the community, Admiral Joseph Prueher, commander in chief, Pacific Command, held an unprecedented meeting with community leaders at his headquarters in Camp Smith. The marines backed down and moved their amphibious landing to Bellows Air Force Station in Waimānalo, where their convoy was also protested.

In 1998 a lawsuit filed by Mālama Mākua and Earthjustice renewed the call for an EIS as required by the NEPA. The army suspended training in Mākua. At first the army refused to do an EIS, claiming that its training had "no significant impact." Later they reached a settlement with Mālama Mākua to suspend training until completing a study that was "compliant with" the NEPA.

In 2000 the army released a flawed and incomplete environmental assessment (EA), which the community rejected. A coalition of groups, Hui Mālama o Mākua, mobilized support for the protection of the valley. The Hui organized numerous meetings, demonstrations, and a petition drive to raise awareness about the army's impacts on Mākua and its implications for community health, cultural preservation, and the environment.

On January 27, 2001, over five hundred people packed a twelve-hour public hearing to testify about the enduring harm of the army's activities in Mākua. The community gave impassioned testimony about family deaths and the high number of cancer cases in Wai'anae, the hazardous waste dumped at Mākua, and the loss of subsistence resources and cultural sites. In all, over fifteen hundred persons testified in support of protecting Mākua.[74]

The army still maintained that its EA was adequate. Mālama Mākua challenged the EA in court and won a preliminary injunction against training until the case could be heard. At that point the community had halted military training in Mākua for three years.

The terrorist attacks on the World Trade Center and the Pentagon on September 11, 2001, changed the political landscape for the Mākua struggle. Evoking "national security" concerns, the army threatened to petition the court for an immediate return to training. Activists knew that the climate of jingoism immediately following the 9/11 attacks would work against their movement in the courts and in public opinion. Mālama Mākua decided to settle the NEPA lawsuit in order to secure certain gains and get a foothold in the valley that would give them leverage in the future. Under the settlement the army was required to complete an EIS within three years, clean UXO from approximately a third of the valley surface, and allow cultural access at least twice a month. The settlement also limited the number of days the army could train. The agreement, like the Kahoʻolawe consent decree, was controversial.

Regaining access to the valley has proven to be vital for cultural restoration and organizing. In December 2001 Nā ʻOhana o Mākua held the first Makahiki ceremonies inside Mākua Valley in perhaps 160 years, signaling the return of Lono and peace to the valley.[75] Since regaining access, hundreds of people have been able to enter and witness the beauty of Mākua and the horror of the military's destructive activities. At the closing of Makahiki season in Mākua, participants chanted:

E iho ana o luna	That which is above shall be brought down
E piʻi ana o lalo	That which is below shall be lifted up
E hui ana nā moku	The islands shall be united
E kū ana ka paia	The walls (nation) shall stand upright
Imua, ke ola pono o Mākua!	Go forward, the pono life (justice) for Mākua![76]

And so the struggle continues.

Conclusion

The attacks on the World Trade Center and the Pentagon on September 11, 2001, signaled the beginning of a new era. Under the pretext of fighting a war on terror, the United States has made an unprecedented bid for global dominance, from the highest reaches of space to the electronic frontiers of cyberspace. The military budget for 2003 reached an astonishing $400 billion, an increase of 30 percent over the previous year's budget. The proposed increase of $48 billion alone is greater than the military budget of every other nation in the world.[77]

However, the 9/11 attacks also revealed a great lie of militarism—that military might equals security. The accelerated pace of globalization and its disruptions and the free flow of ideas and people, as well as resistance it enables, cannot be contained by military force. The new wave of militarization will make its inherent contradictions more pronounced and the world less secure. These sites of potential conflict provide opportunities for intervention and positive social change.

The U.S. military in Hawai'i is mighty but not invincible. Many scholars now argue that the United States is in an unsustainable state of imperial overreach. People's movements have successfully challenged the military and made significant changes in Hawai'i. Kānaka Maoli and their concerns for land, culture, and sovereignty are central to demilitarization efforts in Hawai'i. As militarism and capitalism have become fully globalized, resistance to these hegemonic forces has also gone global. There is a growing movement to close and clean up U.S. military bases in Okinawa, Korea, the Philippines, Guam, Vieques/Puerto Rico, Diego Garcia, Greenland, Germany, Great Britain, and in various locations within the United States. Progressive forces in Hawai'i have joined these networks.[78]

This nascent international/global movement proclaims a radical new vision for the world where genuine security is based on human needs, human dignity, cultural integrity, environmental preservation, and global solidarity. In June 2000 the International Women's Summit to Redefine Security concluded that "military security is a contradiction in terms. The present militarized international security system is maintained at the expense of the natural environment, the economic and social needs of many people, and fundamental human rights. This is a price we refuse to pay."[79]

It is a price Hawai'i cannot afford.

Notes

1. See Gavan Daws, *Shoal of Time: A History of the Hawaiian Islands* (Honolulu: University of Hawai'i Press, 1968). Also Noel Kent, *Hawaii: Islands under the Influence* (New York: Monthly Review Press, 1983).

2. Ian Lind, "Ring of Steel: Notes on the Militarization of Hawaii," *Social Process in Hawaii* 31 (1984/1985): 25–47.

3. Kathy Ferguson and Phyllis Turnbull, *Oh, Say, Can You See? The Semiotics of the Military in Hawai'i* (Minneapolis: University of Minnesota Press, 1999), xiii–xviii.

4. Lind, "Ring of Steel," 27.

5. Lind, "Ring of Steel," 27.

6. "Kanaka Maoli" will be used as an adjective to denote ideas, concepts, and things "Hawaiian." "Kānaka Maoli" with the kahakō, or macron, will be used to refer to the plural noun "Hawaiian peoples."

7. Brian McAllister Linn, *Guardians of Empire: The U.S. Army and the Pacific, 1902–1940* (Chapel Hill: University of North Carolina Press, 1997), 6.

8. The infamous "Bayonet Constitution" was never ratified by the people. It effectively shifted power to the white foreigners, barred Asian immigrants from voting and imposed property and income requirements for voting, which resulted in the disenfranchisement of the majority of Kānaka Maoli.

9. General Macomb, quoted in Lind, "Ring of Steel," 25.

10. See J. Garner Anthony, *Hawaii under Army Rule* (Honolulu: University of Hawai'i Press, 1955).

11. Gary Okihiro, *Cane Fires: The Anti-Japanese Movement in Hawaii, 1865–1945* (Philadelphia: Temple University Press, 1991), 201.

12. Lind, "Ring of Steel," 36–37.

13. Sanford Zalburg, *A Spark Is Struck! Jack Hall and the ILWU in Hawaii* (Honolulu: University of Hawai'i Press, 1979).

14. Matsuo Takabuki, *An Unlikely Revolutionary: Matsuo Takabuki and the Making of Modern Hawai'i* (Honolulu: University of Hawai'i Press, 1998), 66.

15. George Cooper and Gavan Daws, *Land and Power in Hawaii: The Democratic Years* (Honolulu: University of Hawai'i Press, 1990), 8.

16. Takabuki, *An Unlikely Revolutionary*, 64.

17. Cooper and Daws, *Land and Power in Hawaii*, 9.

18. Lind, "Ring of Steel," 17.

19. Currently, Senator Inouye is the co-chair of the powerful Defense Appropriations Committee; Senator Akaka is the ranking member of the Armed Services Committee; and Representative Abercrombie sits on the House Armed Services Committee and the Readiness Subcommittee and Tactical Air and Land Forces Subcommittee.

20. Haunani-Kay Trask, "Settlers of Color and 'Immigrant' Hegemony: 'Locals' in Hawai'i," *Amerasia Journal* 26 (2) (2000): 2–3.

21. U.S. Pacific Command, *Hawaii Land Use Master Plan*; U.S. Pacific Command, *Hawaii Military Installations and Training Areas* (Honolulu, 1998).

22. Lind, "Ring of Steel," 36–37.

23. James Albertini et al., *The Dark Side of Paradise: Hawaii in a Nuclear World* (Honolulu: Catholic Action of Hawai'i/Peace Education Project, 1980).

24. U.S. Pacific Command, *Hawaii Military Installations and Training Areas*.

25. U.S. Pacific Command, *Hawaii Military Installations and Training Areas*.

26. State of Hawai'i, Department of Business, Economic Development, and Tourism, *State of Hawai'i Data Book* (Honolulu: State of Hawai'i, 2000).

27. The proposed army transformation in Hawai'i would entail an increase of 480 troops, 400 armored vehicles, 32 construction projects, and the acquisition of 23,000 acres of land on Hawai'i island and 2,000 acres of land on O'ahu. See "Most Recent Public Scoping Meeting Presentation of U.S. Army Transformation in Hawaii" as delivered by Ron Borne at Nānākuli High and Intermediate School, April 30, 2002; William Cole, "Army to Transform on O'ahu," *Honolulu Advertiser*, April 22, 2002, B1.

28. Despite the fact that there has been a Department of Defense moratorium on training land acquisitions since 1990, the army claims it would need 98,000 contiguous acres of maneuver land. The largest contiguous parcel they currently have is 19,000 acres at Pōhakuloa. It defies common sense for the army to expand its land holdings in Hawai'i by 79,000 acres, when much larger military installations are available on the continental

U.S. See Peter J. Offringa, Major General, U.S. Army, Assistant Chief of Engineers, *Memorandum for SEE Distribution, Subject: Major Land Acquisition Moratorium,* DAEN-ZCI-A (405-10), November 30, 1990; 25th ID(L) and U.S. Army, *Hawaii Land Use Requirement Study,* prepared for USARPAC, USARHAW, 1997.

29. Cynthia Enloe, *Maneuvers: The International Politics of Militarizing Women's Lives* (Berkeley: University of California Press, 2000), 3.

30. Ferguson and Turnbull, *Oh, Say, Can You See?* xiii.

31. Lilikalā Kame'eleihiwa, *Native Land and Foreign Desires: Pehea Lā E Pono Ai?* (Honolulu: Bishop Museum Press, 1992), 25.

32. Sheryl Miyahira, "Hawaii's Ceded Lands," *UH Law Review* 3–4 (1981–1982): 101–148.

33. Judy Lee Rohrer, "Hawaii and the Military: The Conflict over Land," unpublished report (Honolulu: American Friends Service Committee Hawai'i Area Program, 1987).

34. Under the Hawaiian Homes Commission Act of 1920, 187,000 acres were set aside for Kanaka Maoli homesteading to "rehabilitate" the race. Kānaka Maoli who met the 50 percent blood quantum requirement were eligible to get homestead leases for a negligible price.

35. Hoaliku Drake, "Statement of Hoaliku Drake, Chair of the Hawaiian Homes Commission," *Hearings Before a Subcommittee of the Committee on Appropriations, United States Senate, One Hundred Third Congress, First Session* (Washington, D.C.: U.S. Government Printing Office, 1993), 193–199.

36. Greg Kakesako, "Lualualei," *Honolulu Star-Bulletin,* December 5, 1998.

37. Forty percent of the homeless or houseless are Kānaka Maoli; 31 percent of Kānaka Maoli receive annual incomes less than $4,000; 32 percent drop out of high school; only 5 percent have college degrees; and approximately 27 percent of welfare recipients are Kanaka Maoli. Office of Hawaiian Affairs, State of Hawai'i, *Native Hawaiian Data Book* (Honolulu: Office of Hawaiian Affairs, 2000), table 5.4. See also David Stannard, "The Hawaiians: Health, Justice, and Sovereignty," and Healani Sonoda, "A Nation Incarcerated," in this volume.

38. Kānaka Maoli have the highest mortality rate, the lowest life expectancy (four years less than all other groups in Hawai'i), the highest cancer mortality rate, the highest stroke mortality rate, the highest diabetes mortality rate, and the highest infant mortality and suicide rates. Kekuni Blaisdell, "The Health Status of the Kānaka Maoli," *Asian American and Pacific Islander Journal of Health* 1 (2) (Autumn 1993).

39. Office of Hawaiian Affairs, *Native Hawaiian Data Book,* table 7.13.

40. *State of Hawai'i Data Book,* tables 10.4, 10.21, 1.03, 1.29.

41. Aimee Houghton and Lenny Siegel, *Military Contamination and Cleanup Atlas for the United States–1995* (San Francisco: Pacific Studies Center and CAREER/PRO, 1995).

42. Cobalt 60, a radioactive waste product from nuclear-powered ships, is found in sediment at Pearl Harbor. Between 1964 and 1978, 4,843,000 gallons of low-level radioactive waste was discharged into Pearl Harbor. Two thousand one hundred eighty-nine steel drums containing radioactive waste were dumped in an ocean disposal area fifty-five miles from Hawai'i. Nadine Scott, "Pearl Harbor Problems with Radioactive Waste," *Honolulu Star-Bulletin,* April 4, 1979.

43. The navy's Low Frequency Active Sonar (LFAS) damages the hearing of whales and

other marine mammals, which can lead to death. The navy conducts sonar tests off Kaua'i, O'ahu, and Hawai'i. Gretel H. Schueller, "Will Navy's New Sonar System Drown Out the Songs of Whales?" *Environment Hawai'i* 12 (2) (August 2001): 6–12.

44. In 1966–1967 the military tested the nerve gas agent GB and incapacitating agent BZ on Hawai'i Island only fourteen miles from Hilo. Albertini et al., *The Dark Side of Paradise*, 19–20.

45. Kīpuka are variations or changes in form. It is commonly used to describe oases of forest that survive lava flows and provide the seeds for the regeneration of life after the flows cool. Davianna Pōmaika'i McGregor writes, "Rural Hawaiian communities are cultural *kīpuka* from which Native Hawaiian culture can be regenerated and revitalized in the contemporary setting. Protection of the natural resources and the integrity of the lifestyle and livelihoods of the Hawaiians in these rural districts is essential to the perpetuation of Hawaiian culture." "An Introduction to the Hoa'āina and Their Rights," *Hawaiian Journal of History* 30 (1996): 14.

46. Ko Hema Lamalama O Kanaloa (Southern Beacon of Kanaloa) is the older name for Kaho'olawe. Some pronounce the name Kohe Mālamalama O Kanaloa (Sacred Refuge of Kanaloa). Noa Emmett Aluli and Davianna Pōmaika'i McGregor, "The Healing of Kaho'olawe," *Hawai'i: Return to Nationhood,* ed. Ulla Hasager and Jonathan Friedman (Copenhagen: International Working Group for Indigenous Affairs, Document no. 75, 1994), 197–208.

47. Rodney Morales, *Ho'iho'i Hou: A Tribute to George Helm and Kimo Mitchell* (Honolulu: Bamboo Ridge Press, 1984).

48. Walter Ritte Jr. and Richard Sawyer, *Na Mana'o Aloha o Kaho'olawe* (Honolulu: Aloha 'Āina o Nā Kūpuna, 1978), 3.

49. Quoted in Morales, *Ho'iho'i Hou,* 55.

50. Quoted in Morales, *Ho'iho'i Hou,* 72.

51. RIMPAC, or Rim of the Pacific, exercises are the largest multinational naval training exercises in the world. Kaho'olawe was once a regular RIMPAC target.

52. *Memorandum of Understanding between the United States Department of the Navy and the State of Hawai'i Concerning the Island of Kaho'olawe, Hawai'i,* 1994, 13.

53. Stu Glauberman, "Long, Winding Road of Controversy over H-3," *Honolulu Advertiser,* April 13, 1992; Kris M. Tanahara, "Halawa Valley Still in Dispute," *Honolulu Advertiser,* April 6, 1993; Kris M. Tanahara, "Marchers Mark Delay in Halawa Valley Work," *Honolulu Advertiser,* August 30, 1993.

54. Pat Omandam, "Rocky Road: Even with the Opening at Hand, Many Hawaiians Say Protests May Not End," *Honolulu Star-Bulletin,* December 4, 1997; Mike Yuen, "Open Road: After Decades of Controversy, the 16.1-mile Highway Will Soon Open for Business," *Honolulu Star-Bulletin,* December 3, 1997.

55. See "Hiiaka-i-ka-poli-o-Pele," *Hoku o Hawaii,* January 12, 1926, quoted in Elspeth P. Sterling and Catherine C. Summers, *Sites of Oahu* (Honolulu: Bishop Museum Press, 1978), 187.

56. Jim Borg, "Ecologists Sue to Halt Big Isle Army Exercises," *Honolulu Advertiser,* October 8, 1981.

57. "Request to Halt Maneuvers Denied," *Honolulu Advertiser,* October 9, 1981.

58. Dennis Kawaharada, ed., *Ancient O'ahu: Stories from Fornander and Thrum* (Honolulu: Kalamakū Press, 2001).

59. Marion Kelly and Sidney Michael Quintal, *Cultural History Report of Makua Military Reservation and Vicinity, Makua Valley, Oahu, Hawaii* (Honolulu: Bernice P. Bishop Museum, 1977), 8–10.

60. Stephen Desha Sr. and Julia Keonaona, "He Mo'olelo Ka'ao no Hi'iaka-i-ka-poli-o-Pele," serial account published in *Ka Hōkū o Hawai'i* (September 18, 1924, to July 17, 1928), trans. Kepa Maly in *Oral History Study: Ahupua'a of Mākua and Kahanahāiki, District of Wai'anae Island of O'ahu*, PACDIV Contract Number N62742-94-D-0006 D.O. 22. PCH Project No. 442.0122, Institute for Sustainable Development (1998), A1–A13.

61. Ian Lind, "The Captive Valley of Mākua: 42 Years of Military Occupation," *Ka Huliau*, May–June 1983.

62. "Mākua Valley Public Meeting Held on January 27, 2001" (Ralph Rosenburg Court Reporters), 59.

63. Lind, "The Captive Valley of Mākua."

64. Pam Smith, "Makua: Valley of the Duds," *Hawaii Observer*, June 16, 1977.

65. Smith, "Makua," 20.

66. Kelly and Quintal, *Cultural History Report*, 48–49.

67. Peter Rosegg, "Quiet Beach Offers Home to Squatters," *Honolulu Advertiser*, April 14, 1975; Helen Altonn, "Makua Beach Squatters Face Eviction," *Honolulu Star-Bulletin*, July 17, 1978.

68. Smith, "Makua," 22.

69. Vickie Ong, "Hawaiians Raise Flag over Makua," *Honolulu Advertiser*, February 29, 1976.

70. Robert W. Bone, "300 Rally Round Makua's Traditional Lifestyle," *Honolulu Advertiser*, January 3, 1983.

71. *Mākua: Sovereignty in Practice* (Kōkua Mākua 'Ohana, 1983).

72. Science Applications International Corporation (SAIC), *Final Report RCRA Facility Assessment for Makua Military Reservation, Oahu, Hawaii*, submitted to the U.S. Environmental Protection Agency, Region IX. EPA ID No. HI7210022227 (1992), 14.

73. *Mākua: To Heal a Nation*, produced by Nā Maka o ka 'Āina, 1996, videocassette.

74. Ka'iu Kauihou, a Wai'anae youth, testified: "If you don't have a connection to the land, you are not going to feel what the land is feeling. And the bombing of Mākua isn't just hurting the land, it is hurting us. . . . And that's why I am here. Because I don't want to hurt anymore." Transcript from "Mākua Valley Public Meeting Held on January 27, 2001," 99–100. Thomas Naki, a kupuna, said: "Stop the outrageous 'military exercises' now. . . . The exercises have taken away the life cycle of our environment as well as depleted our resources. To say that Mākua would surely become a ghost town is absurd and a vicious drum up of lies that's been a repeated pattern again and again to somehow justify the continued bombing of Mākua." "Mākua Valley Public Meeting Held on January 27, 2001," 247–248.

75. Makahiki is the season of Lono, god of agriculture, peace, and creative arts. The season is marked by offerings to Lono, feasting, games, cultural activities, and a prohibition on war.

76. *Oli Ho'oikaika* (Prophesy of the nation) is a traditional chant documented by David Malo. The last line was added for the Mākua Makahiki ceremony.

77. James Carroll, "Bush's Radical Shift in Military Policy," *Boston Globe,* February 19, 2002.

78. Some of the noteworthy groups working to end U.S. militarism are the East Asia-U.S. Women's Network Against Militarism, the Military Toxics Project, the Filipino American Coalition for Environmental Solutions, Arc Ecology, the Center for Public Environmental Oversight, the Comite Pro Rescate y Desarollo de Vieques (Committee for the Rescue and Development of Vieques), the Fellowship of Reconciliation, the U.S.-Japan Committee for Racial Justice, I Tano-ta I Linala-ta (Our Land is Our Life), Nuclear Free and Independent Pacific, and the American Friends Service Committee Peacebuilding and Demilitarization Program Concentration Network.

79. East Asia-U.S. Women's Network Against Militarism, *International Women's Summit to Redefine Security: Final Statement, June 22–25, 2000.*

KAREN K. KOSASA

Sites of Erasure

The Representation of Settler Culture in Hawai'i

> As I say, everything Western is hegemonic in Hawai'i: styles of
> speech, television, radio and film, clothing, dance, food, habits of
> daily life, and more. So, too, the monsters of concrete, high-rise
> urbanization, land development, mass-based tourism, naval and air
> force bases, and so on.
>
> —Haunani-Kay Trask, "Feminism and Indigenous
> Hawaiian Nationalism"

In this volume photographer Stan Tomita and I would like our
works, "whose vision, 2006" (fig. 1) and "Colonial Crimes: Settlers in Hawai'i"
(figs. 2 and 3), to ask uneasy questions about ourselves and other settlers. We are
sansei, third-generation Japanese settlers, educators, and visual artists. Since the
early 1990s several of our collaborative art projects have represented struggles
over land use in Hawai'i, including the expropriation of Native land for the development of suburban homes, shopping malls, tourist complexes, and geothermal
energy.

Although many long-time settlers in Hawai'i are critical of the ways the land
has been overbuilt by real estate developers and overrun by commercial enterprises, disentangling ourselves from the resulting "amenities" is no easy task. As
settlers, many of us are reluctant, even unwilling, to consider how the pleasures
of everyday life—dining out, shopping in malls, watching television, and living
in suburban communities—can be part of a larger colonial problem. How can
these seemingly innocent activities be "hegemonic"? The words of Hawaiian
nationalist Haunani-Kay Trask in the epigraph above are sobering. In the essay
from which they were taken, she underscores the point that only Hawaiians can
fully understand the destruction of their culture and land.[1] Settlers, she explains,
have been too busy benefiting from the dominance of the American culture and
its exploitative practices. Our very privileges blind us from recognizing the lethal
nature of Western culture. In a particularly vivid passage from one of her writ-

ings, Trask emphasizes the "cruelty" and "stench" of colonial life by describing a Western dystopia where human excrement floats in offshore waters, disgorged from overloaded sewer systems, and where pesticides and herbicides contaminate groundwater sources and endanger fragile wetlands.[2]

In *Culture and Imperialism* Edward W. Said argues for the necessity of looking carefully at the cultures that nurture the "imagination" of empires. Geographical conquest, he emphasizes, is not only about physical violence, "but also about ideas, about forms, about images and imaginings."[3] His objective is to situate "culture" within its historical context and reveal the affiliations between it and the more sordid acts of oppression we associate with the expansion of empires. Inspired by the work of Said and Trask, Stan and I have tried to represent in several art projects the links between the settler society in Hawai'i, its colonization of Native Hawaiians, and confiscation of Native land.[4]

Perhaps one of the most difficult challenges that Stan and I face is understanding how our activities as settler visual artists and educators contribute to supporting the hegemony of the colonial culture. In the first half of this essay I offer a rough sketch of the "settler imaginary" in Hawai'i—the concepts and images we use to imagine, guide, and navigate our lives. This settler imaginary encourages settlers to "misrecognize" the colony as a democratic space of opportunity, but in doing so it allows us to avoid the fact of colonialism and the subjugation of the indigenous people. In the latter half of this essay I describe a few of our visual projects and the ideas that inspired and troubled their making.

Acts of Erasure

Settler colonialism in Hawai'i is composed of "acts of erasure." These "erasures" help to maintain the colonization of Native Hawaiians by creating a "settler imaginary" that continuously eliminates all references to colonialism. This process of erasure naturalizes the United States' illegal presence in Hawai'i. It also creates a perplexing situation where many settlers are unaware of the existence of colonialism and their participation in it.

Settler erasures are integral to colonial life. First, settler leaders in political society sanction the dominance of the United States and its local agent, the State of Hawai'i, by "erasing" or dismissing the connection between the maintenance of colonialism *and* the coercive activities of the military, police, judicial, and legislative bodies.[5] Beginning with the 1893 overthrow of the Hawaiian nation, "crimes of colonialism" in both political and civil societies led to the hegemony of the American settler society; American values and ideology became everyday knowledge for settlers, even for the large, nonwhite settler population.

Second, settlers avoid references to colonialism or use oblique statements to allude to its political existence. These rhetorical erasures and tactics of avoidance are strategic. They deflect and deny references to (or acknowledgments of) crimes committed by the colonial society. Hence although many settlers supported the passage of Public Law 103-150, or the "Apology Law," by the U.S. Congress in 1993 to apologize to the Hawaiian people for the 1893 overthrow, or sympathized with Hawaiian protests against other judicial rulings threatening Hawaiian entitlements and compensatory programs (e.g., *Rice v. Cayetano* 2000; *John Doe v. Kamehameha Schools* 2005), they seldom linked their support with a condemnation of colonialism.

Settler acts of erasure are denials of wrongdoing. They are an intrinsic and necessary part of settler life—sanctioning colonialism by avoiding references to it or disavowing knowledge of it. These denials allow settlers to participate in everyday life as if it were unconnected to the political subjugation of Hawaiians. Although the settler society's hegemony in Hawai'i is maintained by interdependent practices in both political and civil society, this essay focuses on practices in civil society associated with visual culture and everyday life. My references to "erasures" and "denials" are not meant to trivialize and overlook the concrete realities of political subjugation in Hawai'i but to offer a framework for analyzing cultural and visual practices and understanding how they underwrite the conquest of Native peoples by "nurturing" a colonial way of imagining and imaging the world.

The Production of Blankness (and Whiteness)

Acts of erasure are not exclusive to Hawai'i but are local versions of similar activities in the continental United States. At the national level, these physical and conceptual erasures allow settlers in the United States to imagine the spaces of their "origins" as uninhabited, despite the bloody conquest of Native nations. While the contradictory logic of the latter has been widely discussed by scholars, I am interested in how it impairs the ability of settlers to recognize the reality of colonialism. For instance, how are settlers educated not to see the colony and its colonial practices? How does their "failure of vision" prevent them from seeing the political differences between themselves as colonizers and the indigenous people as colonized?

Acts of erasure produce an American imaginary where concepts and images of "blankness" and blank spaces proliferate. Within these imaginative spaces settlers visualize their work as always beginning within a primordial emptiness and innocence. Here, blankness is assumed to represent an uninhabited terrain. But this blankness has been produced to meet a need, much like a commodity. And like many commodities, it is involved in numerous dissimulations and misrepresentations.[6]

Acts of erasure and the production of blankness are highly motivated actions. They engage settlers in performing necessary acts of amnesia—"forgetting to remember" or "remembering to forget"[7] the colonization of Native peoples. These erasures allow settlers to clear an ideological space and construct an American imaginary where the United States is represented as a preeminent democracy and a land of opportunity. Blankness thus provides an imaginative "ground" or fertile terrain for creating and circulating heroic images of America and Americans. It allows settlers to visualize their activities as beginning positively from a *terra nullius* and not negatively over the ruins of another culture.

This imaginary site of blankness is particularly appealing to settlers. They are educated to believe that within this space no one group is privileged over others, that everyone starts from a level playing field. However, this leveled field is a deceitful space. In order to represent itself as a land of opportunity the United States must erase and forget the political and historical differences between settlers and indigenous peoples and repeatedly misidentify and misrepresent the latter as one among many ethnic groups in the United States. A putative space of equality and opportunity is thus offered to settlers at the expense of Native peoples and a recognition of their colonization and political status as colonized subjects.

In the middle of the Pacific, generations of settlers in Hawai'i are thus educated and encouraged to see the geographic terrain as sites/sights of opportunity similar to those in the continental United States, as blank spaces to be filled with localized versions of the American Dream. The situation in Hawai'i, however, is complicated by the presence of a large, nonwhite settler population with a high percentage of people of Asian ancestry. The production of spaces of "blankness" requires the ideological education of settlers of color and their interpellation into American society as champions of democracy for settlers (but not Natives). Ironically, then, the maintenance of the colonial society where Euro-American values dominate was and is accomplished with the assistance of nonwhite settlers and their production of whiteness, of white American culture.

Visualizing Colonial Culture

In many of our mixed-media works made between 1990 and 2000, Stan and I focused on portraying and utilizing strategies of obfuscation. We intentionally covered up photographs of landscapes and written texts behind layers of white paint, wall spackle, plaster, tracing paper, and various kinds of tapes. We utilized these visual strategies to represent settler attempts to whitewash or obscure wrongdoing and to mimic (or "perform") these very activities by making parts of the text and imagery difficult to decipher.

As previously mentioned, many of our past works referred to problems connected to land use like the endangering of indigenous wildlife and flora and the disturbance of Native burials through development projects. We often included phrases from commercial advertisements promoting hotels, restaurants, and real estate firms ("thatched hut for your dining pleasure," "building the home of your dreams"), with references to our family histories ("our grandparents were immigrants/settlers from Japan"). In addition, somewhere in each work we included references to aesthetic concerns—our own ideas and those suggested by art manuals—to signal our activities as settler artists and highlight our physical manipulation and aesthetic arrangement of "raw" materials.

In all but one of our collaborative projects up until 2000, we simultaneously made references to two different settler activities: the commercial development of real estate and the artistic imaging of a particular landscape. In both activities the indigenous culture and its needs were subordinated to the desires and visions of the settler developer and artist; concerns important to the Hawaiian community were dismissed or remained out of sight and out of focus. For example, in a diptych titled *Visual Clutter* (1991) we contrasted a photograph of an open field and a solitary ʻōhiʻa tree with a panel of superimposed texts. The first text was large in size and covered by layers of white paint. It referred to the problems faced by archaeologists hired by developers to identify and assess the importance of Hawaiian objects uncovered on property slated for real estate projects. Although a state policy required the preservation of important cultural items, archaeologists were often pressured by their employers to minimize the significance of any discoveries to facilitate the completion of a project.[8] Developers were sometimes accused of trying to eliminate the problem by bulldozing over sites, thus avoiding costly delays in the documentation, recovery, and preservation of secular and sacred remains.

In the second text, written in small type between the lines of the larger first text, Stan scribbled photographer's notes about film stock, aperture setting, depth of field, and the compositional arrangement he used to photograph the land and ʻōhiʻa tree. The third text was taken from an introductory book on photography with instructions for eliminating "visual clutter" by manipulating the depth of field and focal point. Here, we wanted to refer to the fact that in many instances Hawaiian concerns (and Hawaiians themselves) are dismissed as unimportant, intentionally obscured, or "backgrounded" by a focus on settler concerns.

In 1997 we turned our attention to working on large-scale wall installations. We utilized blue chalk snap lines and small visual and textual "footnotes" on the gallery walls, the first to refer to the business of construction and the second to refer to different kinds of settler practices. The footnotes were generally small in size and placed on the lower half of a wall. We used them to complicate viewers' experiences of images, to trouble the usual pleasure they had while viewing aesthetic images in a gallery. For instance, by providing fragments of text ("certified kitchen designers" or "complimentary validated parking") we hoped to undermine a viewer's ability to dissociate what she or he saw—an enigmatic landscape image—from the everyday world of commercial transactions. As with earlier work we also paralleled the construction of the settler culture and the construction of art. For example, in two exhibitions we referred to "clearing" spaces "to build a home" and "to create our art" in small type silkscreened onto a wall.

As part of an exhibition on global tourism in 2001 we developed a postcard project titled *whose paradise? a Didactic (de)Tour project,* which we continue to produce.[9] In the first postcard we highlighted the fact that most visitors do not know about the 1893 overthrow of the Hawaiian nation by foreign businessmen and the U.S. military. The front of the postcard depicted a map of the islands and a detail of three hotel façades with the words "whose paradise?" On the back we asked, "Can the United States be a democracy and a colonial empire at the same time?" The second postcard included a snapshot of Waikīkī Beach with tourists lazily floating on rafts or swimming in the ocean in front of a wall of concrete, multistoried hotels. On the back we referred to the government's battle to protect the islands from a "silent" invasion of alien plant and animal species. But why, we asked, is there no concern about the entry of millions of pleasure-seeking tourists and the tourist industry's relentless commodification of the Hawaiian culture and the destruction of the land to accommodate the desires of visitors?

In the third postcard we paired a photographic image of a small thatched "hut" (used in a Polynesian revue for tourists) against a backdrop of hotels with a written excerpt from the 1993 "Apology Law." On the back we explained that the Hawaiian people and culture are hostages of the settler society. We also noted that the financial health of the settler state is dependent on the exploitation of the Native culture and land. Subsequently, these postcards have become popular teaching aids—augmenting the work of some educators as they introduce the problem of settler colonialism in Hawai'i to their students.

Crimes of Colonialism

> In Hawai'i, land has always been a political battleground and prize. Those who have held land have generally occupied the high ground in politics. If those out of political power have managed to come into power, they have usually set about using their new position to get hold of land.
>
> — George Cooper and Gavan Daws, *Land and Power in Hawai'i: The Democratic Years*

"whose vision, 2006" (fig. 1) is a heavily revised version of a photographic collage Stan and I first created for the cover image of a special issue of *Amerasia Journal* in 2000.[10] As in the original, the revised image depicts a settler photographer surveying the volcanic terrain around Kīlauea crater on the island of Hawaiʻi through the lens of his/her camera. The "lines of sight" emanating from the photographer's eyes and camera capture a particular vision, an aesthetic framing of the landscape. In the revised work these sightlines also double as lines carving up the terrain, suggesting another kind of work where the photographer will be replaced by the surveyor. Once printed and released into the settler culture, the photographer's vision circulates as a commodity. It serves up the land to settlers for their aesthetic consumption and visual pleasure, triggering or inspiring an endless number of fantasies. This settler image thus makes the land available and vulnerable to the settler imaginary as a resource, as raw material to incorporate into settler visions and desires.

Kīlauea crater and the land immediately surrounding it are sacred to the Hawaiian people. It is not currently the site of real estate development because it lies within a national park. But this does not mean it remains safe from commercialization or commodification. It already serves as an important tourist destination.

Fig. 1. "whose vision, 2006"; Karen K. Kosasa and Stan Tomita.

When George Cooper and Gavan Daws' *Land and Power* was first published in 1985, it created a stir.[11] It identified local Asian politicians, especially those of Japanese ancestry in the Hawai'i State Legislature, their families, and business partners, as collaborators who worked with white landowners in large-scale real estate projects in Hawai'i. A controversial feature of the book was the publication of extensive "tables" listing the names of individuals connected with major land developments and their connections with state or federal offices. The number of financial partnerships (called hui) between "local" Japanese, Chinese, Filipino, and Korean settler men, their relatives and friends, and haole landowners or other Asian settlers is striking.[12] For many of the people listed the exposure was culturally humiliating. However, this exposure did little to hinder the continuation of their lucrative business arrangements. And although the book underscored the centrality of land in the struggle over settler power, its harsh indictment of the Asian settlers was effectively quashed when it was systematically ignored by Asian settler communities.

How, then, does one "expose colonialism" when it is disguised to look like "business as usual" or when its very exposure is immediately erased? How do we expose the fact that those of us who are settlers are linked back in time to the historical expropriation of land and forward to contemporary and future expropriations?

In 2006 Stan and I exhibited "Colonial Crimes: Settlers in Hawai'i" (figs. 2 and 3) in a small gallery/nightclub in Honolulu as part of a group show.[13] Our work consisted of two life-size images of Stan and myself holding signs. Each sign included the word "Settler" printed in our own handwriting next to a black and white photograph. Stan's photograph depicted a sugarcane plant, while mine displayed an enlarged detail of the façade of a building in downtown Honolulu. To the right of the images of Stan and myself we included three visual/textual "footnotes" on the wall. The first note consisted of a chart for the "General Population in Hawai'i" with the population broken down into two categories, "Hawaiian" and "Settler." It displayed the population numbers for seven years, between 1853 and 2000, beginning with Hawaiians numbering 71,019 and settlers 2,118 in 1853. By 2000 the ratio of Hawaiians to settlers had reversed. Hawaiians constituted 254,911 of the population, while settlers were listed at 901,104. Under the "Settler" category, population figures for the different ethnic populations (Haole, Portuguese, Chinese, Japanese, Korean, Filipino, and Others) were listed for seven years.[14]

The second footnote consisted of a miniature image of the sugarcane plant (held by Stan) and a quotation from an essay by Candace Fujikane, editor of this anthology on Asian settler colonialism: "The presence of Asian settlers in Hawai'i was made possible by American colonial efforts to secure a labor base for a settler plantation economy. The Kōloa Plantation was established in 1835, and as the first large-scale plantation in Hawai'i, it intensified foreigners' desire for title to Native land."[15]

The third footnote consisted of a miniature image of the building façade (held by myself) paired with the quotation from an essay by Trask on the hegemonic presence of the Western culture that appears as an epigraph at the beginning of this essay.

The large images of Stan and myself were taken from a series in progress in which we are depicted in two sets of clothing. Stan is wearing "local" wear that people in Hawai'i often refer to as "aloha attire," and I am wearing Western clothing that is not marked by the specificities of Hawai'i as a place. In the gallery book available to visitors we included a discussion of our work.

> The two artists, Karen Kosasa and Stan Tomita, hold signs that identify them as part of the dominant settler (non-Hawaiian) population in Hawai'i. Their eyes are hidden to prevent their real identities—as perpetrators of colonial crimes—from being widely circulated. Ms. Kosasa and Mr. Tomita are teachers and artists. Despite their good intentions, their everyday practices support the colonial government in the islands and in the United States. Here in Hawai'i, every settler benefits from the colonization of Hawaiians, the theft of their lands and resources, and the commercialization of their culture. Why is it so difficult for settlers to recognize their participation in colonial crimes?
>
> Mr. Tomita and Ms. Kosasa hold pictures of a sugar cane plant and a building façade. These images are references to the development of the colonial economy through the sugar cane plantations in the past and multi-national finances today. The "footnotes" along the sides of the main images reveal a glimpse of the colonial problem through a population chart, the words of Hawaiian activist and scholar Haunani-Kay Trask, and Asian American scholar Candace Fujikane.

With "Colonial Crimes" we decided to use a straightforward and didactic approach. Hence the work appears simplistic, like a page from a primer on island life. The handwritten "Settler" sign illustrates and defines the meaning of the person depicted. Knowing full well that settlers do not want to be recognized as settlers—as colonial criminals—we use the signs to stabilize the work's meaning(s) and limit its ability to float ambiguously. In fact, our hope is that the more the "Settler" sign is interpreted as a simple descriptor, the more it will serve as an inescapable indictment of our criminal behavior, equating settlers with the maintenance of colonialism.

"Colonial Crimes: Settlers in Hawai'i, 2006"; Karen K. Kosasa and Stan Tomita

Fig. 2. (Left) "The presence of Asian settlers in Hawai'i was made possible by American colonial efforts to secure a labor base for a settler plantation economy. The Kōloa Plantation was established in 1835, and as the first large-scale plantation in Hawai'i, it intensified foreigners' desire for title to Native land."—Candace Fujikane, "Introduction: Asian Settler Colonialism in the U.S. Colony of Hawai'i"

Fig. 3. (Right) "As I say, everything Western is hegemonic in Hawai'i: styles of speech, television, radio and film, clothing, dance, food, habits of daily life, and more. So, too, the monsters of concrete, high-rise urbanization, land development, mass-based tourism, naval and air force bases, and so on."—Haunani-Kay Trask, "Feminism and Indigenous Hawaiian Nationalism," *SIGNS* 21 (4) (Summer 1996)

Table 3. General Population in Hawai'i

	1853	1890	1900	1920	1940	1960	2000[1]
Hawaiian	71,019	40,622	39,656	41,750	64,310	102,403	254,911
Settler	2,118	49,368	114,345	214,162	359,020	530,369	901,104
Haole	1,600	6,220	8,547	19,708	103,791	202,230	243,626
Portuguese	87	12,719	18,272	27,002			
Chinese	364	16,752	25,767	23,507	28,774	38,197	66,839
Japanese		12,610	61,111	109,274	157,905	203,455	253,475
Korean				4,950	6,851		
Filipino				21,031	52,569	69,070	183,292
Others	67	1,067	648	8,690	9,130	17,417	153,872

Note: All statistics except for the year 2000 are from Robert C. Schmitt, *Historical Statistics of Hawaii* (Honolulu: University Press of Hawai'i, 1977), 25.

[1] Statistics for the year 2000 are from State of Hawai'i, Department of Health, Office of Health Status Monitoring (OHSM), Health Surveys, and Disease Registry (HSDR).

This new work raises questions for both Stan and myself. What does it mean to work against the aesthetic and conceptual ambiguities and subtleties that we have been trained to value and wield as visual artists? What does this say about the possibility of mounting anti-hegemonic visual projects in Hawai'i at a particular moment in history when settlers continually erase all evidence of colonialism and evade their recognition of it? Can we afford to be subtle and artfully veil our meanings behind obscure images and forms?

Strategies of Exposure

To counter the problem of settler erasures in Hawai'i and the invisibility of colonialism, I would like to argue that *everything* in the settler culture—images, objects, people, events, social and political practices, and public and private institutions— should be exposed as colonial products, things generated by the colonial culture. This strategy of exposure should "bring to light" the simultaneous pervasiveness of colonialism and the problem of its invisibility.

By continually exposing colonialism, settlers involved in visual culture can work against acts of erasure and the production of blankness by affirming the prior presence and priority of Native people and their land and culture. As would be expected, the problem is much more complicated and my proposal inadequate. A number of settler artists have been "exposing" different aspects of the colonial problem for more than a decade through their art works and teaching.[16] However, the effect of their work, I believe, is routinely undermined when it is *not* linked to a larger discussion of colonialism and is associated with or dismissed as either "political" or "socially conscious" art. Its significance is furthermore minimized when it is attributed to the opinion of an individual, one among many artistic visions.

One of the problems, then, is the reception of so-called politically or socially minded work, especially those dealing with the colonization of Native Hawaiians. Because we are just beginning to grapple with the problem of settler colonialism in Hawai'i, our ability to understand the critical work that has already been mentioned above is limited, as is our understanding of the work of Hawaiian artists who have been mounting criticisms of the settler culture for years. Such artists include Maile Andrade, Kimo Cashman, Herman Pi'ikea Clark, Kaili Chun, April Hōkūlani Drexel, 'Īmaikalani Kalāhele, Puni Kukahiko, Kapulani Landgraf, Meleanna Aluli Meyer, Carl Pao, and Chuck Kawai'olu Souza.[17] Which brings me to the problem of visibility.

While vision is privileged in Euro-American culture and seeing is knowing, the significance and meaning of what is visible will always exceed what is immediately apprehended. In other words, to understand what is visible requires knowledge of what is not visible—generally historical, cultural, political, social, and economic contexts—against which the visible can be read or "deciphered." Thus the "strategy of exposure" proposed here is a strategy of contextualization, of placing settler activities within the context of colonial histories beginning with the 1893 overthrow. Like many projects influenced by postcolonial and indigenous studies, exposures are crucial exercises in remembering.

The work of Trask is particularly relevant here. Her writings and nationalist work have consistently served to expose the problem of the U.S. presence in the islands. Her argument that "everything Western is hegemonic" points to the problem that settlers are unable to recognize the oppressiveness of the colonial society. I take her words as a warning: settlers cannot be trusted to detect and identify colonial injustice. Hence we must find ways to alter our settler imaginary, recognize the lethal nature of quotidian settler life, and work against our desires to continue business as usual.

Colonialism and the colonial context, then, should serve as the primary interpretive framework against which the settler culture is interpreted and assessed.

"Colonial exposure" is offered as an anti-hegemonic gesture—of revealing the hidden presence of colonialism in all areas of settler life. It is, however, only one among other suggestions asking settlers to acknowledge and remember that they/ we live in a colony where the indigenous people are colonized and still demanding their rights as a nation for self-determination. It should be followed by other anti-hegemonic activities based upon the direction of the indigenous people.

Notes

This essay is an expanded version of an earlier essay, "whose vision, 2000," published in *Whose Vision? Asian Settler Colonialism in Hawai'i*, a special issue of *Amerasia Journal* 26 (2) (2000): xii–xiv. I would like to acknowledge Eiko Kosasa and Tina Takemoto for their helpful comments on early versions of this essay, and Stan Tomita for our collaborative work, which inevitably affects my thinking about visual culture in Hawai'i. I would also like to thank Candace Fujikane for invaluable editorial comments and suggestions and for her encouragement. Of course, any problems posed by my words are my own.

1. Haunani-Kay Trask, "Feminism and Indigenous Hawaiian Nationalism," *Signs* 21 (4) (1996): 912.

2. Haunani-Kay Trask, *From a Native Daughter: Colonialism and Sovereignty in Hawai'i*, rev. ed. (1993); reprint, Honolulu: University of Hawai'i Press, 1999, 19.

3. Edward W. Said, *Culture and Imperialism* (New York: Alfred A. Knopf, 1993), 7.

4. "Native Hawaiian" and "Hawaiian" will be used interchangeably to refer to the indigenous people in Hawai'i. These terms also refer to anyone of Hawaiian genealogical descent regardless of blood quantum.

5. My ideas here are influenced by Antonio Gramsci's description of two different spaces—political and civil societies—and the coercive and consensual activities taking place within them respectively. Taken together, these interdependent activities enable the hegemony of a social class or group. See Gramsci's discussion of the "dual perspective" in *Selections from the Prison Notebooks of Antonio Gramsci*, ed. and trans. Quintin Hoare and Geoffrey Nowell Smith (1971); reprint, New York: International Publishers, 1989, 169–170.

6. I am drawing here on the work of social theorist Henri Lefebvre and his explanation that space is "produced," much like the capitalistic production of a commodity. His analysis of spatial illusions is provocative and helpful. While space is generally perceived as "empty," it hides the fact that it is "full" of the social relations between men, including relations of power. See Lefebvre, *The Production of Space*, trans. Donald Nicholson-Smith (Oxford: Blackwell, 1974).

7. Building on Ernst Renan's work, Homi K. Bhabha explains that amnesia is a critical element in a nation's construction of its official history. "Forgetting to remember" or being "obliged to forget" for Bhabha is not simply a matter of lapsed memory but "the construction of a discourse on society that *performs* the problematic *totalization of the national will.*" Historical amnesia thus becomes a way for citizens to patriotically remember their nation by performing a necessary elision. Bhabha, "DissemiNation: Time, Narrative, and the Mar-

gins of the Modern Nation," in *Nation and Narration*, ed. Homi K. Bhabha (New York: Routledge, 1990), 310.

8. John Heckathorn, "Before It All Disappears," *Honolulu* (February 1985), 52–64.

9. "Paradise in Search of a Future, Part Two," September 21–December 22, 2001, *CEPA Gallery*, Buffalo, New York.

10. See *Whose Vision? Asian Settler Colonialism in Hawai'i*, ed. Candace Fujikane and Jonathan Y. Okamura, a special issue of *Amerasia Journal* 26 (2) (2000): xii–xiv.

11. George Cooper and Gavan Daws, *Land and Power in Hawai'i: The Democratic Years* (1985); reprint, Honolulu: University of Hawai'i Press, 1990.

12. While this book raises an important political critique, the authors do not link their arguments to colonialism. Hence they are unable to situate the activities of the Asian men (and women) within a settler society that enabled and supported their exploitative practices as they pursued their dreams of becoming Americans.

13. "MetroHAWAI'I: Gridlock and Other Local Traditions," *thirtyninehotel* Gallery, April 7–May 20, 2006, curated by Trisha Lagasso Goldberg.

14. The "Settlers" and "Hawaiians" figures for this chart were assembled by Eiko Kosasa from two sources for handouts in political science courses. All statistics except for the year 2000 were from Robert C. Schmitt, *Historical Statistics of Hawai'i* (Honolulu: University of Hawai'i Press, 1977), 25. Statistics for the year 2000 were from the State of Hawai'i, Department of Health, Office of Health Status Monitoring (OHSM), Health Surveys and Disease Registry (HSDR), "Table 1.1: Gender, Age, Ethnicity by County—Population of Hawai'i," Hawai'i Health Survey (HHS) 2000.

15. Cited from an earlier draft of the introduction to this volume.

16. Mark Hamasaki's collaborative work with Kapulani Landgraf (see her images in this volume) is particularly notable, as is the work of Gaye Chan alone or in collaboration with art historian Andrea Feeser. Chan and Feeser's recently published book, *Waikīkī: A History of Forgetting & Remembering* (Honolulu: University of Hawai'i Press, 2006), is an excellent example of a visual and textual project that exposes how colonialism and capitalism drastically changed the terrain and the social relations in a specific place. Over many years printmaker, sculptor, and installation artist Laura Ruby has been referring to interactions between Hawaiians and non-Hawaiians.

17. All but two of these artists were part of an important 1997 exhibition of works by twenty Hawaiian artists, Ho'okū'ē (Resistance), at the East-West Center Gallery in Honolulu, curated by Cashman and Drexel. Ho'okū'ē highlighted the vibrancy of contemporary Hawaiian art and the interdependence of political and cultural issues and was quickly followed by other exhibitions like Nā Maka Hou: New Visions (Honolulu Academy of Arts, 2001). The following is a description of the Ho'okū'ē exhibition from a publicity announcement: "Inspired by the theme of resistance, twenty contemporary artists from the island of O'ahu will address issues pertinent to Native Hawaiians. Some of the artworks will refer to the problems of colonialism, race, genocide and ethnocide while others assert the inherent right of Native Hawaiians to reclaim control over their language, land, natural resources, history, values and practices."

Ideological Images

U.S. Nationalism in Japanese Settler Photographs

Modern Hawai'i, like its colonial parent the United States, is a settler society; that is, Hawai'i is a society in which the indigenous culture and people have been murdered, suppressed, or marginalized for the benefit of settlers who now dominate our islands.

—Haunani-Kay Trask, *From a Native Daughter: Colonialism and Sovereignty in Hawai'i*

What is earned at great price is treasured the most. This truth is reflected in the American experience of those of Japanese ancestry in Hawai'i, as it has been for so many others in this great immigrant nation of ours founded on ideals of human freedom and dignity, rather than on a prevailing blood line.

—Spark M. Matsunaga, "Introduction," *Kanyaku Imin*

In 1985 the Japanese settler community in Hawai'i commemorated one hundred years of settlement on the islands with the Kanyaku Imin Centennial. It held numerous festivities, published an array of literature, and mounted photographic exhibitions to celebrate the rise of the Japanese people from poverty to financial success and from plantation laborers to respected professionals, businessmen, scholars, and state and federal legislators. Not only did members of the Japanese settler community improve their own lives, but they also made significant contributions to the larger colonial society. From the turn of the twentieth century the Japanese, in solidarity with other ethnic groups, organized sugar strikes, unionized the labor force, and revived the local chapter of the Democratic Party. The latter significantly altered the political landscape in Hawai'i by providing a platform for nonwhite voters in Hawai'i to raise issues pertinent to their communities. The Kanyaku Imin Centennial thus publicly served to acknowledge and celebrate the achievements of these Japanese settlers as "American" immigrants.

Several of the centennial publications use archival and contemporary photographs to illustrate and document the positive trajectory of the Japanese "immigrant journey."[1] On the island of Oʻahu[2] the pages of the Oʻahu Kanyaku Imin Centennial Committee's "official" publication, *The Japanese in Hawaii: A Century of Struggle,* are filled with acknowledgments from prominent political and financial figures—who themselves represent the attainment of the American Dream.[3] Among the notables paying tribute are U.S. President Ronald Reagan and Hawaiʻi Governor George Ariyoshi. As the first Japanese American governor, Ariyoshi honors the issei (first generation Japanese) as "pioneering immigrants" and credits the Japanese settler community with building "the beautiful Hawaiʻi we have today."[4] Local businesses use advertisement space to commend Japanese settlers on their "proud heritage." The collective theme throughout these commemorative books is Japanese settler history as an American success story.

One publication, *Kanyaku Imin: A Hundred Years of Japanese Life in Hawaii,* narrates the "struggles to triumph" story of Japanese Americans, primarily through photographs interwoven with short articles.[5] It documents both historical and contemporary events and also presents the works of several Japanese artists, including photographers, painters, and sculptors. Covering two pages, the first photograph begins the book with a startling image: "head shots" of thirty-two sugar plantation laborers, each identified by a number pinned to her/his clothing. It is difficult to look at these photographs without visualizing contemporary posters of criminals. One can only speculate that the editor of the book wanted to re-create for the reader a sense of the racist attitudes and conditions the issei endured on the plantation.[6]

As nisei (second generation Japanese) introducing this book on the Japanese settler experience, U.S. Senators Daniel Inouye and Spark Matsunaga depict themselves as travelers on the immigrant journey within the United States. Both nisei speak of their humble beginnings and praise the economic and political opportunities offered by this "great immigrant nation." Inouye refers to the issei as that "pioneer contingent" whose sacrifices gave Japanese the lifestyle they now all enjoy. The book narrates the history of the Japanese settlers within the larger story of American immigration, thereby denying the history and presence of Native peoples.[7]

The third chapter of *Kanyaku Imin* is devoted to the photographic works of Usaku Teragawachi. Found only four years prior to the publication of the book when the building once housing Teragawachi's studio was torn down, these glass-plate images capture the issei settlers and their families. Teragawachi, an issei who worked during the early twentieth century, was considered a master portrait photographer for his effective use of natural studio light.

During the 1920s and 1930s in Hawaiʻi it was common practice for the issei to send family portraits to Japan. Many had arrived as unmarried contract laborers; it was important to document the wealth and health of their new families. Thus Japanese families would travel to the studios to have their family portraits taken.[8]

However, when private photographs are collected and presented in a public forum, their meaning enlarges. Transferred from a personal context to a social and political context, family portraits of people once identified as one's own parents or grandparents become significant representatives of the entire ethnic group. Although Teragawachi's portraits may not have been offered for public viewing by the subjects' descendants, nonetheless, these photographs were chosen by Japanese settlers in the 1980s to become part of the Japanese settler discourse. These images embodied important aspects of the American "nation of immigrants."

In this essay I will analyze four Teragawachi portraits. Neither their technical nor formal aspects will be considered. Rather, I will examine three photographs' inclusion within *Kanyaku Imin* for the purposes of upholding the American immigrant experience. Hence I will describe the first three Teragawachi photographs (figs. 1, 2, and 3) as evoking the concepts of American nationalism for Japanese settlers in the late twentieth century. The fourth photograph (fig. 4) was not included in any of the celebratory books of 1985. I will speculate on its exclusion and argue that the photograph did not properly represent the ideological beliefs that underlie the narratives of the "nation of immigrants."

My mother presented *Kanyaku Imin* to me as a gift when it was first published. At the time I quickly scanned the book and then placed it on my bookshelf. As a sansei (third generation) woman, I did not need to read the entire text to know its "success" message about the Japanese settler community. This is the familiar message that most sansei, yonsei (fourth generation), and now gosei (fifth generation) accept as reality.

With the rise of the Native Hawaiian sovereignty movement, however, I have come to recognize the hypocrisy of the dominant ideology of the United States as a pluralistic, egalitarian "nation of immigrants" and the denial that it is a settler colonial nation. Native Hawaiian nationalists teach us that Hawai'i was overthrown by the United States in 1893 and subsequently forcibly annexed in 1898. Through these acts of imperialism, Native Hawaiian people lost their human rights to self-determination and self-government. Furthermore, the United States continues to occupy Native Hawaiian ancestral lands and enforce a colonial system that benefits all settlers at the expense of the indigenous people. Consequently, the Japanese settler community did not become successful within a "democratic" and "egalitarian" system but within a colonial one. Japanese are therefore not "immigrants" in a "nation of immigrants," but settlers in a colony like all other foreigners and their descendants in the islands.[9]

The concept of the United States as a "nation of immigrants" is one of the cornerstones of American imperialism. This ideological construct is so powerful that most settlers are unable or unwilling to recognize any notions or evidence that counter it. Italian intellectual Antonio Gramsci would call this unshakable belief in a "nation of immigrants" part of the hegemonic control the United States exerts over its citizens. Gramsci argues that a nation-state does not maintain its hegemony over its citizens solely through the direct and obvious enforcement of laws and judicial rulings. The state also utilizes an indirect approach, gaining its citizens' consent for its dominant political policies and interests through the dissemination of national ideologies in private institutions such as film and television corporations, schools, and churches. National ideologies (as opposed to personal ones), then, organize the citizenry.

On one level, ideologies create the reference points from which people define who they are, locate their place in society, and accept a particular worldview. In other words, ideologies structure the "terrain" upon which citizens "acquire consciousness of their position, struggle, etc."[10] State ideologies are not about individual ideas such as whether a person agrees with specific political issues related to the American government but about whether citizens collectively support the larger political framework (i.e., interests of the state and the dominant social groups) through which they define themselves. On another level, ideologies are the "cement" that holds society together. Ideas such as the United States as a "nation of immigrants" or as a defender of "freedom" bind U.S. citizens together with shared values and worldviews that set them apart from the citizens of other nations. National ideologies, then, create an "us versus them" (self/other) construct. In this way patriotism connects citizens to each other. Hence national ideologies are part of the state's strategy to maintain its existing hegemonic order over society.[11]

To understand the hegemonic process as a relationship between the ideological beliefs of the state and the support of its citizens, we can think of this relationship as an instructional one. Applying this analysis to the United States, the U.S. state (the teacher) tells its citizens (the students) that we live in a "nation of immigrants" (the lesson). We, in turn, use the "immigrant" worldview (ideological lesson) to define who we are. To show our participation in U.S. nationalism we narrate our ethnic histories within the ideological framework set up by the state (i.e., we respond with personal examples). Thus to determine students' level of comprehension, the teacher calls upon students to recite the lesson back to her and to other classmates, and students respond with their own illustrations of the lesson. The 1985 Kanyaku Imin celebration can be understood as the Japanese settler community's response to a nationalist ideology, or the call to American nationalism.

My argument, then, is that the ideologies of the nation-state shape the way we think about the world and ourselves. Through these ideas, we interpret photographs in ways that affirm political ideologies of the United States as a "nation of immigrants." We reinforce these ideas when we write about or display photographs of ourselves. Photographs, then, are not passive, benign objects in the world; they are actively used to elicit our support for the ideas and interests of the dominant societal group. In this sense, photographs are political tools, ideological aids to maintain (or overturn) the hegemony of a nation-state.

Photographs depicting "pioneers" settling the West, or settler groups entering Ellis Island in New York or Angel Island in San Francisco evoke notions of the United States as the land of opportunity, equality, and freedom. In other words, the photographs are used to educate or persuade people that the continental United States was "empty" of indigenous peoples. Such ideas of nationalism both define who we are individually as members of various ethnic groups and collectively as a people and nation. As citizens we respond to the lesson of the United States as a "nation of immigrants" by producing photographic narratives found in books like *Kanyaku Imin*. Hence photographs aid in the two ideological phases of nationalism—the state's call phase and the citizens' response phase.

The State's Call to Nationalism: Educating Citizens

Before analyzing the four Teragawachi glass images, I will expand upon the definition of the state and its educative nature to clarify the links between photographs and the political force of ideologies. Gramsci argues that if one wants to overturn state power, one must study the state in terms of hegemony. Gramsci was a Marxist and acknowledged that the economic system organizes society. However, he was also influenced by the writings of V. I. Lenin, who pointed out that exploitation does not only come from abuse caused by the ruling class, but also from the societal structure itself. State hegemony does not only organize our physical lives, but our intellectual lives as well. Hence to accomplish revolutionary change, an entire new state structure must be built. A change in a state's hegemonic control will not happen when the controlling party in office is replaced with another party. Only when state hegemony is overturned will an entire historic period end and another begin.[12]

Gramsci shows the means by which a state maintains its hegemonic control over its citizens through his expansion of Lenin's concept of hegemony. Emphasizing that a modern nation-state's political influence over its citizens does not extend from public/government institutions alone, he explains how the state preserves its control through the work of private institutions (schools, churches, film industry, news media). Within a capitalist society like the United States, the ruling class that owns the private industries also runs and influences the direction of the government. Hence, Gramsci argues, when one studies the hegemonic control of the state, one must include the private institutions as being part of the state's apparatus. For example, the American news media interpret the world for us. The media determine what is "newsworthy" and what is not and report the events from particular political perspectives—that is, patriotic, white, middle-class male worldviews. Scholar and activist Noam Chomsky writes that the news media are "corporations" owned by the elite who expect their news to reflect their interests. Journalists who do not "conform" to the ideologies of the dominant class, and thus of the nation-state, are rarely promoted to prime time. Hence the nightly news we receive reflects the government's perspective. Whether the journalists are covering wars abroad or poverty at home, they rarely present alternate viewpoints from which to understand the issues.[13]

The American educational system is another example of private institutions that "steer" citizens toward the acceptance of state interests. Schoolchildren are educated to think within the U.S. nationalistic perspective. For example, elementary and secondary education define America's acquisition of its national land base in the west as "Manifest Destiny" instead of an imperial and genocidal campaign to seize the national lands of Native nations. Another example is the teaching of schoolchildren that the United States is an outstanding defender of human rights. In reality, the U.S. state violates Native peoples' human rights by denying them the right to choose their nationality. Native peoples were not asked to become U.S. citizens but were forced to be so through their colonial status.[14] If one recognizes the educational system as part of the state apparatus, then one begins to understand that the knowledge base of a citizenry is indeed political.

Hence Gramsci argues that to understand the state's maintenance of hegemony, one must look beyond political society to civil society. He argues that there are two hegemonic producers of laws and ideologies—public and private institutions of the state—and these producers are always in a dialectical relationship. Gramsci calls this hegemonic process the dual perspective.[15] The public institutions in political society exert *coercion* on a nation's citizens through the passage of laws and judicial rulings, while private institutions in civil society *win* the public's support through news reports, educational lessons, films, and other methods. Thus Gramsci argues that the dual perspective is accomplished through a dialectic of force and consent. The state "forces" compliance from its citizens through legislative laws and judicial rulings, and at the same time the state gains "consent" for its rule from its citizens through ideological concepts disseminated through schools, churches, and television networks. These dual processes constantly *dominate* and *direct* the citizens of a nation to accept particular ideas and worldviews. If citizens disagree with the dominant ideologies, the state has laws in place to limit their ability to dissent. Thus laws make clear just who has political power and who does not. In other words, if citizens resist the state, they are legally harassed and/or incarcerated. Public institutions therefore coerce citizens into obedience, while private institutions educate them to support the existing hegemony of the modern state and its dominant group.[16]

A simple way to visualize this hegemonic movement is to think of a shepherdess moving her herd of goats down a path. If the goats (citizens of a society) stray too far to the right or left of the path (national ideologies), the shepherdess (the state) sends her dog to redirect their course. The shepherdess possesses a variety of methods to control her herd. For example, the shepherdess can command her dog at a running pace to move one side of the herd. The dog's speed and sudden presence (laws/force) intimidates the goats, through the threat of violence, to run back to the center of the herd. For a more subtle approach, the shepherdess can send the dog out at a walking pace (ideologies/consent). The straying goats will continue to graze, but upon noticing the dog's presence, will slowly and "voluntarily" change their direction at their own pace. Whether the individual goats are moving from left to right or vice versa, the larger herd is moving steadily forward on the path. While the goats sometimes choose which leaf or blade of grass to eat, or which part of the path to walk on (citizens have limited agency), the shepherdess controls the overall direction of her herd.

Using this analysis, I want to show how, as a colonial state, the United States "herded" the Japanese settlers in Hawai'i down the path of American nationalism. I will only highlight a few events to illustrate the transformation of Japanese settlers from contract laborers in 1885 into "successful immigrants."[17] The U.S. state implemented two acts in the late nineteenth century that radically changed the political and social life of Hawai'i. Even though the Hawaiian Kingdom was an ally of the United States and was recognized as an independent nation by many world powers, the U.S. military overthrew it in 1893. Five years later the U.S. state annexed Hawai'i against the opposition of the Native Hawaiian community.[18] These two actions from public institutions—the U.S. military and Congress—are the direct "force" (laws) that Gramsci describes in his dual perspective. Whatever the issei thought about the United States before the beginning of the twentieth century, their attitudes were radically altered by these imperial acts.

Shortly after the turn of the century Japan stunned the world with its military victory over Russia (1904–05). This singular event inspired revolutionaries fighting against colonialism in Africa and Asia and frightened the public in Europe and the United States. Never before in modern history had a nonwhite nation succeeded militarily over a white nation. American anxieties over the "yellow peril" increased, and the "Japanese Question" was publicly discussed on the continental United States and in Hawai'i.[19]

By 1900 the Japanese were already the largest racial group in the Hawaiian islands, composing one-third of the population. Discussions on the "Japanese Question" in Hawai'i centered on this large population and the increasing number of its offspring, nisei children. Even though the settler population in 1910 vastly outnumbered the Native Hawaiian population by 153,362 to 38,547,[20] U.S. Territorial leaders feared that nisei settlers would become a formidable voting constituency. While they needed the Japanese as laborers and servants, the white population did not want the former to gain in economic, social, and political status. Thus the "Japanese Question" became the contentious subject of discussion throughout the islands in churches, at conferences, and in the daily papers.[21] It was the beginning of what Native Hawaiian political leader Haunani-Kay Trask identifies as the "intra-hegemonic" struggle. Complicated by the racist beliefs of the white settlers against Asians and the desires of Japanese to become successful Americans equal to haole (whites), these two settler communities would battle over the dominance of colonial Hawai'i and eventually form effective but uneasy alliances.[22]

By the mid-1920s the United States' public institutions had passed two laws that affected Japanese settlers: (1) the 1908 Gentlemen's Agreement restricting the immigration of Japanese from Japan to Hawai'i and from Hawai'i to the continental United States, and (2) the 1924 Immigration Act severely restricting immigration from non-European nations. Within the civil society of the settler colony, the Japanese settlers organized major strikes in 1909 and 1920 against their sugar planter employers. The purpose of the strikes, which involved thousands of workers, was to obtain decent wages from the colonial plantation owners. However, the English-language papers demonized the strikers as "conspirators" and characterized their activities as "unAmerican."[23] As producers of ideological beliefs, the local newspapers educated their readers about what it meant to be an "American"—that is, what it meant in the interests of the white colonial economy and government. Do not strike against one's employer, they preached. While the front pages heavily criticized the striking Japanese laborers, the following pages included business advertisements placed by people of Japanese ancestry. Hence one needs to recall Chomsky's analysis of the media and their production of ruling-class perspectives. Hawai'i English-language papers were prime examples. An efficient and competitive capitalist economy was pivotal for the white settlers—their profits and presence in Hawai'i were dependent on the labor of the Japanese and, to a lesser degree, the cooperation of the Japanese business community.

Lorrin A. Thurston, one of the architects of the overthrow of the Hawaiian Kingdom, was also the publisher of the daily *Pacific Commercial Advertiser,* which reflected his pro-American colonial politics. During the six months of the sugar strike initiated by the Japanese in 1920, Thurston's paper conducted two essay contests for children. The contests asked children to respond to the questions "How I Earn My Money" and "What It Means to Be an American."[24] Given the concerns of the Territorial leaders about nisei children's political viewpoints, it is not too difficult to recognize the ideological tactic used by Thurston's newspaper to teach children, especially the nisei, not to sympathize with the strikers, their own parents, and providers.

In the 1920s the Territory of Hawai'i (the colonial government), through three legislative bills, forced most of the Japanese-language schools to close their doors. Territorial leaders and the haole community believed that the nisei children were being educated to be Japanese nationalists at these schools. Placing these schools under Territorial scrutiny through such means as testing language teachers for their knowledge of American history, Territorial elites thought they could disrupt the Japanese community's centers of learning. Japanese settlers eventually took the Territorial government to court over this closure and won their case in the U.S. Supreme Court. Of interest here is the fact that the Japanese community framed their case and their contentious internal debates over the issues within American ideological beliefs about the democratic rights of immigrants in an "immigrant nation." Neither the Japanese who felt the need to appease the haole community by eliminating anything "Japanese" from their lives nor those who felt America guarantees them the right to educate their children in their own manner ever questioned the legality of the colonial Territorial government's presence in the islands or its ideological beliefs about democracy toward the Native people. The Japanese, by this time, were on their way to becoming American colonialists, educated to think of themselves as "immigrants."[25]

During the 1930s and early 1940s haole editors of English-language papers stepped up their discussion of the "Japanese Question." These editors often concluded that nisei with dual citizenship were disloyal to the United States.[26] Hence when Japan's military bombed Pearl Harbor in 1941, many Japanese settlers destroyed personal items from Japan or possessions associated with Japanese culture such as language books and clothing. They even closed their temples to signify their loyalty to the United States. Nisei volunteered in large numbers to join the U.S. colonial military that had declared war with Japan.

In summary, the overt and subtle "herding" tactics by the settler colonial government and its haole citizens are methods used to maintain American hegemony in Hawai'i. By asserting particular laws and ideological beliefs, the U.S. state continually pressured the Japanese, transforming them from uncooperative laborers into "voluntarily" patriotic American citizens-as-immigrants. Like that of other ethnic groups of color, the Japanese path toward economic, social, and political "success" in the United States was paved with the reality of racist laws and illusions of morality.

Gramsci's concept of dual perspective is useful for any examination of a state's maintenance of hegemony. His insights on the dialectical relationship between institutions in political and civil societies are instructive because they demonstrate how the modern state inundates its citizens with the interests of the state. There is never a moment when the state is not "steering" the public to support particular kinds of policies, legislation, or beliefs that benefit the dominant group, with the help of contentious debates that give the illusion that there is room for oppositional views and "democracy."[27]

In this political landscape photographs can be used as a tool to disseminate and perpetuate the ideological beliefs of the state. Most people consider photographs as personal, benign objects, beyond political suspicion. But a photograph of the Statue of Liberty is found in many schoolbooks because it symbolizes ideas about American nationalism. The photograph "cements" U.S. citizens together as a nation because they believe they live in the only nation that protects individual rights to "freedom" and "opportunities." American adults continue to believe in that political myth, even though the gaps between various races and classes are widening. Photographs, in short, are powerful ways to convey a nationalist message. During the 1909 sugar strike in Hawai'i, a photograph of the arrest of the Japanese strike leaders ran on the front page of the *Pacific Commercial Advertiser*.[28] The photograph, placed so prominently in this English-language daily, served as a warning to the larger Japanese community that people acting against the settler economic system would end in the colonial jailhouse.

Teragawachi's Photographs: Japanese Settler Response to U.S. Nationalism

Kanyaku Imin is an excellent example of the immigrant ideological perspectives the nisei settlers wanted to pass on to the sansei and yonsei. The book is the Japanese response to U.S. nationalism, representing the Japanese as *willingly traveling* on the American "immigrant" journey—beginning in poverty and ending in riches, moving from a simple, rural culture on the plantations to the sophistication of Western urban culture. Never is there mention of the constant coercion or "herding" by the United States. In *Kanyaku Imin* the majority of Teragawachi's photographs depict the Japanese in Western clothing. There is even one of a man smartly attired in a formal coat and top hat; whether the clothing belonged to him is of little concern. Within the pages of *Kanyaku Imin* the wearing of Western clothing becomes a signifier of the early immigrants' participation in American culture. Every sign of Western culture found within the visual details of specific portraits becomes the visual evidence for another, more public story about immigrant success and, because one is reading retrospectively, of an unquestioned patriotism, as if it had always existed.[29]

Figure 1: "Woman By Herself"

The Japanese settler community in Hawai'i is a patriarchal society. The existence of this social and cultural hierarchy is often criticized from within and without the community and contrasted with the American ideals of social equality and democracy. This photograph of a woman in Western attire, gracefully dressed in a patterned and solid apparel and tentatively posed, is forced to speak to this difficult problem. In *Kanyaku Imin* her portrait is placed directly opposite the photograph of the man in formal dress and top hat. This simple pairing seems to suggest that in America this woman is of equal social rank. Within the larger text, her portrait (and his) becomes the visual evidence that the Japanese in Hawai'i successfully transformed themselves from Asians to Americans. Moreover, this exquisitely photographed woman—looking slightly uneasy in a luminous white hat—becomes a sign of opportunity. The image suggests that in America a woman, even a shy one, can attain the gender equality unavailable to her in Japan.

If one were to read this photograph not within the U.S. ideological immigrant perspective but against it—acknowledging the reality of colonialism—what would one see? A well-to-do settler woman (unwittingly) engaged in the support of a colonial economy and lifestyle. The success of the Japanese settlers did not take place within a system of equality but within the inequalities of a colonial society. One could compare the role of the Japanese settlers with the role of foreign settlers in South Africa who supported the Afrikaner regime during apartheid. When unencumbered by immigrant ideologies, one can begin to see the existing economic and political systems in Hawai'i as colonial, functioning to subjugate the Native peoples for the benefit of white and nonwhite settlers alike.

Figure 2: "Two Women and Children"

This group portrait is probably of a mother, her children, and another single adult woman, perhaps the mother's single sister. They are dressed in their best attire. The lei, or flower garlands, on the three children immediately locate the image in Hawai'i and are probably the reason the photograph was selected for the centennial. Among the Japanese communities in the United States, Hawai'i is recognized for the relatively rich opportunities it gave immigrant settlers of Asian ancestry. More important, the Japanese in Hawai'i identify their immigrant experiences as serving a pivotal role in leading the islands to a strong economic and political future, including statehood in 1959. Placing this portrait in the book thus acknowledges the importance of Hawai'i as a site of opportunity for settlers of color, especially for the Japanese in Hawai'i who were able to "accomplish" more as a group than the Japanese in the continental United States.

Fig. 1. Unidentified woman, standing. Photograph by Usaku Teragawachi (courtesy of Bishop Museum Archives).

Fig. 2. Two women with three children, wearing paper lei. Photograph by Usaku
Teragawachi (courtesy of Bishop Museum Archives).

If one resists reading this photograph through U.S. national ideologies, the lei could signify the colonial possession of Hawai'i by the United States. The reality of colonialism in Hawai'i lies in the exploitative relationship of settlers over the Native people and islands—that is, anything Hawaiian (people, resources, lands, culture) becomes available for settler subjugation and commodification. The Japanese settlers (issei and nisei) wearing these lei thus represent their acceptance, support, and participation in the colonial system that subjugates Native peoples.

Today the multinational tourist industry in Hawai'i is an excellent example of settler appropriation of Hawaiian culture and hospitality. The stores and hotels in Waikīkī—many of which are owned or managed by Japanese and other settlers—profit from anything Native. Japanese settlers in the tourist industry and in the larger island community have built their successful lives off the loss of Native Hawaiian government, lands, and people.[30]

Figure 3: "Family Portrait in Front of Car"

This family portrait was probably selected to represent the attainment of the American Dream—the ownership of a house and car. While the children are awkwardly dressed in Western clothing, the family proudly stands in front of a beautiful, large, open-air home. This portrait evokes the dreams of freedom of all American immigrants by including a car, which symbolizes American "prosperity" and "mobility." Perhaps at the time of the portrait the family did not own the house and car, as suggested by the presence of the white boy sitting in the backseat of the car, but within the context of *Kanyaku Imin* the photograph documents the early stages of Japanese "dreaming" of a better life. The "hardships" and "sacrifices" the issei and nisei endured as a community are justified in the process of turning this American Dream into a reality. Today the Japanese settler community has ascended to become the co-ruling class with white settlers in Hawai'i.

When reading the photograph against the "nation of immigrants" ideologies, one sees a Japanese family mimicking haole settler greed. The portrait attests to the Japanese settlers' acceptance of the unjust colonial system because of the opportunities it provides them. Whether there was any recognition of this conflict of interests by the Japanese—that they had benefited from a system that exploited Native Hawaiians—the 1985 Kanyaku Imin celebration shows no evidence. Even though Japanese had to overcome unrelenting racist policies and practices perpetuated by the haole settler community and government, they never questioned the inherent racism built into the U.S. colonial structure against the Native peoples. Thus while Japanese congratulate themselves as "successful" immigrants, they do not acknowledge that they uphold, and thus enforce, racist colonial laws against the colonized people of the islands, the Native Hawaiians.

Fig. 3. Japanese family in front of a car with a house in the background. Photograph by Usaku Teragawachi (courtesy of Bishop Museum Archives).

Figure 4: "Front of a Hotel"

Perhaps this photograph was excluded from *Kanyaku Imin* because it was unable to evoke any aspects of U.S. nationalism. The large Japanese kanji characters written on the building's façade make this picture "unworkable" within the "nation of immigrants" ideological framework. The first question that comes to the viewer's mind is, Where is this building located? Is it in Japan? Hawai'i would probably not be the first answer, let alone the continental United States.

For the sansei and yonsei, this photograph could prompt reflections on the loss of Japanese culture and heritage in becoming "Americanized." It is a sad thought. Statehood has always been regarded as a watershed moment for the Japanese. It supposedly brought political equality for all "races" within the American system. However, the presence of the large ideographic sign disturbs that ideological assumption of a better world. The photograph makes one compare and contrast the nature of the political space back in the early twentieth century to the one we

Fig. 4. View of Onomichiya Hotel at 226 N. Beretania Street, Hawaiʻi, ca. 1918.
Photograph by Usaku Teragawachi (courtesy of Bishop Museum Archives).

live in today. Are we politically freer today? U.S. statehood further entrenched Hawaiʻi in the U.S. colonial regime rather than liberating it. Instead of a smooth immigrant trajectory from oppression to liberation, this photograph reveals a political reversal—that Japanese were freer to express themselves culturally in the past than they are today. For example, we may speak the Japanese language freely in the twenty-first century because it is a language of commerce in Hawaiʻi. However, it is unlikely that large signs composed of Japanese characters would be displayed in the fiftieth state because it may be construed as an "unAmerican" activity. Hence while Japanese settlers currently seem to have more opportunities than their issei ancestors, these political and economic opportunities are limited to those defined by the U.S. colonial system. The photograph, then, touches upon the idea that the Japanese were "herded" down the path to statehood. The passage of statehood in 1959 gave the illusion of choice, but in fact it narrowed Japanese settler options to only America and everything American.[31]

Conclusion

> Asian Americans need to question not only what the American
> nation-state is doing, but also their own complicity in maintaining
> and furthering the West's [neo]colonialist policies.
>
> —Ruth Y. Hsu, "'Will the Model Minority Please Identify Itself?'
> American Ethnic Identity and Its Discontents"

Today, in this new millennium, Hawai'i remains a colonial possession of the
United States. The Japanese settler community was "herded" down this path of
U.S. nationalism and continues to be "directed." However, at this pivotal moment
in history, we must find another path. As settlers who have benefited from the
colonial system, we must support Native Hawaiian leaders like Mililani and Haunani-Kay Trask to regain control of their homeland. This means Native Hawaiian
nationalists will lead their struggle, and we settlers will follow and endorse their
Native initiatives. The indigenous struggle is not a domestic policy issue between
the U.S. government and a group of citizens but a foreign policy one between two
nations: the colonizing nation (United States) and its colony (Native Hawaiian
nation).

We, as Asian settlers, are not members or citizens of any Native nations occupied by the United States; therefore, we cannot represent Native or "neutral" interests. It is colonialist to think that Asian settlers could participate in any process
that decides Native self-determination or sovereignty or to think that Asian settlers could accept any positions/posts on any colonial government panel or committee that is discussing Native interests. Any settler, Asian or haole, in a colonial
situation can represent only colonial interests. We must understand the depth of
our immigrant indoctrination and hence the implications of our ideological education that structures our worldview in terms of settler interests. We do not live in
a multicultural or multiracial or immigrant nation but a colonial one. The Native
struggle for sovereignty will be decided between the Native nation and the colonizing one (the United States).

It is our responsibility to identify and write about the United States as a settler colonial nation and to do the same for Asian settlers who protect colonial
interests by interfering with Native self-determination. U.S. Senator Daniel Inouye
is the prime settler example. Inouye has been in Congress for over forty years
yet has never introduced legislation to change the political status of wardship for
Native Hawaiians. As past chair of the U.S. Senate Select Committee on Indian
Affairs, Inouye could have introduced legislation establishing a federal relationship between Native Hawaiians and the federal government, but he refused to do
so. This is because Inouye wants to maintain settler dominance and his personal

power. Therefore, he actively uses his knowledge and tremendous political power to undermine, discredit, or in other ways corrupt the process for Native Hawaiian self-determination.[32]

We sansei and yonsei currently have the political and economic means to assist in terminating the U.S. imperial hold on the islands. As Japanese settlers, we have ascended from being collaborators in a colonial system to being enforcers and keepers of that system. Therefore, it is our obligation, our responsibility, to the Native Hawaiian people and to our own community to change this unequal, colonial situation. We must begin to examine the ideologies that blinded our vision in the past, and we must organize in the present against U.S. colonialism.

The Japanese have a saying, *kodomo no tame ni,* meaning "for the sake of the children"; one acts not for one's self but for future generations. For the sake of future generations, the Japanese settler community needs to reevaluate our so-called "successes." Does our comfortable lifestyle come from the theft of Native lands and the genocide of Native peoples? What communities did we step on to get where we are today? Is this the legacy we want to leave our children and children's children? Are we willing to see the evidence of our successful participation in the "American Dream" as a sign of our past collaboration with and our present enforcement of an oppressive colonial system?

Notes

I would like to thank Haunani-Kay Trask for her political analyses, which constantly inspire and guide me, and for reading the initial version of this paper; Ida Yoshinaga for her careful reading and suggestions; Allison Yap and Janice Otaguro for their assistance; Candace Fujikane and Lynn Davis for their support; and finally, a special thank you to my sister, Karen Kosasa, without whom I could not have written this essay.

The first epigraph is from the work of Native Hawaiian nationalist, political organizer, poet, and professor at the University of Hawai'i at Mānoa, Haunani-Kay Trask, who is one of the most outspoken critics of the occupation of Hawai'i by the United States. It is through her work that Native Hawaiian and settler communities have come to recognize Hawai'i as a colony of the United States. It is also through Trask's insightful analysis that local Asians have become recognized as settlers. Haunani-Kay Trask, *From a Native Daughter: Colonialism and Sovereignty in Hawai'i,* rev. ed. (1993); reprint, Honolulu: University of Hawai'i Press, 1999, 25.

The second epigraph quotes former U.S. Senator Spark Matsunaga, a nisei who volunteered for active-duty service in the U.S. military after the bombing of Pearl Harbor. Matsunaga served in the famed 442nd Regimental Combat Team, composed of Japanese settlers, before he became a U.S. senator. Spark M. Matsunaga, "Introduction," in *Kanyaku Imin: A Hundred Years of Japanese Life in Hawaii, 1885–1985,* ed. Leonard Lueras, centennial ed. (Honolulu: International Savings and Loan Association, Ltd., 1985), 10.

1. For other community-history books published for the Kanyaku Imin centennial

celebration, see Roland Kotani, *The Japanese in Hawaii: A Century of Struggle* (Honolulu: The Hawai'i Hochi, Ltd., 1985); Franklin Odo and Kazuko Sinoto, *A Pictorial History of the Japanese in Hawai'i, 1885–1924* (Honolulu: Bishop Museum Press, 1985); Dennis M. Ogawa and Glen Grant, *To a Land Called Tengoku: One Hundred Years of the Japanese in Hawai'i* (Honolulu: Mutual Publishing, 1985); and the republication of Dennis M. Ogawa, *Kodomo No Tame Ni: For the Sake of the Children, The Japanese American Experience in Hawaii* (Honolulu: University of Hawai'i Press, 1985 [1978]).

2. Hawai'i is composed of eight main islands. O'ahu island is the third largest in acreage and holds approximately 80 percent of the state's 1,211,537 residents. It is also the site of Honolulu, the capital city, and Waikīkī Beach, the famed tourist destination. Tourism adds to the congestion and population density of O'ahu island. In 1997 alone over five million tourists visited this island. State of Hawai'i, Department of Business, Economic Development & Tourism, *The State of Hawai'i Data Book 1997, A Statistical Abstract* (Honolulu: State of Hawai'i, 1998), 16, 182, 198.

3. The "American Dream" is a settler ideological belief that the United States provides its citizens with equal access to political and financial prosperity. Cultural studies critic Stuart Ewen writes,

> According to the dream, this privileged existence is open to anyone who really wants it. Those who do not believe in the dream, do not deserve it. Those who do believe, but have not yet achieved it, must try harder. . . . This dream resonates through much of American social history. . . . The notion that each individual has fair access to status and recognition, and therefore can escape the anonymity and conditions of the common lot, has shaped the meaning and understanding of American democracy.

Stuart Ewen, *All Consuming Images: The Politics of Style in Contemporary Culture* (New York: Basic Books, 1988), 58–59.

4. George Ariyoshi, "Message from Governor George R. Ariyoshi," in Kotani, *The Japanese in Hawaii*, 5.

5. Lueras, *Kanyaku Imin.*

6. Walter Dillingham, a powerful white settler industrialist and spokesman for the Hawaiian Sugar Planters Association, represented the racist attitudes of sugar plantation owners when he testified before the U.S. Senate Committee on Immigration in 1921. Responding to the question of why white laborers were not recruited for the plantations, Dillingham replied, "When you are asked to go out in the sun and go into the cane brake, away from the tropical breeze, you are subjecting the white men to something that the good Lord did not create him to do. If He had, the people of the world, I think would have had a white pigment of the skin, and not variegated colors." Quoted in Lawrence H. Fuchs, *Hawaii Pono: An Ethnic and Political History* (Honolulu: Bess Press, 1961), 228.

7. U.S. Senator Daniel Inouye, one of the highest-ranking senators in the U.S. Congress, has directed millions of federal dollars into Hawai'i's economy in the form of military infrastructure to maintain the colonial presence of the United States. Inouye characterizes himself as a supporter of Hawaiian sovereignty, but in fact he consistently undermines the process for Native Hawaiian self-determination and self-government in the islands. Inouye instead works to reinforce and ensure the continuation of American subjugation of Native Hawaiian people and their lands. In 1998 Pat Zell, an Inouye staff member, flew to Hawai'i

to gather support for a draft legislation Inouye wanted to pass in the U.S. Congress in 1999. The Inouye bill asked that the Hawaiian nation be restored, but it did not provide this nation with any "lands, revenues, or powers." In other words, Inouye appeared to be supporting Hawaiian sovereignty with his bill, but instead was coercing Native Hawaiians to settle for a "paper nation." See Kiaʻāina (Governor) Mililani Trask's analyses on the Zell/Inouye tactic in Ka Lāhui Hawaiʻi's "Action Alert" of May 13, 1998, and letter of June 16, 1998, to Ka Lāhui Hawaiʻi officers and to other Hawaiian organizations.

8. In her research, Lynn Davis documented 330 commercial Japanese photographers in the first half of the twentieth century. Lynn Davis, "Directory of Photographers in Hawaiʻi, 1845–1945," unpublished draft, 1997.

9. For further information on colonialism in Hawaiʻi, see Trask, *From a Native Daughter;* for colonialism on the U.S. continent, see Ward Churchill, *Struggle for the Land: Indigenous Resistance to Genocide, Ecocide and Expropriation in Contemporary North America* (Monroe, Maine: Common Courage Press, 1993); for broader understanding of indigenous rights, see Sharon Helen Venne, *Our Elders Understand Our Rights: Evolving International Law Regarding Indigenous Rights* (Penticton, B.C.: Theytus Books Ltd., 1998).

10. Antonio Gramsci, *Selections from the Prison Notebooks of Antonio Gramsci,* trans. Quintin Hoare and Geoffrey Nowell Smith (New York: International Publishers, 1971), 377.

11. Gramsci, *Selections from the Prison Notebooks,* 328, 333, 375–377.

12. Although Lenin argues that his work is an expansion of Marx's original ideas, he has uniquely elucidated the concept of "the dictatorship of the proletariat" as an essential step in overturning state hegemony. For further readings on Lenin, see V. I. Lenin, *State and Revolution* (New York: International Publishers, 1932 and 1943).

13. For an in-depth analysis of the relationship between capitalism, the U.S. government, and the media, see Noam Chomsky, *Necessary Illusions: Thought Control in Democratic Societies* (Boston: South End Press, 1989); Edward S. Herman and Noam Chomsky, *Manufacturing Consent: The Political Economy of the Mass Media* (New York: Pantheon Books, 1988); and Michael Parenti, *Inventing Reality: The Politics of the Mass Media* (New York: St. Martin's Press, 1986).

14. For an insightful analysis of the violation of Native Hawaiians' human rights by the United States, see Trask's chapter on "Hawaiians and Human Rights" in *From a Native Daughter.* Trask argues that the document that underlies the legitimacy of America—the U.S. Constitution—imposes a colonial structure that "declares ownership over indigenous lands and peoples." This U.S. foundational document, then, does not protect the human rights of Native peoples to self-determination and self-government but rather formally allows and legitimizes the abuses. Trask sharply assesses that the overthrow and subsequent annexation by the United States "cannot be raised within the context of the U.S. Constitution." Trask, *From a Native Daughter,* 26–40.

Also see Louis Henkin's article on the ratification of various human rights conventions by the United States. Although the United States signs international human rights conventions, it exempts itself from adhering to those agreements. Henkin points out the United States appends each convention with a "package" of amendments that excuses itself from implementing any obligation or international standards should the convention be "inconsistent" with the U.S. Constitution. The United States refuses to submit to any rulings by the

International Court of Justice that may find it in violation of human rights. Louis Henkin, "U.S. Ratification of Human Rights Conventions: The Ghost of Senator Bricker," *American Journal of International Law* 89 (2) (April 1995): 341–350.

15. Gramsci, *Selections from the Prison Notebooks,* 169–173.

16. For a definition of the state as "state = political society + civil society," see Gramsci, *Selections from the Prison Notebooks,* 262–264.

17. The Native Hawaiian population collapsed through its contact with the West (beginning in 1778). Historian David Stannard estimates the pre-Western contact population to be 800,000 to 1,000,000 people. This number mirrors the current population of Hawai'i in 2008. Yet within fifty-six years after Western contact, the 1832 missionary census recorded the drastic decline of the Native Hawaiian population to approximately 132,000. Fifty years later, when the first Japanese contract laborers arrived, the Native Hawaiian population had dropped to approximately 44,000. For more information on the population collapse, see David Stannard, *Before the Horror: The Population of Hawai'i on the Eve of Western Contact* (Honolulu: University of Hawai'i, Social Science Research Institute, 1989). For a comparison of the Native Hawaiian population to settler populations, see State of Hawai'i, Office of Hawaiian Affairs (OHA), *Native Hawaiian Data Book* (Honolulu: State of Hawai'i OHA, 2002), 9.

18. Noenoe K. Silva, "Kānaka Maoli Resistance to Annexation," *'Ōiwi: A Native Hawaiian Journal* (December 1998): 40–75; and Silva, *Aloha Betrayed: Native Hawaiian Resistance to American Colonialism* (Durham, N.C.: Duke University Press, 2004).

19. In studying the political status of settler groups within the United States, we need to examine the international relationship between the settler group's homeland-nation and the United States. For example, the United States was very concerned that Japan's imperialist interests in Asia and the Pacific would clash with its own. By 1910 Japan included Korea and Taiwan under its colonial possession. Adding to concerns over Japan's imperialistic interests were the large numbers of issei who were openly patriotic toward Japan and its imperialist policies and military victories. This combination alarmed Hawai'i Territorial leaders. Historian John Stephan cites several factors that contributed to strengthening issei ties to Japan, among them the fact that the issei were excluded from U.S. citizenship. John Stephan, *Hawai'i under the Rising Sun: Japan's Plans for Conquest after Pearl Harbor* (Honolulu: University of Hawai'i Press, 1984), 14–15. Also see Gay Satsuma, "Immigrant Patriotism: Hawai'i Japanese and Imperial Victories, 1895–1905," *International Journal of Historical Studies* 1 (2) (March 1989): 59–82; Akira Iriye, *Pacific Estrangement: Japanese and American Expansion, 1897–1911* (Cambridge, Mass.: Harvard University Press, 1972); and Ernest Wakukawa, *A History of the Japanese People in Hawaii* (Honolulu: Toyo Shoin, 1938).

20. See table 1.12, "Ethnic Stock, 1853 to 1970," in Robert C. Schmitt, *Historical Statistics of Hawaii* (Honolulu: University of Hawai'i Press, 1977), 25.

21. While this discussion began in the early twentieth century, the "Japanese Question" continued into World War II. For early discussions, see M. M. Scott, "The Japanese Conquest of Hawaii," *Munsey's Magazine* (October 1904 reprint); letter to the editor by an unnamed observer, "Why the Oriental Seems Cheaper Than the White," *The Sunday Advertiser,* March 14, 1909, 12; Theodore Richards, "The Future of the Japanese in Hawaii: Things Problematic, Things Probable, Things Potential," *The Journal of Race Development*

2 (4) (April 1912): 399–423; Lorrin A. Thurston, "The Japanese Problem in Hawaii," in *Americanization Institute Papers* (Honolulu: Citizenship Education Committee, 1919), 11–34. The Japanese also participated in the discussion on the "Japanese Question" with their own papers and publications: A. K. Ozawa, "Opportunities for American-Born Japanese," *Olympus* 1 (3) (1916): 1–11; Takie and Umetaro Okumura, *Hawaii's American-Japanese Problem: A Campaign to Remove Causes of Friction between the American People and Japanese* (Honolulu: self-published, 1922).

22. Although Japanese settlers suffered under American racist laws and practices, those experiences do not alter the larger political status of Japanese as settlers in a colony. This is a confusing fact for American settlers of color, for they see white settlers as different from themselves. However, in a colonial situation, racism between settlers is racial oppression among settler groups. Irrespective of racial differences among settlers, both settlers of color and white settlers are in the same category and in opposition to the Native peoples of a colony. In Haunani-Kay Trask's keynote address at the First International and Eleventh National Multi-Ethnic Literatures across the Americas and the Pacific (MELUS) Conference in Honolulu on April 18, 1997, she described an "intra-hegemonic" struggle between Asian and haole settlers. Many Asians in the audience were stunned to be labeled as settlers. See Trask's speech reproduced in "Writing in Captivity: Poetry in a Time of De-Colonization," in *Navigating Islands and Continents: Conversations and Contestations in and around the Pacific*, ed. Cynthia Franklin, Ruth Hsu, and Suzanne Kosanke, *Literary Studies East and West* 17 (Honolulu: University of Hawai'i, College of Languages, Linguistics and Literature, 2000). Also see her essay, "Settlers of Color and 'Immigrant' Hegemony: 'Locals' in Hawai'i," *Whose Vision? Asian Settler Colonialism in Hawai'i*, ed. Candace Fujikane and Jonathan Y. Okamura, a special issue of *Amerasia Journal* 26 (2) (2000), reprinted in this volume.

23. Scholar and professor Gary Okihiro documents white racism against the issei and nisei in Hawai'i in his book, *Cane Fires: The Anti-Japanese Movement in Hawaii, 1865–1945* (Philadelphia: Temple University Press, 1991), 78–79. However, like much Asian settler scholarship, he situates his argument outside of the colonial context of Hawai'i and within American national immigrant ideologies. Also see the works by Ronald Takaki, *Pau Hana: Plantation Life and Labor in Hawaii* (Honolulu: University of Hawai'i Press, 1983); and *Strangers From a Different Shore: A History of Asian Americans* (New York: Penguin Books, 1989); Kotani, *The Japanese in Hawaii*; Odo and Sinoto, *A Pictorial History of the Japanese in Hawai'i*; and Ogawa, *Kodomo No Tame Ni*.

24. "How I Earn My Money," *Pacific Commercial Advertiser*, March 28, 1920, Feature Section, 2; and April 1, 1920, 3; "What It Means to Be an American," *Pacific Commercial Advertiser*, April 29, 1920, Section 2, 2.

25. For further readings on the closing of the language schools, see Compilation Committee for the Publication of Kinzaburo Makino's Biography, *Life of Kinzaburo Makino* (Honolulu: n.p., 1965), 38–70; Rev. Takie Okumura, *Seventy Years of Divine Blessings* (Honolulu: Okumura, 1939), 43–47, 127–149; Wakukawa, *A History of the Japanese People in Hawaii*, 265–302; Eileen H. Tamura, *Americanization, Acculturation, and Ethnic Identity: The Nisei Generation in Hawaii* (Chicago: University of Illinois Press, 1994), 146–161; Yōichi Hanoka, "The Japanese Language School: Is It a Help or a Hindrance to the Americanization of Hawaii's Young People?" in Ogawa, *Kodomo No Tame Ni*, 180–182 (article

originally published in *Friends* in 1927); "Unity Essential," in Ogawa, *Kodomo No Tame Ni*, 183–185 (editorial originally published in *Hawaii Hochi*, April 21, 1923).

26. For in-depth discussion on dual citizenship up until the 1930s, see Wakukawa, *A History of the Japanese People in Hawaii*, 303–325. For a general discussion, see Tamura, *Americanization, Acculturation, and Ethnic Identity*, 84–88. For various English-language newspaper articles in the 1930s and 1940s, see "Expatriation Is Backed by New Citizens," *Honolulu Star-Bulletin*, July 23, 1938, 1; "Dual Citizens Urged to Clarify Loyalties," *Honolulu Star-Bulletin*, November 18, 1939, 1; "New Citizens Advised to Be All American," *Honolulu Star-Bulletin*, July 19, 1940, 1; "Crawford Calls on Nisei to End Dual Citizenship," *Honolulu Advertiser*, July 19, 1940, 1; "Steadman Raps Dual Citizenship: Language Schools Again under Fire," *Honolulu Advertiser*, July 20, 1940, 4; "Achi Takes Strong Campaign Stand against Dual Citizens," *Honolulu Advertiser*, October 15, 1940, 1; "Where the Advertiser Stands," *Honolulu Advertiser*, October 3, 1940, Editorial Page; "Advice to the Alien Press," *Honolulu Advertiser*, October 14, 1940, Editorial Page; "Dual Citizenship Bill Wins Support of Island Leaders," *Honolulu Star-Bulletin*, November 21, 1941, 13; and "They Seek to End Dual Citizenship," *Honolulu Star-Bulletin*, May 27, 1946, 6.

27. Scholars Bob Hodge and Vijay Mishra argue that settler states (i.e., the United States, Australia, New Zealand, etc.) create foundation myths in order to legitimize their ownership of the land. Because settler states have conquered other peoples' national lands, mythologies must be produced in order to reinterpret the colonization process in terms of nation building. For example, the United States characterizes its birth within an "empty" continent and as a "host" nation to an immigrant population. The genocidal policies of the United States are absent from these mythologies. Hodge and Mishra argue that to maintain a settler state's hegemony, new forms of the foundation myth need to be generated. Hodge and Mishra, *Dark Side of the Dream: Australian Literature and the Postcolonial Mind* (Sydney: Allen and Unwin, 1991), 26.

28. "Yamashiro (the prisoner): Yamashiro, Under Arrest, Being Escorted to an Automobile, en Route to Jail," *Pacific Commercial Advertiser*, June 11, 1909, 1.

29. I would also like to point out that many of the photographs in the larger Teragawachi collection at the Bishop Museum show women wearing traditional Japanese clothing. For issei women living in the early twentieth century, wearing a kimono or *yukata* was a way of life. Among the photographs selected for the *Kanyaku Imin* publication, over half show Japanese dressed in Western clothing.

30. See Trask's insightful chapter on tourism. Through statistics and political analysis, she compares the selling of the Native culture by settlers to prostitution. Trask, "Lovely Hula Hands: Corporate Tourism and the Prostitution of Hawaiian Culture," *From a Native Daughter*, 136–147.

31. After World War II Hawai'i was on the United Nations' list of nations to be decolonized. The United States was obligated to turn in yearly reports to the U.N. on Hawai'i's progress toward decolonization. However, for a number of complicated political reasons, the United States removed Hawai'i from that list when it conducted its statehood vote. In violation of its trust obligations, the United States gave voters only two political choices: to remain a Territory under the United States or to become a state within the United States. Neither choice gave voters the option for decolonization. The only "choice" the United States

offered was the degree to which Hawai'i would remain a colonial possession: as a Territory or as a state. For Native Hawaiians, the choice of statehood furthered their colonial subjugation, as the Admissions Act of 1959 reclassified their status as wards of the state. Under international law, a colony must be given several choices, including independence and free association. See also Mililani Trask, "Hawai'i and the United Nations," *Whose Vision? Asian Settler Colonialism in Hawai'i*, ed. Candace Fujikane and Jonathan Y. Okamura, a special issue of *Amerasia Journal* 26 (2) (2000), reprinted in this volume.

32. See endnote 9 above; Mililani Trask, "Inouye's Legacy to Hawaiians," *Ka Wai Ola O OHA* 17 (2) (February 2000); and Ida Yoshinaga and Eiko Kosasa, Local Japanese Women for Justice (LJWJ), "Local Japanese Should Understand Inouye's Real Agenda," *Honolulu Advertiser,* February 6, 2000, Focus Section, 1; and reprinted as "Local Japanese Women for Justice (LJWJ) Speak Out against Daniel Inouye and the JACL" in this volume.

JONATHAN Y. OKAMURA

Ethnic Boundary Construction in the Japanese American Community in Hawai'i

In 1996 a former University of Hawai'i baseball player, who is a haole (white) raised in the islands, requested permission to play in the Japanese-only O'ahu AJA (Americans of Japanese Ancestry) Senior Baseball League (hereafter AJA League). The player, Bill Blanchette, indicated he wanted to play in the AJA League because it is the most competitive league for former college and professional players like himself.[1] His request was denied by the league's Board of Directors without any formal explanation given to Blanchette. The league president and others who supported the board's unanimous decision against changing its rule to admit non-Japanese players later cited as their reason the "cultural tradition" of exclusively Japanese American baseball teams and leagues in Hawai'i since the 1900s.

In 1998 the Board of Directors of the Honolulu Japanese Junior Chamber of Commerce (hereafter Jaycees) voted unanimously to reduce the blood quantum requirement of queen contestants in its annual Cherry Blossom Festival pageant from 100 percent Japanese to 50 percent. This rule change, which became effective in 1999, allowed women of part-Japanese descent to compete for the first time in the then forty-seven-year history of the Cherry Blossom Festival. While noting that the rule change was "overdue," then Jaycees president Keith Kamisugi provided the rationale for the change: "If we want to have a festival that reflects the Japanese American community, which is multiethnic, the queen and court should reflect that multiethnicity."[2]

I am interested in these two cases because they both are concerned with constructing the ethnic boundaries of the Japanese American community through formal descent-based rules governing participation in organized activities conducted in public arenas, although both the AJA League and the Jaycees are private, not-for-profit organizations. As such, both cases can be viewed in the larger social and political context of the status and relations of Japanese settlers in multieth-nic Hawai'i rather than as issues pertaining solely or primarily to the Japanese American community, such as defining who is or is not considered to be Japanese. The larger political significance of these two cases extends beyond that community since they generated considerable public interest and, in the case of the AJA League, substantial criticism from non-Japanese.

For comparative purposes, I also will discuss the *Rice v. Cayetano* decision of the U.S. Supreme Court on February 23, 2000 (and its ongoing aftermath), which similarly involved a descent-based eligibility rule, in this case concerning Native Hawaiian rights.[3] In response to a suit filed by Hawai'i resident Harold "Freddy" Rice, the court decided in his favor that a Hawai'i state law that gave only Native Hawaiians the right to vote in elections for trustees of the Office of Hawaiian Affairs (OHA, a state government agency) violated the Fifteenth Amendment of the U.S. Constitution, and therefore non-Hawaiians also have the right to vote in OHA elections. Despite Native Hawaiians having a unique political and legal status and rights as the indigenous people of Hawai'i (rather than being an ethnic minority), in its decision the Supreme Court considered them to be a race and thus applied the Fifteenth Amendment, which prohibits restrictions on voting based on race. While Japanese Americans, along with other settler groups in Hawai'i, and Native Hawaiians differ substantially in historical experience and contemporary political and economic status insofar as the former are a privileged ethnic group and the latter are a disempowered Native people, in both the AJA League and OHA cases I contend that neoconservative arguments focused on individual rights, individual equality, and "racial discrimination" were used to challenge their respective descent-based eligibility requirements. Those cases can be seen as local manifestations of the nationwide neoconservative political movement that seeks to establish a "color-blind" society in which race has no legal, political, or other formal significance in the distribution of rights and benefits.[4] However, the ultimate consequences of this movement in Hawai'i are far more severe for Native Hawaiians, who are being threatened with the loss of their rights to self-determination.

Playing Hard Ball

After it became known that the Board of Directors of the AJA League had voted not to change its Japanese-only rule to allow Blanchette to participate, the decision became the subject of quite contentious public discussion and was no longer an issue of concern only to the Japanese American community. A substantial amount of public commentary appeared in the print media, including the two Honolulu daily newspapers and the Japanese American community newspaper, *The Hawaii*

Herald, over a period of several months in the fall of 1996. Editors and columnists of the Honolulu newspapers expressed strong opposition to the board decision, while letters sent to the newspapers from the general public, including Japanese Americans and non-Japanese, were either opposed to or supportive of the decision. Disagreement with the board decision centered on whether the AJA League had engaged in racial discrimination when it prohibited Blanchette from playing solely because he is not Japanese. Blanchette, who was an anthropology major at the University of Hawai'i, himself recognized the racialized nature of the controversy in his observation: "It's a baseball issue that unfortunately became a race issue." [5] Such racialization of seemingly nonracial issues is quite common in Hawai'i given the pervasive significance of ethnicity as the dominant organizing principle of social relations. That is, ethnicity regulates the distribution of socioeconomic status and maintains the institutionalized inequality among ethnic groups with Chinese Americans, Japanese Americans and haole holding dominant positions, while Filipino Americans, Native Hawaiians, and Sāmoans remain in a subordinate status. [6] The degree of public interest given to an unannounced decision by a private organization concerning an amateur baseball league that attracts little attention except among a relatively small group of followers clearly demonstrates that the controversy extended well beyond the Japanese American community.

As noted above, the primary argument advanced by those who supported retaining the AJA League for Japanese only is that the league is part of the "cultural tradition" of Japanese Americans in Hawai'i. They emphasized the "history" of Japanese-only teams and leagues since the 1900s and viewed the AJA League with considerable pride as a long-time community institution developed and maintained by Japanese Americans. In noting that most of the players in the league would not be opposed to a non-Japanese being allowed to join, a player nonetheless remarked, "But that's because we're not in touch with the history of the league. But the [older] officials of the league are. They know the history. Would you want to be the person to end a tradition that's been standing for 30, 40, 50 years?" [7]

In a letter to the *Honolulu Advertiser,* one writer contended that the controversy over the Japanese-only rule was due to "outsiders from the mainland" not understanding local cultural traditions that are not racist in nature.

> People from the Mainland do not understand the diverse cultures, traditions and ways of the Islands. We respect one another's ways of doing things that an outsider does not understand. The board of the AJA League is not prejudiced but is upholding our cultural tradition. Hopefully, the newcomers to the state will try to learn the traditions and local ways of the diverse cultures of Hawaii and not judge it [*sic*] to be racial. Let's try to live together without causing any controversy. [8]

Another letter writer commented that other groups in Hawaiʻi have ethnically exclusive institutions such as the Kamehameha Schools for Native Hawaiians, the Narcissus Queen contest for Chinese Americans, and the Miss Hawaiʻi Filipina contest for Filipino Americans.

Thus in advancing their argument, supporters of the Japanese-only rule can be seen to invoke principles based on cultural pluralism—that is, racial and ethnic minorities have the right to maintain and practice their cultural traditions, beliefs, and values, especially if they are part of the historical legacy of a group. Similar arguments are made by other ethnic groups in Hawaiʻi in support of their being allowed to continue various cultural traditions and practices, such as exploding firecrackers on New Year's Day.

In contrast, critics of the Japanese-only rule contended that it is a form of racial discrimination insofar as it denies individuals from playing in the league solely on the basis of race. They especially pointed out that the league uses City and County of Honolulu parks for its games and therefore should be subject to government laws that prohibit such discrimination in the use of public facilities. An opponent wrote, "If the single qualifying factor [for playing in the league] is race, how far have we come after all toward a melting pot where all persons are created equal and have equal rights?" A sportswriter for the *Honolulu Star-Bulletin* maintained, "This is the United States of America, and I have no sympathy for any organization that argues to maintain ethnic purity in its membership. Especially not when that organization is using public parks funded by my tax dollars."[9]

Thus critics of the Japanese-descent rule can be seen to have expressed their arguments according to the well-established and accepted principles of equal rights and equality of opportunity. They considered the AJA League to be a racial anachronism that somehow has been allowed to continue despite the formal end of government-supported racial segregation in the United States. However, opponents of the eligibility rule also can be said to have rearticulated the meaning of racial equality from a group to an individual concern in their emphases on a person's right to participate in the AJA League without regard to his race and on discrimination against individuals rather than disadvantaged racial minorities. Their arguments thus are quite similar to neoconservative attacks against affirmative action that reinterpreted the meaning of racial discrimination as a violation of individual rights that, as such, could apply to both whites and nonwhites.[10] However, as race relations scholars Michael Omi and Howard Winant have observed, "By limiting themselves to considering discrimination against *individuals* . . . the neoconservatives trivialized the problem of racial equality, and of equality in general."[11] This trivialization of racial inequality from the group to the individual level explains why critics of the Japanese-only rule limited the scope of their concern solely to the controversy itself—that is, to the AJA League and its rule—and did not address other social arenas in which racial inequality and discrimination persist in Hawai'i.

The neoconservative opponents of the Japanese-only rule are either unable or unwilling to see other, far more significant forms of racial and other discrimination prevalent in Hawai'i such as in employment, education, government, and the law. If they are seriously concerned with eliminating racial discrimination, as the contentious tone of their editorials and letters to the editor seem to indicate, then their efforts would be better spent attacking these much more critical manifestations of institutional discrimination that severely restrict the opportunities and access of groups such as Sāmoans, African Americans, Filipino Americans, and Native Hawaiians. But their rearticulation of the meaning of racial equality and discrimination as issues concerning individual rights served as a convenient means for them to avoid having to confront collective inequalities and injustices based on race faced by minority groups.

An editorial in the *Honolulu Advertiser* argued that opening the AJA League to non-Japanese Americans "should spur other 'institutions' to look anew at their ethnically based policies."[12] But instead of citing as examples of such institutions those government agencies and private corporations that continue to discriminate against racial and ethnic minorities in their hiring, promotion, and contracting practices or that have done little to recruit and advance minorities despite their avowed equal employment opportunity and affirmative action policies, the editorial provided a trivial and incorrect example of the Cherry Blossom Festival pageant that supposedly required its contestants to have Japanese surnames.[13] If the *Advertiser* and other media agencies are seriously concerned about ongoing racial discrimination in Hawai'i, there are obviously many more significant cases for them to investigate and publicize than amateur baseball leagues and ethnic beauty contests. But rearticulation of the meaning of racial discrimination enabled the *Advertiser* to criticize a baseball league and thereby take up the cause of an individual white male so that he could play baseball on Sunday afternoons for three months of the year while many far more economically and politically disadvantaged groups are regularly denied equal opportunity solely because of their race in their pursuit of much more basic rights and services such as jobs, education, health care, and legal justice. As one of the strongest advocates of the "Hawai'i multicultural model" that represents island society as uniquely distinguished by ethnic tolerance and equality,[14] the Honolulu dailies do not want to draw attention to the intolerance and institutionalized inequality that persist in Hawai'i, and therefore they address less significant issues such as AJA baseball that will not disrupt the status quo of ethnic stratification in Hawai'i.

Opening the Cherry Blossom Festival Pageant

As stated above, in 1998 the Board of Directors of the Honolulu Jaycees voted to allow part-Japanese (at least 50 percent blood quantum) women to compete in its annual Cherry Blossom Festival pageant for the first time in the nearly fifty-year history of the contest. While noting that it was overdue, Jaycees officials gave as the primary reason for the rule change that the queen needed to represent the multiethnic nature of the Japanese American community.

The Cherry Blossom Festival was notable as the only remaining major ethnic "beauty pageant" that required its contestants to be of "pure" descent. Participants in the Chinese Narcissus Festival must be at least 50 percent Chinese, while those in the Miss Hawai'i Filipina pageant need only be of Filipino descent, without any minimum percentage specified. These more liberal eligibility rules reflect the high degree of intermarriage historically in both the Chinese American and Filipino American communities, both of which were dominated by males during their respective periods of plantation labor recruitment. In contrast, Japanese Americans historically had one of the lowest out-marriage rates and since 1900 have been the largest or second largest ethnic group in Hawai'i. Thus the rule change by the Jaycees was not due to an increasing difficulty in finding sufficient numbers of full Japanese American women to compete in the pageant, as has been the case with similar Japanese American beauty contests on the West Coast.[15]

Although they occurred much earlier, public acknowledgment and acceptance of the multiracial/ethnic composition of the Japanese American community are evident in the Historical Gallery of the Japanese Cultural Center of Hawai'i in Honolulu, which opened in 1994. The very last exhibit in the gallery, which is concerned with the Japanese American historical experience in Hawai'i since labor migration in the late 1800s, is a five-by-four-foot mural consisting of black-and-white photographs of the faces of four generations of male and female Japanese, with each generation arranged in a column of twelve photographs. What probably is apparent even to non-Japanese as one views the photographs is the increasing presence of faces of individuals of multiracial or multiethnic descent, beginning particularly with the sansei (third generation) and becoming very obvious with the yonsei (fourth generation). The significant number of these photos among both the sansei and yonsei generations clearly is meant to represent the considerable presence of part-Japanese among those generations and their acceptance in the Japanese American community.

Thus the Jaycees' change in its descent-eligibility rule to allow part-Japanese women to compete in its Cherry Blossom Festival pageant constitutes an established organization trying to catch up with the social and cultural reality in the larger community. Then Jaycees president Keith Kamisugi acknowledged this delay in his comment that "the pageant was behind the times. The community is already extensively multi-ethnic. We should have done this years ago."[16] Changing the descent rule had been formally discussed in 1984 and again in 1993, but on both occasions the proposed change was defeated by the Jaycees Board of Directors on the basis that "if it's not broken, why fix it?"[17] Another reason given in the past for not allowing part-Japanese women to participate was that it would diminish the "ethnic integrity" of the pageant.[18] However, while the rule and the pageant may not have appeared to be in need of fixing, there was an obvious non-correspondence between the pageant contestants (and queens) and the larger Japanese American community they were supposed to represent; thus the Jaycees could be said to have been in denial about the substantial presence of part-Japanese in the community.

Given the resistance in the past to changing the 100 percent Japanese descent requirement, it is not surprising to learn that the rule change was not welcomed by all Jaycees members. Kamisugi acknowledged that the rule change resulted in "a great deal of skepticism among quite a few of our members and at least some of our past leaders."[19] The continued resistance to making such a long overdue change is unfortunate because as a prominent and established organization in the Japanese American community, the Jaycees should be leading the community by establishing precedents for the rest to follow. More than twenty years ago, the selection of the first Cherry Blossom Queen with an Okinawan name was noteworthy. Again, the Jaycees were following the example of the community and not leading it. However, it cannot be denied that the Jaycees have provided vanguard leadership to the Japanese American community since it began in 1949. In the late 1950s they admitted non-Japanese as members, and in 1969 they elected a Filipino American as their first non-Japanese president.[20]

In 1999 several part-Japanese women competed in the Cherry Blossom Festival pageant for the first time, and in the following year the first part-Japanese queen, Vail Soyo Matsumoto, who is part-Italian, was selected. Catherine Elizabeth Toth, who is of Japanese and Hungarian descent, won the title in 2001 as the first queen without a Japanese last name. In 2002 Lori Akiko Lokelani Okinaga, who is of Hawaiian ancestry, was chosen as the fiftieth queen. The very quick and multiple selections of part-Japanese women as Cherry Blossom Queen following the rule change could be taken as indicating that it was considered long overdue by the Japanese American community.

Baseball and Beauty Queens

A comparison of the respective decisions made by the AJA League and the Jaycees concerning their descent-based eligibility rules needs to consider that the baseball league already had been allowing part-Japanese (at least those with Japanese surnames initially) to participate since the early 1950s.[21] The decision that league officials faced of whether to permit non-Japanese to play went much further than that of the Jaycees Board of Directors, who could be said to have finally followed a precedent established more than forty years before by the baseball league. However, unlike a beauty pageant, which selects an individual winner, baseball is a team activity, and a few part-Japanese team members do not have the same social impact as would a solitary, part-Japanese Cherry Blossom Queen. Having a non-Japanese member of a baseball team, who may not necessarily even play in a given game, is perhaps a less controversial issue for the AJA League, especially since it was known that non-Japanese had been playing in the league since the 1980s in open violation of its eligibility rule, albeit without formal approval. League officials could have considered various ways by which non-Japanese players could join a team without their having a major impact on the game, such as allowing only one player on each team.

The invoking of Japanese cultural tradition and culture in both cases is also instructive in accounting for the difference in positions taken by the AJA League and the Jaycees. In expressing approval of the rule change permitting part-Japanese women to participate in the pageant, 1999 Cherry Blossom Queen Lori Murayama observed that "anyone can embrace the [Japanese] culture if they go in with an open heart and mind."[22] Similarly, former Jaycees president Keith Kamisugi maintained that the rule change "gives opportunity to more people of Hawaii to participate in learning about the Japanese culture."[23] Thus the Jaycees' position is based on the generally accepted view of culture as being learned and not linked exclusively with a particular racial or ethnic group, while supporters of the Japanese-only rule in the AJA League case held an ethnically exclusive notion of cultural tradition.

One possible explanation for the difference in decisions made by the AJA League and the Jaycees concerns generational and age differences in their leadership. The leaders of the league are predominantly older nisei (second generation) and sansei, while Jaycees leaders and members are primarily yonsei, since by nationally established Junior Chamber of Commerce rules they must be less than thirty-nine years old.[24] While the nisei were at the forefront of opening up a highly racialized Hawai'i society in the 1950s and 1960s as labor leaders, legislators, union members, and supporters of a revitalized Democratic Party, they may not necessarily espouse the same progressive values of social justice and equality and economic reform that distinguished them during those decades. A letter writer, who identified himself as Japanese American, emphasized this change in social values in noting that the Japanese-only rule of the AJA League "runs counter to what the boys in the 100th [Infantry] Battalion and 442nd Regimental Combat

Team fought for: fair play the American way."[25] Those Japanese American soldiers in World War II were overwhelmingly nisei and became staunch supporters of the Democratic Party in the 1950s as it gained political power from the haole-dominated Republican Party that had a stranglehold on local politics and government since Hawai'i formally became a U.S. territory in 1900. Along with other nisei, a significant number of Japanese American World War II veterans were elected to office during the 1950s and 1960s and led the Democrats in the Territorial and State legislatures in passing progressive legislation.[26]

However, the great majority of the nisei is in their seventies and eighties and represent the grandparent generation of the yonsei, who are generally in their twenties and thirties. While the yonsei are not viewed as being as liberal a generation in social values and political beliefs as the sansei were when they were about the same age, the yonsei may be considered far more open and progressive in their views concerning ethnic relations compared to the nisei in the 2000s. Most of the players in the AJA League, who are generally yonsei, were not opposed to permitting non-Japanese into the league.[27] This difference in values and attitudes toward other ethnic groups between the nisei and older sansei leaders of the AJA League and the yonsei leaders of the Jaycees very likely contributed to the different decisions made by those organizations concerning their respective descent-based eligibility rules. As noted by one of the AJA League team managers who had been inclined to allow Blanchette to play, "After talking with the older guys—the guys who have been with [the AJA League] a long time—I was convinced we should keep it closed."[28] If the decision had been theirs to make, the yonsei players in the league may very well have voted to permit non-Japanese to play.

The Politics of Ethnic Boundary Construction

The decisions by the AJA League not to admit non-Japanese into the league and by the Jaycees to include part-Japanese in the Cherry Blossom Festival pageant must not be viewed as issues of interest only to the organizations concerned or to the Japanese American community. The decision by the league received extensive coverage in the sports section of the two Honolulu dailies and was the subject of an editorial in one of the newspapers and of numerous letters to the editor to both by Japanese Americans and non-Japanese. Although less controversial, the rule change by the Jaycees was literally "front page news" in the Honolulu daily newspapers, in addition to the Japanese American community newspaper *The Hawaii Herald*. The reason that the decisions by these organizations were of interest and concern to the larger society is because Japanese Americans are one of the larger and more privileged and powerful ethnic groups in Hawai'i, and the decisions themselves have implications for the relations between Japanese Americans and other island groups. Thus interest on the part of non-Japanese was not primarily focused on the AJA League or the Cherry Blossom Festival pageant but on the larger Japanese American community, particularly in the case of the more controversial decision by the AJA League.

In voting to uphold its Japanese-only rule, the directors of the AJA League acted to protect its interests, resources, and privileges in response to a perceived threat from external forces. Commenting on a telephone call he received from a City and County of Honolulu attorney after the controversy over the league's decision had developed, AJA League president Homer Sheldon stated, "It got me on the edge because we're going to have to start protecting the league. I mentioned to the field managers . . . that we're going to take a stand. And if they force us to allow another nationality in our league, we're going to fold the league. We're not going to give in."[29] This hard-line stance also was evident in the unanimous vote of the Board of Directors, apparently with no discussion of the issue, against allowing Blanchette into the league. While such a reaction is understandable on the part of disadvantaged minorities in order to protect their limited resources, a more politically and economically dominant group such as Japanese Americans could have responded to such a request by seeking a compromise resolution to the issue.

Franklin Odo and Susan Yim had predicted that the Japanese American community would respond in such a "defensive" ethnicity manner by seeking to "protect their steadily diminishing areas of influence" by engaging in greater favoritism rather than becoming more egalitarian and inclusive if they perceived their political and economic interests were being threatened.[30] Obviously, it is one thing to deny entry into an amateur baseball league and quite another to limit access to other far more significant economic and political arenas in which Japanese Americans exert a considerable degree of power and control as evident from their substantial representation or positions of authority. These areas include as Department of Education teachers and principals, state and county government white-collar workers, state legislators, and appointed state administrators.[31] Japanese American overrepresentation in those and in other areas in the private sector already has been criticized for some time by other ethnic groups as an indication of Japanese American favoritism for members of their own group and discrimination against other groups.[32]

In the mid-1980s former ethnic studies instructor and state legislator Roland Kotani observed that "faced by anti-Japanese sentiments, AJA politicians and government officials often reacted defensively." He cited a "powerful" member of the state House of Representatives who argued, "The white man is the minority in Hawaii politics. There is a tinge of envy because there are so many Orientals in office. But we shouldn't be ashamed. The governor makes appointments. Why should he have to make excuses for the large numbers of Orientals in office? If we went to the mainland . . . the reverse would be true." [33]

Many Japanese American engineering, contracting, architecture, and other firms seek to enhance their access to lucrative state and county government contracts by contributing to the election campaigns of gubernatorial and mayoral candidates. However, between fall 2001 and 2003, 60 percent of the firms fined or prosecuted for making excessive or false-name campaign contributions in Hawai'i were owned or co-owned by Japanese Americans. In another example of defensive ethnicity, in 2002 several Japanese American state government officials and private contractors were arrested and later convicted of theft and bribery charges in an alleged kickback scheme at the Honolulu International Airport.[34] According to the state attorney general, the scam allegedly involved providing kickbacks to airport administrators in return for state contracts for maintenance and repair work at the airport. It resulted in more than doubling the annual cost of airport maintenance projects from $3 million to $7 million in 1999 and could be the largest misuse of taxpayer funds in state history. Other criminal incidents of abuse of power by Japanese American elected officials became evident in the early 2000s.[35]

As evident from the AJA League and other cases, it would be extremely unfortunate for Hawai'i's people if Japanese Americans continue to respond to such challenges in a defensive manner by seeking to maintain their power and privilege, for example, by favoring Japanese American applicants for jobs or government contracts, while denying fair and equal access to non-Japanese. Given their undeniable dominant socioeconomic and political status in Hawai'i (together with Chinese Americans and haole), Japanese Americans as individuals and organizations should use their privileged positions to work toward the creation and maintenance of equality of opportunity for disadvantaged groups in the state. As noted by English professor Candace Fujikane, "To speak out against local Japanese racism and colonialism is not to malign local Japanese communities but rather to hold ourselves accountable to a broader vision of justice." [36]

Post-Rice Hawai'i: Racializing Native Hawaiians

Japanese Americans are certainly not the only ethnic or racial group in Hawai'i and the continental United States that has established formal descent-based rules for determining eligibility to participate in organized programs or activities. Other groups in Hawai'i such as Chinese Americans and Filipino Americans have developed comparable rules to ascertain eligibility for beauty pageants, sports activities, and scholarships. In contrast to ethnic minorities that have immigrated and settled in the islands, Native Hawaiians are distinctive insofar as they are the indigenous people of Hawai'i, and descent-based eligibility rules have been established by and for them in both the private and public sectors. Among private organizations, the Kamehameha Schools admit students of Native Hawaiian ancestry in accordance with the 1884 will of Princess Bernice Pauahi Bishop that established the schools. Public institutions such as the Hawai'i state and federal governments have mandated descent-based requirements in order for Native Hawaiians to be eligible to receive certain entitlements designated for them such as tuition waivers at the University of Hawai'i and homestead land through the State Department of Hawaiian Home Lands for which recipients by federal law must be at least 50 percent Hawaiian. But as law professors Eric Yamamoto and Chris Iijima point out, as the Native people of Hawai'i, Native Hawaiians "are not seeking privileges or handouts. Nor are they seeking racial preferences. Rather they are asserting international human rights: not simply the right to equality, but the right to self-determination . . . not a right to 'special treatment,' but to reconnect spiritually with their land and culture; not a right to participate in the U.S. polity, but a right to some form of governmental sovereignty."[37]

The U.S. Supreme Court decision in the *Rice v. Cayetano* case threatens those state and federal rights specified for Native Hawaiians only. In response to Rice's lawsuit, filed initially in 1996, which claimed he was subject to racial discrimination because as a non-Hawaiian he was not allowed to vote in elections for trustees of the Office of Hawaiian Affairs (OHA), the court's decision in 2000 granted non-Hawaiians that privilege.[38] In this case, the descent-based rule restricting voting for OHA trustees (who at that time had to be Native Hawaiian) only to Native Hawaiians was not established by Native Hawaiians themselves but by the majority of voters of the state of Hawai'i when they approved the constitutional amendment that created OHA in 1978.

The lawsuit challenging the Native Hawaiians–only voting rule filed by Rice, a wealthy descendant of a missionary family that came to Hawai'i in the early nineteenth century, and the criticisms of that rule expressed after the Supreme Court decision can be viewed as attacks against Native Hawaiians and not the rule per se. Given the absence of much public discussion, I do not believe that there was a great interest, at least prior to the Supreme Court ruling, among non-Hawaiians to vote in the elections for OHA trustees. Thus the attacks against the restricted nature of the voting extend beyond the OHA elections and are really directed against what are referred to as the "special benefits" and "racial preferences" that Native Hawaiians have been receiving and are currently seeking, particularly sovereignty. While Rice and his attorneys may have invoked the need to ensure equality and equal rights in their legal arguments claiming "reverse racial discrimination" against him, the principal goal of their suit was to keep Native

Hawaiians in their subjugated and disempowered status in the United States and thereby to maintain colonial rule over them.

That this was really their ultimate objective became clear the day after the Supreme Court decision was announced when one of Rice's attorneys, John W. Goemans, emboldened by their victory, declared that all "race-based" government programs for Native Hawaiians would be legally challenged: "What the Supreme Court has done with this ruling, narrow as it may seem, is say [that] Native Hawaiian is a racial characterization . . . and that means that all government programs, state and federal, for Native Hawaiians are race-based, presumptively unconstitutional and up for challenge."[39]

Goemans continued that potential cases could include challenging programs for Native Hawaiians that provide homestead land, housing grants, gathering rights, and health and education services. A month later, he maintained that several non-Hawaiians wanted to run in the OHA trustee election and that he would sue on their behalf if their candidacy was denied on the basis that they are not Hawaiian.[40] After a white male, Kenneth Conklin, was denied nomination papers in June 2000 to seek office as an OHA trustee because he is not Hawaiian, such a suit was filed the next month by attorney William Burgess. In that case, *Earl Arakaki et al. v. the State of Hawai'i,* Arakaki and other Hawai'i residents claimed the Rice decision gave non-Hawaiians the right to run for OHA trustee. In September 2000 a U.S. district judge decided in their favor that non-Hawaiians could seek office as OHA trustee, and in her ruling quoted Supreme Court Justice Antonin Scalia in his concurrence with the court's *Adarand* decision: "to pursue the concept of racial entitlement—even for the most admirable and benign of purposes—is to reinforce and preserve for future mischief the way of thinking that produced race slavery, race privilege and race hatred."[41] The citing of this statement to support a legal decision concerning Native Hawaiians clearly captures how successful the opponents of Native Hawaiian rights have been in distorting those rights as resulting in "race privilege and race hatred."

That same month all nine OHA trustees resigned their positions rather than be forced out by then Governor Ben Cayetano, who had earlier indicated he would seek to have them removed from office after the Hawai'i Supreme Court ruled the state could challenge their authority as trustees by filing a petition with the high court.[42] Within a little more than a week of their resignation, Cayetano appointed an interim OHA board that included a Japanese American businessman and 442nd Regimental Combat Team veteran, Charles Ota, as the first non-Hawaiian to serve as a trustee. Ota, together with more than a dozen non-Hawaiians, ran for OHA trustee in the November 2000 elections and was the only one elected after receiving more than 100,000 votes.

On another front, in April 2000 another of Rice's attorneys announced that his law firm would file a "reverse discrimination" suit within the next six months to eliminate educational and other programs for Native Hawaiians.[43] Referring to the *Rice* decision, he added, "So I see this as a milestone in the sense that it has brought realization to the people of this state that nothing is sacred anymore, that all programs are going to be looked at, going to be revisited." Two such programs, OHA and the Department of Hawaiian Home Lands (DHHL), were targeted in a federal lawsuit filed on October 3, 2000, on behalf of a white male, Patrick Barrett, which challenged the constitutionality of Article 12 of the Hawai'i Constitution that established OHA, adopted the federal Hawaiian Homes Commission Act, and provided for Hawaiian gathering rights on private property. Barrett's attorney, Patrick Hanifin, contended that since the *Rice* decision defined Hawaiian as a "racial classification" and government programs cannot discriminate on the basis of race, services and benefits provided by OHA and DHHL should be open to all Hawai'i state residents without regard to race.[44]

Barrett's lawsuit was dismissed in July 2001 on the basis that he had no legal standing to file it because, among other reasons, he could not demonstrate he would benefit from an OHA business loan and had admitted he had never attempted and had no plans to gather natural materials on private property.[45] In February 2002 another suit against OHA filed by John Carroll, former chair of the Hawai'i Republican Party and a Republican candidate for governor in 2002, was similarly dismissed in U.S. District Court on the grounds that he lacked legal standing since he had not attempted to obtain any benefits from OHA.[46] In very likely a coordinated campaign, Carroll had sued on October 2, 2000 (the day before Barrett's suit was filed), to prohibit the state from making revenue payments from the Ceded Lands Trust to OHA and to stop the latter from funding its programs because, according to him, OHA provides services only to Native Hawaiians and thus violates his Fourteenth Amendment rights to equal protection.

Following the rulings in the Barrett and Carroll lawsuits, yet another suit against OHA and DHHL was filed in 2002 by William Burgess and Patrick Hanifin, the attorneys who had represented plaintiffs in previous cases against Native Hawaiian rights. This federal lawsuit again challenged the constitutionality of OHA and DHHL and sought to abolish both state agencies. The suit (sometimes referred to as "Arakaki II") was filed on behalf of sixteen plaintiffs from various ethnic groups, most of whom were parties in the *Arakaki et al. v. State of Hawai'i* case.[47] It was dismissed in 2004 because of the then pending consideration by Congress of the "Akaka Bill" that would provide for federal recognition of Native Hawaiians comparable to that afforded Native Americans and Alaska Natives. The plaintiffs appealed that ruling to the 9th U.S. Circuit Court of Appeals later in the year, and the court ruled in 2005 that they have legal standing to contest State of Hawai'i funding of OHA with state taxes but lack such standing to challenge similar funding of DHHL. The case has been returned to the U.S. District Court in Hawai'i for trial.[48]

Burgess has described OHA and DHHL as the "motherships of racial discrimination" because, according to him, they use taxpayer funds to serve unequally only Native Hawaiians in violation of the equal protection clause of the Fourteenth Amendment.[49] Burgess and his wife Sandra, who is Hawaiian, have been at the forefront of what has clearly emerged as a political movement, sometimes called "Aloha for All" by its leaders, to eliminate state agencies and programs for Native Hawaiians following the *Rice* decision. He explains their position: "We believe in advocating for aloha for all, which means that all citizens, whatever their ancestry, are entitled to equal protection of the law. The Office of Hawaiian Affairs and Department of Hawaiian Home Lands not only divide people according to race, they send a message to Hawaiian people that they cannot be successful or make it on their own in the world without help from government."[50]

As evident from the above, Burgess and his followers are strong advocates of neoconservative racial politics, a major objective of which is to eliminate the formal significance of race toward the establishment of a "color blind" America in which race has no legal basis in the allocation of resources or benefits, and everyone is treated equally as individuals by the state. Like other neoconservatives, including those who accused the AJA League of committing racial discrimination against Blanchette, Burgess and his group emphasize individual rather than group equality and thus view racial discrimination as fundamentally a denial of individual rights, whether those of whites or nonwhites. In keeping with neoconservative arguments, they also contend that economic success results from individual hard work and achievement and personal responsibility rather than from what they contend are government "handouts" and special "race-based privileges" being bestowed upon Native Hawaiians through OHA and DHHL.

To garner support for their views and to obscure their perpetuation of the political and economic subjugation of Native Hawaiians, Burgess and his followers appropriate elements of the Hawai'i multicultural model that maintains the islands are a setting of especially tolerant, harmonious, and egalitarian ethnic relations.[51] They contend that such harmony and equality are being threatened by the "racial discrimination" and "racial preferences" of the state government in its provision of Native Hawaiian rights through OHA and DHHL. On a website maintained by Burgess and his wife, they contend, "Hawaii's gift to the world is the Aloha spirit embodied daily in the beautiful people of many races living here in relative harmony. . . . It is not in keeping with the spirit of Aloha for the government to give one racial group land or money or special privileges or preferences from which all other racial groups in Hawaii are excluded."[52]

They also direct specific criticism to Hawaiian sovereignty advocates and their supposed "racial agenda": "In the activists' demands for 'sovereignty' or 'entitlements' we hear echoes of apartheid, ethnic cleansing, white supremacy and other concepts based on racial discrimination." While Burgess and his followers argue that race should have no legal significance in society in the distribution of rewards and privileges, they nonetheless racialize Native Hawaiians by categorizing them as a race so that programs established for their benefit can be contested as racially discriminatory. The misrepresentation of Native Hawaiians as a "racial group" seeking to maintain "racial preferences" for themselves prevents Burgess and his followers, the U.S. Supreme Court, and supporters of the court's *Rice* decision from acknowledging that Native Hawaiians are Kānaka Maoli, the indigenous people of Hawai'i, with consequent unique rights that ethnic groups cannot claim. Instead, Burgess and his wife maintain that "individuals of Hawaiian ancestry are just like the rest of us. Hawaiians are not a 'people' separate from the state's other citizens. They are not a 'tribe,' not a 'sovereign nation.' They are one among many ethnic groups in the state, entitled to the same respect we give all those groups and their valued culture—but not more."[53]

The problem with this line of thinking is that the "rest of us" are settlers in Hawai'i and thus cannot claim Native status or rights as can Native Hawaiians. The latter therefore have a unique political and legal status in Hawai'i rather than being "one among many" ethnic groups and cannot be treated as though their historical experiences, especially sovereignty, are comparable to those of other groups. However, from the neoconservative perspective, Native Hawaiians and Japanese Americans are equally "ethnic groups," and hence both OHA and the AJA League came under their attack as racially discriminatory.

Rice's suit and some of the other lawsuits against Native Hawaiian rights were funded by right-wing organizations such as the Campaign for a Color Blind America and were assisted by law firms based on the U.S. continent, indicative of the larger political significance of the issue beyond Hawai'i and Native Hawaiians.[54] The emergence of these suits was very likely encouraged by the anti-affirmative action movement that gained substantial ground in the 1990s with the prohibition of race-based affirmative action in California, Florida, Georgia, Texas, and Washington and with ongoing legal challenges in courts across the nation.[55] Thus the *Rice* decision, as narrow as it was in ruling only on who can vote in OHA elections, has ushered in a new era in social relations in Hawai'i—that is, "Post-Rice Hawai'i." The decision already has resulted in the elimination of Native Hawaiians-only rights to vote and seek office in OHA elections and in ongoing legal and political challenges to their remaining rights and may result in similar lawsuits against programs and services designated for ethnic minorities in Hawai'i.

As a notable example, in 2001 the Kamehameha Schools indicated that it would no longer apply for or accept federal funds that amounted to more than two million dollars annually for programs such as college scholarships and free and reduced-price school lunches.[56] In a far more controversial decision in 2002, the schools announced that its Maui campus had accepted a non-Hawaiian student for the coming school year because the pool of academically qualified Native Hawaiian applicants had been exhausted.[57] These decisions very likely were made because of a concern that the schools' admissions policy, which gives "preference" to Native Hawaiians "to the extent permitted by law and the rules governing tax-exempt organizations,"[58] and its tax-exempt status would be legally contested by neoconservative organizations, since institutions that receive federal monies are prohibited from discriminating on the basis of race. Cognizant of this threat, J. Douglas Ing, then chair of the Board of Trustees of Ke Ali'i Pauahi Foundation, which oversees the Kamehameha Schools, stated, "There are those in this country that would like to erode if not eliminate rights for indigenous and native people. We're attempting to protect the admissions policy. To do that it may be necessary for us to give up a pawn here and a pawn there."[59] In fact, in 1997 "Freddy" Rice had filed two federal lawsuits against the schools' admissions policy; one challenged it as a violation of civil rights, and the other charged the policy as violating tax laws.[60] Both suits were later withdrawn by Rice's attorneys because he lacked sufficient funds to proceed with them in addition to his suit against OHA.[61]

In 2003 the Kamehameha Schools were sued by a non-Hawaiian student whose mother had falsely claimed she was Native Hawaiian in her son's school application. The student charged the admissions policy was racially discriminatory against non-Hawaiians. Seeking to protect its policy from further legal challenge, the schools' Board of Trustees agreed to let the seventh-grade student continue through the twelfth grade if he dropped his lawsuit.[62] Another suit was filed in 2003, *John Doe v. Kamehameha Schools,* by an anonymous non-Hawaiian student who also challenged the schools' admissions policy as racially discriminatory after twice being denied acceptance because he is not Hawaiian. In a 2004 ruling in the case, a U.S. District Court judge in Hawai'i found that Kamehameha's admissions policy "serves a legitimate remedial purpose by addressing the socioeconomic and educational disadvantages facing native Hawaiians . . . and revitalizing native Hawaiian culture."[63] However, in 2005 the decision by two of the three judges on a 9th U.S. Circuit Court of Appeals panel in San Francisco overturned the previous ruling and found that the schools' admissions policy "constitutes unlawful race discrimination" and results in "an absolute bar to admission for non-Hawaiians."[64]

Commenting on the court's decision, attorney John Goemans contended that it "is a reaffirmation of everything found in Rice, that all these programs are all race-based. This case sets precedents for other cases [challenging programs only for Native Hawaiians] and dramatically raises the national visibility of what exists in Hawaii and has grown since the 1970s, this pernicious racism." [65]

Goemans' observations underscore the significance of the *Rice* decision as itself a major precedent in providing the legal basis for challenging other programs, both private and public, designated for Native Hawaiians. His reference to "racism" in Hawai'i is ironic insofar as he views non-Hawaiians as somehow victims of racism and racial discrimination by Native Hawaiians because non-Hawaiians are denied the privilege of benefiting from programs such as the Kamehameha Schools that are fully funded by Native Hawaiian financial resources. Shortly after the decision in the John Doe case was announced, the Kamehameha Schools sought and was granted an "en banc" hearing of the case by a larger panel of judges. On December 5, 2006, the en banc panel, in an 8–7 vote, reaffirmed the original judge's decision. The case was subsequently settled out of court by the trustees of the Kamehameha Schools and John Doe in 2007, resulting in the withdrawal of his petition to the U.S. Supreme Court. As is evident, the legal challenges to Native Hawaiian rights since the *Rice* decision are very much part of the overall neoconservative shift in racial politics since the 1970s that seeks to eliminate race-based programs particularly in education and employment. But they also, and perhaps more significantly, represent a gigantic leap backward in efforts to abolish racial inequality, injustice, and discrimination in society.

Conclusion

The three cases discussed above—that is, the AJA League, the Cherry Blossom Festival pageant, and the Native Hawaiian rights court cases—were all focused on descent-based rules that determine eligibility to participate in those activities. As I have argued, ethnic boundary making in Hawai'i is not an issue limited to the group concerned but has important implications for the political and economic relations between that group and other ethnic groups since the constructed boundary may restrict the participation of the latter in an organized activity or program and thus may be subject to challenge.

Economically and politically dominant groups such as Japanese Americans have the power to exclude others from participation in activities and organizations they control, as in the Cherry Blossom Festival pageant and AJA League cases. The latter incident constituted an opportunity for Japanese Americans to respond by upholding principles of social equality and inclusiveness, but such was not the case because of the increasing defensive ethnicity of the community to retain control over its interests and resources. The unwillingness of the AJA League to revise its eligibility rule reinforced the view among many non-Japanese that Japanese Americans are primarily concerned with maintaining their political and economic power in social arenas they control without regard to the status or concerns of other groups.

In the case of Native Hawaiians, descent-based eligibility rules previously established by the state and federal governments for their sole benefit are being contested because, despite their continuing subordinate political and economic status, the sovereignty movement to establish a self-governing Hawaiian nation has gained substantial Native Hawaiian community support since its emergence in the 1970s. Thus driven by the neoconservative political movement, the objective of lawsuits against rights designated specifically for Native Hawaiians, as in the Rice, Arakaki, Barrett, Carroll, "Arakaki II," and Kamehameha Schools cases, and of other legal and political challenges that are very likely to follow, is to maintain Native Hawaiians in their colonized and disempowered status in their homeland by abolishing rights that had previously been granted only to them or that they had enjoyed as a sovereign nation.

Notes

I would like to thank Candace Fujikane and John Rosa for their critical and very useful comments and suggestions for revision of an earlier draft of this essay.

1. Cited in Dave Reardon, "Schutter: AJA Discriminates But That Isn't Against Law," *Honolulu Star-Bulletin*, August 30, 1996.

2. Quoted in Gwen Battad, "Too Little, Too Late?" *The Hawaii Herald*, August 21, 1998, A1, A5.

3. I use the term "descent-based" instead of "race-based" because Native Hawaiians are not a race or an ethnic minority but the Native people of Hawai'i.

4. Michael Omi and Howard Winant, *Racial Formation in the United States: From the 1960s to the 1990s*, 2nd ed. (New York: Routledge, 1994), 117, 128–132.

5. Quoted in Dave Reardon, "AJA Directors Vote to Keep Out Non-Japanese Players," *Honolulu Star-Bulletin*, October 1, 1996.

6. U.S. Census Bureau, 2001. Summary File 1 Hawai'i. See also J. Y. Okamura, "Social Stratification," *Multicultural Hawai'i: The Fabric of a Multiethnic Society*, ed. Michael Haas (New York: Garland Publishing, 1998), 187, 200–201.

7. Quoted in Mark Santoki, "AJA Baseball Today," *The Hawaii Herald*, June 21, 1996, A15. While supporters of the Japanese-descent rule note that the Oʻahu AJA Senior League is the premier amateur baseball league in the state in terms of the level of competition and organization, they do not mention that the level of baseball skill and knowledge attained by Japanese Americans over the years is likely another reason that supporters of the Japa-

nese-only rule would like to maintain the AJA League only for Japanese Americans, since baseball is commonly acknowledged as "their game" in Hawaiʻi.

8. Sachi Sugino, "Pendulum Swings on Racism—But Enough, Already," *Honolulu Advertiser,* October 18, 1996.

9. Pat Bigold, "'Pure' AJA Has No Place in Public Parks," *Honolulu Star-Bulletin,* October 4, 1996, C1. However, City and County of Honolulu officials stated that any not-for-profit organization can use its facilities, and this position was affirmed by the Hawaiʻi Civil Rights Commission. Stacey Kaneshiro, "AJA Will Keep Ethnic Requirement," *Honolulu Advertiser,* October 2, 1996, C4.

10. Omi and Winant, *Racial Formation in the United States,* 131.

11. Omi and Winant, *Racial Formation in the United States,* 131, emphasis in original.

12. Editorial, "AJA Baseball League Should Open Its Doors," *Honolulu Advertiser,* October 3, 1996.

13. At that time, Cherry Blossom Festival pageant contestants were required to be full Japanese by descent, whatever their last name might be.

14. Jonathan Y. Okamura, "The Illusion of Paradise: Privileging Multiculturalism in Hawaiʻi," *Making Majorities: Constituting the Nation in Japan, Korea, China, Malaysia, Fiji, Turkey, and the United States,* ed. D. C. Gladney (Stanford, Calif.: Stanford University Press, 1998), 264–284.

15. Rebecca C. King, "'Eligible' to be Asian American: Counting on Multiraciality," *Intersections and Divergences: Contemporary Asian Pacific American Communities,* ed. Linda Vo and Rick Bonus (Philadelphia: Temple University Press, 2002). King has noted that in order to increase the pool of possible candidates Japanese American pageants in Los Angeles and San Francisco require contestants to be only half-Japanese or even less, as in Seattle.

16. Quoted in Kathryn Bender, "Queen Says Culture Is a State of Mind," *Honolulu Star-Bulletin,* March 22, 1999, A3.

17. Battad, "Too Little, Too Late?" A1.

18. Another possible reason for the resistance to permitting part-Japanese to compete in the pageant is that Japan-based corporations are major pageant sponsors and provide an expenses-paid trip to Japan for the queen and her court. Concern has been expressed about how representatives of these corporate sponsors in Japan would react to a visit by a part-Japanese queen. Catherine Toth, personal communication, December 5, 2001.

19. Cited in Esme M. Infante, "Japanese Pageant Breaks Tradition," *Honolulu Advertiser,* March 18, 1999, A5.

20. The Jaycees extended membership to women in 1984 and elected their first woman president five years later.

21. Karleen Chinen, "Hawaii's AJAs 'Play Ball!' A Look Back at AJA Baseball," *The Hawaii Herald,* June 7, 1996, A1, A10–A11

22. Quoted in Bender, "Queen Says Culture Is a State of Mind," A3.

23. Quoted in Bender, "Queen Says Culture Is a State of Mind," A3.

24. Jaycees members, including officers and board members, consist of a significant number of non-Japanese.

25. Harvey Hakoda, "AJA Baseball League Defies What Japanese Fought For," *Honolulu Star-Bulletin,* October 4, 1996, A13.

26. George Cooper and Gavan Daws, *Land and Power in Hawaii: The Democratic Years* (Honolulu: Benchmark Books, 1985).

27. I base this statement on interviews conducted with current and former AJA League players who were predominantly yonsei.

28. Quoted in Kaneshiro, "AJA Will Keep Ethnic Requirement."

29. Quoted in Santoki, "AJA Baseball Today," A15.

30. Franklin Odo and Susan Yim, "Ethnicity," *The Price of Paradise, Vol. II*, ed. R. W. Roth (Honolulu: Mutual Publishing, 1993), 228.

31. See Jonathan Y. Okamura, "Introduction: The Contemporary Japanese American Community in Hawai'i," *The Japanese American Contemporary Experience in Hawai'i*, a special issue of *Social Process in Hawai'i* 41 (2002). See also Candace Fujikane's introduction in this volume.

32. For example, in 1976 the state government settled out of court and paid $325,000 to more than one hundred white dental applicants who had sued the state claiming racial discrimination as the reason for their lower passing rate on the dental board examinations compared to Asian Americans. Roland M. Kotani, *The Japanese in Hawaii: A Century of Struggle* (Honolulu: Hawaii Hochi, 1985), 160.

33. Kotani, *The Japanese in Hawaii*, 159.

34. "Airport Boss Arrested in Kickback Scheme," *Honolulu Star-Bulletin*, July 4, 2002, A1, A10; for more information on such cases, see "AJA of the Year, Bob Watada," *Hawaii Herald*, December 19, 2003, A6.

35. In July 2001 former Honolulu city councilman Andy Mirikitani was convicted on federal charges of bribery, theft, extortion, wire fraud, and two counts of witness tampering in a salary bonus kickback scheme with two former members of his staff and received a sentence of four years and three months. In April 2002 another former city council member, Rene Mansho, pleaded guilty to felony theft of city funds and her campaign funds and was sentenced to one year in prison.

36. "Sweeping Racism under the Rug of 'Censorship': The Controversy over Lois-Ann Yamanaka's *Blu's Hanging*," in *Whose Vision? Asian Settler Colonialism in Hawai'i*, ed. Candace Fujikane and Jonathan Okamura, a special issue of *Amerasia Journal* (2000): 187.

37. Eric K. Yamamoto and Chris Iijima, "The Colonizer's Story: The Supreme Court Violates Native Hawaiian Sovereignty—Again," *ColorLines*, May 2000.

38. OHA was created in 1978 to develop and administer programs and services for Native Hawaiians. Formerly led by an elected Native Hawaiians–only Board of Trustees, it controls more than half a billion dollars in assets from the "ceded lands" that were Hawaiian government and crown lands seized by the United States when Hawai'i was annexed in 1898. Upon statehood in 1959, these lands were returned to the state to be held in trust partially for the benefit of Native Hawaiians (Yamamoto and Iijima, "The Colonizer's Story").

39. Quoted in Christine Donnelly, "Lawyer: Rice's Win Will Mean More Suits," *Honolulu Star-Bulletin*, February 24, 2000, A1.

40. Christine Donnelly, "Non-Hawaiians Will Sue to Run for OHA," *Honolulu Star-Bulletin*, March 30, 2000, A1.

41. Quoted in "The State of the Hawaiian," *The Honolulu Advertiser*, January 7, 2001. In *Adarand Constructors, Inc. v. Federico Pena, Secretary of Transportation*, the U.S. Supreme

Court substantially restricted federal contracting preferences, or "set-asides," for minority-owned small businesses.

42. Richard Borreca, "Cayetano: OHA Trustees Must Step Down," *Honolulu Star-Bulletin,* August 30, 2000, A4.

43. Pat Omandam, "Lawyer May Sue against Hawaiian Benefits," *Honolulu Star-Bulletin,* April 8, 2000, A3.

44. "Hawaiian Benefits Face Legal Challenge," *Honolulu Star-Bulletin,* July 1, 2001, A12.

45. Pat Omandam, "Barrett Loses OHA Lawsuit," *Honolulu Star-Bulletin,* July 13, 2001.

46. Curtis Lum, "Federal Judge Rejects Suit against OHA," *Honolulu Advertiser,* February 20, 2002.

47. The press release regarding the lawsuit states that the plaintiffs represent Chinese, Filipino, Hawaiian, Japanese, Okinawan, Portuguese, and various European "ethnicities," including English, French, Spanish, and Polish.

48. Sally Apgar, "Supporters of OHA Decry Latest Court Ruling," *Honolulu Star-Bulletin,* September 1, 2005.

49. Pat Omandam, "Suit Alleges OHA Discrimination," *Honolulu Star-Bulletin,* March 5, 2002, A3.

50. Quoted in Malia Zimmerman, "Challenging OHA with Aloha for All," *MidWeek,* January 2, 2002, 6.

51. Jonathan Y. Okamura, "The Illusion of Paradise," 264–284.

52. http://aloha4all.org

53. http://aloha4all.org

54. The plaintiffs in the suit to allow non-Hawaiians to seek office as OHA trustee also were represented by a Houston law firm, Magenheim, Bateman & Helfand, which has challenged race-based programs in North Carolina and Florida, before it withdrew from the case.

55. Peter Schmidt, "Next Stop, Supreme Court?" *The Chronicle of Higher Education,* May 24, 2002, A24–A28.

56. Trina Shapiro, "Kamehameha Schools to Voluntarily Concede Federal Educational Funds," *Honolulu Star-Bulletin,* September 8, 2001.

57. Until 1962 the schools had admitted the children of non-Hawaiian faculty, and while its admissions policy did not formally exclude non-Hawaiian students, none had been accepted in the past forty years.

58. Quoted in Timothy Hurley and Walter Wright, "Kamehameha Schools Admits Non-Hawaiian," *Honolulu Advertiser,* July 12, 2002, A5.

59. Quoted in Jennifer Hiller, "Kamehameha May Alter Its Admissions Policy," *Honolulu Advertiser,* July 16, 2002.

60. Nainoa Thompson, another trustee of the Ke Ali'i Pauahi Foundation, stated that a 1992 audit by the Arthur Andersen accounting firm indicated that if the foundation lost its tax-exempt status, it would have to pay $1 billion in back taxes and 42 percent of its earnings each year in federal taxes. Jennifer Hiller, "Kamehameha Trustees Torn between Duty and Law," *Honolulu Advertiser,* July 17, 2002, A6.

61. "Hawaiians First, Alumni Say," *Honolulu Advertiser,* July 13, 2002, A2.

62. Rick Daysog, "School Lets Non-Hawaiian Stay," *Honolulu Star-Bulletin*, November 29, 2003.

63. Quoted in Sally Apgar, "Court Will Rehear School Case," *Honolulu Star-Bulletin*, February 23, 2006.

64. Quoted in Debra Barayuga, "Kamehameha Will Fight Ruling," *Honolulu Star-Bulletin*, August 3, 2005, A1.

65. Quoted in Sally Apgar, "Appeals Court Lets Group Challenge State Funding of OHA," *Honolulu Star-Bulletin*, August 31, 2005, A6.

Colonial Amnesia

Rethinking Filipino "American" Settler
Empowerment in the U.S. Colony of Hawai'i

A history that serves as a guide to the people in perceiving present
reality is itself a liberating factor, for when the present is illumined
by a comprehension of the past, it is that much easier for the people
to grasp the direction of their development and identify the forces
that impede real progress.

— Renato Constantino, *The Philippines: A Past Revisited*

There has been deliberate, intentional, purposeful miseducation
and disinformation by the government, by the schools, and by
the communications media to hide the truth of this [colonial]
exploitation, and to promote the fairy tale that Hawai'i is a
democracy, that everyone has equal opportunity, and that it's a
paradise with racial harmony.

— Kekuni Blaisdell, *Autobiography of Protest in Hawai'i*

As a result of the countereducation afforded Hawai'i residents
by the Native Hawaiian sovereignty movement, Hawai'i's history of conquest by
the United States has resurfaced, exposing numerous contradictions and questions for those who claim Hawai'i as their home. Previous studies of race relations and popular ways of imagining Native Hawaiians have employed a domestic
"civil rights" framework, framing Native Hawaiians as an ethnic "minority group"
within Hawai'i's multicultural state competing for their fair share of the proverbial
American pie.[1] On the other hand, the body of work produced by many Native
scholars and Native sovereignty supporters uses a broader discourse of "indigenous human rights" that recognizes Native Hawaiians as a "peoples" who have a
genealogical continuity with Hawai'i distinct from other racial or ethnic groups.[2]
This latter framework situates Hawai'i within an international political arena, calling for a reconceptualizing of Native Hawaiians as a colonized indigenous people
with specific human rights that have been violated by the United States.

As the Native Hawaiian sovereignty movement reminds people in Hawaiʻi of a history of colonialism, how can Filipino communities in Hawaiʻi use these challenges to rethink our own past, present, and imagined futures? How do our beliefs, actions, and investments in the U.S. system collide with the aims of the Native Hawaiian sovereignty movement? What are the continuities between Filipino struggles in Hawaiʻi and the various anti-imperialist movements in the Philippines? How can we link these movements to the Native Hawaiian movement for self-determination? In this essay I attempt to show how the U.S. settler state conceals its colonization of Hawaiʻi, maneuvering historically oppressed groups against indigenous peoples. Specifically, I examine the apparent contradictions and implications of a Filipino settler identification with the United States in a U.S. colony. I situate this contradiction within the context of colonial miseducation to show how this identification is the product of a history of U.S. colonialism in both the Philippines and Hawaiʻi. As a fourth-generation settler in Hawaiʻi of Filipino and Japanese descent, I would like to add a different point of reference, one that is in dialogue not with the U.S. settler state but instead with the indigenous peoples under colonial domination. As Vicente Diaz, Pacific studies scholar, has stated regarding Filipinos and Chamorros in the U.S. colony of Guam, "If the history of relations between Chamorros and Filipinos is one of a shared struggle within colonial and neocolonial realities, then it is we who should be orchestrating the history, not allowing it to play us."[3]

For Filipinos in the United States, marginalization and subordination seem to be requisite for U.S. citizenship. The newspapers, books, articles, and journals that focus on racism against Filipinos in Hawaiʻi have pointed out the inequities and systemic structures of racism ingrained in Hawaiʻi's society.[4] Ethnic studies scholar Jonathan Okamura analyzes socioeconomic data from the 2000 U.S. census to show that Hawaiʻi's unique ethnic/racial stratification of power consists generally of whites, Japanese, and Chinese holding dominant positions in the state, and Filipinos, Sāmoans, and Native Hawaiians constituting the lower levels of ethnic/racial stratification.[5] Compared to more dominant groups, Filipinos in Hawaiʻi lack social, economic, and political power, yet we often seek empowerment as "Americans" within a U.S. settler state. While Filipino communities must continue to resist oppressive systems that perpetuate various inequalities, we must also be aware of the colonial structures ingrained in U.S. nationalism that render invisible the U.S. violation of Native Hawaiians' human rights to self-determination.

By shifting our perspective from viewing Hawaiʻi as the fiftieth state of the United States to recognizing Hawaiʻi as a colony under U.S. domination, terms that at one time seemed commonsensical now ring hollow and look perversely constructed as rhetoric that functions to obscure the colonial domination of Native Hawaiians. As Native Hawaiian nationalist and Hawaiian studies scholar

Haunani-Kay Trask points out, words such as "immigrant" and "local" contribute to dominant ideologies that paint Hawai'i as a multicultural utopia, eliding the colonization of Native Hawaiians and the collaboration of non-Natives with this subjugation.[6] Thus Trask has introduced the term "settler" in Hawai'i to describe the non-Native community. The usefulness of the term is that it shatters U.S. paradigms by forcing non-Natives to question our participation in sustaining U.S. colonialism while making important political distinctions between Natives and non-Natives. I do not see the term as derogatory or, as some critics suggest, as pitting Natives against settlers. Instead, I appreciate the term because it exposes how Native and settler interests are often in opposition and consequently presents non-Natives with a clear choice, as Trask points out, "Either they [Asians and haole] must justify their continued benefit from Hawaiian subjugation, thus serving as support for that subjugation, or they must repudiate American hegemony and work with the Hawaiian nationalist movement."[7] Because the United States invaded Hawai'i, Filipinos, like other settlers who immigrated to Hawai'i, live in a colonized nation where the indigenous peoples do not possess their human right to self-determination, and because of this Filipinos are settlers. The word "settler" is a means to an end. The goal is not to win in a game of semantics or to engage in name calling, but rather for settlers to have a firm understanding of our participation in sustaining U.S. colonialism and then to support Native Hawaiians in achieving self-determination and the decolonization of Hawai'i.

The concept of settler colonialism also disrupts notions that minorities who are racially oppressed are incapable of simultaneously participating in the colonial oppression of Native Hawaiians. Because Filipinos in Hawai'i live in a colony, our citizenship and desires for equality within a U.S. political system are crucial components of a complex hegemonic colonial structure that must be carefully questioned. For instance, although the term "Filipino American" combats the racist notion that only haole (whites) are Americans, it also asserts a U.S. nationality within a U.S. colony. For those committed to social justice, identification with the United States is deeply problematic because it is a colonial identity. I use the term "Filipino settler" in this essay not to reproach Filipinos but instead to challenge us to think critically of our position in the U.S. colony of Hawai'i.

Through an analysis of contrasting visions of Hawai'i and diverse narrations of Filipino settler history emerging out of contemporary politics, I will attempt to show how these narrations maintain and resist colonialism in Hawai'i. I begin with Virgilio Menor Felipe's biography, *Hawai'i: A Pilipino Dream*, which tells the life of Bonipasyo, one of the *sakada* (contract workers) who arrived in Hawai'i from the Philippines between 1906 and 1946.[8] While in the Philippines Bonipasyo was told stories by the elders about the violence of U.S. colonization, and he also labored on Hawai'i's sugar plantations and participated in labor unions. Through this text I attempt to show how the American colonial system maneuvers colonized groups against each other. I will then look at an account of Americanization written by Joshua Agsalud, former cabinet member in the administrations of governors George Ariyoshi and John Waiheʻe and also a former superintendent of the State of Hawaiʻi's Department of Education. Agsalud speaks of his experience as a second-generation Filipino growing up on a sugar plantation in Waipahu and of the American educational system's role in shaping his views and subject position as an American. I then examine the narration of "Filipino American" history through Philippine Independence Day in the writings of Zachary Labez, a journalist and activist in Filipino communities. Although the celebration is anticolonial it still celebrates a national identification with America within a remaining colony of the United States. I then contrast two examples of the ways Filipinos have made choices about their roles as settlers. I analyze the artwork of Native Hawaiian artist Kēwaikaliko titled *Benocide,* which offers a critique of former governor Benjamin Cayetano's anti-Hawaiian acts as governor. I contrast this with the anti-imperialist activism of an informal collective of ten Filipinas from the island of Oʻahu who through a "politics of diaspora" link the U.S. colonial domination of Hawaiʻi with the U.S. imperial domination of the Philippines. These activists organized a statement of solidarity to support Native Hawaiians. I end with these Filipina settler activists to show that we need not be paralyzed by colonialism but instead can take positive political action in supporting Native Hawaiians in their movement for decolonization.

Colonial Miseducation in the Philippines

Filipino migration to the United States is due largely to the U.S. colonization of the Philippines. As ethnic studies scholar Yen Le Espiritu states,

> U.S.-bound Filipino migration takes place within the context of the (neo)colonial association between the Philippines and the United States. The glorification of the United States through the colonial educational system; the historically specific recruitment of Filipino nationals to serve in the U.S. armed forces as health practitioners and as low-wage laborers; and the differentials in wage and job opportunities between the two countries: all provide pressure to migrate to the United States.[9]

As Espiritu points out, the Filipino communities in the United States are founded on and shaped by the colonial relationship between the United States and the Philippines. The historical recruitment of Filipino laborers is often coupled with romanticized colonial images of the United States as a "land of opportunity," peddled in the Philippines by the colonial educational system, the media, and relatives and friends already in or returning from the United States.[10] Espiritu, however, also makes clear that Filipinos migrating to the United States "are neither passive victims nor homogenous 'pools of migrant labor' responding mechanically and uniformly to the same set of structural forces. Instead, they are active participants in the process of migration who vary by gender, generation, class, and culture."[11] As "active participants" in the migration process, Filipinos have settled in the colony of Hawai'i, many imagining it as an escape from imperial violence in the Philippines. Filipinos and other Asian settler groups are fed illusions that Hawai'i, because it is portrayed as "America," offers escape from the poverty caused by U.S. imperialism. Yet as Native Hawaiians have argued, Hawai'i is not America. Hawai'i is under colonial occupation by the United States, and Native Hawaiians, engaged in a struggle for decolonization, suffer the consequences of the oppression of settler groups like Filipinos who have their own vested interests in the American dream.

One example of how U.S. colonialism conceals itself is in Virgilio Menor Felipe's biography *Hawai'i: A Pilipino Dream*, which tells the story of an aging *sakada* named Bonipasyo who migrated from Laoag, Ilocos Norte, in 1925 to work on the sugar plantations in Hawai'i. Felipe's book weaves together the narratives of Lilo Bonipasyo's life in both the Philippines and Hawai'i, situating it within these historical contexts. In the Philippines Bonipasyo questions the colonial violence of the United States.

We heard from elders that many barrios were destroyed by cannons of the Amerikanos. This was to hunt the Katipuneros and to scare the civilians from helping them. Many civilians were killed because they were not on guard. They were not hiding—only working to farm a living. And this is what I can't understand and I believe it is the same with a lot of Pilipinos today—why were Amerikanos hunting down our Katipuneros who were already fighting for our independence? Someone has been lying on this. All I know is that we Pilipinos do not come to America with guns and armies. We come to work in America.[12]

Bonipasyo is describing the little-known yet devastating Philippine-American War (1899–1902), in which approximately a million Filipinos died as a result of the U.S. campaign to colonize the Philippines. Comparing what his elders told him of U.S. soldiers killing innocent civilians and fighting against the Katipuneros with the soldiers' portrayal of themselves as "liberating" the Philippines from the Spaniards, he states that "someone has been lying on this," and he is able to see the United States as a colonizing nation.[13] His words, however, also reveal two things about Bonipasyo's understanding of his migration to Hawai'i. First, he describes Hawai'i as "America" when he states that "we Pilipinos come to work in America," which indicates the power of colonialism to equate the two, eclipsing the related struggles against U.S. colonization of Filipinos and Native Hawaiians. Second, he says that Filipino *sakada* traveled to Hawai'i for economic reasons, with no intention of subordinating another colonized group. Yet the colonial system in Hawai'i often maneuvers Filipino settlers to align themselves with the U.S. colonial state, leading them to support colonialism in Hawai'i, however unintentionally.

One of the results of colonial miseducation is that it erases the connections between anti-imperialist struggles of Filipinos and Native Hawaiians. Felipe notes in his introduction,

> Sometime while going around the island is when I began taping our talk stories. When we were past Kaneohe town by the Heeia Boat Harbor, we could see the numerous picket signs protesting to save their farming community from urban development. As I read them off loudly, "Keep the Country Country!" "Hawaiian Lands in Hawaiian Hands!" "Stop Imperialism!" and "U.S. Military, Get Out!" Lilo began to remember the first days when he arrived in Hawai'i.
> "Wen I came hea in Hawaii, you cannot took like dat, you know," Lilo said. And I asked, "What do you mean, Lilo?"
> "Da oldtimers told us when we had meeting dat making oonyoon, union, was against da law. Da govahment can arrest you or shoot you. As wot dey said. In Kauai, dey said plenty people get shot and killed," Lilo said.[14]

The picket signs protest against urban and military development on the windward side of the island of Oʻahu. In this moment where we might expect Bonipasyo to speak about the connection between the struggles of Native Hawaiians and those of his own family against the Spanish and U.S. imperialists in the Philippines, Bonipasyo instead speaks about his experiences with the labor union and the violence suffered by Filipinos during the 1924 Hanapēpē strike where sixteen Filipino strikers and four policemen lost their lives. While Bonipasyo is able to make the connections between the sugar planters' oppression of the Filipino laborers and Native Hawaiians' colonial oppression, he is unable to see that the aims of Native Hawaiians, unlike those of Filipino strikers, is to reclaim their land and nation, similar to the aims of the Katipuneros in the Philippine revolution.

As Melinda Tria Kerkvliet explains, the 1924 labor strike used U.S. patriotic narratives to gain Filipino workers' rights.

> On July 27 [1924] about 1,000 Filipinos took part in a parade through the streets of Hilo. The parade started from the strike headquarters. At the head of the parade were strikers carrying a poster of Abraham Lincoln and a large American flag. . . . Why Lincoln and the American flag? The strikers, by displaying the American flag, probably wanted to reaffirm their recognition

not only of the United States' authority over Hawaiʻi but also their avowal of American values, including justice and a fair deal for everyone.[15]

Kerkvliet's analysis indicates that Filipino protests against labor exploitation also participated in affirming the authority of the United States over Hawaiʻi. Although resistant Filipino laborers suffered blacklisting, imprisonment, beatings, deportation, and even death, their use of U.S. symbols such as Lincoln and the U.S. flag had ideological significance in providing support and legitimacy to U.S. colonization.

As I have pointed out, it is the concealment of U.S. colonialism in Hawaiʻi that leads to these deep contradictions. Dean Alegado, a scholar of Filipino studies in Hawaiʻi, explains that the early Filipino labor leaders such as Pablo Manlapit, Cecil Basan, Epifanio Taok, and Antonio Fagel were "militant labor reformists and ardent nationalists" who "passionately supported the demands of their countrymen in the Philippines for 'immediate, absolute and complete independence' from the U.S."[16] Alegado also writes about the leading Filipino community newspaper in Hawaiʻi during 1940s and 1950s, the Ti Mangyuna, which reported on international events that highlighted the anticolonial liberation struggles in Asia, Africa, and Latin America and the civil rights struggles of African Americans on the U.S. continent.

Colonial miseducation in the Philippines and Hawaiʻi thus led to a contradiction: Filipinos who took a strong stance against the colonization of the Philippines and other places unintentionally supported the colonial authority of the United States over Hawaiʻi. Although Filipinos in Hawaiʻi at that time may have been unaware of Native Hawaiian resistance to colonization, Filipino settlers today know that the Native Hawaiian sovereignty movement seeks self-determination. Because it is easier to see the blindness of the past than of the present, we can learn from and build on the anticolonial struggles of these *sakada*.

Colonial Miseducation in Hawaiʻi

> Spurred by parents who had no intentions to return to the Philippines, the children all considered themselves natives of the land where they were born—there was nothing else to be but American. . . . The primary drive, for the time-being was to speak English, learn about America, practice American morality and espouse American values.
>
> —Joshua Agsalud, "My Perceptions of the Plantation Experience: Influences that Shaped My Views on the Americanization Process"

Today, modern Hawaiʻi, like its colonial parent the United States, is a settler society. Our Native people and territories have been overrun by non-Natives, including Asians. Calling themselves "local," the children of Asian settlers greatly outnumber us. They claim Hawaiʻi as their own, denying indigenous history, their long collaboration in our continued dispossession, and the benefits therefrom.

—Haunani-Kay Trask, "Settlers of Color and 'Immigrant' Hegemony: 'Locals' in Hawaiʻi"

Joshua Agsalud, former cabinet member and chief of staff under governors George Ariyoshi and John Waiheʻe and a Department of Education superintendent, and Haunani-Kay Trask, a Native Hawaiian nationalist, express differing visions of Hawaiʻi and its relationship to the United States, and of the Americanization or U.S. colonial process. Trask points out the current status of Hawaiʻi and Native Hawaiians as colonized by the United States and cogently argues that Asian settler groups in Hawaiʻi collaborate with and benefit from that U.S. colonial project. Agsalud's statement, written twenty years prior to Trask's 2000 essay, is an example of Trask's contention, but Agsalud further explains that when he was growing up on the sugar plantations in the late 1940s and 1950s, there was no other known option for a national identity afforded to Filipinos besides being American.[17] Stating that his family never expected to return to the Philippines, Agsalud explains that he was educated by the assimilationist philosophy of the American colonial education system in Hawaiʻi to "speak English, learn about America, practice American morality and espouse American values." In this section I use Agsalud's essay not to critique it but to provide a historical context for further understanding the colonial influences that shaped a Filipino national identification with the United States. Since the writing of Agsalud's 1981 essay, Hawaiian activists have worked to make Hawaiʻi's history of colonialism far more visible.

Agsalud describes his experiences as a second-generation Filipino growing up on a sugar plantation in Waipahu and speaks specifically to the various state apparatuses that shaped his views about "America" in the 1940s and 1950s.

All the influences which shaped my views on the Americanization process were natural outcomes of the plantation experience. They were congruent to the scenario that was evolving. These influences—family, church, school and the plantation itself, along with a major world event taking place at that time, World War II—the views that were shaped, and the process, were all American. They were not conflicts among the variables, one pulling or pushing against the other—they all seemed to flow in the same direction, a direction which was inevitable under the circumstances . . . Americanization.[18]

Agsalud states that the Americanization of Hawaiʻi was often viewed as "inevitable," a natural process toward "modernity." By portraying everything that is good, civilized, and modern as products of the U.S. presence in Hawaiʻi, the proj-

ect of Americanization declared to its colonized Native subjects and diverse settler populations that their participation in building and maintaining a U.S. system
would be in the best interests of every hardworking American. It offered an avenue
of success but elided the fact that the avenue of success was paved over a stolen
Hawaiian nation. In the 1940s and 1950s Hawaiʻi was going through quick and
tremendous change as a result of specific events; the fervor attached to each of
these—the attack on Pearl Harbor, World War II, labor strikes, martial law, statehood, the Democratic Party's capture of the state, the Cold War—underpinned
American ideologies that attempted to justify U.S. colonial control of Hawaiʻi. The
U.S. system rewards its citizenry for being colonialist yet masks this colonization as
American exceptionalism. American exceptionalism denies that the United States
participates in colonialism or empire building and instead argues that it brings
U.S.-fashioned civilization and democracy to peoples even if they oppose it.[19]

As a result of the massive immigration of Asian laborers to Hawaiʻi's colonial sugar plantations and racist representations of people of color as biologically
and culturally inferior, the U.S. educational system in Hawaiʻi acculturated both
Natives and settlers of color to becoming American. Agsalud explains that though
"the family and church contributed immensely to the Americanization process,
unequivocally, it was the educational system which influenced the process more
than any other variable."[20] This educational system was intimately tied to the sugar
plantations, as Agsalud points out: "Even the schools were dominated by the plantation influence; plantation managers were consulted regarding faculty appointments, especially the principalship."[21] Agsalud goes on to explain that

> the schools were almost perfect in molding my views on being a good, success-
> ful American. As an educator, I have always subscribed to the philosophy that
> the public schools serve as tools for the national purpose. While some may
> question the effectiveness of the educational system today in meeting this goal,
> I am fully convinced that the schools of my time met this aim. The skills and
> attitudes that I developed have indeed made me a confident American.

Agsalud describes himself as a "confident American," representing his American identity as fully formed and unquestionable. I would like to suggest that
Agsalud's description of himself as a "confident American" constitutes a strategy:
he uses a hyper-American discourse to disprove a white supremacist construction
of Filipinos as incapable of becoming fully "American" and colonial stereotypes of
Filipinos as being backward, ignorant, and unassimilable. Through this strategy
Agsalud finds a way to assert his humanity and civility in a racist and colonialist
society. But because Agsalud himself was a state official who held high-powered
positions and who had vested interests in the U.S. political system, he and his

success should not be taken as representative of the experience of Filipino settlers of his generation. Although I have no intention of faulting Agsalud for such an antiracist strategy in that historical moment, antiracist projects that celebrate an American nationality must be rethought, for the grim reality is that U.S. citizenship and "success" as a good citizen is contingent upon the success of U.S. settler colonization of indigenous peoples.

Philippine Independence Day

> An American establishment usually considers these ["minority newspapers"] to be in opposition simply because they appear in languages other than English or represent ethnic cultures. Their dual function, however, is peculiarly American: fostering assimilation into the new society while helping to preserve ethnic identity.
>
> —Helen Geracimos Chapin, *Shaping History:*
> *The Role of Newspapers in Hawai'i*

As a journalist and former president of both the United Filipino Council of Hawai'i and the Filipino Coalition for Solidarity, Zachary Labez was a well-respected community organizer and also one of the first Filipinos to support Native Hawaiian sovereignty publicly in the community newspapers. In a March 1996 issue of the *Hawaii Filipino Chronicle,* Labez asked Filipinos in Hawai'i to question their role in the Native Hawaiian sovereignty movement. In an interview with Native Hawaiian nationalist Pōka Laenui, Labez writes that though "most people are apprehensive if not outrightly against the separation from the United States . . . every citizen in Hawaii today could have a stake in the new nation, giving the native Hawaiians special privileges that are due to them while still remaining true to the aloha spirit for all in a multi-ethnic society." [22] Though I here point to the limitations of his writings on the Philippine Independence Day celebrations, I wish to acknowledge first that Labez was a key voice asking Filipinos to support Native Hawaiians. His writings would influence other Filipinos, including myself, to support Native Hawaiian sovereignty. The problem in his writings is not that Labez did not support Native Hawaiian self-determination but that he failed to recognize the centrality of the U.S. colonization of Hawai'i when interpreting the major events narrated in Filipino "American" settler history.

In June 2001 the *Fil-Am Courier,* a Filipino community newspaper with a circulation of fifty thousand in Hawai'i, celebrated the 103rd anniversary of the anticolonial Philippine Independence Movement with a three-part series of articles designed, as Labez wrote in the series' "Foreword," to "re-visit the past in order to understand where we *Pinoys* are at now." [23] Labez's articles, specially prepared for the Talakayan Community Forum, a part of Hawaiʻi's Kalayaan celebration on May 17, 2001, in Honolulu (*kalayaan* is Tagalog for "freedom"), contextualize the Filipino community's history of oppression and resistance in both the Philippines and Hawaiʻi. Their primary objective is to combat Filipino marginalization by developing a strategy for empowerment within U.S. society. Labez states, "Here in the United States, we Filipino Americans find ourselves reflecting on the historical milestones perennially reminding us of how inextricably linked both countries are—our ancestral homeland we call *Pilipinas* and our adopted homeland of America." While Labez alludes to the fact that Filipinos' "ancestral homeland" and the United States are linked by a history of colonialism, the "adopted homeland," Hawaiʻi, is erased from this discussion. The statement equates Hawaiʻi with the United States, not acknowledging the current status of Hawaiʻi as a U.S. colony or the fact that in 1898 both Hawaiʻi and the Philippines were colonized. The contradiction of the Kalayaan celebration of anticolonial Philippine independence was that it took place in a colony of the United States where Filipinos were participating in the perpetuation of U.S. colonial patriotism. When Hawaiʻi's history of colonialism is obscured by an immigrant narrative of Filipino settler history, both Hawaiian and Filipino historical and contemporary resistance to colonialism are bound yet concealed.

Labez's first article, "*Pinoys* in Paradise: From the Sugar Plantations to the State Capitol," opens, "The first 15 Filipino pioneers ventured to the fabled land of Hawaiʻi on December 20, 1906." [24] By dating Filipino settler history in Hawaiʻi to the 1906 entry of Filipino laborers, we are unable to contextualize our presence within a larger history of crimes committed earlier against indigenous peoples. Some have argued that Filipinos are free from complicity because they did not arrive until after Hawaiians had been dispossessed of their land and government. To focus only on the labor exploitation of Filipinos on the sugar plantations, however, is to obscure the connection of Filipino labor oppression to the colonial dispossession of Native Hawaiians. While the overtly racist sugar plantations were exploiting Filipinos, among them members of my family, Filipino laborers, who were also U.S. colonial subjects, were maneuvered hegemonically within the colonial machine of the sugar plantations. Between 1906 and 1935 approximately 120,000 Filipinos traveled to Hawaiʻi, and while almost half went back to the Philippines or on to California, our presence in Hawaiʻi was critical to building and maintaining the sugar plantations and thus the colonial system. As Bonipasyo recounts in *Hawaiʻi: A Pilipino Dream*, "With my bare hands I helped build Hawaiʻi. I plowed lands for the canefields with mules, I cut cane, I hapaiko, carried cane and watered sugarcane." [25]

In the second article, "*Pinoys* in America: From Philippine Sovereignty to Empowerment in America," Labez writes,

Long before "empowerment" became a buzzword in political, economic and academic coteries of American society, Pinoys already understood its significance in the quest for dignity, acceptance and equal opportunity. Our story was, after all, a story of continuing struggle for self-determination, from the fight for political sovereignty after over 300 years of absolute rule by our Spanish colonial masters in the Philippines to the quest for a fair share of the proverbial pie in [the] "Land of Immigrants." [26]

Labez refers to two ideas relevant to my arguments here: "empowerment" and the problems that arise when Filipinos seek empowerment without addressing colonialism, and the colonial ideology attached to the term "Land of Immigrants."

Filipinos have long asserted their human right to self-determination by opposing the colonial domination of the Philippines by Spain, the United States, and Japan. The primary difference in Hawai'i is that Filipino settlers are not the colonized people since it is not our land, resources, and government that is under occupation. Yet we live within a colonial system, and in our attempts to become "American" we align ourselves with the colonial state. "Empowerment," or our quest for our "share of the proverbial American pie," becomes oppressive because the American political and economic system relies on denying Native Hawaiians their right to self-determination. I am not saying that we Filipinos in Hawai'i should not resist our oppression, but rather that our framework for understanding Hawai'i's political and economic system and consequent actions needs to contend with issues of colonialism.

"Land of immigrants" is an imperialist term that in three words erases fifteen hundred years of pre-contact Hawaiian history, Hawaiians' rights as indigenous peoples, and their claims to sovereignty. The use of the term exposes a U.S. narrative that constructs a phantasmatic land with no indigenous people, vacant land where immigrants have settled to construct a "modern" democratic society. Often implicit in such a narrative is the argument that indigenous peoples also are immigrants, that Native Hawaiians immigrated to Hawai'i some fifteen hundred years ago. This reclassification of Native peoples as "immigrants" attempts to justify conquest. The use of the term "land of immigrants" reinforces a U.S. ideology that erases indigenous peoples from history and clears the way for foreign settlement.

Labez's third *Fil-Am Courier* article, published in June 2001, "Filipino Americans: Empowered Citizens in the Making?" challenges Filipinos in Hawai'i to realize our full political potential by organizing and becoming involved in politics: "Population growth augurs hope for greater empowerment of the Filipino community, specifically in the political area. Given the increasing visibility of the Fil-Am community, the dynamic economic opportunities in this market, and, most importantly, the rapid growth of its population, it is just a matter of time that full empowerment will be achieved."[27] Because Filipinos in Hawai'i remain divided by generational, linguistic, and regional affiliations, solidarity is a crucial component to successful organizing, yet an important question we must ask of ourselves is whether our political leaders will advocate protest or accommodation to a U.S. colonial nation-state. One example of a Filipino settler leader who has not advocated protest but rather accommodation to the political system that colonizes Hawaiians is former governor Benjamin Cayetano.

Whose Side Are We On?

The Honolulu Academy of Arts held an art exhibition titled Nā Maka Hou: New Visions from May 13 until June 17, 2001, featuring more than one hundred works of art by fifty-eight Native Hawaiian artists, an overview of the artistic expressions of Native Hawaiians in a variety of media. A piece by artist Kēwaikaliko, *Benocide,* explicitly addresses the violent effects of colonialism, specifically the collaboration of Filipino settler and former governor Benjamin Cayetano (1994–2002) with legal assaults on Native Hawaiian entitlements.[28]

Kēwaikaliko uses art as a weapon to depict a Hawai'i that often goes unseen. Central to *Benocide* is a loaded illustration of a lynched Native Hawaiian man and his executioner, Cayetano. The powerfully built Native man is being lynched on a tree with leaves made of money; Death, smoking crystal methamphetamine, or "ice," is figured as its trunk. A haole man stands wearing a swastika-covered aloha shirt and waving the State of Hawai'i flag, formerly the flag of the Hawaiian Kingdom. I read this figure as a representation of neoconservative haole settlers who have been seeking to dismantle Native entitlements. Next to him is a pua'a (pig) in Western-style clothing—possibly a colluding Native—who appears to be fondling the haole man's rear. Depicted in black and gray and making up the ground beneath this mob are Natives who appear in all manner of suffering. The black and gray envelop the green mountain that overlooks the urban sprawl of Waikīkī. On the horizon is a nuclear mushroom cloud rising into the sky, a direct reference to nuclear testing in the Pacific and more generally to the U.S. military's devastating impact in Hawai'i and the Pacific. A note from the artist accompanied this aptly named piece: "This artwork was created in October 2000. It was completed in a week and has been getting both positive and negative feedback. Grandma hates it."

There are numerous issues interwoven in Kēwaikaliko's artwork, but I wish to focus on Cayetano's collaboration in the lawsuits that have sought to dismantle Native entitlements. At the 1978 State of Hawai'i Constitutional Convention, the Office of Hawaiian Affairs (OHA) was formed to oversee the trust assets of Native Hawaiians designated in the Admissions Act of 1959. The Admissions Act trans-

Kēwaikaliko, *Benocide, 2000*. Pastel and fluorescent marker on paper. (Courtesy of the artist)

ferred an estimated 1.8 million acres of ceded lands—lands stolen by the United States at the time of annexation—from the U.S. federal government to the State to be administered in a trust-ward relationship, with "the betterment of the conditions of Native Hawaiians" listed as one of the five responsibilities of the "ceded public lands trust." In 1980 a Native Hawaiian–only vote was established to elect nine trustees who would administer OHA assets.

On February 23, 2000, the U.S. Supreme Court in *Rice v. Cayetano* opened all

Native Hawaiian entitlements to legal assault. The court struck down the1980 voting scheme, ruling that the elections were "race based" and consequently discriminatory on the grounds of the Fifteenth Amendment. In spite of the more than 150 federal laws passed by Congress acknowledging Native Hawaiians alongside American Indians as beneficiaries of federal programs for indigenous peoples, the court ruled that Native Hawaiians are not a federally recognized Indian tribe.[29] On October 3, 2000, a settler resident of Hawai'i, Patrick Barrett, filed a complaint in the Hawai'i federal district court alleging that Article XII of the Hawai'i State Constitution violated the Equal Protection Clause of the U.S. Constitution insofar as it created the Hawaiian Homes Commission and OHA and protected Native Hawaiian gathering rights. Barrett's lawsuit followed John Carroll's similar lawsuit, which also alleged that the creation of OHA was illegal on equal protection grounds. These lawsuits were eventually thrown out of court because the plaintiffs had never applied for any Native Hawaiian entitlement program. Kēwaikaliko's *Benocide,* completed in October 2000, is a response to these lawsuits; the caricature represents other settlers who use the court system to legally terminate an indigenous category.

While Cayetano is physically hanging the Native, he does not gaze at the hanging Hawaiian, but rather looks to the haole for recognition of his act.[30] This is a subtle but apt illustration of the performative role that Cayetano as a "Filipino American" must play in order to maintain his political position. Ida Yoshinaga and Eiko Kosasa, founders of the community action group Local Japanese Women for Justice (LJWJ), exposed the chain of command in the state where soon after the U.S. Supreme Court ruled in favor of the plaintiff in the *Rice v. Cayetano* case, Hawai'i's U.S. Senator Daniel Inouye issued a statement to both OHA and Cayetano requesting the removal of all OHA trustees. Inouye wrote in his letter: "I believe that the Governor has authority under a separate State of Hawaii statute to appoint interim trustees so that the important work of the Office of Hawaiian Affairs need not be interrupted."[31] Cayetano, under Senator Inouye's instructions, called for the nine trustees to step down voluntarily or risk OHA's termination and then appointed his own trustees to office. As Yoshinaga and Kosasa point out, "The intended result of Inouye's statement was to facilitate the control of OHA by the state and away from the electoral process. Later, Cayetano released a statement repeating Inouye's analysis as his own." In *Benocide* the pua'a and Cayetano choose not to look at the lynching but instead both look to the haole as they work within the constraints of the system struggling for subordinate supremacy. In other words, Cayetano, as a member of a subordinated group in a political position of power, affirms the colonial order that makes his position possible.

Providing historical depth to the scene, Kēwaikaliko places at Governor Cayetano's feet the bearded and bloodied skull of Sanford B. Dole, the first territorial governor of Hawai'i and a colonial official intimately involved in the 1893 overthrow and 1898 annexation of Hawai'i to the United States. Cayetano is positioned over Dole's remains and appears to have Dole's blood on his hands. The settler contest between representative figures Dole and Cayetano frame the art piece. In what Haunani-Kay Trask describes as an "intra-settler struggle for hegemony," the victor holds the noose.[32] Cayetano stands where Dole once stood, exercising political power that is made possible only by maintaining a U.S. colonial order.

By holding the noose and looking to the haole, Cayetano represents the collusion of the State of Hawai'i with the legal assaults. Since the appearance of the legal challenges, the State of Hawai'i has been in the peculiar position of having to defend Native entitlements from lawsuit while being negligent in administering these same entitlements. In *Benocide* Cayetano lynches the Native on a tree with leaves made of money. In 1991 the Hawai'i Advisory Committee to the United States Commission on Civil Rights published a report titled *A Broken Trust* stating that both the Territory and State of Hawai'i had been negligent for seventy-three years in fulfilling their fiduciary duties as trustees of the Ceded Lands Trust.[33] As a result of the report the State of Hawai'i and OHA throughout much of the 1990s were tied up in court attempting to resolve back payments the State of Hawai'i owed OHA. In 1990 the Hawai'i State Legislature passed Act 304 to provide a mechanism for determining the amount of ceded land revenues owed to OHA.[34] The law specified that OHA was entitled to 20 percent of revenue from the ceded lands. Three years later the State paid OHA $19 million and agreed to make annual revenue payments. OHA filed a lawsuit in 1994 to resolve all remaining back-payment issues. On September 12, 2001, the Hawai'i Supreme Court ruled that Act 304 conflicted with the 1998 Forgiveness Act passed by Congress, which prohibited further payment of airport revenues for claims related to ceded lands, and was therefore invalid. Based on the ruling, Cayetano ordered state departments to stop payments to OHA. He instead offered to settle the issue of repayment in 1999 with a global settlement of $251 million and 360,000 acres of ceded lands, but OHA declined.

One article in the *Fil-Am Courier* describes Cayetano as "the son of immigrants from Kalihi to Washington Place. . . . The American Dream come true."[35] This master narrative of a working-class boy from Kalihi who after hard work and sacrifice becomes governor is very much a part of a dominant Asian settler ideology in Hawai'i that functions to justify the positions of power held by settlers, where the descendants of hardworking laborers on the plantation now control the state.[36] This model minority narrative consequently implies that Native Hawaiians and unsuccessful Filipino settlers just need to work harder. On the contrary, as a commentary on the oversimplified dominant ideologies that cast Hawai'i as the American Dream, a "multicultural paradise," and a "land of aloha," the Native Hawaiian man hung in *Benocide* is scaled realistically compared to Cayetano, the haole, and the pua'a, who are drawn as cartoons with short, round, and stubby features. *Benocide* reveals what these ideologies are designed to conceal: the State of Hawai'i is neither democratic nor utopic but instead is a colony whose existence depends on the violent subjugation of Native people. In the face of Native suffering and colonization, romanticized representations of Hawai'i have as much relevance as a cartoon. Hidden in plain sight, the Native Hawaiian man is being lynched by these three while they themselves bask in the ideologies of American democracy and equality and the political and economic power attached to them.

Kēwaikaliko's *Benocide* forces the viewer to see the often uncomfortable and harsh realities of colonialism in Hawai'i while asking one to bear witness to the contemporary situation of Hawaiians. I would lastly like to point out that the artwork frames the viewer as a spectator to the lynching. In much the same way that lynchings in the United States were viewed publicly and necessitated general public support or at least silent complicity, we view the lynching as it happens, from the same perspective as the other spectators, which implicates the viewer in the symbolic lynching of Hawaiians. Framing the viewed in this way, the artwork poses a difficult question: What are you going to do about this? As Hawaiian scholar Manulani Aluli Meyer asserts in an essay that accompanied this exhibition, "We speak to you in shapes, colors, and metaphors. We view angles distinctly; we prioritize contours differently; we have different politics based on our experience of rape, pillage and transformation. We are speaking in the language of imagery and you are learning more about the passion and priorities of a people. The time demands it of all of us. And I believe we are ready to listen." [37]

Benocide offers a vision of Hawai'i that reveals the current consequences of the blinding ideologies underpinning the current legal assaults against Native Hawaiian trusts and assets. Hawaiian artwork such as Kēwaikaliko's demystifies the illusions of settler colonialism, revealing the current violent effects of the legal challenges and the continued U.S. settler colonization of Hawai'i.

Filipina Settler Activism against U.S. Imperialism in the Philippines and Hawai'i

In 2002, as a result of the 9/11 attacks on the World Trade Center and Pentagon, as well as U.S. President George W. Bush's reactionary "global war on terrorism," an arrangement ensued that illustrates the unequal relationship between the constrained Philippines and the imperialist United States. Philippine President Gloria Macapagal-Arroyo invoked the Visiting Forces Agreement and the

Mutual Defense Treaty to invite U.S. troops to help suppress the so-called terrorist group Abu Sayyaf, a Muslim group that may have had ties to al-Qaeda. With the Philippine government's collaboration in exchange for much-needed U.S. aid, the Philippines received, as President Arroyo stated, "over $4-billion and counting" from U.S. government and private firms. President Arroyo said that in a meeting on November 20, 2001, with President Bush, Bush repeatedly asked her what the Armed Forces of the Philippines needed to eradicate Abu Sayyaf. President Arroyo added, "What's important is that we're getting military and economic assistance that will help us in the fight against terrorism and help us in our battle against poverty." [38]

After two joint U.S.-Philippine military operations failed—Balikatan '02-1 and Balikatan '03-1 (*balikatan* in Tagalog means "shoulder to shoulder")—the United States attempted to train U.S. soldiers for a third joint U.S.-Philippine military operation to hunt down the so-called terrorist group. Native Hawaiian groups protested to stop the military from carrying out the training in the Waiāhole and Waikāne valleys on the windward side of the island of Oʻahu, chosen for their similarities to the rainforests in Mindanao. [39]

During World War II the U.S. Army had used the Waiāhole and Waikāne valleys for military training, which was continued by the marines in 1953. The Kamaka family, who has ancestral links to the valley, was granted a settlement in a disputed land title case and farmed that land from 1976 to 1983. [40] The marines, however, had failed to clean the land before vacating it in 1976; because the land was contaminated with unexploded ordnance, the marines condemned it in 1989 and the Kamaka family lost their land.

Linking the presence of the U.S. military in the Philippines and in Hawaiʻi, an informal collective of ten Filipinas released a statement in March 2003 titled "Filipinos Stand in Solidarity with Native Hawaiians in Opposing United States Military Expansion." As Grace Alvaro Caligtan, Darlene Rodrigues, Melisa S. L. Casumbal, Catherine Betts, Grace Duenas, Gigi Miranda, Cindy Ramirez, Sonya Zabala, Tamara Freedman, and Maile Labasan state,

> As Filipino co-habitants of Oahu, we strongly oppose the U.S. military's proposal to expand its training sites to include Waikane, Kualoa, Hakipuu, and Kaaawa, or any other sites in the Hawaiian archipelago. We demand that the U.S. military take full responsibility for the human displacement and environmental damage caused by its usage of Hawaiian lands. We fully support the Kamaka family's struggle to hold the U.S. military accountable for its failure to properly clean up their land. We join with Kanaka Maoli groups in calling for a return of control of all land in use by the U.S. military to its rightful ancestral stewards and descendants. [41]

Through a politics of diaspora that locates itself within the specificities of the history and anticolonial struggles of both Mindanao and Hawai'i, these Filipina activists stated their opposition in detailed and concrete terms. For instance, the activists voice support for the nationalist struggles in Mindanao, stating that the Balikatan operations "destabilized the fragile and ongoing process of peace talks" and resulted in the deaths of innocent civilians in Zamboanga and Basilan. They argued that the joint U.S.-Philippine military operations were in "violation of the terms of the Mutual Defense Treaty and the Visiting Forces Agreement" and that its earlier joint operations had "not achieved their purported goal of ridding the Philippines of Abu Sayyaf." Stating that the military has created devastating environmental pollution in the Pacific and that "native Hawaiians and other indigenous peoples and nations have shouldered the brunt of military build-up," the activists assert that the "colonization of the Philippines and Hawaii are intimately tied together."

Given that Filipinos in the U.S. comprise a diaspora and, as Jonathan Okamura argues, maintain "cultural, social and economic linkages" with the Philippines, the statement of these activists helps us to realize that U.S. imperialism in the form of U.S. militarism in the Philippines is part of imperialist global forces colonizing Native Hawaiians.[42] The activism of these ten Filipina settler activists illustrates the positive role Filipinos in Hawai'i can play in supporting the anti-imperialist struggles of Native Hawaiians and Filipinos in the Philippines—as Filipino settlers in Hawai'i, we are historically bound by both struggles against U.S. imperialism.

Particularly significant to note is the combination of strength and humility in the politics of the Filipina activists. By calling for a return of all land in use by the U.S. military to its "rightful ancestral stewards and descendants," they locate themselves in Hawai'i in a way that respects Native Hawaiians' right as indigenous peoples to be self-determining. For Filipinos in Hawai'i to support Native Hawaiians in their struggle for self-determination, it is important that we be supporters and not leaders in this movement.[43] Here, the role of ally is not to make decisions for Native Hawaiians but to speak out against colonialism while challenging others in our communities to do the same. Members of our communities have a variety of resources, skills, and talents to offer, and the movement for self-determination occurs on numerous fronts. Identifying our own spheres of influence—including family, friends, institutions or organizations—can be a critical way to begin to consider how we might together interrupt the cycle of colonialism.[44]

As a result of protests in Manila and elsewhere in the Philippines, the United States was not allowed to land troops in the Philippines. In 2003 government officials in the Philippines were able to stop the joint U.S.-Philippine military operations by enforcing the Philippine constitution's stipulation that foreign troops cannot engage in combat against Philippine citizens on Philippine soil. Although the fact remains that the Philippines continues to conduct joint U.S.-Philippine exercises also termed "Balikatan" in the Philippines while receiving military aid from the United States to fight the "war on terrorism," this effort to stop U.S. troops from engaging in combat against nationalist movements in Mindanao was an important victory in resisting U.S. imperialism.

Conclusion

The Philippines and all of its more than seven thousand islands with diverse languages, customs, and epistemologies, had no conception of a Philippines or a Filipino people before colonization or anticolonial resistance. In 1521 Ferdinand Magellan, like Christopher Columbus three decades earlier in the Americas, named the indigenous peoples of the Philippine islands *indios,* a name that stuck for more than 350 years in the Philippines. The term was eventually dropped in the late nineteenth century when a "Filipino" national consciousness began to take shape and the Native peoples who referred to themselves as "Filipinos" united to resist the domination of Spanish colonizers. In an analysis of Philippine revolutionary Andres Bonifacio's poem "Pag-ibig sa Tinubuang Bayan" (literally, "Love for the country of one's roots"), Philippine historian Reynaldo Ileto explains that Bonifacio sought to "release the people's energies in the right direction" by evoking memory to dissolve *utang na loób* (feelings of indebtedness) toward Spain and to foster *utang na loób* for the anticolonial movement: "To have compassion and *utang na loób* for the mother country means participating in the act of freeing her, and by this one becomes 'Filipino.'" [45] According to Bonifacio, identifying as "Filipino" meant committing oneself to resisting colonial oppression.

Filipino settler communities in Hawai'i possess a fierce history of resistance to colonization and can become powerful supporters for the Native Hawaiian movement for decolonization. Racism against Filipinos in Hawai'i is a problem; I encountered it in numerous forms as I was growing up. While these issues hurt, anger, and hinder us, as long as Native Hawaiians remain colonized, empowerment through the colonial system means that we stand on the backs of indigenous peoples. My hope is that we instead combat the discrimination and marginalization that Filipinos in Hawai'i face while also working toward a new consciousness that supports the Native Hawaiian struggle for self-determination. To adopt an ideology of empowerment as "Americans" while knowing that the American political system is colonial suggests that colonialism is justified as long as we are not the colonized. To remain silent or neutral is to support the status quo; if we opt for such escapism, we turn our backs on the people to whom we are most indebted. In

Hawai'i, *utang na loób* belongs to Native Hawaiians, not to the U.S. government, because we live in a stolen Hawaiian nation, and it is Native Hawaiian people who are being subjugated.

Notes

An earlier version of this essay was first published in *Positively No Filipinos Allowed: Building Communities and Discourse* (Philadelphia: Temple University Press, 2006). I thank the editors, Tony Tiongson, Ricardo Gutierrez, and Edgardo Gutierrez, for allowing me to publish this version here. My deep appreciation also goes to Kēwaikaliko for allowing me to use his artwork. I would also like to thank the following people for their thoughtful comments at different stages of this project: Dean Alegado, Rosie Baldonado, Tracy Lachica Buenavista, Duane Champagne, Vicente Diaz, Candace Fujikane, Jason Luna Gavilan, Theodore Gonsalvez, Eiko Kosasa, Roderick Labrador, Don Nakanishi, Jonathan Okamura, Christine Quemuel, Darlene Rodrigues, Sarita See, Haunani-Kay Trask, Julkipli Wadi, Erin Wright, Henry Yu, Dick and Drew Saranillio, Eloise Yamashita Saranillio, Shelley Takasato, and Sharon Heijin Lee. All errors are my own.

1. See, e.g., Ronald Takaki, *Pau Hana: Plantation Life and Labor in Hawaii, 1835–1920* (Honolulu: University of Hawai'i Press, 1983); and *Strangers from a Different Shore: A History of Asian Americans* (New York: Penguin Books, 1989).

2. See Haunani-Kay Trask, *From a Native Daughter: Colonialism and Sovereignty in Hawai'i*, rev. ed. (1993); reprint, Honolulu: University of Hawai'i Press, 1999, 25.

3. Vicente Diaz, "Bye Bye Miss American Pie: Chamorros and Filipinos and the American Dream," *ISLA: A Journal of Micronesian Studies* 3 (1) (Rainy Season 1995): 160.

4. Ruben R. Alcantara, *Sakada: Filipino Adaptation in Hawaii* (Washington, D.C.: University Press of America, 1981); R. R. Cariaga, *The Filipinos in Hawaii: Economic and Social Conditions 1906–1936* (Honolulu: Filipino Public Relations Bureau, 1937); Luis V. Teodoro Jr., *Out of This Struggle: The Filipinos in Hawaii* (Honolulu: University of Hawaii Press, 1981); Bernadette Suguitan Ledesma, *Ating Tao/Our People: The Filipinos in Hawaii* (Honolulu: General Assistance Center for the Pacific, 1976).

5. See Okamura, "Ethnic Boundary Construction in the Japanese American Community in Hawai'i," in this volume.

6. Haunani-Kay Trask, "Settlers of Color and 'Immigrant' Hegemony: 'Locals' in Hawai'i," *Whose Vision? Asian Settler Colonialism in Hawai'i*, ed. Candace Fujikane and Jonathan Y. Okamura, a special issue of *Amerasia Journal* 26 (2) (2000), reprinted in this volume.

7. Trask, "Settlers of Color and 'Immigrant' Hegemony," 20.

8. Virgilio Menor Felipe, *Hawai'i: A Pilipino Dream* (Honolulu: Mutual Publishing, 2002).

9. Yen-Le Espiritu, *Home Bound: Filipino American Lives across Cultures, Communities, and Countries* (Berkeley: University of California Press, 2003), 44.

10. Espiritu, *Home Bound*, 24.

11. Espiritu, *Home Bound*, 24.

12. Felipe, *Hawai'i: A Pilipino Dream*, 29.

13. Felipe, *Hawai'i: A Pilipino Dream*, 28.

14. Felipe, *Hawai'i: A Pilipino Dream*, xvi.

15. Melinda Tria Kerkvliet, *Unbending Cane: Pablo Manlapit, A Filipino Labor Leader in Hawai'i* (Honolulu: University of Hawai'i Press, 2002), 47–48.

16. Dean Alegado, "The Legacy and Challenge of *Ti Mangyuna*" (Honolulu: Union of Democratic Filipinos [KDP], 1981), 5.

17. Joshua Agsalud, "My Perceptions of the Plantation Experience: Influences That Shaped My Views on the Americanization Process," 12, paper presented at the Philippine Studies Conference at the Center for Asian and Pacific Studies at the University of Hawai'i "in commemoration of the 75th anniversary of the coming of Filipinos to Hawai'i," June 28, 1981.

18. Agsalud, "My Perceptions of the Plantation Experience," 12.

19. Michael Ignatieff, *American Exceptionalism and Human Rights* (N.J.: Princeton University Press, 2005).

20. Agsalud, "My Perceptions of the Plantation Experience," 12.

21. Agsalud, "My Perceptions of the Plantation Experience," 11.

22. Zachary Labez, "Hawaiian Sovereignty and the 'Non-Hawaiian' . . . Another Viewpoint," *Hawaii Filipino Chronicle* (March 16, 1996), 13. Also see Zachary G. Labez, "On Statehood: Sovereignty and the Search for Justice," *The Fil-Am Courier* (August 2003).

23. Zachary G. Labez, "The *Pinoys'* Quest for Political Empowerment in America," *The Fil-Am Courier* (June 2001).

24. Zachary Labez, "*Pinoys* in Paradise: From the Sugar Plantations to the State Capitol," *The Fil-Am Courier* (June 2001).

25. Felipe, *Hawai'i: A Pilipino Dream*, xix.

26. Zachary Labez, "*Pinoys* in America: From Philippine Sovereignty to Empowerment in America," *The Fil-Am Courier* (June 2001).

27. Zachary Labez, "Filipino Americans: Empowered Citizens in the Making?" *The Fil-Am Courier* (June 2001).

28. Kēwaikaliko, *Benocide*, in *Nā Maka Hou: New Visions, Contemporary Native Hawaiian Art* (Honolulu: Honolulu Academy of Arts, 2001), 81.

29. Jeanette Wolfley, "*Rice v. Cayetano:* The Supreme Court Declines to Extend Federal Indian Law Principles to Native Hawaiians' Sovereign Rights," *Asian-Pacific Law & Policy Journal* 3 (2) (Summer 2002).

30. Mieke Bal, "Seeing Signs: The Use of Semiotics for the Understanding of Visual Art," *The Subject of Art History: Historical Objects in Contemporary Perspectives,* ed. March Cheetham, Michael Ann Holly, and Keith Moxey (Cambridge: Cambridge University Press, 1998), 81.

31. As cited in Ida Yoshinaga and Eiko Kosasa, "Local Japanese Women for Justice Speak Out against Daniel Inouye and the JACL, *Honolulu Advertiser,* February 6, 2000, reprinted in *Whose Vision? Asian Settler Colonialism in Hawai'i,* ed. Candace Fujikane and Jonathan Y. Okamura, a special issue of *Amerasia Journal* 26 (2) (2000); and in this volume.

32. "Writing in Captivity: Poetry in a Time of De-Colonization," *Navigating Islands and Continents: Conversations and Contestations in and around the Pacific,* ed. Cynthia Franklin, Ruth Hsu, and Suzanne Kosanke, a special issue of *Literary Studies East and West* 17 (Honolulu: University of Hawai'i, College of Languages, Linguistics, and Literature, 2000), 17.

33. Hawai'i Advisory Committee to the United States Commission on Civil Rights, *A Broken Trust: The Hawaiian Homelands Program: Seventy Years of Failure of the Federal and State Governments to Protect the Civil Rights of Native Hawaiians* (Honolulu: Hawai'i Advisory Committee to the United States Commission on Civil Rights, 1991).

34. Debra Barayuga, "OHA Sues to Resume Land Revenues; The Agency Says that the State Failed in Its Fiduciary Duties as Trustee of the Lands," *Honolulu Star-Bulletin,* July 22, 2003.

35. Zachary Labez, "Mabuhay . . . and Salamat, Ben," *Fil-Am Courier* (December 16–30, 2002).

36. Trask, "Settlers of Color and 'Immigrant' Hegemony," 2.

37. Manulani Aluli Meyer, "Hawaiian Art: A Doorway to Knowing," *Nā Maka Hou, New Visions Contemporary Native Hawaiian Art* (Honolulu: Honolulu Academy of Arts, 2001), 12.

38. "President Arroyo Brings in $4 Billion in Pledges from U.S. Visit," *Hawaii Filipino Chronicle,* December 1, 2001, 9.

39. Darlene Rodrigues, phone interview, October 30, 2003.

40. See Kyle Kajihiro, "The Militarizing of Hawai'i: Occupation, Accommodation, and Resistance," in this volume.

41. Grace Alvaro Caligtan et al., "Filipinos Stand in Solidarity with Native Hawaiians in Opposing United States Military Expansion," posting to indyhawaiilist, March 15, 2003, http://archives.lists.indymedia.org/imc-hawaii/2003-March/000715.html.

42. Jonathan Okamura, *Imagining the Filipino American Diaspora: Transnational Relations, Identities, and Communities* (New York: Garland, 1998), 8.

43. Eiko Kosasa, "Ideological Images: U.S. Nationalism in Japanese Settler Photographs," *Whose Vision? Asian Settler Colonialism in Hawai'i,* ed. Candace Fujikane and Jonathan Y. Okamura, a special issue of *Amerasia Journal* 26 (2) (2000); and reprinted in this volume.

44. See Beverly Daniel Tatum, *"Why Are All the Black Kids Sitting Together in the Cafeteria?" and Other Conversations about Race* (New York: Basic Books, 1997), 105.

45. Reynaldo Ileto, *Filipinos and Their Revolution: Event, Discourse, and Historiography* (Manila: Ateneo De Manila University Press, 1999), 24.

Anatomy of a Dancer

Place, Lineage, and Liberation

Long ago when tigers smoked pipes and rabbits had long tails.
. . . This is the way many Korean stories begin—tales of wise actions based on compassion and devotion or of foolish actions based on selfishness and greed. These stories also relate the lesson that justice is within reach for even the humblest when one acts out of generosity on behalf of others. The necessity to act on behalf of others has been a theme of my own family's stories. I have inherited this legacy—both as a burden and an inspiration—which has in turn guided not only the creation of my own artistic lineage as a dancer, but also my perceptions of place, action, and transformation. My family's vision of justice has been defined and constrained by their own diaspora—by leaving their homeland for Hawai'i and carrying out actions to fit their vision as settlers on land not their own.

So a long time ago, or so it seemed to me, my *jeong-jobu,* my great-grandfather, Choy Choon Yee, embarked on a journey from Korea to Hawai'i, across the Pacific from one colonized state to another. The Choy family was of the Kyungju Choy lineage; Choy Choon Yee's immediate family, however, had moved to Kyungsan-namdo. There, they carried out an action that created havoc. My *jeong-jobu*'s family buried their grandfather in the Choy family cemetery in Kyungsan-namdo without seeking proper permission. There were threats from other family members to kill Choy Choon Yee's oldest son, Doo Wook, my grandfather. To save the boy, Choy Choon Yee took his son and hid him in a cave on a nearby hillside. Meanwhile, news that Koreans were being recruited to work on the Hawai'i sugar plantations reached my *jeong-jobu*'s ears. In 1904 Choy took his wife and eldest son out into the dark of night and began the long walk to the port of Pusan in order to board a ship for Hawai'i.[1] They were sent to work on a sugar plantation at Hanapēpē, Kaua'i, and they lived in Camp Four with other Koreans.

My great-grandfather was part of the second group of immigrants recruited by the Hawaiian Sugar Planters' Association in 1904.[2] According to Wayne Pat-

Mary Choy and Barry Nakamura at a demonstration against French nuclear testing in the Pacific. The demonstration took place at the McCoy Pavilion at Ala Moana Park, where the French consulate was celebrating Bastille Day on July 14, 1995. Photograph by Ed Greevy.

terson they were hired with three-year, nonbinding work agreements. With Japan's colonialist annexation of Korea as a protectorate in late 1905, life in Korea had become chaotic. Affected by armed conflicts, famine, poverty, and loss of sovereignty, Koreans were uprooted from their homes. They were then in a position to break away from adherence to the Confucian principle that disapproved of leaving one's home country.

The sugar planters' strategy of "dividing and conquering" the immigrant laborers by ethnic group exploited the existing divisions between groups and was apparent in not only the layout of the segregated plantation camps, but also in the racist, essentialist attitudes of the planter elite. Patterson quotes a planter who went to Korea to recruit workers in 1902: "I feel as confident as I can without positively knowing, that the Koreans will prove good laborers if we can get them to the islands. . . . They are lusty strong fellows and physically much the superior of the Jap. In rice culture and mining work they excel [sic] any other nationality and I can't for the life of me see how it is possible for them to prove other than good laborers for us."[3]

Like other Koreans, my great-grandfather left the plantation for the city more quickly than the Puerto Ricans, who arrived at about the same time, and, in fact, faster than any other group of plantation workers. There were reasons for this rapid urbanization. The Koreans had certain advantages. Compared to other immigrants, Koreans had a relatively high literacy rate. They were from different walks of life with a variety of skills, which assured more economic stability for their community as a whole when compared with other Asian immigrants. In fact, according to Patterson Koreans were more often than not unused to farming. They turned out to be mediocre laborers, whereas most of the Chinese and Japanese recruits were skilled farmers in their home countries.[4]

Unlike other Korean immigrants, Choy Choon Yee arrived with some resources. After fulfilling his labor agreement, he left the plantation and moved to Honolulu. Supplementing his own resources through the means of *gye,* a collective economic strategy of pooling resources with others who contributed on a rotational basis, he leased out the upstairs of a building at the corner of King and Alakea Streets and began a lodging rental business. He was a man of few words who smoked and liked his liquor and whose authority was law. He had knowledge of herbal medicine used to sustain the body under difficult conditions.

My great-grandfather, like many in his community, helped other Koreans in their efforts to survive. They came together regularly because of religious affiliation (primarily Christian) and felt a bond of solidarity as an ethnic group. It was also less difficult for some Korean settlers to see Hawai'i as a permanent home.[5] Unmarried men left Korea because of the promise of employment as a means to escape poverty. Others were impelled by a strong desire to fight colonialism from a safe haven abroad, albeit from another colony. However, many of those who did not return to Korea stayed in Hawaiʻi not simply because they saw Hawaiʻi as home, but because they felt that as long as Japan ruled Korea, a return home was an impossibility.[6]

My grandfather, Doo Wook, at eighteen years of age, felt that he himself lacked the physical strength for plantation labor.[7] To compensate for his inadequacy, he set up his own business selling men's work clothes to plantation workers. Rising at four in the morning, he made his rounds peddling clothes to Filipinos as well as other plantation workers and town residents. On payday he would hitch up his horse, put on a revolver, and collect payments.[8] On his trips to Oʻahu he learned about the presence of U.S. Navy and Army military bases, and acting upon what he sensed could be a lucrative market for military uniforms, he moved the entire family to Honolulu to begin a new business. The main tailor shop was downtown, and he managed to open branch shops at Fort Shafter, Schofield Barracks, Fort DeRussy, and Pearl Harbor. In this way he was able to support his own family as well as the Korean independence movement. I would spend Saturdays sitting on the large canvas-cutting table watching Grandpa Choy and his other workers cut khaki with heavy scissors. The Korean women would patiently sew uniform after uniform on big, black Singer sewing machines. I would have small conversations with army and navy officers who came in to buy their supplies. Little did I know that my grandfather's work was but a small piece of the powerful U.S. military establishment.

Along with the development of the U.S. capitalist economy with Hawaiʻi as a dependent satellite, the islands were also a crucial strategic link in the U.S. "Pacific Strategy" of empire building. Even prior to annexation in 1898, then later as a territory and state, Hawaiʻi was not only a site that America could mine for its natural resources and labor, but was also a strategic site in the Pacific serving the purpose of U.S. "national security." Because the plantation elite had secured the islands as a U.S. territory and military outpost in the Pacific, the United States gave them free rein over the islands.[9] My grandfather's business served America's strategic and security interests. Sitting on the canvas-cutting table, playing with army and navy patches, and putting military studs on the sailor hats I would wear, I had no idea of this larger picture.

While Choy Doo Wook himself had not been educated, he financed the college education of his siblings, Doo Hwan, Soon Hee (Priscilla), and Bong Kun (Martha). He sent funds home to Korea. Active in the community, he belonged to a group of businessmen who financially supported the Korean independence movement. The Korean National Association had regular meetings that the whole family would attend.[10] My grandfather appeared to be an active member of the

Korean Methodist Church, which we would also attend each Sunday. On January 16, 1932, the Hawai'i Korean Association dissolved and reformed as the Association of People, of which my grandfather was vice president. He also served on the Committee of the Korean Association Abroad as a cabinet member of its financial division, and he was one of fourteen community representatives of Americans for Independence. On April 20, 1941, he founded the Korean Association in America's Hawai'i chapter. In September 1944 he was elected vice president of the Party of Korean Independence, Hawai'i Headquarters. In 1945 he was on the cabinet of the Association of People.[11] In June 1997 he was posthumously awarded a patriotic medal, which my father Duke accepted on his behalf in Seoul.[12]

I was oblivious to my grandfather's position in his community. Grandpa Choy was silent with us and only smiled. He would engage in lively discussions in Korean only with friends. No doubt these conversations included heated debates about Korea's occupation by Japan and the possibilities for independence.

Hawai'i as Meeting Ground: The Whang Family

My father's family was joined to the Whang family through his marriage to my mother, Mary. In an interview published in *Autobiography of Protest in Hawai'i*, my mother explains that she was aware of her family's strong female lineage: "Traditionally, Korean women keep their own surnames when they are married. They play a major role in family decisions. In my auntie's family, the eldest of the eight siblings was a sister. When both parents [who were farmers] died at an early age, she became the undisputed head of the family."[13]

The Whang family in Honolulu had a strong woman as its head: Whang Ha Soo, my mother's *go-mo*, or aunt on her father's side.[14] I knew her simply as "Tūtū."[15] Whang Ha Soo had traveled to Alabama to study at Athens Women's College. On her way home to Korea in 1919 she stopped in Honolulu, where she was offered a job as a social worker at the YWCA's International Institute. Later, my mother and her sister Elizabeth were sent from San Francisco to live with their *go-mo* while their father Whang Sa Sun recuperated from his grief over the death of his wife, Chang Tae Sun. The temporary stay became permanent. Whang Ha Soo adopted my mother and Elizabeth.[16] My mother describes her education under Whang's guidance.

My sister and I often accompanied aunty as she made her rounds visiting families, skillful as interpreter, mediator, teacher. An outstanding contribution she made was her pioneering efforts to keep Korean culture alive. She organized Korean young women's clubs where Korean music and dance were taught by the elders in the community. She created dramatic stage productions based on

Korean folktales, which were presented in the beautiful setting of the central court of the Honolulu Academy of Arts. With this connection to my Korean heritage, I have never lost sight of understanding and appreciating my identity. But at the same time, I now realize that I was caught in the process of American "assimilation."[17]

A 1924 newspaper article on the YWCA's International Institute includes a description of Whang's work: "Miss Whang, the Korean worker, recently had an interesting case when she was called upon to find a home for a young Korean picture bride who went to the institute for protection from a cruel and much older husband."[18] Her fearless advocacy on behalf of Korean picture brides came from her own strong cultural identity as a Korean woman and her rootedness in Christian belief. Nevertheless, by working for the International Institute she gave support to their "internationalist" perspective that was an extension of the colonizer's view.

The International Institute was located at 1562 Nuʻuanu Street, and the sign over the door of the building read "Ka Hale Kōkua," translated by a journalist as "The House of Friendly Help."[19] This "help" rested on the premise that the women who came to the International Institute needed "protection" and guidance to become good Americans. Said to have "a remarkable representation of the races of the Pacific," the International Institute did not appear to include anyone from the indigenous Hawaiian group. Nutrition classes were taught "where mothers of all races learn the use of American foods" in addition to other classes in English, sewing, and cooking. The leadership was haole (white), with the institute's executive committee consisting of Mrs. Doremus Scudder as executive secretary and Mrs. Arthur Withington as chair of the executive board. An annual "Rally Day" organized every fall served as a recruitment device to publicize what the institute offered. The October 1924 rally day featured a "model house" set up in a second-floor room at the institute wherein "proper and sanitary" American living habits were exhibited.

Mrs. Russell and Miss Cooke demonstrated that four people could live in two rooms and have proper sanitary arrangements. . . . This model house is a striking illustration of the manner in which the work of the institute is dovetailed with that of other agencies. As the result of this demonstration, the central committee on child welfare has voted to give $300 towards the erection and furnishing of a two-room cottage on wheels which will travel from one section of the city to another. Miss Anna Cooke will demonstrate the proper use of "haole" furniture, what foods can be best cooked in a small space and what a growing child should eat.[20]

While the YWCA's purpose was to change the "primitive immigrants" into good Americans, Whang's own contribution to the Korean community is nevertheless clear—she underscored the need to know one's roots in a multicultural colonial context. She founded the Hyung Jay (Sisterhood) Club and the Korean Mother's Club in order to bridge political divisions that existed within the local Korean community. The YWCA was the vehicle by which she provided a haven for Korean women so they could gather together and be active outside the household. One must understand the liberating impact of being part of the Hyung Jay Club for some of the young picture brides who faced violence and troubled relations with frustrated spouses who were sometimes less educated than they were.

From as early as the 1920s until 1939 Whang utilized her knowledge of Korean dance, which she had studied in Korea, and her understanding of her native customs and stories to institute programs to support Korean women. Adapting her cultural knowledge to the circumstances of the women she worked with, Whang produced and directed, advised, and oversaw dance and music concerts, pageants, and festivals. The O Wol Dan O (Fifth day of the fifth month, or Korean Spring Festival) were covered by the media from at least 1934 through 1937 and featured Korean dances and different plays produced, written, and directed by Whang.[21] The plays were adaptations from Whang's own store of Korean stories or legends and included stories she herself created to make an ethical point to instruct young women on how they should live. The titles of the plays she directed bear witness to her advocacy for women: *The Spirit of Womanhood* (May 11, 1929), *My Sister* (1932), and *Little Women* (May 18, 1935). She also encouraged others to create and direct their own plays, dances, and musical performances. Productions often featured a variety of music and dance, such as tap, hula, and Polish dances.[22] She also wrote and directed another spectacle, *Honin-Yaybi* (Wedding ceremonials of Korea), which was sometimes paired with the O Wol Dan O in an evening's program. *Honin-Yaybi* was apparently an adaptation of a Korean story, "Nyu Cha Sung Han" (A Korean girl's cycle of joy). Productions could involve large numbers of women, such as in the 1934 Spring Festival, which included a "cast of 75 girls of Korean ancestry." [23] Whang wrote and directed productions of O Wol Dan O in 1936 that featured a reader, a singer, dancers, and Korean games such as *neul-duigi* (seesaw riders) and *su bak chigi*.

The contents of O Wol Dan O changed over the years. In 1938 the O Wol Dan O festival included the dramatization of "Shim Chung," a story included in the *pan sori* (folk opera) canon about a daughter's filial devotion to her blind father, which was adapted and directed by Margaret Kwon. By this time Whang's status appears to have been that of overall director. In this same 1938 program my aunt, Elizabeth Whang, was the "reader," and Shim Chung was played by my father's sister, Jane

Choy. My father appeared in scene IV, the "Market Scene," as an attendant, and my mother Mary Whang was a dancer in scene VI.[24] Whang's advocacy efforts provided a foundation for my parents' later activism, an activism that extended beyond the Korean community to focus on issues of importance to those Native to Hawaiian soil.[25]

For Whang, cultural productions produced largely by women were one means for community cohesion, women's pride, and empowerment in the context of settler colonial society. In this context performances represented "Korean-ness" without the context of feudal courts and Confucianism, a context that allowed women vehicles for expression, organization, and social relations not possible in their home country. Why the productions included "hula" taught and performed by Koreans and not hula 'auana taught and performed by Hawaiians substantiates the view that the YWCA was a microcosm of the larger racist colonial society.

This dominant perspective seeped into my own home. We were reminded to be proud of being Korean, and yet at the same time we spoke "standard English" instead of pidgin (Hawai'i Creole English), ate meatloaf more often than *bul ko gi*, and did not eat *gim-chi jji-gae* whatsoever.[26] Instead of Korean dance I learned ballet at the YWCA, a "natural" place for me to go considering Whang's commitment to its activities. Ironically, at the end of her tenure at the YWCA Whang herself was left unprotected by the institution to which she had given so much and was relegated to a lowly staff position of secretarial help by the administration until 1942. With the coming of World War II the Hyung Jay Club and the International Institute ceased to exist.

Mary and Duke Choy: "Home" as a Site for Struggle

Whang Ha Soo devoted her energies to advocacy for Korean women's identity in a multiethnic context—however colonial and ultimately disempowering for her own life's work. Her vision was grounded in Christianity. In 1948 she left the organized church and felt that her beliefs were best expressed through her own daily ethical actions.[27] Whang's strong sense of ethical purpose to work for the disempowered—with or without the backing of organized religion—provided the ethical grounding for the family life of her nieces, whom she singlehandedly raised from childhood into adulthood.

Whang Ha Soo's independent spirit had a great influence on my mother's own transformation. From being an active member of the Korean Methodist Church as choir director and a housewife, my mother became a Buddhist and, almost simultaneously, a political activist, a woman liberated from the household.[28] Her political actions began with her anti–Vietnam War stance through the Church of the Crossroads. Both she and my father supported "local" antiwar draft resisters and participated in antiwar demonstrations. She and my father supported not only the formation of ethnic studies at the University of Hawai'i, but also people's movements to stop the tide of development in the 1970s and into the 1980s. She explains,

> We studied Mao, liberalism, monopoly capitalism, etc. Our inspiration came from the Black and Puerto Rican movements. Leaders from the revolutionary Black Panthers and the Young Lords parties were invited by the Ethnic Studies Program to come to Hawai'i to share their experiences with us. What a consciousness raising time that was!
>
> With the Kalama Valley and the Ethnic Studies Program conflicts still vivid in our memories, some young people gathered their forces to help the Chinatown community people to contend with the problems of urban redevelopment—in other words, the destruction of their communities. Our daughter, recently graduated from the University of Wisconsin, a hotbed of antiwar protest, helped to organize The Third Arm. She enlisted the help of her father to open a Free Chinatown Medical Clinic. It became the center for political education. It was a stimulating experience for us. We had parties, fundraisers, potlucks, forums—Chinatown and the wider communities coming together as comrades.[29]

My mother became a member of Kōkua Hawai'i, which was organized to stop development in Kalama Valley. Both of my parents supported other community struggles in Chinatown, Ota Camp, and Hale Mōhalu in Waimalu.[30]

My father, Duk Cho Choy (or "Duke"), had also been active in the Methodist Church laity. His Christian beliefs did not alter even in his openness and acceptance of my mother's new political and spiritual path, upon which she embarked in the early 1970s. He became involved in the sanctuary movement, which gave sanctuary to draft-dodgers and was based at the Church of the Crossroads in Honolulu, and he was a draft counselor along with my mother. He supported the other struggles, particularly through his medical knowledge. When Third Arm opened a free clinic, he volunteered his services as a doctor there for twelve years. His own pediatric practice was supplemented with alternative therapies including hypnotherapy, healing touch therapy (Reiki), and acupuncture. He has always freely aided those in need, including activists and family friends.

Because of her past involvement in movements dealing with land rights, my mother took the next step in the 1990s to learn about the indigenous struggle for Hawaiian sovereignty. She educated herself about the history of how Native Hawaiian lands came to be illegally occupied by the U.S. government, about indigenous worldviews, and their rights to governance over their own lands. She tried to study the Hawaiian language (she kept a Hawaiian-language dictionary in the cupboard by our dining table at home) and would teach me Hawaiian words she had come to know. She joined with Native Hawaiians struggling for independence and sovereignty, helping with the landmark Ka Hoʻokolokolonui Kanaka Maoli-Peoples' International Tribunal Hawaiʻi in 1993.[31] In an interview, she tells us, "There is a growing realization that Kanaka Maoli and non-Kanaka Maoli must come together in support of independence for the Hawaiian nation, which includes complete control of their lands and resources. It affects us all and I am glad to be a supporter."[32]

As much as my mother came to respect the indigenous right of independence from the colonizer, she also engaged in an inner debate related to the responsibility of settlers such as herself to aid in the struggle for that right. She was critical of Asian American communities, including Korean American ones, and their lack of attention to the question of Native Hawaiian sovereignty.

Her political activities were consistently synchronized with her Zen Buddhist practice of mindful action and her love of the ʻāina, or Native land. When driving into Mānoa Valley, she would frequently express her awe at the beauty of the mountains, and toward the end of her life it was a daily and deeply felt expression of appreciation. Two of the high points in the last years of her life were connected to this love of the land. One experience was her hike up Kum Gang San, or the Diamond Mountains in North Korea.[33] The other moment took place when she went with long-time ethnic studies and community activist Marion Kelly to visit the opening of Waiāhole-Waikāne lands for a return to taro cultivation. She hiked into the valley and felt a fulfillment in bearing witness to the land and its indigenous fruits. Kelly writes,

> There was a decision by the State that the water that belonged to Waiāhole Valley would be sent to the lands in central Oʻahu and that the water coming down the stream at Waiāhole would be cut off at the mountain. The taro farmers in Waiāhole depended on that water and were willing to set up camp at the head of the valley, deep in the forest (about three miles inland from the gate where the people had gathered [in protest]). The group camped at the head of the valley needed some supplies, so Mary and I volunteered to take them in. We walked the three miles in the forested valley and arrived at the camp. They were grateful for the supplies we had brought to them, and then they showed us exactly where the water was coming from, which way it was being sent, and how they were going to make sure that it would not be sent away from Waiāhole Valley. They had set up camp and were ready to stay until the State pulled back.

Then we walked all the way back to the group at the big gate to report to them. It was a wonderful experience, and we talked together about our various experiences in the movement to support Kanaka Maoli rights of way to access the sea and the inland areas of the valleys and their rights to have water.[34]

Dancing in the Steps of My Ancestors

Like old Korean tales, my own family's real-life stories offer us lessons. In this moment of reflection I see connections between these lessons and my own life journey in dance. As Whang inspired my mother, in turn my mother inspired me. She encouraged me to choreograph something about the *jeong-sin-dae*. During World War II between 80,000 and 200,000 Korean women were forced to become sex slaves for Japanese soldiers. Officially, they were labeled "military supplies" and were sent off to the battlefields like grenades or rifles. Unofficially, the soldiers called them "public lavatories." The *jeong-sin-dae* were raped, assaulted, and tortured. They were considered female kamikaze (literally, "divine wind") to be sacrificed for the glory of the emperor of Japan. Many were murdered, died of venereal disease, suffered from mental disorders, or committed suicide.[35] My mother had first heard about these women through feminist activist, scholar, and family friend Alice Chai, who also informed me about the issue. At first it seemed impossible to attempt to deal with this subject through dance, but my mother's urgency taught me that to ignore the hidden and painful stories of these women would be to ignore the need for justice.

I choreographed "*Jeong-Sin-Dae*/Comfort Woman" as part of a suite, *Seung-Hwa: Rape/Race/Rage/Revolution,* which premiered in New York in 1995.[36] The process of choreography was interwoven with music by composer and baritone saxophonist Fred Wei-han Ho in collaboration with drummer Royal Hartigan and soprano saxophonist Allen Won. We spent hours debating and discussing a range of issues from the historical circumstances of the *jeong-sin-dae* to related issues of sexism and militarism, what the *jeong-sin-dae* might have thought and felt, as well as what the Japanese soldiers might have thought and felt and what sounds and movements could help to express the devastating torment and inhumanity. The musicians not only played their respective instruments, but also acted as the Japanese soldiers dressed in army hats and dark glasses, encircling the *jeong-sin-dae,* danced by myself. My own process was that of reaching an understanding of the inner terrain of the *jeong-sin-dae*. The image of a puppet first came to me to express the need to distance oneself from one's body, to divorce oneself from the inflicted violence. Then the idea of dancing with my legs in the air became the means to express the violation, the defenselessness, and lack of control over one's own body.

The dance movements were inspired by other Asian movement or dance forms I have studied: Korean *tal-chum* (mask dance), Zen Dance/Son Mu, and yoga.[37] I am in the process of creating my own technique inspired by several Asian movement forms, all of which have the common element of *gi* (life force) energy. Telling such devastating stories requires that I perform in such a way that does not deplete my energy but rather renews it. The Zen Dance/Son Mu technique has as its primary focus breathing from the *dan jeon*, the point approximately two inches below one's navel, and this focus of breath allows my *gi* to flow.

My grandfather Choy Doo Wook supported efforts for an independent Korea. Whang Ha Soo focused on the struggles of Korean women settlers. My mother and father were supportive of ethnic groups in the islands that struggled for land and civil rights. Finally, while my mother had great interest in issues of justice for Koreans in the homeland, she felt the sovereignty of the Hawaiian people held the key to the future health and longevity of all people in Hawai'i. Like my mother, I believe that justice for one's own people is integrally linked to the struggles of indigenous peoples. In 1997 I was inspired by my colleague Fred Ho to choreograph a piece about Sarraounia, the great indigenous Hausa queen of Burkina Faso. In 1899 she successfully led her people against the French colonial forces of Voulet and Chanoine through superior tactical maneuvers and her indigenous spiritual knowledge. The dance was part of my suite, *Gi-Aché: Stories from the Belly,* which premiered at the Danspace Project in New York. I collaborated with dancer and choreographer Dyane Harvey, who brought to the piece her own knowledge of some forms of African dance and the Afro-Brazilian martial art of *capoeira.*

Another dance in the same suite tells of Non-gae and her act of resistance to save her land and people from Japanese imperialism. From a poor family, Non-gae served as a *gi-saeng,* or female entertainer, for Korea's Yi dynasty elite. In 1593 the Japanese general Motani and his troops ravaged Non-gae's town, pillaging and killing both soldiers and civilians. Non-gae danced for the drunken Motani, drawing him outside to a cliff overlooking a river. Wearing ten silver rings that she had requested from the general himself, she locked her hands, grasped Motani, and jumped into the river to her death, drowning the general with her. At the end of the suite it is Sarraounia who lifts up the body of Non-gae and mourns for her.

By bringing these women of courage together in my suite through dance movements inspired by Korean and African/Afro-Brazilian forms of movement, I could explore the intercultural connections between different peoples engaged in resistance out of love of their own land. I coined the term *gi-aché,* which combines the Korean notion of internal life-force energy with the Yoruba notion of *aché* (the spiritual power that makes things happen, life-force energy), brought together through dance in the moment of performance.

Lessons of the Ancestors

In essence, what are the lessons conveyed by these stories?

Lesson 1: As settlers, we must know who we are. As Koreans on Hawaiian soil, we need to challenge the myth that we can live as an ethnic group insulated from other groups, and we can transform that myth into a memory of where we came from and a vision of what we need to do to move forward.

Lesson 2: We must tell stories of exploitation and oppression as a means to liberation. Grandpa Choy was silent with his grandchildren, but he was articulate in his native tongue, speaking out against Japanese imperialism. Tell what is necessary by whatever means necessary to see history for what it is. Then, whether we speak through performance or other acts of political resistance, we can more precisely walk in the footsteps of our ancestors.

Lesson 3: Before walking in the steps of our ancestors, we need to listen to see if we are missing crucial stories. My own family's stories took place not on their own soil but on Hawaiian soil. They did admirable things for their own community as well as for the home country. They were, however, living at a time when the islands were going through a transition from territory to state, a time during which U.S. colonial control over the islands was made more complete. The wider context of colonial domination cannot be ignored. The legacy of their own lives—as ethically as they lived—was tainted with unavoidable complicity. The deliberate separation of ethnic groups in the islands made it easier to ignore Native Hawaiian struggles for self-determination and sovereignty.

This millennium's challenge will be for Koreans and other Asian groups living in the islands to begin to listen to Hawaiian stories, danced or otherwise told—not just our own people's stories—in order to see history for what it is, and then we can better see what transformations need to occur for future generations.

Notes

Dedicated to my parents, Mary and Duke Choy, and their grandchildren, Noa Duke Fujimura, Maya Caroline Haesoo Choy-Sutton, and Tony Duke Choy-Sutton.

1. My uncle Herbert Choy said that "they walked to the departure point for Hawai'i." It is likely that this departure point was the port of Pusan.

2. The first group of Koreans came in 1903, and the third came during the first half of 1905. Wayne Patterson, "Upward Social Mobility of the Koreans in Hawaii," *Korean Studies* 3 (1979): 82.

3. Quoted in Patterson, "Upward Social Mobility of the Koreans in Hawaii," 89.

4. Patterson, "Upward Social Mobility of the Koreans in Hawaii," 89.

5. Patterson, "Upward Social Mobility of the Koreans in Hawaii," 84, 86–88.

6. I am grateful to Brenda Kwon for this point of view, which problematizes the notion of "immigration." Personal communication, January 25, 2000.

7. He was born on May 4, 1891, and died on June 20, 1956.

8. He learned his trade through two correspondence courses: Cybick School of Garment Design in New York and the Trafhagen School of Garment Cutting and Design. He hired and trained workers at his tailor shop to mass-produce the clothing. Herbert Choy, interview, July 23, 1999.

9. Noel J. Kent, *Hawai'i, Islands under the Influence* (New York: Monthly Review Press, 1983), 67–69.

10. Herbert Choy, interview, July 23, 1999.

11. Choy Doo Wook's penchant for sharing his income extended to the University of Hawai'i and its Center for Korean Studies.

12. He was one of two Americans to be awarded this medal by the South Korean government.

13. Mary Choy, "Mary Choy," *Autobiography of Protest in Hawai'i*, ed. Robert H. Mast and Anne B. Mast (Honolulu: University of Hawai'i Press, 1996), 181.

14. Whang Ha Soo was born in 1889 and died in 1984.

15. "Tūtū" means "grandmother" in Hawaiian

16. "Hanai" means "to adopt" in Hawaiian. It does not necessarily mean legal adoption, but rather a more informal adoption, which is often of members of one's extended family.

17. Choy, "Mary Choy," 180–181.

18. *Honolulu Star-Bulletin*, November 15, 1924. While Whang Ha Soo's contributions are the focus of this article, my mother also acknowledged the outstanding leadership provided by other women employed at the International Institute: "The women who worked alongside my aunty were equally strong and committed, and well respected in their communities. I remember them so well: Mrs. Kishimoto, Mrs. Yee, Mrs. Avecilla." Choy, "Mary Choy," 181.

19. *Honolulu Star-Bulletin*, November 15, 1924.

20. *Honolulu Star-Bulletin*, November 15, 1924. Mrs. James Russell was "head nutrition worker" at the institute. Miss Anna Cooke was a volunteer.

21. O Wol Dan O translates as "fifth month day five" but was translated in the media and programs as "fifth day of the fifth month," or "Korean Spring Festival."

22. E.g., a program from circa 1932 included the following: *My Sister* presented a "Polish Dance" (danced by my Aunt Elizabeth, my mother Mary, and four other women), a play called *The Obedient Princess* and another play called *My Sister*, a "Korean Dance," "Tap Dance," and concluding with "Additional Numbers" of singing with piano accompaniment. Another Hyung Jay Club program held at the YWCA on May 8, 1937, included a "Korean Spring Song," a play called *The Woon Soo* (Fate) directed by Miriam Kang, a "Hula Dance," directed by Eunice Song, with Durshton Kim as vocalist and Mary Whang on piano. Another program was sponsored by the Morning Music Club for the benefit of its scholarship fund. The Hyung Jay Club was featured, presenting O Wol Dan O Korean Spring Festival and Honin-Yaybi Wedding Ceremonials of Korea on Tuesday, March 31, 1936, 8:30 p.m., at Dillingham Hall.

23. *Honolulu Star-Bulletin*, May 18, 1934.

24. Program, O Wol Dan O Korean Festival, Honolulu Academy of Arts, May 5, 1938.

25. I thank Brenda Kwon for this insight. Personal communication, January 25, 2000.

26. My mother had attended Roosevelt High School, which was an "English Standard" school. My father attended McKinley High School, which did not have this reputation, and he felt freer to speak pidgin inside and outside of the home.

27. In a letter written to Kay Paik, February 3, 1952, Ha Soo wrote: "I decided to follow him like his true servants or preachers who do not receive salary or live in luxury, but sacrifice themselves as Jesus did . . . then love your neighbors as thyself. The 'Christians' are not only hearers and preachers, but living and doers of the 'words.' I have left the false way . . . in fact all the churches of any kind are in one way or another gone out of the true meaning of Christianity."

28. Her Buddhist name was "Sister of the Clouds."

29. Choy, "Mary Choy," 182–183.

30. The struggle at Ota Camp involved the eviction of a Filipino community by the landowner. Eventually, Ota Camp families secured a piece of land to build their homes on. Hale Mōhalu was an intermediate care center for leprosy (Hansen's disease) patients. The State decided to use the land the center was on for other purposes and issued patients notices of eviction. After ten years of struggles for alternative housing, the State divided the property into a home for people with disabilities and a baseball field. Choy, "Mary Choy," 183–184.

31. "Kanaka Maoli" is the indigenous term for "Native Hawaiian." The tribunal convened in August 1993 and brought the United States and the State of Hawai'i to trial for crimes committed against the indigenous Hawaiian peoples.

32. Choy, "Mary Choy," 184.

33. The Diamond Mountains hold special meaning for all Korean people and are considered one of the natural treasures of the peninsula.

34. Personal communication from Marion Kelly, March 21, 2000.

35. Alice Chai, "Asian-Pacific Feminist Coalition Politics: The *Chongshindae/Jugunianfu* ('Comfort Women') Movement," *Korean Studies* 17 (1993): 67–91.

36. The performance was presented by the Dance Theater Workshop and the National Performance Network, March 16–19, 1995, at the Bessie Schönberg Theater in New York. A year prior I had received the first commission for the suite through Cornell University.

37. I am a certified teacher of Zen Dance/Son Mu taught to me by its creator, Lee Sun Ock, a choreographer based in Seoul and New York/New Jersey and performer of her own Zen Dance/Son Mu style as well as traditional Korean dance.

Local Japanese Women for Justice (LJWJ) Speak Out against Daniel Inouye and the JACL

The following is a reprint of an op-ed piece we published in the *Honolulu Advertiser* on February 6, 2000. There, we criticized U.S. Senator Daniel Inouye and the Japanese American Citizens League–Honolulu (JACL–Honolulu) for their roles in obstructing the process for Hawaiian sovereignty. We spoke out after a politically motivated media smear campaign against Native Hawaiian nationalist Mililani Trask, who had objected to Inouye's act of overriding an agreed-upon process for the U.S. federal reconciliation hearings for Hawaiians. Ignoring the content of Trask's objections, the media sensationalized a comment she made in a private meeting, referring to Inouye as the "one-armed bandit." As the result of this campaign, many non-Hawaiians, including the JACL–Honolulu, took the opportunity to attack Trask and Hawaiians in general with American patriotic rhetoric.

We publicly supported Trask, a respected and prominent leader who advocates for a self-determined sovereignty. Many in the local Japanese and larger Hawaiʻi communities were shocked that sansei women broke the political and cultural silence by publicly criticizing other Japanese. Moreover, we spoke out against Inouye, generally considered the "godfather" of Hawaiʻi politics and the embodiment of Asian immigrant success. We received supportive letters, including many from people who said the newspapers refused to print any positive responses to our article. The papers ran only letters attacking Hawaiians and the sovereignty movement.

Why are non-Hawaiians—that is, Inouye, the JACL, and the media—compelled to control the direction and process of the Hawaiian sovereignty movement? In their own homeland Hawaiians do not control their national lands, resources, and political processes—these are dominated by settlers from Asia, Europe, and the U.S. continent who run the colonial state structure and economy. Settlers benefit every day from this unequal, unjust situation and constantly discredit Hawaiian nationalists who try to overturn it.

Under international law, Native Hawaiians have the right of self-determination because their nation was invaded and annexed by a colonial country, the United States. In contrast, Asian settlers do not have that right, as we migrated to Hawai'i to participate in and help build the U.S. colonial empire. Different settler groups may be oppressed (due to racism, sexism, heterosexism, classism, and other forms of discrimination), but we are not colonized. Japanese settlers, in particular, have ascended to the ruling class and compete with the haole (whites) to control the colony of Hawai'i.

Thus Inouye's and the JACL's actions against Trask were not "harmless" deeds but instead served colonial interests. These acts obstructed attempts by Native Hawaiians to control and direct their own sovereignty process. Here it is crucial to draw the distinction between social issues involving civil rights, and Native struggles for the rights of nationhood. Racism, discrimination against gays and lesbians, and other inequalities are domestic problems to be resolved among the citizenry within the settler colonial nation. The right of self-determination, however, is a principle of international law—to be addressed at the level of foreign policy between nations, between colonizer and colonized.

We therefore asked why Inouye, who is not in the State Department (which is responsible for negotiating with Hawaiians as one nation to another), continues to interfere with the Native self-determination process. We also questioned the role of the JACL in policing the sovereignty process, telling Trask how to act while defending Inouye's continued control over the movement.

Why are these settlers interfering in the sovereignty movement?

As we noted, Senator Inouye has long supported the American government's interests in maintaining Hawai'i as a colony, rather than allowing the establishment of a self-determined Native Hawaiian nation. Strategically, Hawai'i is the linchpin for U.S. imperialism in Asia and the Pacific, and Inouye ensures America's global power through enormous military funding. Hawai'i ranks second nationally in per capita expenditures from the Department of Defense, and the Commander in Chief, U.S. Pacific Command (or USCINPAC—the combined four branches of the American military) patrols 50 percent of the earth from its base in Honolulu.[1]

Japanese settlers must see past Inouye's self-promoted, sacred-war-hero image to his tremendous power over politicians and businessmen. Inouye's behind-the-scenes manipulation of the Hawaiian reconciliation process did not end with the Trask-Inouye debate. After the U.S. Supreme Court ruling on the *Rice v. Cayetano* case in 2000, Inouye issued a statement to the Office of Hawaiian Affairs (OHA) and to Governor Benjamin Cayetano (but interestingly, not to the press) that stated the following: "I believe that the Governor has authority under a separate

State of Hawaii statute to appoint interim trustees so that the important work of the Office of Hawaiian Affairs need not be interrupted."[2] The intended result of Inouye's statement was to facilitate the control of OHA by the state and away from the electoral process. Later, Cayetano released a statement repeating Inouye's analysis as his own.[3] As usual, the media refused to report this chain of events, despite being apprised of it.

The JACL–Honolulu—contrary to its official mission as a civil rights organization—operates as an adjunct committee for the interests of Hawai'i's settler-dominated Democratic Party. Past and current JACL members connect in political networks extending to the State legislature, Hā Hawai'i (the state "sovereignty" initiative), the State of Hawai'i Commission on Civil Rights, OHA, the William S. Richardson School of Law (University of Hawai'i), and other state agencies and private businesses. Despite their rhetoric supporting Hawaiian sovereignty, the JACL–Honolulu never challenges Japanese political dominance in the state.

Not surprisingly, the JACL–Honolulu perpetuates colonialism by assimilating immigrants into the American settler mindset—that is, to completely dominate one's new environment. The JACL lauds the "success" of our Japanese settler community, fronting it as the model for others. As the Japanese community's self-appointed "leader," the JACL offers to educate other immigrant communities striving to establish themselves in Hawai'i and the United States.[4] Encouraging new settler groups to prosper on and govern Native land is not supporting sovereignty.

Finally, we believe that settlers must challenge, not deny our participation in, colonial structures. For example, the JACL ignores a key critique about the Japanese community's corrupt political influence and patronage networks. Bob Stauffer, for one, argues that the 1954 Democratic "revolution" did not bring equality for all, but rather it mainly elevated Japanese settler leaders and their cronies.[5] But the JACL's response to Stauffer, by Brian Niiya, addresses just minor points on prewar history and the dangers of "'yellow peril' stereotypes." Raising the old ghost of yellow peril stereotypes is a frequent JACL strategy to deflect power analyses. Not only do Japanese dominate our political and economic institutions, but no one can say this—or s/he is inciting "racial tensions." This is precisely the strategy the JACL used to attack Trask.[6]

We settlers must stop seeing our benefits as a result of our "hard work" within a fair system. Let's not fool ourselves by listening to JACL member Bill Hoshijo, who says, "Less for Hawaiians does not mean more for non-Hawaiians."[7] Hoshijo, along with his liberal Japanese colleagues, strategically misdirects us to believe that our political and economic gains do not come at the expense of Native Hawaiians. In other words, this is the Democratic Party's (read: Inouye's) position, where "Hawaiian sovereignty" will not entail any change to the colonial power structure.

These Japanese settlers are protecting their own interests while pretending to support Native rights.

It is not up to Asian settlers to predetermine the limits of Hawaiian government, lands, and resources. As Asians we must hold those who represent and support the U.S. government accountable for its continued genocidal actions against Native peoples. We must recognize that whether those in charge of this colonial system are whites, Asians, or other settlers of color isn't the point. Nor is it how we divide the spoils of colonialism.

Sovereignty is not about "race." It is about nationhood.

"Local Japanese Should Understand Inouye's Real Agenda," *Honolulu Advertiser*, February 6, 2000

We belong to a group of local Japanese women who have come together over the Trask-Inouye controversy. We come from families who served in World War II, small business, labor, education, and public service. We are speaking out now because we remained silent during the Lenore Kwock–Inouye sexual harassment controversy.[8] Because of the tremendous power Senator Inouye holds through networks of monies and influence, no one dared criticize him.

This time, we want to apologize to Lenore Kwock for not supporting her publicly in the Kwock-Inouye controversy and to former State legislator Annelle Amaral for not supporting her when she protected the identities of nine women who made a similar claim. Now we support respected Hawaiian sovereignty leader Mililani Trask against the public smear campaign by Inouye and those he influences in the media, the Japanese American Citizens League (JACL), and the Office of Hawaiian Affairs (OHA). As local Japanese we are living and prospering on Native Hawaiian ancestral lands. Can we imagine Japan being occupied by a foreign government and foreign citizens whose ways of life, culture, and language subjugate Japanese people? Because grievous wrongs were committed by the U.S. government against Native Hawaiians when it overthrew their nation in 1893 and annexed it to the United States in 1898, we have the ongoing obligation to support Native Hawaiians in obtaining their self-determination.

As Japanese community members, we want to address the JACL's recent public letter condemning Mililani Trask "and others who disagree" with Inouye's views on sovereignty.[9] As women, we are inspired by OHA Trustee Trask's integrity and strength in holding Inouye accountable. She's worked tirelessly for over two decades to make state and federal agencies responsible to Native Hawaiians and to the larger public. Over the years we have witnessed her leadership in helping not just Native Hawaiians, but also other groups, obtain justice. Internationally, Trask assists indigenous peoples in fighting for their rights for self-determined sovereignty. Yet the media has portrayed this Trask-Inouye controversy as Trask's personal "disrespect" for Inouye, describing her in such terms as "disparaging" him or "complaining" about him.[10] The JACL has uncritically accepted this view and jumped on the anti-Trask bandwagon. We believe, however, that it is Inouye who needs to be respectful of Native Hawaiians' quest for sovereignty and accountable for his continued attempts to block Hawaiians from obtaining their own nation.

The *Advertiser*'s focus on the "one-armed bandit" phrase is evidence of how Inouye's power influences the media's selective reporting.[11] Control over land and power is at stake, not nicknames. The substantive issue that Trask raised was Inouye's influence in the reconciliation process and in Hawaiian federal legislation.[12]

Local media have a responsibility to readers to research the background of this debate. As long-time reporter Ian Lind has said, Inouye is more an institution than an individual.[13] The only elected Hawai'i official to serve continuously from statehood, he has built up patronage networks of money and influence over the last forty years. During that time Inouye has been one of the most influential U.S. senators, as he sits on the powerful Senate Appropriations Committee. As the Senate's largest committee, Appropriations controls the U.S. federal budget, including the Department of the Interior (which oversaw the Hawaiian reconciliation hearings).

This position allows Inouye to dole out monies for education, health, housing, the military, and so on. This is part of his job as a public servant and an elected official. This position gives him tremendous power over the politics and commerce of this state. But isn't Inouye accountable to the public for the ways in which he has used and abused his power? Specifically, what has Inouye done in his long tenure in the U.S. Congress to change the political status of Native Hawaiians?

Inouye claims he supports sovereignty. But Native self-determination means that Hawaiians would determine their own future and have direct control over their lands, revenues, and government. In other words, Hawaiians would no longer be wards of the state and federal governments, as they are currently. Under international law, self-determination is a basic human right for all peoples. Thus the United States is violating Native Hawaiians' human rights by not allowing them self-government.

Bill Was Merely an Apology

Like the U.S. government, Inouye claims he supported the 1993 U.S. Apology Bill.[14] However, as Haunani-Kay Trask argues, what good is an apology without returning political power, lands, and rights to Native Hawaiians? In Inouye's own words, recorded in the *U.S. Congressional Record*, October 27, 1993, the bill is only an apology and nothing more: "To suggest that this resolution is the first step toward declaring independence for the State of Hawaii is a painful distortion of the intent of the authors . . . if it calls for an apology we do so. That is all we are asking for."[15] According to the March 21–April 3, 1997, edition of the *Pacific Citizen,* the JACL's national newsletter, the Apology Bill "doesn't force Congress to reconcile the past." In that same article, Inouye states, "It is very clear that it [the Apology Bill] was just an apology. It doesn't confer any substantive rights to the Native Hawaiian people."[16]

These two sources show that Inouye's de facto position does not support the return of lands to Native Hawaiians. In fact, he is interfering in the process for self-determined sovereignty for Native Hawaiians, as Mililani Trask has charged. Inouye states in that same *Pacific Citizen* article, "I cannot envision any Congress approving an act that would propose the seceding of a segment of the state of Hawaii or the state of Hawaii from the Union." By defining the process as a domestic policy rather than an international human rights issue, he is determining the outcome.

Inouye defends his record by saying he's allocated monies for existing Native Hawaiian health, housing, and education programs. Yet Inouye as a public servant does not provide ongoing reports of the Native Hawaiian agencies that receive these funds and the amounts of monies that go specifically to each agency. Which individuals and agencies are getting these monies? Surely not the majority of Native Hawaiians. We asked his D.C. office for a chart of agencies and the money each is allocated, but we didn't receive that information. Instead, we received a list of acts (a format that makes it difficult, if not impossible, to track the monies.)

Moreover, limited appropriations to a handful of programs does not change Native Hawaiians' overall political status. Inouye is keeping control and power in his hands and away from Native Hawaiians. This pattern is not new. In the past Inouye has supported the $1.2 billion construction of a military highway, the H-3, against the opposition of small farmers, Native Hawaiians, and environmentalists. He supported the bombing of Kahoʻolawe Island for thirty-one years. When the bombing was stopped, cleanup monies went largely to the military, not to Native Hawaiians for preservation of sacred sites. Inouye supported big business against labor during the 1971 dock strike when he introduced the Public Interest Protection Act, considered by the International Longshore and Warehouse Union (ILWU) to be a major strike-breaking move.[17]

The JACL Touts Inouye Line

The JACL–Honolulu supports Inouye's position on sovereignty. In a recent public letter to Trustee Trask and the two dailies, Clayton Ikei, 1999 president of the

JACL–Honolulu, emphasizes Inouye's position as "evidence of leadership in support of indigenous rights and principles of sovereignty."[18] The JACL also says it passed a formal resolution on Hawaiian sovereignty and held educational workshops on sovereignty issues.

But what is the JACL–Honolulu's real record on key sovereignty issues? A JACL national resolution adopted in 1992, in fact, does not specify the returns of lands, resources, and government to Native Hawaiians.[19] This resolution mirrors Inouye's version of a Hawaiian "paper nation." And if the JACL has done community workshops on sovereignty, why haven't we heard about them? Furthermore, the Hawai'i Newspaper Index and the state archives indicate that the JACL has not taken any formal position on Senate Bill 8 (Native gathering rights) or House Bill 2340 (Ed Case's bill co-opting "sovereignty" by making it a corporation). The entire Native Hawaiian community united against these two bills. Organizers against Senate Bill 8 included, among others, the Sierra Club Legal Defense Fund, Hawai'i Green Party, Native Hawaiian Legal Corporation, Hawai'i Audubon Society, and American Friends Service Committee. Where was the JACL, whose mission, as its own literature states, is to "secure and uphold the human and civil rights of Americans of Japanese ancestry and others"?

The JACL has consistently not supported civil and human rights violations by powerful Japanese and Japanese American citizens. Why didn't the JACL support Lenore Kwock? Why didn't it support Annelle Amaral, who tried to raise the issue of sexual harassment by public officials? If the JACL is so concerned with the return of Native Hawaiian lands and justice, why did it oppose a ban on foreign purchase of land in Hawai'i while so many Native Hawaiians have died waiting for Hawaiian Home Lands?[20]

How credible is the JACL's position on the Trask-Inouye debate? They told Trask where to focus her criticism,[21] when they hadn't even verified her side of the story before firing off a letter to the media. As a professional organization, they should have checked into the issues she raised about the reconciliation process. This would have been a contribution to the sovereignty movement. Instead, the JACL attacked a woman who has worked with the Japanese community for over thirty years. She began as a law student and member of the Asian Pacific Islander Student Association (APISA) working on the Japanese reparation claims in California. And even today Trask assists the indigenous Ainu of Japan in their claims for a self-determined sovereignty.

Compared to the JACL, Mililani Trask's record on indigenous rights is without question. For example, Nobel laureate Rigoberta Menchu chose Mililani Trask to head an indigenous delegation to lobby the U.N. General Assembly in New York. Trask addressed the General Assembly representing all the indigenous peoples of the world.[22]

Trask Didn't Demean Inouye

Indeed, we ask why the JACL is making public statements regarding Hawaiian sovereignty. Bill Kaneko, a past president of JACL–Honolulu, has stated that one reason the JACL issued the sovereignty resolution is because it doesn't want to be viewed as a "one issue" (internment camp reparations) organization.[23] However, sovereignty is not about a Japanese organization diversifying its public image but about Native Hawaiians regaining self-government and a land and resource base that they control.

As local Japanese women, we suggest the JACL clean its own house before interfering in the affairs of another community. Although the JACL takes pride in itself as a civil rights organization, its history in this area is terrible. During World War II the JACL colluded with U.S. camp authorities against the Japanese resisters who demanded that their civil rights be respected.[24] Despite the fact that the JACL sansei supported the reparations movement, the JACL has never apologized to these resisters. The organization did not officially acknowledge its collaborator role in the internment of its own people. It was finally forced to discuss this issue in 1999 after a critically acclaimed documentary, *Rabbit in the Moon,* revealed its role. To this date the JACL has never apologized to its own people for the pain, suffering, and division it inflicted on the interned Japanese community or compensated the resisters for their civil rights violations. Even though many members of the larger continental Japanese community call on the organization to apologize, it has yet to do so.[25]

Finally, the JACL's reckless, shallow statement about racial stereotyping in referencing the Trask-Inouye controversy is an embarrassment. Ikei criticizes Trask for referring to Inouye as the "Japanese senator." As everyone in Hawai'i knows, we often identify each other according to our racial group, such as "that Japanese man" or "the Chinese woman." Trask did not use any "demeaning and simplistic"[26] racial stereotypes, such as "slant eyes" or "buck tooth." Her use of the term "Japanese" was merely descriptive—just as it is in the name "Japanese American Citizens League."

Sovereignty Is Long Overdue

The JACL owes a most sincere apology to Trustee Trask for its thoughtless, unsubstantiated public letter. Furthermore, the JACL should apologize to the Japanese community for its role in internment during World War II. This would begin a healing within our community that is long overdue.

The Japanese community, including the JACL and Inouye, must support real self-determination of Native Hawaiians. Hawaiians need a workable sovereignty.

Our role as Japanese should be to support Native Hawaiians rather than preclude the outcome of their movement. Native Hawaiians, including Mililani Trask, supported Japanese during our drive for Japanese reparations. Now it is our turn to do the same for Native Hawaiians.

Hawai'i voters should hold Inouye accountable for the ways in which his networks of power and patronage divide communities. No matter how much Inouye denies this, he is a very powerful, negative force in the state. The lack of public criticism of Inouye testifies to the power he wields. While writing this essay we were asked by many of our Japanese friends, "Aren't you afraid to speak out against Inouye?" Yes, some of us are afraid of criticisms and attacks on ourselves and our families. We don't want to be harassed like Lenore Kwock. But we need to put our fears aside because these are important political and social issues.

Note: As of January 2008 the JACL–Honolulu had not apologized to Trask.

Notes

Local Japanese Women for Justice is an organization of nisei, sansei, and yonsei women in Hawai'i. It aims to fight oppression in the Japanese and larger communities. If you would like to contact us, please do so at Local Japanese Women for Justice, P.O. Box 62144, Honolulu, Hawai'i 96839.

1. United States Department of Defense, *Hawai'i Military Land Use: Master Plan,* July 1995, A1, B2; for ranking on federal spending, see State of Hawai'i, Department of Business, Economic Development and Tourism, *The State of Hawai'i Data Book, 1998: A Statistical Abstract* (Honolulu: State of Hawai'i, 1999), 296.

2. U.S. Senator Daniel Inouye, press release, "Statement of Senator Inouye on the Supreme Court's Ruling in *Rice v. Cayetano,*" February 23, 2000.

3. State of Hawai'i Governor Benjamin Cayetano, press release, "Governor Takes Steps to Comply With *Rice v. Cayetano Ruling,*" February 23, 2000; OHA Trustee Mililani B. Trask, press release, March 1, 2000.

4. Since our public statements challenging the JACL–Honolulu's sovereignty record and the JACL's history of collaborating against interned Japanese during World War II, the JACL–Honolulu began a monthly column in the *Hawai'i Herald* called "Leading the Way." The *Herald* is Hawai'i's main Japanese American newspaper. See message from Allison Tanaka, current president of the JACL–Honolulu, to the Japanese community on JACL leadership, "What is 'Leading the Way?'" *Hawai'i Herald,* June 16, 2000, A13.

5. Bob Stauffer, "Our Father? A New Biography on Governor Jack Burns Fails to Get beyond the Machine and Its Myths," *Honolulu Weekly,* 10 (21) (May 24–30, 2000), front page.

6. See Clayton Ikei's letter in endnote 9 below; also see endnote 19 below.

7. See Bill Hoshijo, "The Shame of the *Rice v. Cayetano* Decision," *Hawai'i Herald,* March 3, 2000, A-2.

8. In his 1992 reelection campaign for the U.S. Senate, Inouye was exposed as a sexual

harasser by his opponent, Rick Reed. See Richard Borreca and Becky Ashizawa, "Reed Ad: Inouye Forced Woman to Have Sex," *Honolulu Star-Bulletin,* October 16, 1992, A1; Becky Ashizawa, "Kwock: Inouye Forced Me to Have Sex with Him," *Honolulu Star-Bulletin,* October 17, 1992, A1; paid political advertisement, "Has Dan Inouye Used His Position to Sexually Exploit Women?" *Honolulu Star-Bulletin,* October 17, 1992, A5; and Allison K. Yap, "Challenging Asian Patriarchal Power and Privilege in Hawai'i: Speaking Up/Out Against Dan Inouye," paper presented at the Tenth National Conference of the Association for Asian American Studies, June 2–6, 1993, Cornell University, Ithaca, New York.

9. JACL–Honolulu, Clayton Ikei, letter to Mililani Trask, November 22, 1999, reprinted in "JACL Opposes Trask's Comments to Inouye," *Hawai'i Herald,* December 3, 1999, A-7. The original public letter by Ikei stated,

> The Japanese American Citizens League (JACL) of Honolulu is deeply concerned about the racial/ethnic remarks attributed to you in your criticism of Senator Inouye and the role he is playing in the pending reconciliation discussions between the federal government and Hawaiians. According to media accounts, in your objection to the timing of congressional hearings to be conducted by Senator Inouye just before scheduled reconciliation talks, you called him a "one-armed bandit" and referred to him as our "Japanese senator." In recent days you have given your assurance that you did not mean to offend either disabled persons or Japanese Americans in Hawaii.
>
> JACL–Honolulu has taken a formal position in support of Hawaiian sovereignty, and has urged the Japanese American community and other non-Hawaiian civil rights organizations to take informed and responsible positions in support of Hawaiians in their struggle for recognition of their sovereignty and rights. These efforts have included outreach and community education, as well as successfully advocating the national JACL to take a position of support for Hawaiian sovereignty. In recent months, JACL–Honolulu offered to submit an amicus brief in support of *Rice v. Cayetano,* to offer the perspective of an Asian American civil rights organization who has faced historical racism, in support of Hawaiians who are faced with civil rights arguments turned on their head by plaintiff Rice.
>
> Despite your stated non-discriminatory intent, your recent reported comments negatively impact our efforts to reach out to Japanese Americans on the sovereignty issue, and hurt your cause. Given the history of Japanese Americans' struggle against historical discrimination and racial injustice, we are particularly sensitive to perceived racial attacks on the Japanese Americans or other racial minorities. There is no denying that Senator Inouye is widely held in high regard and respected in the Japanese American community and the broader community. Attacks on Senator Inouye, particularly racial characterizations and references to his Japanese ancestry, tend to rally support for him. Many in the Japanese American community view his work on Native American and Hawaiian issues in the U.S. Senate as evidence of leadership in support of indigenous rights and principles of sovereignty. For you and others who disagree with this assessment, it better serves us all that your criticism to be discussed on the merits, rather than to be dismissed as demeaning and simplistic personal attacks.
>
> As a policy maker and public figure, Senator Inouye and his positions are appropriately the subject of public debate. The JACL raises these concerns in a constructive spirit,

in the hope that your future criticisms of Senator Inouye be focused on the merits, and that you will avoid future resort to divisive racial and ethnic characterizations.

10. Yasmin Anwar, "OHA Member Disparages Inouye: Senator Saddened by Trask Remark," *Honolulu Advertiser,* November 10, 1999, A1. By crafting stories of personal drama, such as Inouye's "sadness" and Trask's "anger" or "frustration," the media redirects readers away from larger societal critiques—e.g., what institutionalized structures allow Inouye to influence the sovereignty and reconciliation processes?

11. Yasmin Anwar, "OHA Trustee Won't Back Down: Trask Defends Her Attack on Inouye," *Honolulu Advertiser,* November 11, 1999, A1. Although the media originally made it sound as if Trask had invented this nickname, later investigations showed that it was used popularly long before her comments—even by Inouye's fellow soldiers in the 442nd Regimental Combat Team and by former state governor John Burns. See Center for Oral History, "Oral History Interview with Mike Tokunaga with Larry Meacham and Daniel W. Tuttle on September 12, 1989," in *Hawai'i Political History Documentation Project, Vol. III* (Honolulu: Center for Oral History, University of Hawai'i at Mānoa, 1996), 1233.

Regardless, "one-armed bandit" and its genealogy became a red herring—neither the media nor the JACL made an effort to check into Trask's concrete criticisms of Inouye.

12. Mililani Trask, letter to *Hawai'i Tribune Herald,* November 23, 1999; Mililani Trask, letter to OHA trustees Colette Machado and Frenchy Desoto, OHA Board of Trustees, Hawaiian community, and media, November 23, 1999. Because the media refused to cover Trask's position addressing her criticisms of Inouye, she had to buy advertisement space to inform the public of her response. See Mililani Trask, "Inouye's Legacy to Hawaiians," *Ka Wai Ola o OHA,* February 2000, 20–21.

13. Ian Lind, "Dan the Man: Three Decades of Dan Inouye," *Honolulu Weekly,* September 23, 1992, 1.

14. Anwar, "OHA Trustee Won't Back Down," A1.

15. *U.S. Congressional Record,* Proceedings and Debates of the 103rd Cong., First Sess., vol. 139, no. 147, October 27, 1993, S14480.

16. Allan Beekman, "Hawai'i Self-Determination Debate Heats Up over Money," *Pacific Citizen,* March 21–April 3, 1997, 1.

17. For more on the H-3 Interstate Highway, see "History of the Construction of the H-3 Freeway," *Island Issues,* host Bob Rees, June 28, 1998; Bruce Dunford, "H-3 Tab Will Pass $1 Billion," *Honolulu Advertiser,* July 9, 1995, A1; and Steven Goldsberry, Clemence McClaren, and Tamara Moan, "Interstate H-3: What Price? What Purpose?" *Honolulu Magazine,* March 1992, 32–37, 44–47.

After years of destructive bombing of Kaho'olawe Island, the U.S. Navy is now allocated the lion's share—89 percent—of the federal funds for the island's cleanup. Since 1995 the navy has received approximately $220 million out of a total of $240 million for this job. In contrast, the State of Hawai'i agency, the Kaho'olawe Island Reserve Commission (KIRC), is allocated 11 percent of this federal budget to restore and care for the island. The KIRC's 2001 budget has allocated $57,000 for what seems to be the preservation of sacred sites, but it is unclear if such past monies were indeed spent for this purpose. See State of Hawai'i, Kaho'olawe Island Reserve Commission's (KIRC) annual report, "Fiscal Year 2001 Budget."

For more information on Inouye's historical position on labor issues, see Karen Winkler, *Daniel K. Inouye: Democratic Senator from Hawaii,* a part of *Ralph Nader Congress Project: Citizens Look at Congress* (Washington, D.C.: Grossman Publishers, 1972), 14–15. Inouye was never part of the labor faction of the Democratic Party but on the side of management and business.

18. Ikei letter.

19. Specifically, the 1992 JACL national resolution commits only to the following:

[B]e it resolved that the JACL determines that 1993 should serve Hawaii, our nation and the world as a year of special reflection on the rights and dignities of the indigenous people of Hawaii; and

Be it further resolved that the JACL recommits and reaffirms its efforts and support of indigenous Hawaiians in their struggles to address the federal government's illegal and immoral wrongdoings committed against them; and

Be it further resolved that the JACL calls upon the government of the United States of America to recognize the sovereign nation of Hawaii to correct the injustices of one hundred years ago.

20. William Kresnak, "Land-Buy Limits Said to Fuel 'Dangerous Racial Tensions,'" *Honolulu Advertiser,* February 27, 1990, A-6. In 1990 the JACL–Honolulu issued a statement in response to State Senator Russell Blair's proposal to limit foreign purchase of land in Hawai'i (see Senate Bill 82 in the 1989 Legislative Session). The chapter protested the measure, saying that Japanese national monies were the main target, and this could result in "scapegoating" effects on local Japanese. Never mind the real economic problem of land prices skyrocketing due to Japanese nationals' purchase of land, or the political reality that local Japanese cannot be scapegoated because we wield power here.

21. Ikei letter.

22. *The Advertiser* did not include this paragraph on Trask's international record and stature on indigenous rights.

23. Arnold Hiura, "AJA Perspectives: Japanese American Community Examines Its Role and Responsibilities," *Hawai'i Herald,* February 12, 1993, A-10.

24. See the 1990 "Research Report Prepared for the Presidential Select Committee on JACL Resolution #7" (also called "the Lim Report") by Deborah Lim, who was commissioned by the JACL to investigate the JACL's role in the internment camps before and during World War II. Lim's highly critical findings so disturbed the JACL leadership that it suppressed her report, rewriting and distributing another report that cleared the organization of any collaborative activities. However, in June 2000, through community pressure, the Lim Report was finally made widely available to the public. To download the report, see http://JAvoices.com and http://www.resisters.com. Although the JACL claimed they never suppressed the Lim Report, for ten years many people did not have access to Lim's findings. See also Alice Yang Murray, "'Silence, No More'": The Japanese American Redress Movement, 1942–1992, Ph.D. dissertation, Stanford University, 1994.

25. In June 2000, at their national convention, the JACL finally passed a resolution apologizing to the resisters, more than fifty years after internment. What offsets this gesture is the JACL's simultaneous support for the controversial Japanese American veterans' war

memorial in Washington, D.C., which includes the words of JACL leader Mike Masaoka, a documented collaborator with the U.S. federal government and against Japanese people before, during, and after World War II. See Martha Nakagawa, "JACL National Council Approves Apology to Resisters of Conscience," *Pacific Citizen,* July 7–13, 2000; and Sam Chu Lin, "JACL Votes to Apologize to Nisei Resisters of World War II: Leaders Work to Heal Wounds after Debate and Reunify Organization," *Rafu Shimpo* and *AsianWeek,* July 7, 2000.

26. Ikei letter.

CONTRIBUTORS

Candace Fujikane is an associate professor of English at the University of Hawaiʻi. Her publications on Asian settlers in Hawaiʻi include, most recently, "Foregrounding Native Nationalisms: A Critique of Antinationalist Sentiment in Asian American Studies." She is expanding on that work in her book, *Colonial Imaginings: Asian Settler Mapping of Native Land in Hawaiʻi*.

Jonathan Y. Okamura is an associate professor in the Department of Ethnic Studies at the University of Hawaiʻi. He is the author of *Ethnicity and Inequality in Hawaiʻi* and *Imagining the Filipino American Diaspora: Transnational Relations, Identities and Communities*. He has researched and written on ethnicity and ethnic relations in Hawaiʻi, the global Filipino diaspora, and minority access to higher education.

Peggy Myo-Young Choy is a choreographer/dancer who supports the demilitarization and independence of Hawaiʻi. Her writings include "Dancing outside the American Dream: History and Politics of Asian Dance in America" and "Return the Islands Back to the People: A Legacy of Struggle and Resistance in Ka Paeʻāina." She is founder and director of The Ki Project, an organization supporting creative thinking and intercultural performance for future generations. Choy teaches in the Dance Program at the University of Wisconsin, Madison.

kuʻualoha hoʻomanawanui is a Native Hawaiian poet and artist. She is a founding and chief editor of *ʻŌiwi: A Native Hawaiian Journal*, a publication featuring Native Hawaiian writers and artists. She is also an assistant professor of Hawaiian literature in the English department at the University of Hawaiʻi specializing in traditional and contemporary Hawaiian folklore, mythology, and literature.

Kyle Kajihiro is the program director for the American Friends Service Committee Hawaiʻi Area Program and has been active in peace building, demilitarization, and human rights work in Hawaiʻi since 1996. He is a fourth-generation Hawaiʻi Japanese.

Momiala Kamahele is a Native Hawaiian nationalist, kumu hula, and chanter. She is an assistant professor of Hawaiian studies and teaches Hawaiian history at Leeward Community College.

Eiko Kosasa, a third-generation Japanese settler, is a lecturer in political science at Leeward Community College. She is completing work on *Predatory Politics: U.S. Imperialism, Settler States, and the Legitimacy of Injustice*, a book based on her dissertation.

Karen K. Kosasa is an assistant professor in the Department of American Studies and director of the Museum Studies Graduate Certificate Program at the University of Hawaiʻi. She is currently working on a book titled *Sites of Erasure: Art, Museums, and Colonial Visual Culture in Hawaiʻi*.

Kapulani Landgraf is a Native Hawaiian photographer. She has published three books of her work: *Nā Wahi Kapu o Maui, Nā Wahi Pana o Koʻolau Poko,* and *E Nā Hulu Kūpuna Nā Puna Ola Maoli Nō.*

Dean Itsuji Saranillio is a doctoral candidate in the Program in American Culture at the University of Michigan. His essay featured in this volume was first published in *Positively No Filipinos Allowed: Building Discourse and Communities.* His current research examines the conflicting interests and relations among Native Hawaiians, Asian Americans, and powerful industrialists through the movement for and opposition to Hawaiʻi statehood.

Healani Sonoda is a Native Hawaiian nationalist advocate for Hawaiian inmates and co-founder of Protect Our Native ʻOhana (PONO), an organization that raises public awareness about issues involving Native Hawaiian inmates. She is actively involved in numerous community-based Native Hawaiian educational programs. She is also a graduate student at the Center for Pacific Islands Studies at the University of Hawaiʻi.

David Stannard is a professor of American studies at the University of Hawaiʻi. His numerous articles and books include *Before the Horror: The Population of Hawaiʻi on the Eve of Western Contact, American Holocaust: The Conquest of the New World,* and *Honor Killing: Race, Rape, and Clarence Darrow's Spectacular Last Case.*

Haunani-Kay Trask is a Native Hawaiian nationalist and the author of four books, including *From a Native Daughter: Colonialism and Sovereignty in Hawaiʻi, Eros and Power: The Promise of Feminist Theory,* and two books of poetry. She is a professor of Hawaiian studies at the University of Hawaiʻi.

Mililani B. Trask is a Native Hawaiian nationalist, civil rights attorney, human rights advocate, and founder of Ka Lāhui Hawaiʻi. She served as the first Pacific Expert to the United Nations Permanent Forum on Indigenous Issues and is recognized globally as an indigenous expert in international human rights law. She has also been a lecturer at the University of Hawaiʻi Center for Hawaiian Studies.

Stan Tomita teaches in the Photography Program at the University of Hawaiʻi's Department of Art and Art History.

Ida Yoshinaga is an assistant professor in sociology and women's studies at Leeward Community College. She writes poetry, plays, and personal essays on Japanese settler history and politics, such as "Pacific (War) Time at Punchbowl: A Nembutsu for Unclaiming Nation," published in the journal *Chain.*

civil rights arguments used against Hawaiians, 14–17; counterhegemonic intervention, 8, 13, 29–31, 36, 171, 189, 205–207, 208n16, 226, 243, 273–275, 291, 296–297, 301–302; definition, 3–6, 9, 50, 120, 295; differences between settler groups, 9, 295; distinction between minority populations and indigenous peoples, 4–5, 11–12, 57; distinction between Native and settler, 6, 9, 295; erasure of indigeneity, 26, 28–29, 144, 197–198; historical overview of large-scale settlement, 5–7, 17–20; historiography, 1–3, 25–29, 46–51, 174, 196–198, 206, 207n7, 210–212; political movements in Asia, 17–20; political power and, 7, 20, 23–28, 47–48, 102, 173, 241, 271; population figures, 21–23, 202, 205; "power sharing" with white settlers, 4, 12, 25, 47–48, 101, 105, 202, 216, 222, 295; power relationships between Asian settler groups, 9; *terra nullius* and nation-building arguments, 2–3, 231n27, 266. *See also* Asian settler colonialism, intrasettler racism; Chinese in Hawai'i; Filipinos in Hawai'i; Japanese in Hawai'i; Koreans in Hawai'i

Bamboo Ridge Press, 120–123, 126–129, 140–141, 144–146, 154n93
beauty pageants, blood quantum requirements for, 238
Bhabha, Homi, 207n7
Blaisdell, Kekuni, 256
Bonifacio, Andres, 275–276

Campaign for a Colorblind America, 248
capitalism, 38n28, 123, 138, 178, 189, 208n16, 289
Case, Ed, 32, 94–95, 97n7, 300
Cayetano, Benjamin: on being "Hawaiian," 16; "Benocide," 268–272; icon of "Amer-

ican Dream," 271; and legal assault on Native Hawaiian rights, 268–272; obstruction of Native Hawaiian rights, 35, 245, 259
Chai, Alice, 289
Chan, Gaye, 208n16
Chinese in Hawai'i: anti-Chinese sentiment, 18; "building" Hawai'i, 37n8; Chinese Exclusion Act (1882), 18; Chinese settlers in government with ties to development, 202; in the Department of Education, 25; immigration history, 17–18, 40n54; intermarriages, high rates of, 238; plaintiffs in *Earl Arakaki et al. vs. State of Hawai'i*, 254n47; political power, 23–25, 235, 243; population figures, 17, 21–23, 40n60; recruitment of Chinese laborers for the plantations, 17, 40n54; rise to political power, 8, 47, 62n3, 174; as settlers, 3–6, 9, 50, 120; in the State Legislature, 22–25; success narratives, 47, 174
Chock, Eric, 63n7, 120, 124, 127–129, 131–132, 135–136, 138, 140, 143
Choy, Duke, 283, 287
Choy, Mary, 30, 35, 280, 286–289
Choy, Peggy, 8, 20, 30, 35
class: class-based frameworks that do not account for indigeneity, 4; class differences that cut across settler groups, 9, 27–28, 295; hegemony of a social class, 207n5; "local" identification as working class with plantation roots, 25–28, 120; "local" middle-class, American colonial values and aspirations, 47, 61, 62n3, 118–119, 122–123, 126, 135, 140, 173–174, 198; production of ruling-class perspectives, 214–216; revolutionary change through new social structure, 213; white, Japanese and Chinese settlers ascend to ruling class, 101–104, 122, 271; working-class Asian settlers, 27–28. *See also* Lenin, V. I.
colonialism: classic forms differentiated

from settler colonialism, 10. *See also* settler colonialism

Curthoys, Ann, 11–12

Democratic Party, 63n9, 72, 209; failure to resolve Hawaiian land claims and demands for self-determination, 13, 72; Japanese settler dominance in, 23, 27–28, 38n21, 47, 52, 54, 102, 209, 240–241, 296; leaders formed partnership with the military, 119; 1954 takeover, 5, 8, 27, 47, 102, 173, 264, 296; promised land reform through land taxes and land-use laws, 5, 28, 73; real-estate hui and Democratic political power structure, 28. See also *Land and Power in Hawai'i*

de Silva, Kahikina, 15

Diaz, Vicente, 257

Docker, John, 11–12

Dudoit, Māhealani, 119, 145

Emerson, Nathaniel B., 152n54

Enloe, Cynthia, 170, 175

Ethnic Studies: differentiation of goals from those of American Indians and Hawaiians, 4; emergence out of domestic civil rights struggles and international human rights struggles, 2; reiteration of *terra nullius* arguments, 2; Third World Liberation Front, 2; Third World Strike, 2, 4; at the University of Hawai'i, 2, 35, 36n5, 287–288

Fanon, Frantz, 31–32, 45, 77–78, 87, 90

Feeser, Andrea, 208n16

Filipinos in Hawai'i: Americanization movement, 35, 257, 263–265; anti-Filipino racism, 9, 257, 275; "building" Hawai'i, 37n8; in the Department of Education, 25; empowerment strategy, 9, 257, 266–267, 275–276; Filipino settlers in government with ties to development, 202; immigration history, 19, 259–260, 266; national identification with America, 9, 259, 261–265; Philippine-American War, 19, 260; plaintiffs in *Earl Arakaki et al. vs. State of Hawai'i*, 254n47; population figures, 21–23, 101, 205, 266; racial profiling and discrimination against, 9, 237; recruitment of Filipino laborers for the plantations, 19, 259–260; resistance as laborers, 261–262; as settlers, 3–6, 9, 50, 120, 258; socioeconomically subordinated, 9, 23, 235, 257; in the State Legislature, 22–25; stereotyped in literature, 135; "success" narrative, 47, 174; support for Hawaiian rights, 35, 265, 273–275; Talakayan Community Forum, 266; *utang na loob*, 275–276

Forman, David, 52

Foucault, Michel, 110, 117

442nd Regimental Combat Team and 100th Infantry Battalion, 13, 16, 51, 173, 226, 240, 245, 304n11

Franklin, Cynthia G., 36n16

Frasier, Frances N., 132–133

Fujikane, Candace, 28–29, 37n6, 48, 63n6, 148n3, 202–204, 243

gender, 139, 142, 170, 219, 260; sexism, 289, 295. *See also* women

genocide, 1, 31, 61, 110, 177, 208n17, 214, 226, 231n27, 297

Gramsci, Antonio, 207n5, 212–215, 217

H-3 freeway, 182, 299, 304n17

Hamasaki, Mark, 208n16

Hamasaki, Richard, 140, 144

Hara, Marie, 136

Hawai'i: annexation of, 5, 46, 71, 73, 76; descriptions of in historical accounts, 3, 6, 123, 196, 198, 219, 256; equated with "America," 260–261, 266; "exceptionalism" as a multicultural state, 3, 4, 47; genealogical relation to, 45; historical relationship to the United States, 72–73;

land base for Hawaiians, 50; overthrow of the Hawaiian government, 5, 14, 17, 19, **46**, 53, 71, 73, 172, 200, 215; population of, 21–23; settlement of, 5, 8–9, 17–21; as a settler colony of the U.S. settler state, 1, 3, 5, 31, 36; State of Hawai'i negligent in management of Hawaiian trust assets, 271; *terra nullius* ("empty," "belonging to no one"), 2, 58, 142, 196–198

Hawaiians. See Native Hawaiians

Hawai'i Creole English (HCE) (also known as "Pidgin"), 117–118, 138–140, 286

Helm, George, 180–181

historiography: Asian settler, 1–3, 25–29, 46–51, 174, 196–198, 206, 207n7, 210–212; developmental narratives in, 3; settler, 1–3, 10–11, 26, 196–198, 207n7

ho'omanawanui, ku'ualoha, 15, 21, 33

Hoshijo, Bill, 296

Ikei, Clayton, 52, 299–301, 303n9

'Ilio'ulaokalani Coalition: formation of, 32, protest against Senate Bill, 8, 88–94; Ua Ao Hawai'i protest concert, 78; union of culture and politics, 88

immigrants. *See* Asian settlers in Hawai'i; settlers; United States, "Nation of Immigrants," ideological representations of

indigenous peoples: definition of, 56–57; distinct from "minority populations," 56–58; United Nations Declaration on the Rights of Indigenous Peoples, 4–5, 55–59, 62. *See also* Native Hawaiians

Inouye, Daniel: control over OHA, 16, 227n7, 270, 296–297; and the Democratic Party, 63n9; icon of Asian success, 113n19, 173, 210, 295; obstruction of Native sovereignty process, 51–52, 54, 63n9, 225, 227n7, 294–295, 298–299; political power, 35–36, 54, 225–226, 298, 302; sexual harassment charges, 270, 297, 302n8; support for big business against labor, 299, 304n17; support for bombing of Kaho'olawe, 299; support for H-3, 182, 299, 304n17; support for military spending, 182, 190n19, 295

International Longshore and Warehouse Union (ILWU), 173

Iwase, Randy, 32, 82, 92–94, 97n8

Japanese American Citizens' League (JACL), 13, 36, 51–55; support for Japanese American internment, 52

Japanese imperialism, 6, 17–19, 40n53, 41n75, 289–291

Japanese in Hawai'i: Americanization movement, 173, 216–217; anti-Japanese racism, 2–3, 18, 172–173, 222, 230n23, 242–243; "building" Hawai'i, 37n8; "defensive" ethnicity, 242, 250–251; in the Department of Education, 25; genealogy in Japan, 21; immigration history, 18; Japanese settlers in government with ties to development, 202; Kalākaua's "invitation," 18, 40n57; land ownership, 28; "local" Japanese investors and developers, 28; military service provides access to political power, 13, 173; plaintiffs in *Earl Arakaki et al. vs. State of Hawai'i*, 254n47; political action against Hawaiians, 16, 27–28, 32, 52; political power, 9, 13–14, 16–17, 22–25, 32, 35, 52, 63n9, 102, 235, 257, 295–296; population figures, 21–23, 40n60, 101, 205; racism, 9, 41n75, 102, 210, 243; recruitment of Japanese laborers for the plantations, 18; rise to political dominance, 5, 8, 13, 47, 62n3, 101–102, 118–119, 174, 226; as settlers, 3–4, 25, 28, 34, 50, 101, 103, 118, 120, 209, 211, 219, 230n22; in the State Legislature, 22–25, 102; "success" narrative, 47–48, 103, 173, 209–210, 217, 296; support of American Indians at Alcatraz and

Hawaiians at Kahoʻolawe, 4. *See also*
442nd Regimental Combat Team and
100th Infantry Battalion; Japanese
American Citizen's League (JACL);
Land and Power in Hawaiʻi; Local
Japanese Women for Justice (LJWJ)
Johnston, Anna and Alan Lawson, 7–8,
10, 26–27

Kahoʻolawe, 179–182, 186. *See also* Protect
Kahoʻolawe ʻOhana (PKO)
Kajihiro, Kyle, 13, 34
Kalāhele, ʻImaikalani, 30–31, 144,
146–147, 147, 154n97
Ka Lāhui Hawaiʻi, Native Hawaiian
sovereignty initiative, 13–14, 32, **46**, 55,
58–62, 70–75, 98, 228n7
Kalākaua, King David, 18, 40n57, 172
Kalama Valley, 179
Kalanianaʻole, Prince Jonah Kūhiō, **100**
Kaluaikoʻolau, 132–133
kamaʻāina: appropriated by white and
Asian settlers, 125–126, 143–144;
definition of, 125
Kamahele, Momiala, 5, 15–16, 32
Kamauʻu, Mahealani, 144
Kameʻeleihiwa, Lilikalā, 1, 17, 176
Kamehameha Schools / Bishop Estates, 12,
28, 74, 82, 197, 236, 244, 249–251
Kanahele, Pualani Kanakaʻole, 92, 98n20,
128
Kanaka Maoli Peoples' International
Tribunal, 30, 288, 293n31
Kaneshiro, Keith, 32, 102
"Kaulana Nā Pua," also known as "Mele
ʻAi Pōhaku" (Rock-eating song), 15,
129–131
Kawaharada, Dennis, 126, 140–144,
149n19
Kekahuna, "Boogie" Kealoha, **109**
Kelly, Marion, 288
Kēwaikaliko, "Benocide," 259, 268–269,
269, 270–272
Koʻolau, Piʻilani, 132–133

Koreans in Hawaiʻi: Americanization
movement, 284–286; in the Department
of Education, 25; immigration history,
18–19, 281; Korean settlers in government with ties to development, 202;
linking struggles for justice for Korean
women sexually enslaved during WWII
by the Japanese and for indigenous
peoples, 289–290; population figures,
21–23, 101, 205, recruitment of Korean
laborers for the plantations, 19, 279,
281; return to Korea difficult, 282; as
settlers, 3–6, 9, 50, 120; in the State
Legislature, 22–25; "success" narrative,
47–48; support for Hawaiian rights, 30,
287–290; support for Korean Independence movement, 282–283; young
women's clubs and cultural productions,
283–286
Kosasa, Eiko, 8–9, 13–14, 16–17, 18, 21,
23, 31, 34–36, 40n60, 52–55, 270
Kosasa, Karen, 12–13, 34, 203
Kotani, Roland, 27, 227n1, 242

Labez, Zachary, 35, 259, 265–268
land. *See* ʻāina.
*Land and Power in Hawaiʻi, The Demo-
cratic Years,* 5–6, 23, 28, 38n21, 62n3,
173–174, 200, 202
Landgraf, Kapulani, 15, 33, 206, 208n16
Lefebvre, Henri, 207n6
Lenin, V. I., 213, 228n12, 287
Liliʻuokalani, 17, 46, **100**, 129–131, 145,
151nn42, 46, 172
Lind, Ian, 171, 173, 180, 298
Linnekin, Jocelyn, 126, 150n30
literature, Kanaka Maoli (Hawaiian)
contrasted with "local" settler literature,
119–123, 126–140
"local": critiques of, 25–29, 48, 118–119,
122–123, 125, 135, 139; definition of, 6,
27; denial of settler status, 48, 119, 123,
139, 258; developmental accounts of, 3,
26; development supported by "local"

developers, 28, 202; erases indigeneity by blurring distinction between Hawaiians and non-Hawaiians, 26, 48, 119, 149n10; geographical marker, 6; gloss for "settler," 4, 26, 46; historical formation of, 25–26; identification as working class with plantation roots, 27, 120; identification strengthened in defensive response to Hawaiian nationalism, 50–51; illusion of "shared struggle" with Hawaiians against white racism, 29, 48, 50, 120; "indigenization of the settler," 27, 139; masks Asian settler political power, 26, 27, 48, 257–258; middle-class American colonial values and aspirations, 61, 118–119, 122–123, 135, 140, 173–174, 198; political stakes differ from Hawaiian nation-building, 6, 119, 122; popular perception of multicultural diversity, 25–26, 29, 31, 235, 258; popular perception of resistance to continental "standards," 27; popular perception of resistance to development (commercial, suburban, resort), 25–26; scholarship on, 3, 6, 148n3; settlers claiming Hawai'i as their own, 4, 6, 46, 50–51, 122, 125, 139, 258. *See also* Hawai'i Creole English (HCE); *Land and Power in Hawai'i*

Local Japanese Women for Justice (LJWJ), 6, 30, 35, 52–55, 270, 295, 297

Lum, Darrell, 120–123, 126–128, 132, 135–136, 138, 140, 143, 146

Mākua Valley, 27, 34, 178, 184–188, 193n74; Mālama Mākua, 187–188

May, Keoni, 101

McGregor, Davianna Pōmaika'i, 192n45

Meyer, Manulani Aluli, 128, 272

military: Asian settler-dominated Democratic Party leaders form alliance with the military, 174; contradictions in providing openings for intervention and transformation, 34, 171, 189; devasta-

tion of land and sea, 85, 155, 177–178, 183–188, 192n44, 193n74; expansion in Hawai'i, 34, 175, 184; Hawai'i key to U.S. economic and military dominance in the Pacific, 171, 295; at Kaho'olawe, 178–182; land seizures and usage, 33–34, 174–177, 183, 184, 190n28, 273; maintenance of colonialism, 171–172, 196, 227n7; at Mākua, 184–188, 194n78; military service provided access to political power for Japanese settlers, 13, 173; naturalization and normalization of, 34, 170–171, 175–176; at Nohili (Pacific Missile Range Facility), 183; overthrow backed by U.S. military, 5, 14, 71, 170, 172, 215; at Pōhakuloa, 183–184; population of, 175; resistance to at Hālawa Valley / H-3 Freeway, 182; second largest "industry" in Hawai'i, 174, 282; support for other settler states like Israel, 34; at Waiāhole–Waikāne Valleys, 273–275; at Waikāne, 183, 261; white Republican oligarchy forms alliance with, 172, 282. *See also* 442nd Regimental Combat Team and 100th Infantry Battalion

Mitchell, Kimo, 181

Morales, Rodney, 126, 140–141, 144, 146

Nakamura, Barry, **280**

Native American. *See* American Indians

Native Hawaiian Government Reorganization Act. *See* Akaka Bill

Native Hawaiians: 'aipōhaku, 15, 155–157, **155**; anti-Hawaiian politics, **vi**, 48, 52, 55, 164–165; artists, 206, 208n17, 268; colonial definitions based on blood quantum, 149n12; colonization of, 3, 5, 7–9, 12, 17, 31–32, 34, 86–87, 105, 174, 197; criminalization of drug addiction, 104–107; in the Department of Education, 25; education, 47, 63n5, 165–166, 174; gathering rights, 16, 76, 81–88, **93**; health, 1, 13, 33–34, 47, 63n5, 149n23, 162–164, 174; houseless and landless,

of Korean women ("Comfort Women"), 289–290; treatment of Hawaiian women inmates, 108, 110. *See also* Local Japanese Women for Justice (LJWJ)

Wood, Houston, 143–144

Wright, Erin, 31

Yamamoto, Eric, 64n15, 244; Akaka Task Force, 53–54; definition of "local," 27, 63n7, 148n3

Yamanaka, Lois-Ann, 135–138

Yoshinaga, Ida, 13, 16–17, 35–36, 52–55, 270

Yu, Peter, 11